Decade of dealignment

Decade of dealignment

The Conservative victory of 1979 and electoral trends in the 1970s

BO SÄRLVIK

and

IVOR CREWE

With the assistance of

NEIL DAY and ROBERT MACDERMID

CAMBRIDGE UNIVERSITY PRESS

Cambridge

London   New York   New Rochelle
Melbourne   Sydney

Published by the Press Syndicate of the University of Cambridge
The Pitt Building, Trumpington Street, Cambridge CB2 1RP
32 East 57th Street, New York, NY 10022, USA
296 Beaconsfield Parade, Middle Park, Melbourne 3206, Australia

First published 1983

Printed in Great Britain at
the University Press, Cambridge

Library of Congress catalogue card number: 83 – 1827

British Library Cataloguing in Publication Data

Särlvik, Bo
Decade of dealignment.
1. Voting – Great Britain – History – 20th century
I. Title   II. Crewe, Ivor
324.941'0856   JN961

ISBN 0 521 22674 0

Contents

Preface

When we set out to write this book, our intention was to prepare a short descriptive report on the findings of the national interview survey which we conducted immediately after the May 1979 general election. But we have come to write a longer book. We could not avoid seeking explanations for the Conservatives' victory, and in doing so found ourselves looking back to the two elections of 1974 and occasionally beyond. Nor could we entirely resist the temptation to look at the 1979 result with the benefit of hindsight and in the light of recent upheavals in Britain's party system.

Our book therefore contains three elements. It serves, firstly, as a reference source of what we trust is authoritative information – as far as national interview surveys allow – about the state of public opinion and electoral behaviour at the time of the 1979 election. Towards this end we have presented numerous tables, some of which are purposely fuller than is perhaps usual for a book of this kind. But we have aimed to write a book which, whilst being informative for the academic specialist, can also be used by senior undergraduates and the interested lay public. We therefore hope that the advanced researcher will bear with those passages in which we describe in deliberately simple terms the nature of certain techniques of statistical analysis.

The book also seeks to explain the Conservatives' victory – or cast light on explanations offered by others – by reference to changes of opinion and voting patterns between 1974 and 1979. For this purpose our survey in 1979 returned to respondents first interviewed in one or other of our surveys at the elections of February and October 1974. Like the 1979 study, the 1974 studies were national surveys, carried out immediately after each of the two elections. We have made use of the resulting 'panel' data, as well as the February 1974 and October 1974 surveys in their own right.[1]

---

[1] Because of the length of this book it was not possible to include the usual appendices on the questionnaire, sampling design, sampling error and other aspects of data collection and analysis. Technical documentation can be obtained from the SSRC Data Archive at the University of Essex. A list of the documents available is given on page xiv.

From time to time the book takes a deeper perspective and examines longer-term changes in the nature of British electoral behaviour. On these occasions we have gone back to the series of election studies carried out between 1963 and 1970 by David Butler and Donald Stokes. Their pioneering study, *Political Change in Britain*, [2] laid a foundation for research on voting and public opinion of such originality and comprehensiveness that almost every path that we have followed in our own research has taken their book as a starting point.

Our book is about the general election in Great Britain. We have excluded Northern Ireland from our study because its party system and electoral politics differ so much from that in the mainland. We have also deliberately forsaken the special analyses of Scotland and Wales that these two countries' increasingly distinctive pattern of voting and opinion in the 1970s merit. This is partly because a strictly representative sample of Great Britain, consisting of about 1,900 respondents, will include too few of them from Scotland and Wales for the purpose of detailed statistical analysis. (Indeed, the problems posed for analyses of the English regions are similar.) But it is also because, in response to this very problem, the Social Science Research Council funded parallel but independent research projects on the 1979 election in Scotland and Wales. [3] The three election studies contained a large common core of identically worded questions to ensure comparability across the three nations of Great Britain, but from the outset it was agreed that results would be reported independently.

The national surveys of the two elections in 1974 were jointly conducted by the authors of this book. For the survey of the 1979 election we were joined by Dr David Robertson, formerly of the University of Essex and now a Fellow of St Hugh's College, Oxford. We all took a full share in the responsibility for the planning and conduct of the 1979 survey. The questionnaire, on which so much ultimately depends in research of this kind, is the result of numerous discussions and meetings among the three of us about the contents and phrasing of almost every item.

David Robertson undertook extensive analysis on the social determinants of the vote, the results of which is being published separately. We therefore decided to devote only one chapter to this aspect of voting in Britain: in this chapter the reader will find a broad, summary description of the social basis of the parties' support. The main themes of our enquiry, however, are the flow of the vote during the 1970s and its relation to positions taken by voters and parties on the issues that dominated the period from 1974 to 1979.

---

[2] David Butler and Donald Stokes, *Political Change in Britain. The Evolution of Electoral Choice* (London: Macmillan, 2nd edition, 1974).

[3] The Scottish Election Study was directed by Jack Brand and William Miller of the University of Strathclyde; the Welsh Election Study by Peter Madgwick and Denis Balsom of the University of Aberystwyth. The SSRC also funded a special study of Scotland at the October 1974 election, under the day-to-day direction of William Miller.

The character of a study of this kind is so heavily determined at the design stage that it is next to impossible to distinguish one investigator's contribution from another's. Nevertheless, when it came to writing the book, the two authors decided that the most practical way to proceed was to divide the work. We agreed upon the plan for the book, discussed all chapters extensively, and are indebted to each other for the intellectual stimulation and insights gained from this collaboration; but each author is responsible for the chapters that bear his name. We are jointly responsible, however, for the concluding Part III.

We have received a great deal of assistance throughout the project from many individuals and institutions. Our greatest debt is to our research officers. Tony Fox was involved in the preliminary stages of the 1979 survey, having worked with us on all stages of the 1974 surveys. He was helped by Bill Aughterson. Neil Day was our senior research officer for most of the planning stage and throughout the fieldwork. He also supervised the checking and coding of the interview data. He was helped for a year by Alastair Gordon. His successor as senior research officer was Bob MacDermid, who carried out almost all the computing for the analyses reported in this book, and who prepared supplementary technical papers on the project (these are listed on page xiv). Towards the end of the project, Dorothy Chase provided invaluable help by checking and editing tables and technical documentation. Finally, we want to mention the important contribution made by our first research officer, Jim Alt (now at Washington University, St Louis) to the 1974 surveys. In the course of the project, when we were often tied down by teaching and other academic responsibilities, much depended on our research officers' enthusiasm, resilience and technical skill. We thank them all.

The secretaries were always important members of our small project team. June Yates was the project's secretary during the planning and fieldwork and assisted with the typing of the book. Nina Elston typed successive drafts of the manuscript for the book. We thank them both for their cheerful and efficient assistance.

A large-scale interview survey also requires extensive assistance on such laborious but essential tasks as coding, data processing, and the checking of interview schedules. We were fortunate to find many students and others who at one time or another were willing to lend a hand. We particularly wish to thank

Jasmine Alterrihi	Halima Hosein
Vanessa Bean	Alan Jabez
Paddy Dale	Anne Kewley
Janet Day	Blanca Muniz
Tom Duncan	Jane Sargent
Barbra Evans	Shirley Thompson
Sandy Holder	Neil Wallace

Drafts of our writing were read by a number of our colleagues. We are particularly indebted to Anthony King, who went far beyond what any author could reasonably expect in his detailed and helpful comments and suggestions. We also wish to express our gratitude to Jean Blondel, Ian Budge, Jill Hills, and Olof Peterson for commenting on parts of the typescript at its various stages of production, and to Hugh Berrington for his support and encouragement when we first embarked on the election studies.

The interview fieldwork for the 1979 election survey was carried out by Research Services Ltd. The February 1974 and October 1974 cross-sectional surveys were conducted by the British Market Research Bureau and Social and Community Planning Research, respectively. We appreciate the co-operation we received from all three organisations in response to the special needs of the 1974 and 1979 studies.

All of the election studies have been funded by grants from the Social Science Research Council, for which we wish to record our appreciation. We are also grateful to the University of Essex for providing office space and computing facilities, to the staff of the University's Computing Centre for advice and practical assistance on many occasions, and to the Educational Technology Unit for the loan of equipment during the pilot stages of the project.

Finally, our list of acknowledgements would be incomplete without a special, personal note of thanks for the encouragement and understanding of our families: Ingegerd and Katarina Särlvik, and Jill, Deborah, Benjamin and Daniel Crewe.

This book represents neither the first nor the last of our writing on the election surveys. The results of the 1974 surveys were reported in a dozen articles appearing in scholarly journals and edited volumes. This time we decided to produce a book before proceeding to publish articles on more specialised and technical topics.[4]

The collection and analysis of data based on large-scale surveys is a time-consuming business, however, even with the aid of powerful computers. The fieldwork for the interviews, their detailed coding, and the checking and organisation of the data files took up the first twelve months after the 1979 election. What we now present is the result of analyses and writing in the following year and a half. There remains much to be done. We intend to return to the problems we have begun to penetrate here in further publications.

[4] Although the following unpublished papers, available from the authors, make some use of the 1979 election study data:
I. M. Crewe, 'The Electoral Decline of the Labour Party'.
B. Särlvik, I. M. Crewe and D. Robertson, 'Why the Parties were Liked and Disliked in the 1979 Election: An Analysis of "Free Answer" Survey Data'.
I. M. Crewe, 'Electoral Volatility in Britain Since 1945'.
I. M. Crewe, 'Party and Public'.

We shall be helped in this task by many other scholars. The data from the 1974 surveys have been available since October 1976 through the SSRC Data Archive at the University of Essex. A large number of books, articles, papers and theses are partially or wholly based on the British Election Study data (a regularly updated list may be obtained from the SSRC Data Archive). The 1979 survey – as well as the Welsh and Scottish sister surveys – have been similarly available since June 1981. We anticipate an equally intensive use of these data by the research community at home and abroad. We hope that these surveys will be regarded, in conjunction with the earlier election studies conducted by David Butler and Donald Stokes, as a research resource for the study of British politics.

Note on documentation about the British Election Studies, 1974 – 1979

The following BES Technical Papers can be obtained from the SSRC Data Archive, University of Essex:

A Comparison of Respondents' Characteristics with Known Population Parameters

A Description of Surveys Conducted by the British Election Study Project

The 1979 British Election Study: The Survey, The Sample Design and The Fieldwork, with a Note on Sampling Error

Continuity Guide to Questions Asked in British Election Studies from 1963 to 1979.

The SSRC Data Archive can also provide a list of publications by members of the British Election Study, as well as a list of books, articles, papers and dissertations based wholly or partly on data collected by the British Election Studies from 1974 to 1979.

The machine-readable data files for the cross-sectional studies conducted in February 1974, October 1974, June 1975 (EEC Referendum) and May 1979, as well as for the 1970 – February 1974 and February 1974 – October 1974 – May 1979 panel studies, can be obtained from the SSRC Data Archive, University of Essex. Accompanying documentation (which can be obtained without the data) includes, for each study, a codebook with frequency distributions, a facsimile of the questionnaire, and a detailed description of the sample design, sampling errors, response rates and fieldwork procedures.

Note on the tables

The number of respondents in the 1979 election survey is 1,893. However, in many tables we have excluded from the per cent distributions small numbers of respondents for whom data were inadvertently missing. Therefore, the tables show a slight variation with regard to the total number of respondents as well as the numbers in the sub-categories.

Unless otherwise stated, the tables display complete per cent distributions. The total for complete per cent distributions is always given as 100 per cent; however, because of decimal rounding the sum of the percentages in a row or column can occasionally differ slightly from 100.

Part I

Political context and electoral change

1

The flow of events

1.1 The result of the 1979 general election

A study seeking to account for the Conservative victory of 1979 must come to terms with an election result marked by contradiction and ambiguity. On the one hand, the result was thoroughly decisive (see Table 1.1). The Conservatives' parliamentary majority of seventy-one over Labour and forty-three over all opposition parties combined ended four and a half years of an occasionally minority and always precarious Labour administration, and was sufficient virtually to guarantee as many more years of Conservative government. Out of eleven post-war elections it was only the sixth to produce a comfortable majority for one party. Indeed, the true margin of the Conservatives' win was even more impressive than its moderate majority suggests. Not since the Labour 'landslide' of 1945 had one major party benefited from so emphatic a turn-round of major party fortunes (a 5.2 per cent national 'swing'[1]), or led the other by such a large margin of votes (7 per cent of the total poll). On both counts the 1979 election was more decisive than the sweeping victories of Macmillan in 1959 or Wilson in 1966: only the malapportionment of constituency electorates and the below average swing in Labour marginals prevented the Conservatives' majority at Westminster from nearing triple figures.[2] This was therefore not an election result that could be plausibly attributed to the chance or fleeting incidents that sometimes determine close-run contests. On the contrary, it raised the possibility that the election marked a turning point in British electoral history: the emergence of a new conservative electorate.

The minor parties all did badly. Liberal representation at Westminster fell from fourteen (which included one by-election gain) to eleven, its vote dropping by over a million from 18.3 per cent to 13.8 per cent. Liberal candidates lost many more deposits (304 as against 130 last time) and came runner-up in fewer constituencies (81 as opposed to 105). The Scottish Nationalists did worse still, losing nine of their eleven MPs and seeing their share of the vote in Scotland almost halved, from 30.4 per cent to 17.3 per cent. They were clearly demoted

Table 1.1 *The results of the October 1974 and 1979 general elections*

	October 1974 general election					1979 general election				
	Vote	Candidates	MPs	% share of total vote	% of electorate	Vote	Candidates	MPs	% of vote	% of electorate
Conservative	10,462,565	622	277	35.8	26.1	13,697,923	622	339	43.9	33.3
Labour	11,457,079	623	319	39.3	28.6	11,532,218	623	269	36.9	28.1
Liberal	5,346,704	619	13	18.3	13.3	4,313,804	577	11	13.8	10.5
Scottish Nationalist	839,617	71	11	2.9 (30.4% of vote in Scotland)	2.1	504,259	71	2	1.6 (17.3% of vote in Scotland)	1.2
Plaid Cymru	166,321	36	3	0.6 (10.8% of vote in Wales)	0.4	132,544	36	2	0.4 (8.1% of vote in Wales)	0.3
National Front	113,843	90	0	0.4	0.3	191,719	303	–	0.6	0.5
Other	802,975	191[1]	12[2]	2.8	2.0	848,895	312[4]	12[5]	2.7	2.1
Total	29,189,104	2,252[3]	635	100.0%	72.8	31,221,362	2,576[6]	635	100.0%	76.0
Difference between Conservative and Labour	Lab +994,514	Lab +1	Lab +43[7]	Lab +3.5	Lab +2.5	Con +2,165,705	Lab +1	Con +71[8]	Con +7.0	Con +5.2

Notes
[1] Including all candidates in Northern Ireland, and 29 Communists.
[2] The 12 members for Northern Ireland constituencies: 6 Ulster Unionists, 3 Vanguard Unionist Progressive, 1 Democratic Unionist, 1 Independent Republican and 1 Social Democratic and Labour. The Speaker counts as a Conservative.
[3] This is the number of candidatures. The number of *candidates* was 2,231: one candidate contested 12 constituencies and another contested 11.
[4] Including all candidates in Northern Ireland, 60 from the Workers' Revolutionary Party, 53 from the Ecology Party, and 38 Communists.
[5] The 12 members for Northern Ireland constituencies: 5 Ulster Unionists, 3 Democratic Unionists, 1 Independent Ulster Unionist, 1 United Ulster Unionist, 1 Independent Republican and 1 Social Democratic and Labour. The Speaker counts as a Labour MP.
[6] This is the number of candidatures. The number of *candidates* was 2,569: one candidate contested six constituencies and another contested three constituencies.
[7] Because the Speaker, who cannot vote in Commons divisions, was elected as a Conservative MP, Labour's majority was increased by one.
[8] Because the Speaker, who cannot vote in Commons divisions, was elected as a Labour MP, the Conservatives' majority was increased by one.

Source: F. W. S. Craig, *Britain Votes 2: British Parliamentary Election Results 1974 – 1979* (Chichester, Sussex: Parliamentary Research Services, 1980). The number of votes shown in the table are based on returns made by Returning Officers to the author, and have been subsequently checked against the *Returns of Election Expenses* compiled by the Home Office. The size of the eligible, registered electorate is calculated by means of the following formula:

(total number of 'dated names' on the Register) × number of days from 17 February to polling day (both dates inclusive) /

plus (total number of 'undated names').

from second to third party in Scotland. Plaid Cymru, the Welsh Nationalists, also fell back. They lost one of their three MPs, and obtained their lowest share of the Welsh vote (8.1 per cent) since they first stood throughout Wales in 1970. Altogether the number of seats won by parties other than Conservative and Labour dropped from thirty-nine to twenty-seven, and their combined share of the vote from 24.9 per cent to 19.2 per cent. The retreat of the minor parties and the return to secure single-party government suggests another possible turning point, therefore: the restoration of the two-party system which prevailed from 1945 to 1970.

But closer inspection of the 1979 figures leads to a more cautious interpretation. As Table 1.2 shows, although the share of the vote and number of MPs secured by the minor parties fell, both remained at their highest level, 1974 excepted, since the war. Despite their reverses, the minor parties were in a better position to make a comeback than at any time since the war. The combined Conservative plus Labour share of the *electorate* – the most telling statistic of major party support – was, at 61.4 per cent, a bit higher than in the elections of February 1974 (59.2 per cent) and October 1974 (54.7 per cent). But it was still substantially lower than for any of the earlier post-war elections, when it averaged 72.2 per cent. In this respect the 1979 election result bore more resemblance to those of 1974 than to those of 1945 to 1970.

The measure of the Conservatives' triumph must be qualified in three ways. Firstly, the Conservative share of the vote, although up from 35.8 per cent to 43.9 per cent, was well below that obtained at their earlier post-war election victories (see Table 1.2). When the Conservatives took office in 1970 under Edward Heath their vote was 46.4 per cent, and in their successive victories of 1951, 1955 and 1959 it averaged 49.0 per cent. The Conservative share of the total electorate shows a similar pattern. In the 1950s it averaged 38.6 per cent; in 1970 it was 33.4 per cent, and in 1979 it fell fractionally to 33.3 per cent. Thus, claims to an overwhelming mandate need to be tempered by the fact that four voters out of seven and as many as two electors out of three failed to vote Conservative. Indeed, no party has gained office with a secure majority on so low a proportion of the vote since the Conservatives under Bonar Law in 1922.

The margin of the Conservatives' win therefore owed more to an exceptionally low Labour vote than to an unusually high Conservative one. Labour's share of the vote dropped from 39.3 per cent to 36.9 per cent, its lowest ebb since its débâcle in 1931. Only one other post-war election has resulted in a smaller number of Labour MPs (258 in 1959) or a smaller total Labour vote (it was 75,000 less in October 1974 – when turnout was lower). This was the third successive election at which Labour failed to obtain 40 per cent of the vote, thus completing its poorest decade since the 1930s. In this sense the 1979 election was lost by the Labour government rather than won by the Conservative opposition. The result spoke more eloquently of the electorate's rejection of Labour than of its embrace of the Conservatives. The second qualification to the Conservatives'

Table 1.2 *Electoral Support for the Conservative and Labour Parties 1950-1979*

Date of general election	Share of *poll* obtained by:				Share of *electorate*[a] obtained by:			
	Conservatives[b]	Labour	Conservatives and Labour combined	Other parties (with no. of MPs)	Conservatives[b]	Labour	Conservatives and Labour combined	Other parties
	%	%	%	%	%	%	%	%
1950	43.4	46.1	89.5	10.5 (12)	36.3	38.6	74.9	8.8
1951	48.0	48.8	96.7	3.3 (9)	39.3	39.9	79.2	2.7
1955	49.7	46.4	96.1	3.9 (8)	38.2	35.6	73.8	3.0
1959	49.4	43.8	93.2	6.8 (7)	38.8	34.5	73.4	5.4
1964	43.4	44.1	87.5	12.5 (9)	33.4	34.0	67.4	9.6
1966	41.9	48.0	89.9	10.1 (13)	31.8	36.4	68.2	7.6
1970[c]	46.4	43.1	89.4	10.6 (12)	33.4	31.0	64.4	7.6
Feb 1974	37.9	37.2	75.0	25.0 (37)	29.9	29.3	59.2	19.7
Oct 1974	35.8	39.3	75.1	24.9 (39)	26.1	28.6	54.7	18.1
1979	43.9	36.9	80.8	19.2 (27)	33.3	28.1	61.4	14.6

Notes
[a] These figures are based on the registered electorate in the UK, which will have included people who died, emigrated or moved out of the constituency by the time the election took place. Adjustment for the age of the register at the time of the election would raise the figures (by 4% on average) but not alter the direction or magnitude of the trend over the period. This table makes no adjustment for the number of Liberal and other minor party candidates. Their steady increase since 1955 partly accounts for the decline of the major party vote, but partly results from it too.
[b] Includes votes for the National Liberal and Conservative party, and for Ulster Unionists up to 1970, after which they no longer took the Conservative whip.
[c] The voting age was lowered from 21 to 18 in 1969.

Source: F.W.S. Craig, *British Electoral Facts 1885 – 1975* (London: Macmillan, 3rd edition, 1976), and Craig, *Britain Votes 2.*

victory was that it fell short of a *national* mandate. This was not only because, as usual, the majority of seats in Scotland and Wales went to Labour. Of more significance were the exceptional regional differences in the swing to the Conservatives – at least by post-war standards. South of a line running roughly from the Humber to the Mersey (including Wales) the average swing was 6.4 per cent. North of that line it was 2.9 per cent (3.8 per cent in Northern England but only 0.7 per cent in Scotland), insufficient on its own to give the Conservatives a workable majority. Within each region, too, there were unusually marked variations of electoral movement from one constituency to another.[3] In the outer suburbs, smaller towns and countryside the Conservatives advanced further than in the major industrial conurbations. And, sub-dividing again, there were consistently higher than average swings to the Conservatives in some types of community such as mining areas, new towns, and 'car-worker' seats, and consistently below average swings in others, such as areas of Asian and West Indian settlement, fishing communities and university towns.[4] (A detailed analysis, based on our survey data, of the relationship between party choice and location in the social structure, is provided in Chapter 3.) Indeed, in no other post-war election have so many different local factors acted as a brake or accelerator on national electoral forces. But the overall picture depicted a 'two-nation' election. The Conservative majority was largely built on the relatively prosperous commuting areas, small towns and countryside of the South and Midlands; it had little foundation in the old industrial and urban areas of the North and Scotland. The Conservatives advanced most where there was economic expansion and security, least where there was deprivation and decline.

The third ambiguity about the election result is that the Conservatives lost some ground during the campaign. Our own survey was carried out immediately after the election. We must turn, therefore, to the opinion polls conducted during the campaign to find indicators of any change during those weeks. The Conservatives' lead over Labour in the polls narrowed from an average of 11.9 per cent in the first week of the campaign to 7.2 per cent by the eve and day of polling. Mr Callaghan was the more popular choice for Prime Minister from the very start of the campaign; his lead over Mrs Thatcher steadily increased as the campaign progressed. (But see Chapter 5's analysis of the impact of the party leaders.) Moreover, according to the polls, the Conservatives' 9 per cent edge over Labour as the party with the 'best policies' in the first week of April had dropped to 5 per cent by polling day.[5] A satisfactory account of their victory must therefore look beyond the few weeks that preceded election day.

1.2 The Labour government 1974–1979

The Labour government elected in October 1974 was committed to an ambitious programme of social and political change.[6] Its election manifesto ended with a pledge to work towards 'a fundamental and irreversible shift of power and wealth

in favour of working people and their families', and many of its specific legislative proposals reflected this general objective. Its proposed measures for bringing more of the private sector into public ownership included the nationalisation
of the ports, and of the shipbuilding and aircraft industries; an increase in the
state's financial stake in the exploitation of North Sea oil and gas; the establishment of a National Enterprise Board with powers to intervene in, and if necessary
purchase, private companies; and a Community Land Act which would oblige
local authorities to purchase (compulsorily if necessary) land for development. Its
policies for the redistribution of wealth consisted of an annual wealth tax and a
capital transfer tax, as well as a variety of new or improved social benefits, including a new scheme of earnings-related pensions containing better provision for
women, a programme of improved benefits for the disabled, and the extension of
family allowances to the first child, payable to the mother. Its proposals for attacking privilege included the withdrawal of tax relief from private education and
the phasing out of pay beds in the National Health Service. The rights of workers
were to be extended by a further dismantling of the Conservative government's
Industrial Relations Act and by a new Employment Protection Bill, which
together would extend the rights to peaceful picketing, and restore the traditional
legal status of the closed shop; in addition there was a commitment to a 'radical
extension of industrial democracy'. Taken together, these measures constituted a
serious programme of moderate socialist reforms. The Labour government's
manifesto promises on constitutional matters were no less extensive. The government would continue to re-negotiate the terms under which Britain had entered
the EEC in 1971, and would then put the question of whether Britain should
remain in or withdraw from the Community to a national referendum. It proposed to bring in a Sex Discrimination Act, a reform of the Official Secrets Act,
and a change in the nationality laws. Most important of all, it was pledged to
devolve administrative and legislative powers to Scotland and Wales, through the
setting-up of elected assemblies in both regions.

But the new Labour government immediately faced two overriding problems
which were to plague it for most of its period of office. The first was its precarious parliamentary position. Labour's majority over the Conservatives was a
comfortable forty-three; but its majority over all opposition parties combined
was a slender three. It was unlikely that all the opposition parties – the Conservatives, the Liberals, the Scottish Nationalists, Plaid Cymru, and the twelve
MPs from Northern Ireland – would frequently come together in the same
division lobby. Nonetheless, there was likely to be a time when all opposition
parties would unite on a vote of no confidence. The government was acutely
vulnerable to by-election defeats and the defection of a handful of dissidents
from its own backbenches.

Its second problem was the state of the economy. Labour returned to office
to face a large balance of payments deficit, a real fall in the Gross Domestic
Product, a slow but persistent rise in unemployment and, most serious of all, a

rapidly accelerating rise in prices. In the first quarter of 1974, when it replaced the Conservative government, the year-on-year rate of inflation was 12 per cent. By the last quarter, despite the February 1974 Labour government's rent freeze and subsidising of essential foodstuffs, the rate was 17 per cent. The primary cause was the Yom Kippur war of October 1973 and the subsequent raising of oil prices by OPEC. But these inflationary forces were reinforced by exceptionally large wage rises negotiated in 1974 and 1975. To get the miners to return to work the incoming Labour administration of February 1974 had approved of a 30 per cent wage rise (followed by one of 25 per cent for rail workers), and this was to set a standard for workers in other industries. By the first quarter of 1975 the price inflation rate had reached 20.1 per cent; by the second, 24.5 per cent; and by the third, 26.5 per cent.

Inflation of this magnitude was unprecedented in twentieth-century Britain. There were fears that it would spiral out of control and into a ruinous hyper-inflation. But although the government had to take counter-measures, it was tightly constrained by its political position. Severe deflation of a conventional kind – raising taxes and cutting public expenditure – would quickly lead to more unemployment and thus be unacceptable to the Labour backbenches. A statutory incomes policy was also ruled out. It had been tried by Mr Heath only a year earlier and failed spectacularly; it was opposed at both 1974 elections by the Labour party; and the trade unions were strenuously hostile. The remaining option was voluntary restraint by the trade unions. Back in February 1974 Mr Wilson had floated the idea of a 'social contract' between a Labour government and the trade unions. The government would repeal the previous Conservative government's industrial relations legislation, control prices, increase pensions and other benefits, and raise the taxes on high incomes and wealth; in return the trade union leadership would recommend their local officials to limit wage claims to levels necessary to maintain their members' living standards.

It was clear from the inflation figures in mid 1975 that the social contract had failed. The trade union leaders could not enforce it, but even if they could have done cost-of-living wage increases in the aftermath of the oil price rises were themselves inflationary. New measures were urgently needed. An initiative came from Jack Jones, the leader of the Transport and General Workers' Union. He proposed that for a twelve-month period wages should be strictly limited to a flat-rate increase of £6.00 a week, with those earning above £8,500 a year receiving no rise at all. The proposal proved attractive to government and unions alike. It was anti-inflationary, obviously just in a crude way, egalitarian, and simple to police. It particularly benefited low-paid workers, although its squeezing of differentials was to store up trouble for the government later. The proposal was quickly taken up by a grateful government and accepted by the trade union movement in the late summer and autumn.

The £6.00 policy was to pave the way for two further annual instalments of negotiated but voluntary incomes restraint. In July 1976 Mr Healey, the Chancellor of the Exchequer, secured the TUC's agreement to Phase II of the policy: a 5 per cent limit to pay increases up to a maximum of £4.00 in return for a lowering of the standard tax rate. Negotiations for a Phase III proved more difficult, but the government imposed a 10 per cent target for the public sector, and threatened sanctions against private firms exceeding the norm. The impact of wages restraint on price rises was marked. In the final quarter of 1975 the annual inflation rate had reached its peak of 26 per cent; in the final quarters of the three following years it dropped to 15 per cent, 12 per cent, and 9 per cent successively. (For the eventual electoral consequences, see Chapter 6.)

Shortly after the government had taken the first serious steps to bring inflation under control, signs of the sterling crisis that was to dominate 1976 became apparent. When the Labour government was elected the pound stood at $2.33. It slipped throughout 1975 to $2.04 by the final quarter. By June 1976 it had fallen to $1.76 and in its worst week in October it reached $1.56. The fall in the value of the pound made price inflation worse still, by raising the costs of essential imports such as fuel and food. Although the reason for the particular timing of the run on sterling was obscure, the source of sterling's long-term weakness was not: an inflation rate worse than that in most comparable industrial democracies, large balance of payments deficits, and high public spending. Rightly or wrongly, it was the latter that took most of the blame in foreign financial circles, and that was therefore the key element in negotiations for international support for the pound.

In June 1976 a short-term, stand-by loan was negotiated with the central banks of the United States and West Germany. Three months later a new loan from the International Monetary Fund was secured. The measures demanded in return involved a massive reduction in government spending. Mr Healey had already cut public expenditure in 1975; in June 1976 further cuts totalling £1 billion were announced (and National Insurance contributions were raised); and by December 1976, when the final terms with the IMF had been settled, it was announced that the public sector borrowing requirement was to be reduced by £1.5 billion and that tighter controls would be imposed on the growth in the money supply.

The sterling crisis disappeared almost as quickly as it had first arrived. By January 1978 the pound touched $2.00 and the IMF credits were never drawn. But whilst the problems of sterling proved fleeting, the remedies were not. The IMF's conditions set the government's economic strategy for the remainder of its period of office. The watchwords became tighter monetary control, cuts in public spending by way of cash limits on local authorities and the nationalised industries, and continued wage restraint, especially in the public sector. The political impact of these measures was a paradox. They were responsible for the widespread feeling in 1978 that the economy had turned a corner, as the rate of inflation came steadily down and real living standards rose again, and this feeling was reflected in Labour's steady recovery in the opinion polls. But these same measures, which had seriously divided the Cabinet in late 1976, also alienated the Labour movement in the country. Local trade union officials and party workers could not reconcile themselves to the inevitable damage inflicted on the social services, on the wages of public sector employees and on overall employment levels by measures carried out at the apparent behest of the international banking community. By 1978 the Labour government had the scent of success amongst the electorate but the smell of failure amongst its own activists.

At both of the 1974 elections the Labour party had promised to replace the conflict and confrontation that marked industrial relations under the previous Conservative government by a new era of co-operation and consultation. It claimed to be the only party that 'could work with the unions'. For the four years until October 1978 this claim had some foundation. Under the preceding Conservative government the yearly average of days lost through industrial stoppages was $15\frac{1}{4}$ million; for the first four years of the Labour government that figure was halved, to 7.6 million. The years 1975 and 1976 were, in fact, amongst the most strike free since the war. The government attributed the industrial peace to the repeal of the Conservatives' Industrial Relations Act and to their regular consultation with trade union leaders through the National Economic Development Council and the TUC-Labour Party Liaison Committee. But opposition critics talked of capitulation rather than consultation. They portrayed the Labour government as a captive of the trade unions, passing legislation at their bidding, notably the Trade Union and Labour Relations (Amendment) Act of 1976, which not only restored the closed shop to its original status but extended it to the newspaper industry. Critics could also point to a number of disputes which, whilst inflicting little damage on the national economy, were reminders of the nature and uses of trade union power. At Grunwick's, a film processing works in North London, a union-recognition dispute attracted crowds of 'flying' pickets, who attempted to stop the workforce entering the premises. Television's daily relay of scenes of mass disorder at the Grunwick site left the clear impression of trade union inspired intimidation and inadequate laws on picketing. Other minor but newsworthy disputes included a drawn-out strike of Glasgow dustmen in 1975 which eventually required the use of troops to clear the mounting refuse, and the firemen's strike in late 1977 which also required the use of military personnel and equipment to put out dangerous fires. Another such dispute occurred sporadically in London hospitals, over the issue of pay beds in NHS hospitals. The media's pictures of bedridden patients being wheeled away from strike-hit wards reinforced the impression – not always an accurate one – made by the earlier disputes that trade unions were prepared to pursue claims even at the risk to human life and health. Thus, although the relatively tranquil industrial scene from 1974 to 1978 was an electoral asset to the Labour government, it was not one based on any popular sympathy for the trade unions. (The electorate's perceptions of trade unions are charted in Chapters 5 and 6.)

Although problems of the British economy dominated the political scene they were not the only concerns of the public or politicians. Growing concern was expressed in the media and amongst Conservatives about an alleged decline of 'law and order'. The phrase was an umbrella term, used to cover everything from petty vandalism to the IRA's London bombing campaign. Prominence was given to the statistics of rising crime, especially violent crime; to an apparent rash of 'muggings' in London; to fighting on the football terraces; to violent picketing, such as that at Grunwick's; and to demonstrations by the National Front and the sometimes violent counter-demonstrations that these provoked amongst the coloured communities and the Anti-Nazi League. The police, seen as struggling to control violent pickets and demonstrators, enjoyed a surge of sympathy.

Discussion of 'law and order' was often linked, not always explicitly, to what was regarded as a wider breakdown of the social and moral order. The break-down manifested itself in various ways. In the aftermath of the Conservatives' election defeat in February 1974 it was for a short time fashionable to worry about whether Britain had become ungovernable, and even to speculate about the possibility of a military takeover in response to a general strike. Education pro-vided another target for those alleging a general decline in standards. The *Black Papers on Education*[7] claimed that the change to comprehensive schools had been accompanied by a deterioration of academic standards, a claim that seemed to be partly backed by Mr Callaghan's and Mrs Williams' call for a 'great debate' on education, and by the revelations of the inquiry into the William Tyndale school.[8] The campaign against pornography led by Mrs Whitehouse was another example of the apparent resurgence of moral and social conservatism. (How the electorate responded to social and cultural change is described in Chapter 7.)

Another issue sometimes linked in the public mind with assumptions about 'declining standards' is coloured immigration. Although not as politically import-ant as in the 1960s, the issue erupted from time to time under the Labour government. The stream of immigrants from the Asian subcontinent had dried up to a trickle of 20,000 by 1977. Yet in that year, perhaps as a result of press stories about local authorities accommodating homeless East African refugees in four-star hotels, the National Front began to pick up electoral support. In the Greater London Council elections its share of the vote approached 20 per cent in some East End constituencies (albeit on an exceptionally low turnout) and in the by-elections at Walsall North, Birmingham Stetchford, Birmingham Ladywood and Lambeth Central it pushed the Liberals into fourth place. In January 1978 the issue re-emerged after a television interview with Mrs Thatcher on the Con-servatives' immigration policies. These were to include a clamp-down on illegal immigration by means of tougher quotas, a register of resident immigrants' dependants living abroad, a review of an immigrant's fiancé's right to enter Britain, and a commitment to pass a new British Nationality Act. The interview was mainly remembered, however, for Mrs Thatcher's off-the-cuff comment that 'people can feel rather swamped' by immigrants. The remark was strongly resented by the immigrant communities and attacked by the Labour and Liberal parties; but the opinion polls registered a sharp, although short-lived, increase in Conservative support.[9] Clearly, immigration and race remained electorally potent issues.

Despite their importance to the electorate, none of these concerns absorbed much parliamentary time. The issue which dominated the parliamentary sessions of 1976–7 and 1977–8 was devolution. At the October 1974 election the Scottish Nationalists did remarkably well. They pushed the Conservative vote into third place, won eleven of the seventy-one Scottish seats, and came runner-up in forty-two more. The Labour party felt particularly threatened by the Nationalist tide because it counts on winning a majority of seats in Scotland, and partly depends on these to muster a majority in the country as a whole. Details of the government's manifesto commitment to establish elected assemblies in Scotland and Wales were set out in a White Paper (*Our Changing Democracy*) in November 1975. The proposals satisfied nobody. The Scottish and Welsh Nationalists regarded the measures as well short of full devolution because of the limits that it was proposed to place on the assemblies. Macro-economic policy, including social security, industrial relations, and, most crucial of all, the power to raise revenue by taxation, would be left in the hands of the central government. Moreover, all legislation passed by the assemblies would be subject to a veto by the Secretaries of State for Scotland and Wales, sitting in the Cabinet. The Nationalists were only prepared to support the proposals as a first step. The Conservative party, which under Mr Heath had briefly favoured devolution, now turned against an elected regional assembly in principle; under Mrs Thatcher, a traditionalist on constitutional matters, it emphasised the political indivisibility of the United Kingdom. And amongst Labour backbenchers there were also serious misgivings: some saw regional devolution as a potential brake on socialist planning; others resented the granting of a constitutional privilege to some regions rather than others; yet others objected to the resulting anomaly whereby Scottish MPs at Westminster would be able to legislate for England, whereas English MPs would not be able to legislate on the same matters for Scotland. Objections such as these slowed down the passage of the Bill so seriously that by February 1977 the government moved a guillotine motion; but as a result of a rebellion by Labour backbenchers the motion was lost and the legislation had to be scrapped – at least for that parliamentary session.

The defeat of the guillotine motion was to threaten the survival of the government and in turn precipitated the Lib-Lab pact. By November 1976 by-election defeats and backbench defections had eliminated the Labour government's majority in the House of Commons.[10] In March 1977 the Conservatives tabled a motion of no confidence which had the support of all the opposition parties. The government was naturally anxious to avoid a defeat, since this would have led to dissolution and an early general election which it would almost certainly have lost badly. It therefore looked around for an understanding with one of the minor opposition parties. The Scottish and Welsh Nationalists were too angry at the delay on legislation for devolution to be considered; and an initial approach to the Ulster Unionists came to nought because the price demanded for support – the replacement of direct rule by a return to one-party (i.e. Loyalist) government from Stormont – was too high. The government therefore turned to the Liberals, who were equally fearful of an early general election, and whose leader, David Steel, was keen to demonstrate the Liberal party's ability and willingness to participate in government. The result was the Lib-Lab pact, an agreement by which Liberal MPs would support the government in major votes in return for regular and advance consultation on the government's parliamentary business and legislative proposals. The government also agreed to bring forward the legislation on direct elections to the European assembly and on devolution, and to allow a free vote on the adoption of proportional representation in both cases. The pact initially ran until the end of the 1976–7 parliament but was renewed for a further year.

The deal proved better for the government than the Liberals. The government gained time in which to allow its standing in the electorate to recover as the economy improved. It sacrificed almost nothing in the way of legislation. By contrast, no major Liberal policy was advanced by the pact. The proposal for proportional representation in the European elections was defeated in a free vote. The pact did allow the Liberals to pitch their claim as a party capable of playing a moderating role in government; but, in the short term at least, this was probably an electoral liability, because it alienated those of its previous supporters who were strongly anti-Labour. The Liberals' performance in by-elections and the polls, which was fairly poor before the pact, slumped still further after it.[11]

The lease of life granted by the pact was largely devoted to a second attempt to steer through parliament the government's devolution proposals. This time there was less dissent from the Labour backbenchers, who knew that the government's survival depended on satisfactory progress on the Bill, and the legislation made steady progress. But opponents to the Bill forced one important concession on the government. The devolution proposals were to be subject to referenda in Scotland and Wales. The referenda would be advisory rather than mandatory on the government, but as a result of an amendment moved by a Labour backbencher, George Cunningham, the government would not proceed with the Bills if less than 40 per cent of the Scottish and Welsh electorates gave their approval.

By the late summer of 1978 the economic and political tide had clearly turned in the Labour government's favour. The devolution legislation was being safely steered through Parliament. The industrial scene was quiet. And, whatever the long-term prospects, short-term developments in the economy were favourable. The annual inflation rate in September was down to 8 per cent, the lowest for over five years. Foreign trade was in balance and sterling stood at only a shade under $2.00 with little expectation of any serious slippage. The seasonally adjusted unemployment rate had been trickling down steadily for nearly a year. And, most important of all, living standards had soared since the autumn of 1977. Whilst take-home pay was accelerating (because of tax cuts in the autumn 1977 budget and the less stringent Phase III pay policy) inflation was braking (partly because price rises lag behind wage rises, partly because the stronger pound meant cheaper imports). The result was an 8 per cent increase in real income in the year up to September 1978. These trends were reflected in the opinion polls. In the third quarter of 1977 the Conservative lead over Labour in the Gallup poll was 10 per cent; a year later it was only 2 per cent. In the third quarter of 1977 the 'satisfaction ratings' of Mr Callaghan and Mrs Thatcher were equal; a year later they put Mr Callaghan 15 per cent ahead. *The Times'* economic correspondent reflected: 'although the overall state of the economy is worse than at any election since the war the recent past is working almost entirely in their (i.e. the Labour government's) favour. By luck and by judgement they have created the very model of a pre-election boom.'[12]

Despite widespread expectations to the contrary in the summer of 1978, Mr Callaghan decided to postpone the general election to the following spring. A detailed account of his reasons can be found elsewhere,[13] but the main considerations appeared to be confidence in the immediate economic trends, a wish to see the economic recovery make itself more apparent to the electorate, the disturbing results of the party's private polls and a naturally cautious disposition.

Soon after the decision to postpone the election, the government's fortune turned. In July the Prime Minister had announced a Phase IV pay policy consisting of a 5 per cent ceiling. By September it was apparent that so low a limit – and probably any limit – would meet strenuous opposition from the trade unions, who were under heavy pressure from their members, especially those angry about narrowing differentials after three years' restraint. The TUC conference in September voted overwhelmingly to restore free collective bargaining. A month later the annual Labour party conference followed suit by a vote of over two to one. In October workers at the Ford Motor Company rejected an offer that stayed within the government's guidelines and struck for nine weeks. The eventual settlement of 17 per cent made a major breach in the policy. The government attempted to repair it by imposing sanctions (such as the cancellation of government contracts) on companies settling outside the guidelines. But even this measure proved ineffective, after the Opposition, with the help of four left-wing Labour backbenchers, won a motion condemning the use of sanctions. Nothing but government exhortation could now prevent other workers from stepping through the breach.

In January 1979 there was an explosion of strikes as one group of workers after another sought wage rises well in excess of the 5 per cent limit. The devastating impact of these strikes on the Labour government's electoral standing is charted in Figure 1.A. In the final quarter of 1978, according to the Gallup polls, Labour was 2 per cent ahead of the Conservatives and Mr Callaghan 17 percentage

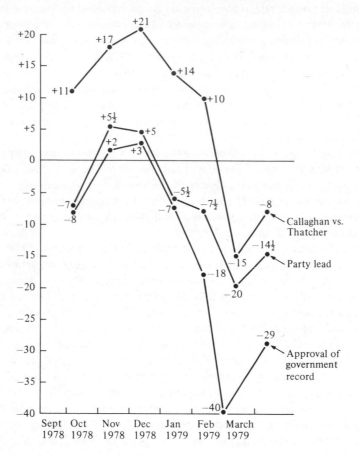

Notes

Callaghan vs. Thatcher: % satisfied with Callaghan *minus* % satisfied with Thatcher

Party lead in polls: % intending to vote Labour *minus* % intending to vote Conservative (including 'leaners' but excluding 'don't knows' from the percentage base)

Approval of government record: % approving *minus* % disapproving of 'the government's record to date'

Data source: Monthly Gallup polls, as reported in the monthly *Gallup Political Index,* Nos. 218–25 (London: Social Surveys (Gallup Poll) Ltd,1978–9).

Figure 1.A *Trends in public opinion, September 1978 – March 1979*

points more popular than Mrs Thatcher. By February 1979 the position had been transformed. Approval of the government's record plummeted from 41 per cent to 23 per cent, Mr Callaghan trailed 15 per cent behind Mrs Thatcher in popularity, and the Conservatives soared into an 18 per cent vote lead. In its forty years of polling, Gallup had never recorded a sharper reversal of party fortunes within a period of two months. There could be no doubt as to the cause: in the last quarter of 1978, 14 per cent mentioned strikes as the country's single most urgent problem; by February 1979, 51 per cent did.

Major strikes rarely win the sympathy of the general public, and usually result in temporary unpopularity for the party in office. This is particularly to be expected for a party with long-held and close ties to the trade union movement. But many strikes have badly inconvenienced the public in the past without the government, even when a Labour one, seeing its public stock fall so low. Why was the damage to Labour's standing so severe this time? One reason was, quite simply, the number of strikes that coincided. The petrol tanker drivers, the lorry drivers, the ambulance drivers, the train drivers, in some regions the bus drivers and water workers, as well as various groups of local authority workers, all stopped work in quick succession. Another reason was the sheer discomfort inflicted on most people's day-to-day existence: the difficulty of getting to or from work (because petrol was unavailable, or because the buses or trains were not running), the shortage of basic items in the shops (because the lorry drivers were not delivering them), the unemptied dustbins (because the dustmen were on strike), the closing of schools (because the caretakers were, too).

But these factors are only part of the explanation. The strikes were also marked by two other unusual features: the vehemence, bordering on violence, of some of the picketing; and, often as a consequence, what appeared as indifference to the safety and health of the ordinary public. For example, local authorities' road maintenance men refused to grit the roads, which had been made dangerously icy by an unusually cold spell. More serious, somebody having an accident might find no ambulance to take him to hospital, because drivers were on strike, in some areas refusing to deal even with emergency calls. People reaching the hospital gates under their own steam faced the possibility of being turned away by pickets of hospital porters or ambulance men. People admitted to hospital found that there were no porters to ferry them to the operating theatre, nor laundry staff to clean their bed linen. And, for those who died, there might be nobody to dig their graves, because the local authorities' cemetery workers were also on strike. This unusual fierceness, moreover, was vividly communicated to the public day after day in the press and on television: shortages in the supermarkets, the turning away of ambulances and the unburied dead were ideal stories for the media. There is no evidence that the health and physical safety of more than a few people were put into danger; yet, as a backbench Labour MP put it at the time, people 'felt the ground slipping from under their feet'.

The public's irritation with the strikers, and perhaps the trade unions generally, is easy to understand. But why was its anger also aimed at the government? The fact that Labour happened to be the party in office, and that it has close associations with the trade unions, was not the only reason. Labour won the two 1974 elections partly on the argument that it was politically and temperamentally better equipped to obtain the co-operation of the trade union movement. Until late 1978 there seemed to be substance to the claim: industrial relations under the Conservative government of 1970 to 1974 had deteriorated badly, culminating in the miners' strike and the February 1974 election itself, whereas between July 1975 and October 1978 the Labour government's 'social contract' with the trade unions did secure a considerable reduction in industrial stoppages.

The winter's strikes put paid to the Labour party's slowly accumulated credibility as the only party capable of handling industrial relations. Despite its much vaunted special relationship with the trade unions, it could not persuade their leaders to call off the strikes, or even to modify the vigour with which they were pursued. This was not only because the government appeared to carry little weight with union leaders but because union leaders in turn appeared to carry little with their own members. The resulting impression of a general loss of control and authority also damaged the government's standing. Mrs Thatcher seized the political opportunity and proposed a set of legal reforms in the practice of industrial relations. These included state-financed but compulsory postal ballots for the election of union officials and for decisions on strike calls, the prohibition of 'secondary' picketing, and the taxing of social security benefits paid out to strikers' families. All three measures were opposed by the Labour government but, according to contemporary polls, all were supported by the vast majority of the British electorate – including trade union members and Labour supporters.[14] The ground appeared to be slipping from under the government's feet, too.

The devolution referenda were held on 1 March 1979. With the winter's strikes still fresh in the electorate's memory, the government, which was campaigning for a 'yes' vote, was very unpopular. The referendum results were a deep disappointment to both the Nationalists and the government. In Wales the proposals were rejected by a majority of four to one; a mere 12 per cent of the Welsh electorate voted 'yes'. In Scotland, the devolution proposals did obtain the approval of a majority of those who voted, but a very slender one – 51.6 per cent. With the turnout in Scotland only 63 per cent, the proportion of Scotland's electors who gave their approval – 32.9 per cent – fell far below the 40 per cent required by the Cunningham amendment. The government's devolution plans were dead. In their bitterness, the SNP in parliament moved a motion of no confidence in the government. With the support of the Conservatives, Liberals, and eight Ulster Unionists[15] it won by one vote. In the election that followed the issue of devolution, which had so dominated parliament from 1976 to 1978, played almost no part in the campaign, even north of the Border.

The events of the winter undoubtedly made it more difficult for Labour to win the general election. Although the Conservatives' lead over Labour, and Mrs Thatcher's over Mr Callaghan, was already narrowing in the March polls (see Figure 1.A), Labour failed to recover all the ground it had lost. Many previously undecided voters must have finally made up their minds, to the Conservatives' benefit, as a result of the strikes; many who had previously considered themselves certain Labour voters must have thought again. The precise extent of the damage done to Labour by issues of industrial relations is estimated in Part II of this book, especially Chapters 6 and 11.

It should not be inferred, however, that Labour would necessarily have won an election held in the previous autumn. The evidence points in both directions. On the one hand, in October 1978 Labour was ahead of the Conservatives by 4 to 5 per cent in both the Gallup and NOP monthly polls; and Mr Callaghan was far more popular than Mrs Thatcher. On the other hand, Labour never managed to sustain a commanding lead in the opinion polls. Moreover, by October 1978 public confidence in the country's economic future – often the harbinger of changes in the electoral climate – was slipping.[16] More telling evidence can be found in the by-election results, which persistently contradicted Labour's lead in the polls throughout 1978. Although the monthly Gallup polls suggested that the swing to the Conservatives since October 1974 was only 2.6 per cent – not enough to guarantee them office – the average by-election swing (outside Scotland[17]) was 7.2 per cent, enough to provide them with a three-digit parliamentary majority. The most one can safely conclude is that Labour stood a better chance of winning in October 1978 than in April 1979, when it was forced to enter into an election campaign.

1.3 The campaign

There is not one election campaign but many, conducted at different levels and through a variety of channels. At the constituency level it is waged by candidates and party workers by means of election addresses, canvassing, small public meetings, and local broadcasts and press releases. Themes and issues vary from one constituency to another, and only a small portion of the electorate comes into direct contact with the candidates. At the national level the campaign is fought by the parties' major figures, of whom the leader assumes overwhelming importance, through the now established routine of morning press conferences, daytime speaking tours and the evening set speech. A study of electoral behaviour must focus on the campaign as conveyed to the mass of ordinary electors; and that essentially means press and television coverage of what the party leaders say and do.

The election was unusually devoid of personal gaffe or dramatic incident. Only two items of news intruded into the campaign: the assassination of Airey Neave, the Conservative spokesman on Northern Ireland and a close aide of Mrs Thatcher, and the riots in Southall, an area of Asian immigration, where the National Front tried to hold a meeting. Both incidents may have marginally raised the saliency of the 'law and order' issue. The campaign was also free from personal attacks. The fact that the Conservative leader was a woman, far from becoming a campaign issue, actively discouraged Labour politicians from criticising Mrs Thatcher for fear of appearing sexist or unchivalrous. (The negligible impact of Mrs Thatcher's sex is described in Chapter 5.2.) In fact the campaign was in general less negative than some of its predecessors: compared with the elections of 1974 and 1970 the party leaders spent more time outlining their future plans and less time attacking those of their rivals.[18]

Thus the 1979 campaign was unusually dominated by the presentation of party philosophy and policy. A party's formal address to the nation is contained in its election manifesto. But the leader's room for manoeuvre within the framework set by the manifesto is considerable. The manifesto's importance rests on the status it carries in the media and amongst the party rank and file (especially Labour's) as a policy programme to which the party would be committed in government. But as a guide to the themes of the campaign it is less important. Its length and detail (and cost) discourage more than a tiny minority of the electorate from reading it, and oblige the party leader to be highly selective about the bits to emphasise. In reality the party leader sets the tone and agenda of the campaign debate.

Labour's campaign

Labour's manifesto, *The Labour Way is the Better Way*, was a detailed document with 133 specific policy pledges. Its overall commitment was almost identical to that at the previous election: 'to bring about a fundamental shift in the balance of wealth and power in favour of working people and their families'. Both at the time of its drafting and since the election its left-wing detractors have portrayed it as a bland and complacent document devoid of socialist commitments. This is not strictly true. Most of the pledges wanted by the more left-wing local activists and officials, and passed at annual conferences, were included in the manifesto, although occasionally in a slightly watered-down form. These included, amongst others, an annual wealth tax on people with a net personal wealth of over £150,000; the abolition of remaining public subsidies for independent schools; an increased national stake in North Sea Oil; the nationalisation of commercial ports and cargo handling; planning agreements with major companies accompanied by the necessary back-up statutory powers; selective import controls; the government's right to take a proportionate share in the ownership of companies receiving government subsidies; the abolition of the delaying power and legislative veto of the House of Lords; a reduction in defence spending; a radical reform of the EEC's agricultural policy; and the establishment of building workers' co-operatives. Although the manifesto was not especially radical, it contained the kind of commitments that are traditional for a democratic socialist party.

Yet the contrast between what a party's manifesto contains and what its leader says was particularly apparent in the case of the Labour party. Mr Callaghan's selection and presentation of party policy – and for all essential purposes this was what the media conveyed as Labour's campaign – concentrated on only a few issues: industrial relations, unemployment, prices, social benefits, and the consequences of the Conservatives' pledge to cut income tax.

Despite the enormous damage done to the Labour government's credibility by the winter's strikes, in his speeches Mr Callaghan set great store on the agreement – known as the concordat – reached between the government and trade unions in the aftermath of the strikes. The agreement included pledges by the government and trade unions to work together to bring about a rapid reduction in inflation, as well as fewer strikes, less vehement picketing, and a more tolerant application of the closed shop. This example of voluntary co-operation was contrasted with the Conservatives' proposals to tackle the problems of industrial relations by the law. Despite the events of the past winter, Mr Callaghan repeatedly insisted that statutory solutions to industrial strife would not work, but would lead to confrontation; the only practical measures were those consented to by a partnership of trade unions, management and government.

On unemployment too the government had a difficult record to defend. In its four and a half years of office, unemployment had doubled from 2.8 per cent to 5.6 per cent. But Labour claimed that the rise was modest in the context of the world recession and by international comparisons; and it pointed to signs that unemployment was coming down, a trend it attributed to the numerous job creation and training programmes it had set up. Mr Callaghan stressed the essential role of government, rather than the market alone, in protecting and creating jobs. He reiterated the many detailed proposals in the manifesto for expanding the government's role: a strengthened National Enterprise Board, which would pay particular attention to micro-electronics and other high technology industries; regional development agencies to be added to those already existing in Scotland and Wales; planning agreements with major companies; a voluntary early retirement scheme and a steady move towards a 35-hour week; selective import controls; and, most publicised of all, a pledge 'to ensure that no one will be unemployed for more than twelve months without receiving either the offer of a job or of re-training'. To bring down unemployment the government needed to intervene more, not less.

Despite the near doubling of prices between 1974 and 1979 the issue of inflation provided more favourable battle terrain. Mr Callaghan could at least point to the government's achievement in reducing the annual inflation rate to single figures (this was confirmed – just – by the April figure of 9.8 per cent). He emphasised the government's overriding commitment to bring down the rate to 5 per cent within three years. This would be done by strengthening the powers of the Prices Commission; through the government's agreement with the TUC; and by a radical reform of the EEC's Common Agricultural Policy. The Conservatives' proposals, on the other hand, would raise prices because they intended to abolish the Prices Commission, and because their cuts in income tax would require a rise in VAT, which was directly inflationary. Mr Callaghan's message was simple: a Labour government had brought inflation down and if it was to be kept down a Labour government had to be re-elected. The evidence from our survey (see Chapters 6 and 11) suggests that the message had some effect.

The Prime Minister also played on Labour's traditional appeal as the party of social welfare and public services (that Labour is seen as such a party is confirmed in Chapter 8). He reminded his audiences that Labour was the party that protected the weak, in particular the old, the young, the sick, the unemployed, the poor, and single parents. He pointed to the raising of the real level of pensions, the creation of a disability allowance, and the new child benefit; and he committed a future Labour government to raising their value again in six months. Other commitments included a major extension of nursery education and the eventual abolition of prescription charges. The Conservative party's promise to cut income tax was used to contrast Labour's concern and compassion for the weak with the Conservative's callous disregard. The tax cuts could only be afforded by the running down of public services, including the National Health Service, the schools and the personal social services, and by the abolition or devaluation of welfare benefits.

These specific references to past results and future plans were not, however, couched in explicitly socialist terms. On the contrary, the overall message was conservative: an appeal to the electorate to stick by a government which, despite a few mishaps, had had some modest success, and not to gamble with the experiment of a radical Conservative government. Mr Callaghan asked voters to choose between his way of co-operation and consent, rather than the Conservative way of confrontation and compulsion. His watchwords were national unity and partnership, not class war; his rhetoric was pragmatic rather than idealistic and concrete rather than philosophical; his appeal was to old loyalties rather than to potential converts. The overall impression was of a politician, and by projection a party, made wise and not a little weary by the hard experience of office.

The Conservatives' campaign

Opposition parties normally contest elections by devoting most of their attention to attacking the government's record, and, as a secondary consideration, by offering a detailed blueprint of what they would do if elected to office. The Conservative party's campaign did not entirely conform to this pattern. Not unnaturally it referred frequently to the alleged influence of 'extremists' in the Labour party; and it exploited the unpopular aspects of the Labour government's record, in particular the winter's strikes, the unprecedented inflation since 1974, and the steadily rising level of unemployment. But the main thrust of its campaign was its own remedies for Britain's ills and the drawing of a contrast between its general political approach and Labour's. Its campaign included a few specific – and probably crucial – pledges, but it avoided a long shopping-list of promises. Its manifesto was less detailed than Labour's; instead it took the 'high ground', emphasising general objectives and the broad principles of free enterprise, competition and individual responsibility. The electorate was to be offered not only a better government and healthier economy, but a different form of government and economy, in which initiative and enterprise would flourish in a bracing climate of untrammelled market forces, free from stultifying state control.

This alternative philosophy was underlined in the five tasks that the Conservative manifesto listed for a future Conservative government:

1. To restore the health of our economic and social life, by controlling inflation and striking a fair balance between the rights and duties of the trade union movement
2. To restore incentives so that hard work pays, success is rewarded and genuine new jobs are created in an expanding economy
3. To uphold parliament and the rule of law
4. To support family life, by helping people to become home-owners, raising the standard of their children's education and concentrating welfare services on the effective support of the old, the sick, the disabled and those who are in real need
5. To strengthen Britain's defences, and work with our allies to protect our interests in an increasingly threatening world

The core of the Conservative campaign – in their broadcasts and in Mrs Thatcher's speeches – consisted of the first two of these themes, notably a cut in public spending, the reform of trade union practices, and the lowering of taxes.

The Conservatives emphatically rejected the Labour government's method of directly controlling prices through the Prices Commission. This was a typical example of the ineffectiveness of state intervention; the Prices Commission would be the first 'quango' to be abolished. The key to counter-inflation was 'sound money' and 'proper monetary discipline'. There would therefore be 'publicly stated targets for the rate of growth in the money supply' and a 'gradual reduction in the size of the government's borrowing requirement'. Prices, interest rates, taxes and unemployment went up when governments spent and borrowed too much; the Conservatives' counter-inflation strategy was to ensure that the government spent and borrowed less. There were two ways this would be done. First, some of the Labour government's new-fangled expenditure would be cut back. What it had nationalised – the aerospace and shipbuilding industries, building development land and the National Freight Corporation – would be denationalised; the financial resources (and powers) of the National Enterprise Board would be severely pruned; and state aid to ailing companies and industries would be rapidly reduced. (The growing electoral popularity of denationalisation is shown in Chapter 8.2.) And secondly, a Conservative government would wage an implacable war against wasteful and unnecessary expenditure by local and central government. Some public expenditure would be exempt from cuts, notably defence, the police, the Health Service, and pensions; and there was no stipulation as to which of the public and social services would be cut back, other than 'expensive socialist programmes'. Nonetheless the manifesto carried a general warning: 'we do not pretend that every saving can be made without change or complaint'.

However, retrenchment of public spending would allow a Conservative government to 'cut income tax at all levels to reward hard work, responsibility and success'. No promise made by any party was repeated so insistently. A precise figure to these tax cuts was not given (except that the top rate would come down to the European average). But commitments to raise the tax threshold, tackle the 'poverty trap', and reduce the burden of the investment income surcharge made the Conservatives' determination to lower everybody's tax bill apparent to all. The Labour party counter-campaigned on the amount by which VAT would have to be raised as a result; but although this appeared to make some impact on the electorate, the Conservatives retained the offensive throughout the campaign by their clear and persistent pledge to cut income tax. But whether this pledge won many extra votes is doubtful, as Chapter 11 shows.

The third major strand in the Conservative campaign was its proposal for changes in trade union law. There were too many strikes, Conservatives argued; too often they were weapons of first rather than last resort. The Conservatives wished to avoid the calamity the Heath government had created for itself by the sweeping nature of the reforms embodied in the ill-fated Industrial Relations Act. It therefore proposed only a small number of highly specific measures which would be difficult for opponents to interpret as a deliberate onslaught on the trade union movement as a whole. It proposed to review the law on picketing, especially secondary picketing – an obvious response to the events of the winter. It promised to protect individuals expelled or excluded from trade unions where a closed shop operated. It guaranteed to provide public funds for the holding of secret ballots. And it stipulated that 'unions will bear the fair share of the cost of supporting those of their members who are on strike' – a veiled reference to the payment of non-taxable supplementary benefits to strikers. In the field of industrial relations, therefore, the normal attitudes of the two main parties to the role of the state was reversed. The Conservatives proposed to use the law as a regulator, whereas the Labour party insisted that changing the law would not work. Chapter 9 demonstrates that the electorate largely agreed with the Conservatives.

But on two further aspects of the economy the Conservatives maintained their scepticism about the benefits of state intervention. In reaction to the miners' defeat of the Conservative incomes policy in February 1974, and to the winter's strikes, it set its face against a statutory pay policy. Yet within the senior ranks of the party were many who had strongly supported the Heath government's attempts to create an incomes policy, and who feared the consequences of free collective bargaining. The issue received little attention by Conservatives, and in the manifesto a vague compromise was fashioned. A Conservative government would seek 'responsible pay bargaining', leaving the private sector to its own devices, whilst ensuring that wage negotiations in the public sector would 'take place within the limits of what the taxpayer and ratepayer can afford'. The aim was wage restraint, but the means would not be found in the law or by other government sanctions.

On the question of unemployment, too, the Conservatives refused to follow the path of direct state intervention. 'Too much emphasis', the manifesto stated bluntly, 'has been placed on attempts to preserve jobs.' A distinction was drawn between genuine jobs, created and sustained by a dynamic private sector, and artificial jobs, subsidised by the state on the proceeds of over-taxed private companies. A Conservative government would not throw money at unemployment, but rely on unburdened private enterprise to create jobs; again, this proved to be in tune with public sentiment (see Chapter 9.1).

The Conservatives' campaign on issues outside the economy also blended old-fashioned principle with a few fairly modest proposals. The need to tackle the rise in crime, especially violent crime, was a frequent theme; and the tone adopted always one of determination and toughness. The specific measures suggested, however, were not particularly sweeping. The police would receive more pay and better equipment. There would be experiments in certain detention centres with 'a tougher regime as a short, sharp shock for young criminals'. And the House of Commons would be given an early opportunity to have a free vote on the restoration of capital punishment – a way of indicating to the electorate that many Conservatives, including Mrs Thatcher, favoured restoration, without committing the party that far. However, the Conservatives came over as the party more concerned about the issue, especially as the Labour manifesto, and Labour politicians, had little to say about it.

On another emotive issue, race, the Conservative campaign was entirely restricted to the question of immigration, with particular reference to illegal immigration. (The section of the manifesto on immigration and race came under the general heading of 'The Rule of Law'.) The Conservatives' general premise was that 'firm immigration control for the future is essential if we are to achieve good community relations'.

To that end the Conservatives promised to take firm action against illegal entry and to restrict immigration further by such means as quotas, fewer work permits, and a register of immigrants' dependants. However, there was to be 'no question of compulsory repatriation' – which was still the call from the former Conservative, Enoch Powell. It was generally believed that the Conservatives' proposals would have only a modest impact on the scale of coloured immigration, which was anyway small. Nonetheless they were in line with the policies announced by Mrs Thatcher in January 1978 (when she made her controversial remarks about 'swamping'), and thus reinforced the impression that the Conservatives were the 'tougher' of the two parties on coloured immigration. (See Chapter 10.3 for a detailed analysis of the relations between the issue of race, perceptions of the parties' positions, and the vote.)

In the field of social policy ('Helping the Family') the Conservatives made fewer commitments and were perhaps less distinctive. They concentrated on housing and education. There was no repeat of the commitment made in October 1974 (by Mrs Thatcher, as opposition spokesman on housing) to bring down mortgage rates; it was simply assumed that along with other interest rates they would trickle down as the government spent and borrowed less. But one housing proposal received a lot of attention. The Conservatives promised to oblige local authorities to allow council house tenants to buy their houses at a substantial market discount and with 100 per cent council-provided mortgages. The Labour party was not opposed in principle to the selling of council houses. But its attitude was never more than lukewarm, and many local Labour authorities were strongly opposed on the grounds that it would deplete the public housing stock in areas where there was a shortage of cheap rented accommodation for families who could not afford a mortgage. The Conservatives could therefore continue to claim to be the party of home-ownership and a 'property-owning democracy'.

The Conservatives' campaign on education stressed standards and quality, which they contrasted with Labour's alleged obsession with the structure of the schools system. They promised to retain schools of 'proven worth' (which meant local grammar schools) and to repeal the provision in the 1976 Education Act which obliged local authorities to submit plans for comprehensive schools (a provision which a number of Conservative local authorities had successfully resisted up to 1979). They would oblige state schools to publish prospectuses and examination results, and would establish an assisted places scheme for bright children from poorer families wishing to attend independent, fee-paying schools. Thus the emphasis of the Conservatives was on strengthening the meritocratic element of the educational system – from which, as the media frequently pointed out, Mrs Thatcher herself had benefited as a child.

Foreign affairs played little part in the Conservatives' campaign. The EEC was treated as an economic issue: the Conservatives pledged themselves to work with Britain's EEC partners, rather than against, as they alleged the Labour government was doing; but in common with all other parties called for a radical change in the Common Agricultural Policy. Whilst leader of the Opposition, Mrs Thatcher had earned herself the sobriquet of 'iron maiden' for voicing her deep distrust of the Soviet Union and for calling for a strengthening of the West's defence. The only other international issue to excite British politicians was Rhodesia, most Conservatives being critical of the attempt by Labour's foreign secretary, Dr Owen, to find a settlement acceptable to the black guerilla forces. But all these matters stayed in the background during the campaign itself. As usual, the election was about domestic issues, and in particular the state of the British economy.

The Liberal campaign

The Liberal party entered the election campaign with two additional disadvan-

tages to those it was accustomed to facing as a minor party with limited resources and little publicity. In August 1978 the party's former leader, Jeremy
Thorpe, was charged with conspiring to murder his alleged, one-time, homo-
sexual lover. The drawn-out committal proceedings, open to the press, included
sordid allegations of sexual exploitation, blackmail, and the embezzlement of
party funds; but Mr Thorpe insisted on defending his seat of North Devon. The
party's second liability was its difficulty in establishing an equal distance from
both main parties, after having sustained the minority Labour government in
1977 and 1978 (although Chapter 12.6 suggests that the Liberals were largely
successful in doing this by election day). Nonetheless, in the campaign the Liberal
party appealed for 'a large wedge' of Liberal MPs to hold the balance between
the two big parties, and defined the choice before the electorate as one between
the failed old two-party system and a new political system.

The Liberal manifesto, which was accurately reflected in Mr Steel's speeches,
concentrated on four areas:

1. 'Fundamental' political and constitutional reform
2. Industrial and economic reform
3. The need to change and simplify 'our over-burdened tax system'
4. The need to 'bring to bear an environmental perspective across the whole
    range of government policies'

The dominant theme, therefore, was institutional reform, and the word 'reform',
alongside 'co-operation' and 'conservation', was the most frequent in Mr Steel's
vocabulary.

The overriding priority was constitutional change, which encompassed a long
list of reforms. First and foremost was proportional representation ('the key to
the lock'). Others included regional devolution within England, as well as for
Scotland and Wales; the eventual establishing of a federal Europe, a written
constitution and Bill of Rights, an elected second chamber, a system of more
powerful select committees in the Commons, and more open government based
on a Freedom of Information Act, and the reform of the Official Secrets Act.
The opening sentences of the manifesto caught the flavour of these sweeping
proposals: 'this election could be about something more important than a change
of government. It could be a chance to change a failed political system.'

The two main proposals for dealing with the economy were industrial democracy and a statutory prices and incomes policy. A sharing by employees in the
profits and decision making of their company was advocated as a way to break
down class divisions and produce a new spirit of co-operation in the workplace.
A statutory prices and incomes policy, given teeth by tax incentives and penalties,
was regarded as the only alternative to high unemployment, or inflation, or both.

Under the third heading of tax reform the Liberals proposed measures which
were markedly more radical, although less well publicised, than those of the
Conservatives. They included the use of tax credits in place of means tests, social
security payments and personal allowances; a 20 per cent standard rate of income

tax and a raising of thresholds, a shift towards the taxation of expenditure and wealth; and the replacement of rates by a local income tax and a tax on land values.

The Liberal party's emphasis on the environment was the most original of its themes; the two main parties virtually ignored the issue. The manifesto advocated the development of a long-term plan for the conservation of energy, land and other non-renewable resources; investment in energy saving; a slow-down in the depletion of North Sea oil, a 'war' on waste and pollution, and the establishing of a permanent Energy Commission.

It was therefore far from true, as it is sometimes asserted, that the Liberal party lacked policies, or put forward no more than a mixture of what was offered by the two main parties. However, these specific proposals were lost in the customary overall appeal which the Liberal party tried to make: that of a centrist and modern party, independent of capital and organised labour, capable of exercising a moderating influence on a government of either party, if sufficient of its candidates were elected to Westminster.

The tone of the campaign

A recital of the parties' specific proposals does not do full justice to the overall impression made by each party in the campaign. The ways in which policies are justified, presented and related to each other also contribute to a party's general image. In this respect the two major parties presented a marked contrast.

The first of these contrasts lay in the ideological coherence of the Conservative party's proposals and the more piecemeal quality of Labour's. The Labour campaign was strictly down to earth, its language concrete and practical, its tone slightly weary and sceptical. No single principle or ideological position tied together its various proposals other than, perhaps, the need for co-operation and partnership. The Conservatives' pledges and policies, however, were presented with evangelical enthusiasm and woven together into a simple ideological frame: the need to tilt the balance of responsibility in society away from the state and towards the individual. Shot through the Conservatives' proposals, too, was the recurring motif of authority and discipline – not only in relation to crime and schools, but also wage negotiations and the government's own responsibility for controlling the money supply. Thus the sum of Conservative policy came to more than its parts, the sum of Labour policy less; the Conservatives presented a long-term programme, Labour a set of immediate measures.

A second, related, contrast lay in the fervour with which the parties campaigned. The Conservatives were emphatic and on the offensive; Labour cautious and on the defensive. This was partly the inevitable result of Labour being in government and the Conservatives in opposition, but partly too a reflection of Mr Callaghan's and Mrs Thatcher's personalities. Mr Callaghan was an apostle of persuasion and consensus, Mrs Thatcher the missionary of fundamentalist truths;

Mr Callaghan the politician of experience, Mrs Thatcher the politician of will.
'I am a conviction politician', Mrs Thatcher claimed. 'The Old Testament prophets
did not say, "Brothers, I want consensus." They said, "This is my faith and
vision. This is what I passionately believe. If you believe it too, then come with
me."' Mrs Thatcher came over as tough-minded, determined and implacable,
Mr Callaghan as gentler and more guarded, and these impressions rubbed off on
to the parties they led.

These two contrasts between the parties resulted in a third. Unusually for
British politics, Labour wore the mantle of the Establishment, offering reassur-
ance and advocating continuity, whereas the Conservatives were the party of
radical change. The Conservatives called for a decisive break, not only with the
outgoing Labour government, but with the policy consensus operated by both
parties since the war. They called for more than the defeat of the Callaghan administration – for an end to Keynesian demand-management economics, for a
rolling back of the corporate state, and for a gradual dismantling of the welfare
system. 'Most people', the Conservative manifesto concluded, 'in their hearts
know that Britain has to come to terms with reality . . . the years of make believe
and false optimism are over.'

Thus the 1979 election campaign appeared to offer the British electorate a
clearer choice than for many years. The parties competed not only in terms of
their leaders, or their managerial competence, or even the specific measures they
proposed, but in terms of deeper differences of philosophical outlook. Which, if
any, of these differences proved decisive with the electorate is the subject of the
remainder of this book.

2

The flow of the vote

In the 1970s the British electorate appeared to be edging away from a pattern of voting it had maintained throughout the quarter century from the Second World War. The eight general elections from 1945 up to 1970 displayed three main, interconnected, features. The first was an almost rock-like stability to the major party division of the vote. From 1950 to 1970 both parties' share of the vote fell within the narrow six-point range of 43 to 49 per cent and the average swing between them was only 2.5 per cent.[1] Elections were therefore decided by tiny fluctuations of Conservative and Labour support. The second feature was that these ripples of change were remarkably *uniform*, in magnitude as well as direction, across the whole of Great Britain. In every election at least three-quarters of the constituency swings were within two per cent of the national median, and usually only a handful of seats swung against the national trend. To know the swing in Cornwall was to know, within a percentage or two, the swing in the Highlands. The third feature was that, partly as a result of the first two, the Conservative and Labour parties enjoyed a seemingly impregnable *two-party dominance* over the electorate, and thus over the House of Commons. Britain has never in fact been a pure two-party system: since 1945 minor parties have not only contested many constituencies, but not infrequently have come runners up, and very occasionally won. But from 1945 to 1970 the two parties won, on average, all but 8 per cent of the vote and all but 2 per cent of the seats. For a quarter-century a stable two-party system was securely rooted in the electorate.

The last three elections – those of February 1974, October 1974 and 1979 – mark a significant departure from each of these three voting patterns. The electoral serenity of earlier elections made way for unusual turbulence. The February 1974 election produced the largest turn-round of party fortunes since 1945, mainly but not entirely at the Conservatives' expense. The Conservative share of the vote slumped by 8.6 per cent, the sharpest loss it, or indeed any party, has incurred since 1945. But Labour's share also fell, by 6.0 per cent, the worst deterioration suffered by the major Opposition party in half a century.

The main beneficiary of this snub to both main parties was the Liberal party, whose share of the vote almost trebled from 7.5 per cent to 19.3 per cent. In Scotland the emergence of the Nationalists was equally dramatic: they doubled their vote from 11.4 per cent to 21.9 per cent. In the election eight months later there was less change (except in Scotland where the Nationalists advanced further still). The discontinuity with 1970 was therefore maintained and in some sense reinforced. But in 1979 there was marked electoral instability once more. The 5.2 per cent national swing was the highest since the war, and there were some unprecedentedly large swings in individual constituencies.[2]

These electoral fluctuations of the 1970s were accompanied by a geographical unevenness unknown since the 1920s. In the two 1974 elections the party system in Scotland was transformed by the rise of the Nationalists from a fringe party to the main contender against Labour; and in rural and suburban England, especially in the South, the party landscape was substantially altered by the emergence of the Liberals as major challengers to the Conservatives. In the 1979 election, as pointed out in Chapter 1, there were marked disparities of swing between the regions and within the regions between the large cities and the hinterland. By the end of the decade there were reasons to doubt the existence of a single *British* general election and to assert 'The End of British Politics'.[3]

But the most significant feature of the elections of the 1970s is that they cracked the Conservative and Labour parties' post-war grip over the electorate. In 1970 the two parties' hegemony looked as solid as ever. They took 90 per cent of the vote, 98 per cent of the seats and first and second place in all but 44 of the constituencies. But in February 1974 the minor parties tripled their representation in Westminster from 13 to 37, and came runners up in a further 169 constituencies – over a quarter of the country. The two-party share of the vote dropped to 74.9 per cent, and of the electorate to 58.5 per cent (from 64.4 per cent in 1970). This grip was loosened further in October 1974, when their share of the electorate slipped further, to 54.7 per cent, and two more minor party MPs were elected – making a post-war record. And although the two-party grip tightened again in 1979 it did not regain its former hold. The two-party share of the electorate rose to 61.4 per cent, falling far short of normal levels in the preceding quarter century. The 1970s therefore mark the decade in which the mass foundations of the two-party system were, if not toppled by electoral earthquakes, at least weakened by electoral tremors.

The purpose of this chapter is to map and measure these tremors. It traces the patterns of net electoral change across two, three and occasionally four elections in the 1970s, estimates their magnitude, reveals their consequences for the major and minor parties, and makes comparisons with the elections of the 1960s. It begins with a description of the components of electoral change, of the ways these can be identified and measured, and of the best means of summarising their contribution to an election result. The section that follows contains summary descriptions of the net electoral change (the 'flow of the vote') registered at the

February 1974, October 1974 and 1979 elections, and proceeds to a detailed description of the criss-crossing pathways by which this change came about. It tells us the exact contribution of various categories of vote changers – not only direct switchers between the main parties, but those moving to and from abstention, or into and out of the electorate itself – to the election result. Our next section ('The Flow of the Vote Across the 1970s') examines vote switching across three and four elections in order to reveal more about selected aspects of electoral change across the decade. In particular we focus on the decline and partial recovery of the Conservatives, the more-or-less continuous decline of the Labour party, and the advance and partial retreat of the Liberals. Our final section ('Patterns of Electoral Change 1959 – 1979') takes a longer perspective still, by comparing the 1974 and 1979 elections with those of the 1960s. Based on an analysis of the complete set of national election surveys going back to 1963, it assesses whether electoral volatility has been on the increase, as commonly supposed, and whether its pattern has significantly changed over the last twenty years. Our analysis leads to conclusions rather different from the conventional wisdom, with some surprising implications for a proper interpretation of the electoral change of the 1970s.

2.1 The components of electoral change

Until now we have described the electoral change of the 1970s solely on the basis of national or constituency election returns. Aggregated statistics of this kind, however, are inadequate for gauging the magnitude and direction of the various components of electoral change. The underlying pattern of vote switching is usually more complex than the net, visible movement suggested by the aggregate statistics. This is partly because vote switching is always multi-directional: the partisan tide might be flowing strongly in one direction but there will always be cross-currents and counter-eddies. We shall come across some spectacular examples of this phenomenon later in the chapter. Aggregate statistics cannot identify these counter-flows, let alone measure their precise strength, especially when the situation is confounded by the advance and retreat of minor parties. What is needed, therefore, is data on individual electors, preferably a record of the vote of an identical set of electors (or 'panel') at two or more successive elections. (For a detailed assessment of the relative merits of using panel rather than cross-sectional data, see Appendix.) We therefore make use of three panel samples. The first consists of the 1,096 respondents from Butler and Stokes' 1970 cross-sectional sample whom we managed to re-interview in February 1974. The second consists of the 1,830 respondents who were interviewed for the *first* time in February 1974 and whom we were able to recontact in October 1974. And the third consists of 765 respondents – of whom all but nine were also respondents in February 1974 – re-interviewed in 1979.

From time to time we also analyse the three-wave February 1974 – October 1974 – 1979 panel of 756 respondents.

Panel data of this kind amply confirms that the real pattern of vote switching at the 1979 election was more complex than the result indicated. Table 2.1 displays the October 1974 – 1979 *outflow*, i.e. the 1979 destination of October 1974 voters. It shows, for example, that a higher proportion of October 1974 Conservatives (89 per cent) than of their Labour (80 per cent) or Liberal (46 per cent) contemporaries stayed loyal to their party five years later. It shows that Liberal defectors were four times as likely to switch to the Conservatives (39 per cent) than to Labour (9 per cent) and that those October 1974 abstainers who voted in 1979 were twice as likely to plump for the Conservatives (33 per cent) as for Labour (16 per cent). This is the pattern one would expect of an election won so decisively by the Conservatives. But the table also reveals that a minority of electors swam against the tide: 3 per cent of October 1974 Conservatives, 9 per cent of October 1974 Liberals and 16 per cent of October 1974 non-voters shifted to Labour in 1979. The electoral stream did not all flow one way.

The outflow table allows the reader to compare the rate and direction of defections from each party. But it does not easily lend itself to precise measures of the relative contribution made by each category of switchers to the election result, because the 'pools' of October 1974 Conservative, Liberal, Labour and other voters from which the defectors flowed vary considerably in size. The Labour pool was a little larger than the Conservative pool, and both were substantially bigger than the Liberal pool. Table 2.1 can therefore provide no more

Table 2.1 *The October 1974 – 1979 outflow: the 1979 vote of October 1974 voters*

October 1974 vote	1979 vote						
	Conservative	Liberal	Labour	Other	Did not vote	Total per cent	Number of respondents
Conservative	89	5	3	–	3	100%	228
Liberal	39	46	9	–	6	100%	118
Labour	8	7	80	–	5	100%	284
Other	(17)	(8)	(21)	(38)	(17)	(100%)	(24)
Did not vote	33	7	16	2	41	100%	82
All	41	13	36	2	9	100%	736

Note: October 1974 vote is as reported in October 1974. Respondents refusing or unable to declare their vote at either election have been omitted from the table.

The percentage figures for October 1974 'Other' voters have been placed in brackets because they are based on a very small number of respondents; interpretation of their meaning must take this into account.

Data source: British Election Study October 1974 – 1979 panel sample (N = 765)

than a rough impression of the pattern of vote changing between October 1974 and 1979; and this impression can sometimes be misleading. For example, the 39 per cent Liberal-to-Conservative defection rate appears to be a far more significant contribution to the Conservative victory than the 8 per cent Labour-to-Conservative defection rate. But its true significance is less impressive once it is realised that there were under half as many Liberals as Labour voters (respectively 16 per cent and 39 per cent of our panel sample) in October 1974. Similarly, the fact that three times the proportion of October 1974 Liberals (9 per cent) as October 1974 Conservatives (3 per cent) defected to Labour in 1979 at first suggests that there were three times as many ex-Liberals as ex-Conservatives amongst Labour's 1979 recruits. But there were not, because the Conservative pool was twice as large as the Liberal pool.

One way of rectifying this capacity to mislead is provided in Table 2.2. This table is based on the identical raw data, but reverses perspective and displays the October 1974 – 1979 *inflow*, i.e. the October 1974 origins of 1979 voters. It shows, for example, that amongst 1979 Conservative voters ex-Liberals were not four times as numerous as ex-Labour voters – as Table 2.1 might have been thought to show – but only twice as numerous. Similarly, it reveals that Labour's small number of recruits from other parties in 1979 were almost equally divided between former Liberal and Conservative voters, and not, as Table 2.1 seems to suggest, twice as numerous amongst the former as the latter. Clearly, an adequate account of the contribution made by different components of electoral change to the 1979 election result requires an amalgamation of inflow and outflow data.

Table 2.2 *The October 1974 – 1979 inflow: the October 1974 vote of 1979 voters*

| October 1974 vote | 1979 vote | | | | | |
	Conservative	Liberal	Labour	Other	Did not vote	All
	%	%	%	%	%	%
Conservative	67	12	3	(–)	9	31
Liberal	15	57	4	(–)	11	16
Labour	8	22	86	(–)	20	39
Other	1	2	2	(82)	6	3
Did not vote	9	6	5	(18)	53	11
Total per cent	100%	100%	100%	(100%)	100%	100%
Number of respondents	305	94	262	(11)	64	736

Note: See Table 2.1.
Data source: See Table 2.1.

However, the amalgamation of inflow and outflow data by itself would not be enough, for two reasons. First, at every election there accrues to each party a net increment or decrement of votes from the continuous turnover of the electorate brought about by comings of age and deaths, and by immigration and emigration. Panel data are necessarily incapable of recording such sources of electoral change. Thus, for a complete picture of the October 1974 – 1979 outflow, Table 2.1 requires an additional row showing the 1979 vote of those who were ineligible to vote because, for example, at the time they were under eighteen or were not resident British citizens. Since a panel sample is drawn from the electoral register it cannot include such cases. Similarly, for a complete picture of the October 1974 – 1979 inflow, Table 2.2 requires an additional column showing the October 1974 vote of those not on the 1979 register because, for example, they had since died or emigrated. Such people, too, cannot be part of the panel sample's second wave even if they were interviewed at the first wave. In addition to panel survey data, therefore, we require independent estimates of the vote cast by those who entered or left the electorate between the two elections.

Figure 2.A displays all the different streams of vote changing that can occur between two elections, including those that arise from people entering or leaving the electorate in the intervening period. The streams inside the dotted circle represent the electoral change attributable to switching between parties. The streams crossing the dotted circle represent the electoral change attributable to other factors, namely the physical replacement of the electorate and shifting rates of electoral participation. The change in the Conservative vote between two elections can be seen to depend on the net outcome of the two-way exchange of electors between the Conservative party and
- the Labour party (marked A on Figure 2.A)
- the Liberal party (B^{con})
- the various other parties (C^{con})
- non-voting at the first or second election ($D^{con} + E^{con}$)
- membership of the electorate at the first and second elections (F^{con})

The change in the Labour vote between two elections depends on the net result of the equivalent set of exchanges (A, B^{lab}, C^{lab}, etc.). The combination of these two sets of vote-switching streams therefore explains the change in lead of one major party over the other between two elections. These components of change can be categorised as follows:

Straight conversion (marked A on Figure 2.A)
The circulation of Liberals ($B^{con} + B^{lab}$)
The circulation of other party supporters ($C^{con} + C^{lab}$)
Differential abstention ($D^{lab} - D^{con}$)
Differential turnout ($E^{con} - E^{lab}$)
The replacement of the electorate ($F^{con} + F^{lab}$)

We shall now proceed to a discussion of each of these six components.

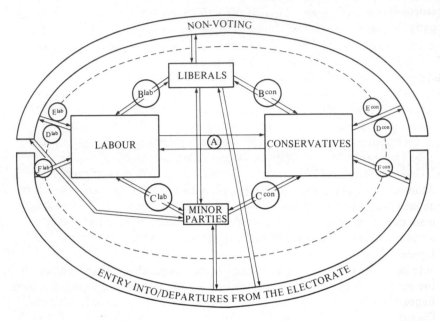

Components of change in the major party lead

A = Straight conversion
$A^{con} + B^{lab}$ = The circulation of Liberals
$C^{con} + C^{lab}$ = The circulation of minor party supporters
⎤ attributable to switching between
⎦ parties (streams within dotted circle)

D = Differential abstention
E = Differential turnout
F = The replacement of the electorate
⎤ attributable to other factors
⎦ (streams cutting across dotted circle)

Figure 2.A *The flow of the vote between two elections*

Straight conversion (A)

Direct switching between Labour and Conservative is the most obvious source of change in the relative strength of the two major parties. In popular commentary on elections it is sometimes assumed to be the only source of such change, and wrongly thought to be the same as 'swing'. But its relationship to major party change is not always simple, or even important. A sizeable national swing between the two main parties is not necessarily caused by straight conversion on a large scale (Butler and Stokes showed that it was in 1966 and 1970, but not in 1964);[4] equally, a negligible national swing can be the net outcome of substantial direct switching, but in both directions, as we shall see for February 1974. However, unlike our other components of electoral change, it makes a *double* contribution to the change in the *major party lead*, since a direct switch of vote is simultaneously one vote extra for the favoured party and one vote less for the losing party. Straight conversion therefore consists of:

$$
\left(
\begin{array}{l}
\text{Number switching} \\
\text{from Labour at} \\
\text{election 1 to} \\
\text{Conservative at} \\
\text{election 2}
\end{array}
\right)
\quad \text{minus} \quad
\left(
\begin{array}{l}
\text{Number switching} \\
\text{from Conservative} \\
\text{at election 1 to} \\
\text{Labour at election} \\
2
\end{array}
\right)
\quad \times\, 2
$$

The circulation of Liberals (B^{con} plus B^{lab})

At most general elections there is discussion in the media and party organisations about the impact of fluctuations in Liberal support on the standing of the two main parties, or of the entry and exit of Liberal candidates on individual constituency results. There have been two grounds for such speculation. First, Liberal strength has varied markedly since the war, from 2.6 per cent of the total vote in 1951 to 19.8 per cent in February 1974. Part of that variation reflects the number of constituencies contested by Liberals: in 1951 it was 109, in February 1974, 517. But the average performance of Liberal candidates has also fluctuated considerably, from 12.1 per cent of the constituency vote in 1950 to 23.7 per cent in February 1974. As both types of variation have an impact on the major party lead, both must be incorporated into accounts of the flow of the vote. Secondly, panel surveys have consistently revealed an exceptional fluidity in the Liberal vote. The typical pattern is for a large fraction of previous Liberals to defect, usually reverting to their major party of origin, in exchange for a smaller proportion (but not necessarily smaller number) of former Conservative and Labour voters.[5] But the exchange is never exactly equal in its relative outcome on the Conservative and Labour parties, or between both parties on the one hand and the Liberal party on the other.

There are particularly compelling reasons for analysing the effect of Liberal traffic in the elections of 1974 and 1979. One reason is the unusually high number of Liberal candidates: up from 332 in 1970 to 517 in February 1974, up again to 619 eight months later (setting two post-war records), and down only a little to 576 in 1979. A second reason is the strong ebb and flow of the Liberal vote in the 1970s: it trebled between 1970 and the two 1974 elections, only to be cut by a third between October 1974 and 1979. There are also grounds for assuming that Liberal circulation might have had a less neutral impact than usual on the two major parties in 1979. One is the consistent way, stretching back over half a century, in which the Liberal vote has fallen sharply under Labour governments to the apparent benefit of the Conservatives; the second is the 1977 – 8 Lib-Lab pact, which will have closely identified the Liberal party with Mr Callaghan's administration in the minds of many voters.

The precise consequences of Liberal circulation for the change in the major party lead can be estimated by the following equation:

$$\left[\left(\begin{array}{c}\text{Number switching}\\\text{from Liberal in}\\\text{election 1 to}\\\text{Conservative in}\\\text{election 2}\end{array}\right)\ \text{minus}\ \left(\begin{array}{c}\text{Number switching}\\\text{from Conservative}\\\text{in election 1 to}\\\text{Liberal in election}\\2\end{array}\right)\right]+\left[\left(\begin{array}{c}\text{Number switching}\\\text{from Labour in}\\\text{election 1 to}\\\text{Liberal in election}\\2\end{array}\right)\ \text{minus}\ \left(\begin{array}{c}\text{Number switching}\\\text{from Liberal in}\\\text{election 1 to}\\\text{Labour in election}\\2\end{array}\right)\right]$$

Circulation of other party supporters (C^{con} plus C^{lab})

From 1945 to 1970 less than a quarter of the electorate in Great Britain were confronted by candidates from other than the three leading parties and less than one in forty gave them their vote. But in the elections of 1974 and 1979 the minor parties made more of a mark. In Wales and Scotland, the Nationalists stood in every constituency (except Orkney and Shetland in February 1974). In Wales, Plaid Cymru's share of the vote hardly changed, slipping from 11.5 per cent in 1970 to 10.8 per cent in both 1974 elections, and down further to 8.1 per cent in 1979. In Scotland, however, the Nationalist tide advanced strongly between 1970 and October 1974 (from 11.4 per cent to 30.4 per cent), and ebbed rapidly in 1979 (down to 17.3 per cent), affecting all three British parties, but not equally, nor in a way that was identical from one type of constituency to another.[6]

The impact of such electoral movements, however dramatic within their own regions, is inevitably limited for Great Britain as a whole by demographic arithmetic: Scotland and Wales between them form less than a sixth of Great Britain's electorate. However, as Table 2.3 shows, to the Nationalists must be added a swelling army of candidates from weaker but geographically less circumscribed parties. From 1945 to 1970 there were, on average, only 88 of such candidates; in February 1974 there were 254; in October 1974, 277; and in 1979, 585, including 303 from the National Front, 38 Communists and 54 from the fledgling Ecology Party.

Altogether the Nationalists and other minor parties took 3.4 per cent of the total vote in February 1974, 4.3 per cent eight months later and 3.3 per cent in 1979. These modest proportions do not suggest that the minor parties had a major bearing on Conservative and Labour fortunes, but they may well mask larger movements at the individual level, and are anyway an increase on the proportion for the preceding elections, which was 1.4 per cent on average. The calculation of the impact of minor party circulation is similar to that for 'Liberal circulation':

$$\left[\left(\begin{array}{c}\text{Number switching}\\\text{from other parties}\\\text{in election 1 to}\\\text{Conservative in}\\\text{election 2}\end{array}\right)\ \text{minus}\ \left(\begin{array}{c}\text{Number switching}\\\text{from Conservative}\\\text{in election 1 to}\\\text{other parties in}\\\text{election 2}\end{array}\right)\right]+\left[\left(\begin{array}{c}\text{Number switching}\\\text{from Labour in}\\\text{election 1 to other}\\\text{parties in election}\\2\end{array}\right)\ \text{minus}\ \left(\begin{array}{c}\text{Number switching}\\\text{from other parties}\\\text{in election 1 to}\\\text{Labour in election}\\2\end{array}\right)\right]$$

Table 2.3 Minor party candidates and vote shares 1945 – 1979

Elections	Scottish National Party		Plaid Cymru		National Front		Communist Party		Other parties		All minor parties		
	Candi-dates	% of GB vote	Candi-dates	% of GB vote	Candi-dates	% of GB vote	Candi-dates	% of GB vote	Candi-dates	% of GB vote	Candi-dates	% of GB vote	% of GB electorate
1945–70 (mean)	15	0.3	16	0.2	n.a.	n.a.	40	0.2	48	0.7	119	1.4	1.1
February 1974	70	2.0	36	0.6	54	0.2	44	0.1	156	0.5	360	3.4	2.7
October 1974	71	2.9	36	0.6	90	0.4	29	0.1	158	0.3	384	4.3	3.1
1979	71	1.7	36	0.4	303	0.6	38	0.1	244*	0.6	692	3.3	2.5

Notes: n.a. = not applicable. The National Front first fielded candidates (10) in 1970, who have been included in the 'other parties' category for 1945–70.
*including 54 candidates for the newly formed Ecology Party.

Data sources: The Times Guide to the House of Commons May 1979 (London: Times Books, 1979);
F.W.S. Craig, British Parliamentary Election Statistics 1918–1970 (Chichester: Political Reference Publications, 2nd edition, 1971); Craig, Britain Votes 2.

Differential turnout (D) *and Differential abstention* (E)

If the electorate was divided into fixed proportions of regular voters and regular non-voters, abstention from the polls would not affect election outcomes. But turnout fluctuates from one election to another. Its official level in Great Britain rose sharply from 71.9 per cent in 1970 to 79.0 per cent in February 1974, fell back to 73.0 per cent eight months later, and recovered slightly to 76.2 per cent in 1979. Most of this variation can be attributed to the age of the register[7] at the time of the election, but whatever the explanation, all movement between voting and non-voting affects the election outcome, and most affects the major parties' fortunes. According to panel data we have analysed elsewhere[8] the large majority of non-voters in any single election are indeed 'once only' abstainers rather than permanent stay-aways, who will have cast a vote at both the previous and following election. To the extent that these votes do not divide identically, at least one party stands to gain and another to lose. And there is no reason to assume that movement to or from abstention will affect the Conservative and Labour parties equally. Indeed, it is part of the common lore of elections that Labour is the less effective at 'getting its vote out', a belief sustained by hard evidence in the case of postal votes.[9] Since most elections are decided on slender changes of net support for the two main parties, the small partisan imbalances in the joint outcome of differential abstention and turnout can be decisive.

In our presentation of this component of major party change we shall separate the impact of *differential abstention* from *differential turnout*. The former refers to movements of electors from a major party vote at one election to non-voting at the next; the latter to movements from non-voting at one election to a vote for a major party at the next. Differential abstention consists of:

$$
\left(
\begin{array}{l}
\text{Number switching} \\
\text{from Labour in} \\
\text{election 1 to} \\
\text{abstention in} \\
\text{election 2}
\end{array}
\right)
\text{minus}
\left(
\begin{array}{l}
\text{Number switching} \\
\text{from Conservative} \\
\text{in election 1 to} \\
\text{abstention in} \\
\text{election 2}
\end{array}
\right)
$$

Differential turnout consists of:

$$
\left(
\begin{array}{l}
\text{Number switching} \\
\text{from abstention in} \\
\text{election 1 to} \\
\text{Conservative in} \\
\text{election 2}
\end{array}
\right)
\text{minus}
\left(
\begin{array}{l}
\text{Number switching} \\
\text{from abstention in} \\
\text{election 1 to} \\
\text{Labour in election} \\
\text{2}
\end{array}
\right)
$$

We make this separation because, although both components reflect the relative abilities of the two main parties to overcome apathy amongst their potential supporters, we shall discover that they do not necessarily work in tandem, or make an equal contribution to overall shifts in major party strength.

The replacement of the electorate (F^{con} plus F^{lab})

The electorate is subject to constant renewal and depletion, a process which is not necessarily neutral in its partisan consequences. Butler and Stokes showed that throughout the 1960s it worked to Labour's advantage. This was partly because there were more Conservative than Labour voters amongst those who died, but more because the Conservatives were markedly less popular than Labour amongst young people and immigrants coming on to the register. And this edge could be crucial: in 1964 it made the difference between a Labour and Conservative victory.[10]

Figures for the physical evolution of the electorate between the three pairs of elections in the 1970s are given in Table 2.4. They show how the modest changes in the size of the registered electorate from one election to the next masked a much larger demographic turnover produced by comings of age and death, and by immigration and emigration. For example, between October 1974 and 1979 the number of registered electors rose by just over one million, a growth of 2.7 per cent. But our estimates – the procedures we adopted are described in the Appendix – show that this small increase was the net outcome of almost three and a half million leaving the 1974 electorate through death and emigration, while almost four and a half million entered the electorate through immigration, naturalisation or reaching their eighteenth birthday. In less than five years eight million people had moved in or out of the registered electorate. Over the decade as a whole the size of the turnover is more dramatic. Of the 1970 electorate nearly one in five was no longer entitled to vote by 1979; of the 1979 electorate just over one in five had not been entitled to do so in 1970; in all, fifteen million people joined or left the electorate, a turnover of one-third in the space of only nine years.[11]

To work out the contribution made by the physical replacement of the electorate to changes in the major party lead we must first estimate the departing electors' vote at the previous election and the entering electors' vote at the current election. How this is done is explained in the Appendix. We can then apply the following formula:

$$\left[\left(\begin{array}{c} \text{Number of} \\ \text{Conservative} \\ \text{voters who} \\ \text{have entered} \\ \text{electorate} \end{array} \right) \text{minus} \left(\begin{array}{c} \text{Number of} \\ \text{Labour voters} \\ \text{who have} \\ \text{entered} \\ \text{electorate} \end{array} \right) \right] + \left[\left(\begin{array}{c} \text{Number of} \\ \text{previous} \\ \text{Labour voters} \\ \text{who have left} \\ \text{electorate} \end{array} \right) \text{minus} \left(\begin{array}{c} \text{Number of} \\ \text{previous} \\ \text{Conservative} \\ \text{voters who} \\ \text{have left} \\ \text{electorate} \end{array} \right) \right]$$

Only one further problem remains to be resolved before we are ready to proceed with the analysis.[12] Our survey data, being based on a random sample, are not perfectly representative of the Great Britain electorate. In most respects it is very representative; the three-party division of the 1979 vote amongst our respondents, for example, is very close to the actual election result. But as in

Table 2.4 *The physical turnover of the electorate 1970 – 1979 (in thousands)*

Pair of elections	Number of electors* at first election	Number *departing* from electorate through:				Number *entering* electorate through:				Number of electors* at second election (% difference between first and second election)
		Death	Emigration	Total	% of old electorate	Reaching 18	Immigration and naturalisation	Total	% of new electorate	
1970 – Feb 1974	38,007	2,298	710	3,008	-7.9%	2,708	732	3,440	+8.9%	38,439 (+1.1%)
Feb 1974 – Oct 1974	38,439	391	121	512	-1.3%	290	–	290**	+0.8%	38,217 (−0.6%)
Oct 1974 – 1979	38,217	2,921	515	3,436	-9.0%	3,839	629	4,468	+11.4%	39,249 (+2.7%)

Notes:
*Great Britain electorate only. The figures are adjusted for deaths and emigration between the base date for compilation of the register and polling day.
**Both elections in 1974 were fought on the same register. Those reaching the age of 18 between the two elections were eligible to vote in October if their name and eighteenth birthday were listed in the 1974 register (as they were entitled to be); immigrants' names could not be added to the register between the two elections.

Data sources: The Times Guide to the House of Commons for 1970, February 1974, October 1974, and 1979; Craig, *Britain Votes 2: Annual Abstract of Statistics 1980* (London: HMSO, 1980), Chapter 2; Office of Population Census and Surveys, *Mid-1979 Population Estimates for England & Wales*, OPCS Monitor PP1 80/1, May 1980.

almost all national election surveys our sample severely under-represents non-voters. The official abstention rate in 1979 was 24 per cent, whereas reported non-voting in our sample amounted to only 9 per cent. In order to measure the exact contribution of different components of electoral change to an election result we therefore need, in addition to an integration of inflow and outflow data, and to independent estimates of the impact of the physical turn-over of the electorate, a weighting of our sample so as to bring the overall distribution of party references in line with the actual result of both elections in question. The Appendix describes the technical details of how this was done.

2.2 The flow of the vote in February 1974, October 1974 and 1979

In this section we shall present a complete picture of the flow of the vote be-tween each consecutive pair of elections in the 1970s. This will be done in Tables 2.5 to 2.8, which are directly comparable to similar tables constructed for the elections of the 1960s by Butler and Stokes in *Political Change in Britain*. How-ever, we have somewhat elaborated upon Butler and Stokes' format for the presentation of the data by adding an 'other party' category, and by including more summary information at the bottom of each table.[13]

A word of caution needs to be added about the interpretation of the flow-of-the-vote tables that follow. Each of these tables is based on too small a number of respondents for all the differences between individual cells (i.e. components of electoral change or constancy) to have statistical significance at the customary levels of confidence. This will not affect the broad conclusions we reach about the flow of the vote at each election, nor preclude generalisations about the typical partisan impact of a component of electoral change. But although our calculation of the net effects of different categories of electoral change on the major party lead remains a legitimate accounting operation, the fragility of our data must be borne in mind when interpreting the significance of a single component of electoral change at any one election.

1970 – February 1974

The turnover of votes between 1970 and February 1974 is presented in Table 2.5. It immediately demonstrates how deceptive aggregate election statistics can be. The Conservative lead over Labour declined by a gentle 0.7 per cent, an 'electorate swing' of 0.35 per cent.[14] Underlying this collective calm, however, was very considerable individual turbulence.

All three parties in February 1974 lost about a third of their 1970 supporters. Of those entitled to vote at both elections only 58 per cent stayed with the same party (or twice abstained). Yet it was not the substantial body of switchers who threw the election to the Labour party. Straight conversion from Conservative to Labour did not help because it was exactly balanced by conversion in the

Table 2.5 *The flow of the vote from 1970 to February 1974*

All entries in this table are expressed as percentages of the total number of electors eligible to vote in one or both elections.

		Con	Lib	Lab	Other	Did not vote	Left electorate	1970 electorate	
1970	Con	19.6	2.6	1.9	0.3	3.6	2.4	30.4	33.2
	Lib	0.5	2.9	0.3	0.2	0.6	0.5	5.0	5.5
	Lab	1.9	3.3	16.7	0.6	4.1	2.2	28.8	31.5
	Other	0.2	0.4	0.1	0.7	0.0	0.1	1.5	1.7
	Did not vote	5.1	3.8	5.3	0.5	9.1	2.1	25.9	28.1
	Entered electorate	1.3	1.5	3.4	0.2	1.9		8.3	
		28.6	14.5	27.7	2.5	19.3	7.3	100.0%	
February 1974 electorate		30.7	15.7	30.1	2.7	20.9		N = 1064	

Components of change in the major party lead

Straight conversion
$(1.9) - (1.9) \times 2$ = 0.0

Circulation of Liberals
$((0.5) - (2.6)) + ((3.3) - (0.3))$ = +0.9

Circulation of other party supporters
$((0.2) - (0.3)) + ((0.6) - (0.1))$ = +0.4

Differential turnout
$(5.1) - (5.3)$ = −0.2

Differential abstention
$(4.1) - (3.6)$ = +0.5

Replacement of the electorate
$((1.3) - (3.4)) + ((2.2) - (2.4))$ = −2.3

Change from 1970 Con lead of
1.6 to February 1974 Con lead
of 0.9   = −0.7

Indicators of change and stability

Of those entitled to vote in 1970 and/or Feb 1974, 84.4 per cent were entitled to vote at both, of whom

41.9 per cent changed their vote
58.1 per cent were constant

February 1974 constancy rate of:

1970 Conservatives : 70.0 per cent
1970 Liberals   : 64.4 per cent
1970 Labour voters: 62.8 per cent
1970 Non-voters   : 38.2 per cent

Notes: For a description of how the flow-of-the vote tables were constructed see Appendix. The major party lead presented in this table, and for October 1974 and 1979 in Tables 2.6 to 2.8, is narrower than the one with which readers will be familiar. This is because the basis of our calculations is not just those who voted, but all those who were in the electorate *at either one of the two elections*. For a normally spaced pair of elections this is likely to add between a third and a half to the percentage base and thus reduce the gap between the two major parties by a similar amount. Readers will also be surprised by the percentage figures for non-voting. They are slightly lower than the customary figures because the size of the registered electorate on which they are based has been adjusted to take account of deaths and emigration between the compilation of the register and polling day. The N refers to the number of respondents entitled to vote, and interviewed, at both elections.
Data source: British Election Study 1970 – February 1974 panel sample.

opposite direction. It accounted anyway for only a small proportion (10.7 per cent) of all those switching between parties or to or from abstention. The circulation of Liberals was a more common form of vote switching, but actually penalised Labour (by 0.9 per cent)[15] because in February 1974 the Liberal party gained more converts from former Labour than from former Conservative voters. The interchange of minor party supporters also gave an edge to the Conservatives (0.4 per cent), for a similar set of reasons. And although differential turnout fractionally assisted Labour, differential abstention more than compensated the Conservatives. The reduction of the Conservatives' lead over Labour was almost entirely due, in fact, to the one remaining source of change – the physical replacement of the electorate.

We can be more specific. The partisan consequences of departures from the 1970 electorate through death or emigration were negligible, providing Labour with a mere 0.2 per cent advantage. What helped Labour, decisively as it turned out, and not for the first time, was its substantially greater popularity than the Conservatives amongst the one-twelfth portion of the electorate entitled to vote for the first time – the eighteen to twenty-two year olds and, to a lesser extent, newly registered immigrants. Amongst new electors Labour enjoyed a 25 percentage point lead over the Conservatives (41 per cent to 16 per cent), and amongst immigrants a massive 49 per cent lead (56 per cent to 7 per cent), as mentioned earlier. The decisiveness of the physical replacement of the electorate may be put this way: had the February 1974 vote been cast by the 1970 electorate, the electoral swing would have been to the Conservatives, and although only of the order of 0.4 per cent, sufficient to provide the Conservatives with an additional twenty or so seats and thus to return them comfortably to office.

February 1974 – October 1974

The election of October 1974 followed so closely upon the last that, at least by outward appearances, little changed. The same party leaders campaigned on similar issues to an almost identical electorate, and in aggregate terms the party division of the vote remained similar, at least outside Scotland. Yet, as Table 2.6 shows, none of the three main parties managed to retain more than three-quarters of their February 1974 vote. For the Conservative and Labour parties this was a superior retention rate to that for 1970 – February 1974; but it was far short of the continuity one might have expected since both parties had been reduced in February 1974 to an unprecedentedly small (and thus, one might have supposed, loyal) portion of the electorate, and only eight months separated the two elections.

These shifts of support, however, cannot match the massive discontinuity of Liberal voting between February and October 1974. A more striking instance of the disparity between net and gross electoral change would be hard to find. Liberal support over the eight months gave every indication of stability, slipping a mere 2 per cent. But Table 2.6 shows that the Liberal party was abandoned by almost half (48 per cent) its February 1974 supporters – about three million voters – a mere eight months later, yet obtained near to this share of the vote by attracting over two million new voters within the same brief interval.[16] Although less than one voter in five was a Liberal at either election, one in three (32 per cent) cast a Liberal vote at least once. No other party, not even the Nationalists, was subject to so much displacement; indeed, even non-voters showed more consistency. Despite its promotion in 1974 to the status of a major third party, the Liberals continued to distinguish themselves from their two major rivals, and from the major third party north of the Border, by the rapidity with which they could simultaneously win and lose large segments of the electorate.

The turnover table for February 1974 to October 1974 reveals that on this occasion the large-scale circulation of Liberals was the single most important source of the 3.0 per cent net change in Conservative and Labour support. On the one hand, more February Liberals defected to Labour than to the Conservatives; on the other, the Liberal candidates in October attracted twice as many February Conservatives as February Labour supporters. Half the 'electorate swing' to Labour can be attributed to this uneven exchange.

By itself, however, Liberal circulation would have been insufficient to give Labour an absolute majority in the Commons. Almost as important, and in contrast to February 1974, was the advantage accruing to Labour through differential abstention and turnout. Whereas unwillingness to vote again put Labour at a fractional disadvantage, this was more than counter-balanced by Labour's greater attraction to former non-voters: of the one elector in fifteen who abstained in February but turned out in October, 44 per cent voted Labour and 27 per cent Conservative.

The remaining three components of major party change were of minimal consequence. The rate of straight conversion from one major party to the other was again the same in both directions and anyway negligible. The circulation of minor party supporters continued to have a miniscule impact, at least on Great Britain as a whole, although it did help Labour fractionally. The short interval between the two elections precluded any significant change arising from the physical replacement of the electorate. In contrast to February 1974, therefore, the swing to Labour came about by conventional means: Labour had the edge in recruiting (or, more probably, re-recruiting) from that relatively uncommitted sector of the electorate composed of former Liberals and non-voters.

1970 – October 1974

We can now proceed to examine the components of major party change over the period 1970 – October 1974. Earlier analyses of panel data have demonstrated that change over successive pairs of elections is not aggregative: switchers of

Table 2.6 *The flow of the vote from February 1974 to October 1974*

		October 1974						February 1974 electorate	
		Con	Lib	Lab	Other	Did not vote	Left electorate		
February 1974	Con	22.0	2.3	0.7	0.7	4.5	0.4	30.6	30.7
	Lib	1.9	8.0	2.3	0.2	3.1	0.1	15.6	15.7
	Lab	0.7	1.2	22.4	0.5	4.7	0.4	29.9	30.1
	Other	0.1	0.1	0.2	1.7	0.3	0.0	2.4	2.7
	Did not vote	1.7	1.7	2.8	0.1	14.0	0.4	20.8	20.9
	Entered electorate	0.1	0.1	0.4	0.0	0.1		0.7	
		26.5	13.4	28.8	3.2	26.7	1.3	100.0%	

October 1974 electorate   26.9   13.7   29.3   3.2   27.0   N = 1754

Components of change in the major party lead *Indicators of change and stability*

Straight conversion
$(0.7) - (0.7) \times 2$ = 0.0

Circulation of Liberals
$((1.9) - (2.3)) + ((1.2) - (2.3))$ = −1.5

Circulation of other party supporters
$((0.1) - (0.7)) + ((0.5) - (0.2))$ = −0.3

Differential turnout
$(1.7) - (2.8)$ = −1.1

Differential abstention
$(4.7) - (4.5)$ = 0.2

Replacement of the electorate
$((0.1) - (0.4)) + ((0.4) - (0.4))$ = −0.3

Change from February 1974
Con lead of 0.7 to October
1974 Con lag of 2.3   = −3.0

Of those entitled to vote in Feb 1974 and/or Oct 1974, 98 per cent were entitled to vote at both, of whom

30.5 per cent changed their vote
69.5 per cent were constant

October 1974 constancy rate of:

February 1974 Conservatives :   72.8 per cent
February 1974 Liberals :   51.6 per cent
February 1974 Labour voters: 75.9 per cent
February 1974 Non-voters: 68.6 per cent

See notes to Table 2.5.
Data source: British Election Study February 1974 – October 1974 panel sample.

Table 2.7 *The flow of the vote from 1970 to October 1974*

| | | October 1974 | | | | | | 1970 | |
		Con	Lib	Lab	Other	Did not vote	Left electorate	electorate	
	Con	17.6	3.4	1.1	0.6	4.9	2.7	30.3	33.2
	Lib	0.3	2.6	0.5	0.2	0.7	0.6	4.9	5.5
	Lab	1.1	2.3	16.9	0.5	5.4	2.5	28.7	31.5
1970	Other	0.1	0.2	0.2	0.4	0.5	0.1	1.5	1.7
	Did not vote	4.2	3.1	4.4	0.8	10.6	2.5	25.6	28.1
	Entered electorate	1.2	0.9	3.8	0.4	2.6		8.9	
		24.5	12.5	26.9	2.9	24.7	8.4	100.0%	
October 1974 electorate		26.9	13.7	29.3	3.2	27.0		N = 2097	

Components of change in the major party lead

Straight conversion
$(1.1) - (1.1) \times 2$ = 0.0

Circulation of Liberals
$((0.3) - (3.4)) + ((2.3) - (0.5))$ = -1.3

Circulation of other party supporters
$((0.1) - (0.6)) + ((0.5) - (0.2))$ = -0.2

Differential turnout
$(4.2) - (4.4)$ = -0.2

Differential abstention
$(5.4) - (4.9)$ = +0.5

Replacement of the electorate
$((1.2) - (3.8)) + ((2.5) - (2.7))$ = -2.8

Change from 1970 Con lead of
1.6 to October 1974 Con lag
of 2.4 = -4.0

Indicators of change and stability

Of those entitled to vote in 1970 and/or October 1974, 82.7 per cent were entitled to vote at both, of whom

41.8 per cent changed their vote
58.2 per cent were 'constant'*

October 1974 'constancy rate'* of:

1970 Conservatives: 63.8 per cent
1970 Liberals: 60.5 per cent
1970 Labour voters: 64.5 per cent
1970 Non-voters: 45.9 per cent

Notes: *These figures are over-estimates because they define as 'constant' those electors who voted the same way in 1970 and October 1974, but differently in February 1974. Also, see notes to Table 2.5.
Data source: British Election Study 1974 cross-section sample. Vote in 1970 is measured by recall in October 1974.

votes at one election are disproportionately likely to switch again at the next, and, moreover, to revert to their party of origin. The turnover figures for 1970 to October 1974 (Table 2.7) will not reveal the total amount of vote changing over all three elections because, for example, an elector switching from Conservative to Liberal and back again to Conservative would be recorded as an unchanging Conservative.

However, the turnover figures do allow us to account for Labour's two-step attainment of power between 1970 and October 1974. Two components of electoral change proved to be important. Of the 4.0 per cent net change in Labour's favour, 2.8 per cent resulted from the physical replacement of the electorate, notably from Labour's marked advantage over the Conservatives amongst new electors. The rest came from the circulation of the Liberal vote, which, although marginally at Labour's expense in February 1974, did more damage to the Conservatives eight months later. Switches to and from abstention first injured Labour, then the Conservatives, the effects cancelling each other out; the impact of the minor parties was negligible, and of straight conversion nil. The flow of the vote can, therefore, be summarised as follows: most of the physical change in the electorate occurred between 1970 and February 1974; whereas Labour only gained from the circulation of Liberal voters after February 1974. The swing resulting from the former was enough to narrow the Conservatives' 1970 lead to almost nothing by February 1974; the swing resulting from the latter was sufficient to turn it into a Labour lead. To simplify a little, what toppled the Conservative government was the new generation of electors in February 1974, and what transformed a Labour government from minority to majority status was the pattern of Liberal gains and losses over the subsequent eight months.

October 1974 – May 1979

Between October 1974 and May 1979 a 2.3 per cent Labour lead in the electorate was transformed into a 5.1 per cent Conservative lead, the sharpest reversal of fortunes for the major parties since 1945. Three separate but not inconsistent accounts of this turn-round can be offered. The first focuses on the most obvious source, the direct conversion of former Labour voters into Conservatives. The Conservative party made unusually strenuous efforts to win over normally Labour working-class voters, as reflected not only in their explicit appeals[17] but in their specific commitments to abandon wage controls, further restrict immigration, and oblige local authorities to offer to sell council houses at favourable terms to their tenants. The above average swings to the Conservatives amongst manual workers, which we discuss in the next chapter, suggest that these efforts met with some response.

The second explanation centres on the decline of the Liberals. Under every Labour government the Liberal vote has fallen and, with the exception of the short-lived 'nursery' Labour administrations of 1964–6 and February – October 1974, the Conservative vote has risen. There were particularly good reasons to expect a repeat of the pattern in May 1979. For one thing, as we have already seen, in October 1974 the Liberal party recruited more Conservative deserters than Labour deserters; the Conservatives would therefore stand to benefit from any general reversion to old loyalties. For another, the Liberal party had been closely associated with the Labour government, to the point of rescuing it from an early election, under the terms of the 1977–8 Lib-Lab pact; thus right-wing Liberals had more reason than usual, and left-wing Liberals less, for abandoning their party in favour of the Conservative and Labour parties respectively.

The third explanation also attributes the Conservatives' victory to indirect gains, but this time to the failure of Labour to mobilise its nominal supporters. This is a traditional lament of Labour party officials, but one given some extra plausibility in 1979 by the Labour government's failure to improve more than marginally the living standards of its natural supporters, and by the spectacular damage done to its overall credibility during the winter's strikes of 1978–9.

From the relative size of the components of major party change (see Table 2.8) it is clear that the Conservatives owed their election victory in about equal measure to straight conversion, Liberal circulation, and movements to and from non-voting. The single most important factor in the 7.4 per cent net change was straight conversion (3.4 per cent); yet it was not, perhaps, as substantial a factor as might have been anticipated. By itself it could not have produced an overall majority in the Commons for the Conservatives.

There was, once again, massive movement in and out of the Liberal camp. The Liberal party was deserted by three-fifths of its October 1974 supporters – almost three million voters – but attracted two and a quarter million new supporters. As expected, the Conservatives benefited from both the inflow and the outflow. For every two October 1974 Liberals who defected to Labour, five defected to the Conservatives; but for every two new Liberal recruits made from the Conservatives, three were made from Labour. The net result was a 2.5 per cent advantage to the Conservatives.

If the contribution of non-voting to the Conservatives' success was not entirely unanticipated, its magnitude and form was. For Labour was not ditched by failing to get its voters out – 'differential abstention' harmed it by a mere 0.5 per cent – but by the Conservatives' superior ability to win over previous non-voters. A fifth of their May 1979 vote, and half of their new recruits, came from this group. Whether they were returning home after a temporary stay-away protest in October 1974, or completing the last leg of a journey from the Labour side that started earlier, will be investigated later.

Not every component of electoral change worked in the Conservatives' favour. Once again, the physical replacement of the electorate helped Labour, and for the usual reasons: of those who died after October 1974 slightly more were Conservative than Labour, whereas of those coming on to the register a clear plurality

Table 2.8 *The flow of the vote from October 1974 to 1979*

		1979						October 1974 electorate	
		Con	Lib	Lab	Other	Did not vote	Left electorate		
	Con	17.3	1.0	0.7	0.1	2.4	3.0	24.5	27.4
	Lib	3.4	4.7	1.4	0.1	1.9	0.9	12.5	14.0
	Lab	2.4	1.5	17.3	0.1	2.9	2.6	26.8	30.0
October 1974	Other	0.3	0.2	0.4	1.3	0.5	0.1	2.9	3.2
	Did not vote	5.7	1.3	3.2	0.6	10.5	1.4	22.8	25.5
	Entered electorate	2.6	1.3	3.6	0.1	3.0		10.5	
		31.8	10.0	26.7	2.4	21.2	8.0	100.0%	
	1979 electorate	34.6	10.9	29.0	2.6	23.0		N = 1528	

Components of change in the major party lead

Straight conversion
$(2.4) - (0.7) \times 2$ = 3.4

Circulation of Liberals
$((3.4) - (1.0)) + ((1.5) - (1.4))$ = 2.5

Circulation of other party supporters
$((0.3) - (0.1)) + ((0.1) - (0.4))$ = −0.1

Differential turnout
$(5.7) - (3.2)$ = 2.5

Differential abstention
$(2.9) - (2.4)$ = 0.5

Replacement of the electorate
$((2.6) - (3.6)) + ((2.6) - (3.0))$ = −1.4

Change from Oct 1974 Con lag
of 2.3 to 1979 Con lead of 5.1   = +7.4

Indicators of change and stability

Of those entitled to vote in October 1974 and/or 1979, 81.5 per cent were entitled to vote at both, of whom

37.3 per cent changed their vote
62.7 per cent were constant

1979 constancy rate of:

October 1974 Conservatives: 80.5 per cent
October 1974 Liberals: 40.5 per cent
October 1974 Labour voters: 71.5 per cent
October 1974 Non-voters: 48.8 per cent

Notes: See Appendix on how this table was constructed. Also, see the notes to Table 2.5.
Data source: British Election Study cross-sectional sample; British Election Study October 1974 – 1979 panel sample.

were Labour. Had voting in 1979 been confined to the October 1974 electorate the 'electorate swing' to the Conservatives would therefore have increased by 0.7 per cent, worth an extra fifteen to twenty seats. But a qualification needs to be made. The Conservatives' traditional demographic liability was less pronounced than usual: in the elections of 1970 and February 1974, for example, the physical re-composition of the electorate was worth 2.3 per cent to Labour in contrast to the 1.4 per cent this time. The reason for Labour's diminished advantage on this occasion can be found amongst the young voters. In February 1974, for example, eighteen to twenty-two year olds gave Labour a 32 percentage point advantage over the Conservatives; in 1979 they voted Labour and Conservative in almost exactly equal numbers. Thus, Labour's advantage from the physical replacement of the electorate appears to be largely due to the overwhelmingly Labour vote of newly registered immigrants.[18]

2.3 The flow of the vote across the 1970s

So far we have confined our analysis to the individual vote changes that occur between two consecutive elections. This can provide a useful account of the short-term electoral movements that contribute to a particular election result, but its narrow focus carries one disadvantage. The significance of a switch between parties from one election to another varies according to the prior and subsequent voting pattern of which it forms a part. Consider, for example, a voter switching from Liberal to Conservative between October 1974 and 1979. The voter could be returning to a normal Conservative allegiance, or could be a life-long Liberal registering a temporary protest, or could be on the last stage of a ten-year ideological drift from the Labour party. Similarly, somebody switching from Conservative in 1970 to Liberal in February 1974 might have been making a permanent conversion, a one-off protest, or the first step towards regular support for the Labour party. Without examining the prior voting history of the first elector, and the subsequent voting history of the second, we have no way of telling.

Our map of the pathways of change between October 1974 and 1979 prompts questions which can only be answered by reference to prior voting patterns. Were most of the Conservative recruits in 1979 simply reverting to an old allegiance, and, if, so, had it been an intermittent or long-lasting allegiance? Or had most of them abandoned long-held Labour and Liberal loyalties, thus providing the Conservative party with genuinely fresh – and perhaps permanent – converts? Were the Conservatives' gains from the non-voters of October 1974 no more than the re-couping of once only abstainers or the mobilisation of a hitherto non-partisan segment of the electorate? Similarly, our maps of the pathways of change between 1970 and the two 1974 elections raise questions which can only be answered by examining subsequent voting histories. What was the outcome of Liberal gains from the two major parties between 1970 and

1974? How many of these Liberal recruits stuck to their new party in its difficult year of 1979 – something that would suggest enduring conversion – and how many returned to their major party colours? What has become of the support Labour lost between 1970 and February 1974 and which, from the appearance of overall election returns, it has never recovered?

We shall attempt to answer these and similar questions by analysing the 1,300 respondents in the 1979 survey on whom we have voting information (which includes the act of not voting) for each of the four elections from 1970 to 1979. Our record of their vote is always based on the respondent's report which was made closest in time to the election in question. This means that the February 1974 and October 1974 votes of panel respondents are taken from the survey conducted immediately after these two elections, whereas the February 1974 and October 1974 vote of non-panel respondents are based on their recollection of how they had voted five years earlier. Because the panel does not extend back to 1970, the 1970 vote of panel respondents is based on recall at the time of their first interview, and that of non-panel respondents is based on recall in 1979. Our sub-sample is confined to those respondents eligible to vote at all four elections. It therefore excludes those aged eighteen to twenty-six in 1979, because they will have been too young to vote in 1970, and it seriously under-represents the older electors of 1970, many of whom will have died by 1979. As a result the discussion that follows does not consider the part played by the physical replacement of the electorate in the four-stage voting patterns.

The major parties' decline 1970 – February 1974: where were the defectors by 1979?

We begin by focusing on the path taken in October 1974 and 1979 by various categories of switchers between 1970 and February 1974. The distinctive feature of the February 1974 election was that *both* major parties lost votes, and at a heavy rate by post-war standards. The Conservative share of the poll dropped from 46.4 to 37.8 per cent, and the Labour share from 43.1 to 37.1 per cent. Our main interest will therefore be in the subsequent history of these major party defectors. How many had returned home by 1979 and how many continued to stay away?

Table 2.9 displays the rates at which the Conservative and Labour parties recovered their February 1974 defectors; for comparison it also gives the rates at which they retained their February 1974 loyalists. It shows, first, that the *immediate* recovery rate was very low: less than a fifth reverted to their 1970 loyalties in October 1974 and remained loyal subsequently. Not surprisingly, the *eventual* recovery rate – the eventual return to 1970 loyalties by 1979 – was larger. Yet it was far from complete. Only half (51 per cent) of the Conservative defectors had been won back by 1979, leaving 40 per cent who continued to stay away. A small portion of these stay-aways will have been regular Labour or Liberal

Table 2.9 *The Oct 1974 and 1979 vote of Conservative and Labour loyalists and switchers in 1970 – Feb 1974*

Vote in 1970 Vote in Feb 1974	Conservative switchers Con Not Con	Conservative loyalists Con Con
	%	%
Conservative recovery/retention		
Immediately		
Voted Con in *both* 1974 *and* 1979	18 ⎤	80
Later	⎬ 51	
Voted Con in 1979 but *not* Oct 1974	33 ⎦	9
Conservative losses		
Voted Con in *neither* Oct 1974 *nor* 1979	40	4
Other		
Voted Con in Oct 1974 but *not* 1979	10	8
Total per cent	100%	100%
Number of respondents	136	429

Vote in 1970 Vote in Feb 1974	Labour switchers Lab Not Lab	Labour loyalists Lab Lab
	%	%
Labour recovery/retention		
Immediately		
Voted Lab in *both* Oct 1974 *and* 1979	19 ⎤	73
Later	⎬ 33	
Voted Lab in 1979 but *not* Oct 1974	14 ⎦	2
Labour losses		
Voted Lab in *neither* Oct 1974 *nor* 1979	57	5
Other		
Voted Lab in Oct 1974 but *not* 1979	10	20
Total per cent	100%	100%
Number of respondents	90	451

Note: Respondents ineligible to vote in any of the four elections from 1970 to 1979, or whose vote at any one of the four elections was not ascertained, have been excluded from the table. The February 1974 and October 1974 votes of panel respondents are based on the survey conducted immediately after the election in question; those of non-panel respondents on their recollection in 1979 of how they voted five years earlier. The panel does not extend back to 1970; the vote recorded for 1970 is therefore based on recall in 1979 in the case of non-panel respondents, and recall at the time of the first interview in the case of panel respondents.
Data source: British Election Study 1979 cross-section sample, incorporating the British Election Study February 1974 – October 1974 – May 1979 panel.

supporters in the 1960s who were temporarily attracted to the Conservatives in 1970; they should not, perhaps, be regarded as 'losses' at all. Nonetheless this still suggests that the Conservative party made a less than full recovery from its nadir in 1974. Amongst Labour defectors the eventual recovery rate was more modest still. Only one in three (33 per cent) had returned to the Labour party by 1979, whereas well over half (57 per cent) continued to stay away. This difference between the recovery rates of the two parties is more intriguing, moreover, than the bare statistics suggest. For whereas not all the Conservative defectors of February 1974 had formerly been regular Conservatives, the large majority of Labour defectors had formerly been regular Labour voters.[19]

The obvious next question is: where did the stay-aways eventually turn up? Here the small numbers in our sample mean that any answers must be tentative. But it is not 'squeezing' the data too hard to suggest that the answer varies, not unexpectedly, according to where the major party defectors in February 1974 first went to (see Table 2.10). Defectors to the Liberals, if they did not revert to their former loyalties, tended to stay Liberal; defectors to the opposite side, if they did not revert, tended to remain with the opposite side. But two qualifications need to be added. First, the *proportion* staying away also appears to have varied with the precise category of defector. As earlier tables have led us to expect, the proportion was lowest amongst switchers to non-voting, highest amongst defectors to the opposite side, and lay in between amongst defectors to the Liberals. And, secondly, there is a hint in the data that Labour defectors were slightly more prone than Conservative defectors to use the Liberal party as

Table 2.10 *Vote in 1979 of different categories of major party defectors in 1970 – February 1974*

Vote in 1970	Conservative			Labour		
Vote in February 1974	Did not vote	Liberal	Labour	Did not vote	Liberal	Conservative
Vote in 1979	%	%	%	%	%	%
Conservative	68	53	37	(1)	17	50
Liberal	7	31	2	(–)	33	11
Labour	–	10	51	(4)	39	21
Other	4	–	–	(–)	–	–
Did not vote	21	6	9	(5)	11	18
Total per cent	100%	100%	100%		100%	100%
Number of respondents	28	62	43	10	46	48

Data source: See Table 2.9.

a stepping stone to the opposite side. Amongst Conservative-to-Liberal defectors, three remained Liberal for every one who moved on to the Labour party; amongst Labour-to-Liberal defectors, only two remained Liberal for every one who moved on to the Conservative party.

The Conservatives' recovery

We shall now reverse perspective and explore the origins of Conservative recruits in 1979. There are two background factors to bear in mind. On the one hand, we already know (see Table 2.2) that recruits formed an unusually large component of the 1979 Conservative vote – 33 per cent if we exclude first-time electors. On the other hand, the Conservative share of the electorate was only slightly higher in 1979 (34.6 per cent) than in 1970 (33.2 per cent). These two facts are logically reconcilable in a wide variety of ways, from which it is useful to pick out two. One possibility is that most Conservative recruits were *homecomers* – regular Conservatives who had nonetheless strayed in either or both 1974 elections but had returned to their true home by 1979. Were this the case, one could regard Conservative gains in 1979 as a *restoration* of Conservative support to something near its normal post-war level; and the Conservative losses in 1974, especially to the Liberals, as a short-lived phenomenon with little lasting impact. Alternatively, most Conservative recruits might be *fresh converts* with no previous record of Conservative support. Were this the case one could regard the Conservative gains of 1979 as a *replacement* of that portion of Conservative support that was lost between 1970 and 1974. It would suggest that in 1979 the Conservative party had made significant inroads into Labour and Liberal support but in turn had lost, probably for good, similar numbers of its own supporters of the 1960s.

Not surprisingly, as Table 2.11 shows, the basis of the Conservatives' recovery in 1979 was a mixture of both restoration and replacement, rather than one to the exclusion of another. Amongst Conservative recruits as a whole, homecomers (i.e. those who had been Conservative in 1970)[20] outnumbered fresh converts (those who had not voted Conservative at either 1970 or February 1974) by 53 per cent to 42 per cent, the remaining 5 per cent falling in neither category. However, this pattern varied sharply according to the particular source of Conservative recruits. The large majority (76 per cent) of recruits from previous non-voters were homecomers, reflecting in part the involuntary nature of much non-voting (through illness, absence abroad, etc.). And amongst Conservative recruits from the Liberals, too, a majority (61 per cent) had been Conservative in 1970. But the background of Labour-to-Conservative switchers was very different: two in three (66 per cent) were voting Conservative for the first time; 45 per cent after three consecutive votes for the Labour party. Summarising broadly, Conservative recruits from former Liberals and non-voters were homecomers; Conservative recruits from Labour were fresh, but not necessarily permanent, converts.[21]

Table 2.11 *The 1970 and February 1974 vote of switchers to the Conservatives in 1979*

Vote in Oct 1974 Vote in 1979	Did not vote	Liberal	Labour	All switchers to Conservative in 1979*
		Conservative		
	%	%	%	%
Homecomers				
Voted Conservative				
in *both* 1970 and Feb 1974	38 }76	28 }61	11 }32	24 }53
in 1970 but *not* Feb 1974	38 }	33 }	21 }	29 }
Fresh converts				
Voted Conservative				
in *neither* 1970 nor Feb 1974	12	33	66	42
Others				
Voted Conservative				
in Feb 1974 but *not* 1970	12	6	2	5
Total per cent	100%	100%	100%	100%
Number of respondents	26	67	56	156
Voted for same party in 1970, Feb 1974 and Oct 1974, before switching to Conservatives in 1979	4%	10%	45%	21%

Note: *includes a few respondents who switched from other parties.
Data source: See Table 2.9.

Labour's defectors in 1979: returning home, or leaving after a long stay?

A different but not inconsistent perspective is provided by focusing on the voting antecedents of Labour defectors between October 1974 and 1979. Once again, the reader is reminded that our interpretations are necessarily based on small numbers and therefore must be regarded as tentative, not definitive. It is again helpful to distinguish between two broad types of Labour defector: the *home-goer*, returning to his normal Conservative or Liberal allegiance, or to his habitual non-voting, after a temporary stay with Labour in October 1974; and the *leaver*, abandoning the Labour party after having voted for it at each of the three previous elections. The arithmetic of the clear decline in Labour's national support from 43.1 per cent of the vote in 1970 to 39.2 per cent in October 1974, and from 31.4 to 28.5 per cent of the electorate – a decline that will have been sharper, moreover, amongst those eligible to vote at both elections – immediately suggests that homegoers will not have accounted for more than a minority of defectors. This suggestion is reinforced by Table 2.12: only 6 per cent of all

Table 2.12 *The 1970 and February 1974 vote of switchers from Labour between October 1974 and 1979*

Vote in October 1974	Labour			All switchers from Labour*
Vote in 1979	Con	Lib	Did not vote	
	%	%	%	%
Voted Labour				
in *both* 1970 and February 1974 (*leavers*)	45	69	79	63
in 1970 but *not* February 1974	7	11	2	6
in February 1974 but *not* in 1970	31	11	10	18
in *neither* 1970 *nor* February 1974	18	10	9	13
Total per cent	100%	100%	100%	100%
Number of respondents	56	39	43	140
Voted for same party in 1970, February 1974 and 1979, having voted Labour in October 1974 (*homegoers*)	11%	3%	2%	6%

Note: *includes two respondents who switched from Labour to a minor party in 1979.
Data source: See Table 2.9

Labour defectors were homegoers in the strict sense of returning to the party they had supported in both 1970 and February 1974. By contrast, 63 per cent abandoned Labour after having stayed with the party throughout its relatively unpopular times of 1970 to October 1974. However, once again the pattern varies, this time according to the destination of Labour defectors. A large majority of Labour abstainers (79 per cent) were Labour in 1970 and February 1974, the main explanation again being that much of the abstention will have been technical rather than political. By comparison, the 45 per cent proportion of leavers amongst the Labour-to-Conservative defectors appears modest. But it is worth noting that they outnumbered the Labour-to-Conservative homegoers (only 11 per cent); and as we know from the previous table this proportion of leavers represents a higher rate of 'fresh conversion' to the Conservatives than that obtained by the Conservative party from former Liberals and non-voters.

The surge and decline of the Liberals: what difference did it make?

Our final exploration of voting pathways from 1970 to 1979 focuses on the longer-term impact of the Liberal surge in 1974. How many of its recruits from the major parties did the Liberal party manage to retain five years later – in the midst of the Thorpe trial and after eighteen months of the Lib-Lab pact? Table 2.13 once again demonstrates the brittle quality of Liberal support. Most

Table 2.13 *Percentage voting Liberal in 1979 amongst those switching to the Liberals in February 1974 or October 1974 and amongst consistent Liberal voters in 1970, February 1974 and October 1974*

Voted Liberal in 1970?	No	No	No	Yes
Voted Liberal in February 1974?	Yes	No	Yes	Yes
Voted Liberal in October 1974?	No	Yes	Yes	Yes
% voting Liberal in 1979	29%	28%	43%	70%
Number of respondents	62	65	70	40

Note: Of the fifteen respondents who voted Liberal in 1970 but in neither of the 1974 elections, only two voted Liberal in 1979. Of the sixteen respondents who voted Liberal in both 1970 and one but not both of the 1974 elections, five voted Liberal in 1979.
Data source: See Table 2.0.

of the Liberal party's 1974 recruits had deserted it by 1979. For every ten who moved to the Liberals in either February 1974 or in October 1974, seven had moved away again by 1979. Of those who switched to the Liberal party in February 1974, and stayed with it in October 1974, over half had left by 1979. Indeed, even amongst the 'core' of thrice-voting Liberals the attrition rate in 1979 was 30 per cent – higher than amongst their Conservative and Labour counterparts (9 per cent and 21 per cent respectively). This is not to deny that the Liberal party's rise in popularity in 1974 produced some enduring gains, but only to suggest that electoral progress for the Liberals takes the slow and frustrating form of three steps forward, two steps back.

The consequences of the 1974 Liberal surge for the major parties in 1979, although limited, was not entirely even-handed. Table 2.14 (which, admittedly, is based on fragile data) suggests that Labour suffered more electoral damage than the Conservatives (see the two right-handed columns in particular). For one thing, the Liberal party was slightly more successful at retaining its Labour recruits than its Conservative recruits. For example, of those who voted Liberal at both 1974 elections, having voted Conservative in 1970, 38 per cent stayed Liberal and 53 per cent returned to the Conservatives; but of those 1974 double-Liberals who had voted Labour in 1970, 45 per cent stayed Liberal and only 25 per cent returned to Labour. These last sets of figures illustrate a second way in which the Liberal surge in 1974 turned out to hurt Labour more than the Conservatives – at least in 1979. Conservative defectors treated the Liberal party as either a permanent resting place or a turn-round point: they either stayed Liberal in 1979 or, more usually, returned home to the Conservatives. But a substantial minority of Labour defectors opted for a third path, using their 1974 move to the Liberals as neither resting place nor turn-round point, but as half-way house on a journey that brought them over to the Conservative party by 1979.

Table 2.14 1979 vote of 1970 major party voters who switched to the Liberals at either or both 1974 elections

| Vote in 1970 | Conservative | Labour | — | — | Conservative | Labour |
| Vote in February 1974 | Liberal | Liberal | Conservative | Labour | Liberal | Liberal |
Vote in October 1974	—	—	Liberal	Liberal	Liberal	Liberal
Vote in May 1979	%	%	%	%	%	%
Conservative	55	17	69	28	53	20
Liberal	30	33	25	36	38	45
Labour	9	39	3	32	–	25
Other/Did not vote	6	11	3	4	9	10
Total per cent	100%	100%	100%	100%	100%	100%
Number of respondents	64	46	32	25	32	20

Notes: '—' = any party.
Data source: See Table 2.9.

In the previous section of this chapter we explored the stability and change in the vote across two elections. In this section we have extended our analysis to the four elections of the 1970s. The impression gained is to some extent contradictory: on the one hand, considerable electoral flux; on the other, a structure to that flux that suggests an underlying stability. Particularly noticeable has been the capacity of both major parties to regain a substantial proportion of their losses in the 1974 elections and the corresponding inability of the Liberals to retain more than a small proportion of their gains. Whether this cyclical pattern was specific to the 1970s or the recurrence of a general phenomenon in British electoral behaviour is the subject of the next and final section.

2.4 Patterns of electoral change 1959 - 1979

The existence of panel data on each of the past six pairs of elections offers a unique opportunity for the analysis of electoral volatility in Britain. Instead of having to rely on one panel survey, we can examine several. Instead of having to base conclusions on only two or three elections, covering a short and perhaps untypical period of a few years, we can explore a much longer period lasting twenty years, in order to unearth lasting regularities and sustained changes. That is the purpose of this final section.

We turn first to questions of magnitude. What is the general level of electoral instability? Is the electorate gradually becoming more fickle, and if so, what form is electoral inconstancy taking? Answers are provided by Table 2.15 which presents the rates of individual constancy and change for each pair of consecutive elections between 1959 and 1979. Change resulting from the entry or departure of electors is excluded since its magnitude is largely a function of the number of electors dying or coming of age between elections, and therefore reflects the length of interval between elections, not changes in individual preference.

Constancy and change between two elections

In recent years commentary on electoral trends in Britain has often referred to the 'growing volatility of the British electorate'. This stock-phrase is based on the increasingly sharp oscillations of support for the Conservative and Labour parties in general elections, by-elections and the regular opinion polls over the last quarter of a century.[22] This growth in *net* electoral change, it is presumed, must reflect a parallel growth in the underlying amount of *gross* electoral change.

Table 2.15, however, casts some doubt on this assumption. The same broad pattern of constancy and change in individual voting appears to have occurred throughout the last twenty years. There has undoubtedly been a substantial volatility of individual voting between consecutive elections. On average one in three electors entitled to vote at two successive elections switched their vote; on no occasion was the proportion less than one in four and at two of the elections

Table 2.15 *Rates of individual constancy and change between each pair of consecutive elections, from 1959 – 1979*

	1959 – 1964	1964 – 1966	1966 – 1970	1970 – Feb 1974	Feb 1974 – Oct 1974	Oct 1974 – 1979
	%	%	%	%	%	%
Remained constant by twice:						
Voting for major party						
Conservative	26 }51	26 }55	24 }47	23 }43	22 }45	21 }42
Labour	25	29	23	20	23	21
Voting for Liberal or minor party	2	4	3	4	10	7
Abstaining	11	15	16	11	14	13
per cent constant	64%	74%	66%	58%	69%	62%
Changed by moving between:						
Conservative and Labour	5	3	5	5	1	4
Conservative or Labour, and Liberal or Nationalist	7	4	4	8	8	9
Voting and abstention*	24	19	25	29	22	25
per cent changing	36%	26%	34%	42%	31%	38%
Total per cent	100%	100%	100%	100%	100%	100%
Number of respondents	1,528	1,340	1,085	1,064	1,754	1,528

Notes: *Also includes a very small number of switchers between minor parties, e.g. Liberal and Nationalist.
The percentage figures in this table are derived from flow-of-the-vote tables that have been weighted according to the procedures outlined in the Appendix.
Data sources: for 1959–64: Butler and Stokes' 1964 cross-section sample
1964–66: Butler and Stokes' 1964–6 panel sample
1966–70: Butler and Stokes' 1966–70 panel sample
1970 – Feb 1974: BES 1970 – Feb 1974 panel sample
Feb 1974 – Oct 1974: BES Feb 1974 – Oct 1974 panel sample
Oct 1974 – 1979: BES Oct 1974 – 1979 panel sample

in the 1970s it was two in five. But it would be mistaken to infer that the individual propensity to switch votes has been on the clear increase. Much of the variation in the amount of vote switching has to do with the different intervals between elections. If that factor is set aside, no more than the mildest of trends can be discerned:[23] the proportion changing their vote did rise from 36 per cent in 1959 – 1964 (and 34 per cent in 1966 – 1970) to 42 per cent in 1970 – February 1974, but fell back to 38 per cent in 1974 – 1979. Fluidity of party choice is not a particularly recent phenomenon amongst British electors. It has existed for at least twenty years.

The pattern of vote switching, moreover, has remained broadly similar over the twenty years. Table 2.15 shows that the amount of straight conversion from one major party to the other remained small throughout the twenty-year period. The direct convert continues to be the exception. The table also shows that, despite the trebling of the Liberal vote between 1970 and 1974, and its continuation at that level eight months later, there was only a small increase in the amount of Liberal circulation; indeed it was no greater than during the earlier Liberal resurgence in 1964. It is movement to and from abstention which continues to account for the large part of all vote changing. In 1959 – 1964 it accounted for one elector in four (and 67 per cent of all vote changers); in 1974 – 1979 the figures are almost identical. The fluidity of the British electorate appears to rest less upon its changing choice of party than upon its choice of whether to vote at all.

What has changed, however, is the amount of constant support for the Conservative and Labour parties. This has never been as large as commonly supposed. The Conservative and Labour icebergs loom large in the sea of the British electorate, but their size and solidity should not be exaggerated. In a typical election of the 1960s and 1970s under half (47 per cent) of the British electorate, excluding new electors, voted for one or other major party twice running. But as Table 2.15 shows, the two icebergs gradually melted over the two decades. Constant support for one or other party dropped from 51 per cent in 1959 – 1964 to 47 per cent in 1966 – 1970, and down again to 43 per cent in 1970 – February 1974 and 42 per cent in 1974 – 1979. This was accompanied, but not entirely counter-balanced, by a small rise in the level of regular voting for the minor parties, which averaged 3 per cent in the three elections up to 1970, and 7 per cent in the three elections after. A comparison of 1964 – 1966 with February – October 1974 is also instructive: although there were fewer, and so one would have supposed more committed, major party voters in February 1974 than 1964, and although the interval between the two 1974 elections was exceptionally brief, consistent Labour or Conservative voting was considerably lower (45 per cent) than between 1964 and 1966 (55 per cent). If proper account is taken of the varying intervals between pairs of elections, the erosion of regular Conservative and Labour voting constitutes clear although undramatic evidence of a declining public commitment to the two governing parties.

From questions of magnitude we turn to the question of partisan advantage, by exploring the contribution of different components of electoral change to the fluctuating fortunes of the Conservative and Labour parties over the last twenty years. Do some components of change regularly help one major party rather than the other, whatever the overall direction of change? Or do all components feed into the general stream of change, albeit in different degrees? Or do both patterns coexist, with some components always helping the same party, and others always conforming to the overall trend? We can begin to answer such questions by inspecting Table 2.16 which presents the magnitude and direction of the components of major party change for each pair of consecutive elections between 1959 and 1979. With no more than six pairs of elections, and a swing to the Conservatives at only two of them, the data are far from ideal. Moreover, the variations of time between elections affect the proportions entering and departing from the electorate and therefore the amount of major party change attributable to such turnover. Nevertheless, a number of patterns over the twenty-year period do emerge.

A glance down each column reveals, first, that in none of the elections did every component of change benefit the same party. The higher-swinging elections (1964, 1966, 1970 and 1979) were marked by relatively more uniformity in the direction taken by the different components of change, but not one escaped counter-trends. In Labour's victory year of 1966, for example, the Conservatives managed to benefit slightly from the circulation of Liberal votes; at its decisive defeat at the following election Labour still gained substantially from the replacement of the electorate. In every election, therefore, runaway victories and humiliating defeats have been partially forestalled by the existence of small electoral movements against the overall trend.

Not only did one or two components of change always flow against the general current; no components conformed to the direction of the net major party change in all six elections. It proved impossible to say, at least for the period under discussion, that whichever party benefited from one component of change would win the election – or even be the party on the upswing. Of all the components of change differential turnout came closest to moving in tandem with the general trend, the only exception being 1970 when its net impact was nil. This probably reflects the susceptibility of intermittent, uncommitted voters to immediate partisan forces rather than the two parties' relative ability to mobilise non-voters.

It is possible, however, to pick out a number of components of change which appear to help one party rather than the other. First, there was an almost continuous trickle of Liberals defecting to the Conservatives' advantage. In addition, differential abstention – non-voting by previous voters – worked against Labour at every election except 1966 (when Labour had its best election in two decades). The element of electoral change most conspicuous for its partisan bias, however, was the physical replenishment of the electorate. At every election the increment of new electors preferred Labour to the Conservatives, usually by a substantial

Table 2.16 Components of major party change for each pair of successive elections, 1959–79

Component of change in major party lead	1959 – 1964	1964 – 1966	1966 – 1970	1970 – Feb 74	Feb 74 – Oct 74	Oct 74 – 1979
Straight conversion	−0.6	−3.2	+4.8	0.0	0.0	+3.4
Circulation of Liberals:						
Defection to Liberals	−1.5 ⎫ −1.2	+0.3 ⎫ +0.8	+0.4 ⎫ +1.2	+0.7 ⎫ +0.9	−1.1 ⎫ −1.5	+0.5 ⎫ +2.5
Recruitment from Liberals	+0.3 ⎭	+0.5 ⎭	+0.8 ⎭	+0.2 ⎭	−0.4 ⎭	+2.0 ⎭
Other circulation	n.a.	n.a.	n.a.	+0.4	−0.3	−0.1
Differential turnout	−1.6 ⎫ −0.8	−0.9 ⎫ −1.6	0.0 ⎫ +2.8	−0.2 ⎫ +0.3	−1.1 ⎫ −0.9	+2.5 ⎫ +3.0
Differential abstention	+0.8 ⎭	−0.7 ⎭	+2.8 ⎭	+0.5 ⎭	+0.2 ⎭	+0.5 ⎭
Replacement of the electorate:						
Entered electorate	−0.6 ⎫ −1.7	−0.4 ⎫ −0.4	−2.4 ⎫ −2.3	−2.1 ⎫ −2.3	−0.3 ⎫ −0.3	−1.0 ⎫ −1.4
Left electorate	−1.1 ⎭	0.0 ⎭	+0.1 ⎭	−0.2 ⎭	0.0 ⎭	−0.4 ⎭
Change in major party lead	−4.3	−4.4	+6.5	−0.7	−3.0	+7.4

Notes: n.a. = not ascertained, + = change in favour of Conservatives, − = change in favour of Labour.
Data source: See Table 2.5.

margin, such as to save it from yet deeper humiliation in 1970 (and, to a lesser extent, 1979) and to hoist it into office in the close-run elections of 1964 and February 1974.

Constancy and change over three or more elections

Investigations confined to pairs of consecutive elections allow for only a limited assessment of the degree and patterns of electoral instability. As explained earlier in this chapter, a switch of votes between two elections takes on a different meaning according to the elector's party choice at earlier and later elections. Moreover, the constancy of voting between only two elections, often no more than three or four years apart, is an unsatisfactory measure of electoral stability, which normally refers to consistency of party choice over a much longer period. We turn finally, therefore, to a consideration of vote-changing patterns over four successive elections.

Table 2.17 shows the proportion of the electorate entitled to vote at any set of three consecutive elections between 1959 and 1979 who consistently voted for the same party, or who persistently abstained. Table 2.18 shows the proportion voting for the same party *four* times running across two sets of elections, those from 1959 to 1970 and those from 1970 to 1979. Both tables reinforce the impression of the electorate that we sketched earlier. The propensity to cast a constant vote is considerably weaker than often supposed, but there is little to suggest a long-term trend in this regard. In the first triad of elections, 1959 – 1964 – 1966, 62 per cent voted consistently; in the most recent triad of February 1974 – October 1974 – 1979, 60 per cent did.

The only concerted change, reflecting the Liberal and Nationalist surges of 1974, was the gentle decline from 57 per cent to 51 per cent in the proportion voting consistently for one of the two main parties. There was a correspondingly modest rise, from 2 per cent to 7 per cent, in the level of consistent Liberal or Nationalist voting – a pale shadow of the two parties' electoral high noons in February and October 1974 respectively.

The absence of any long-term change is even more strikingly illustrated by comparing the four elections from 1959 to 1970 with the four from 1970 to 1979. The pattern of stability and change that emerges for the 1970s is almost identical to that for the 1960s. It suggests that in both decades the British electorate could be divided into four groups. The largest consisted of exactly half the electorate, who changed votes – or moved to or from abstention – on at least one occasion. The remaining half consisted of two blocks, representing a little under a quarter of the electorate each, who consistently voted Conservative and Labour, and a tiny residual group of persistent Liberals, Nationalists and non-voters.[24] The miniscule level of constant support for the minor parties (3 per cent) is a conspicuous reminder of the capacity of the Liberal and Nationalist parties to both win and lose large numbers of major party supporters in rapid

Table 2.17 *Constancy and instability of voting over triads of consecutive elections 1959–1979*

		1959– 1964–1966	1964– 1966–1970	1966– 1970–Feb 74	1970– Feb 74–Oct 74	Feb 74– Oct 74–1979
		%	%	%	%	%
Voted Conservative	3 times	28 ⎫ 57	26 ⎫ 53	25 ⎫ 55	24 ⎫ 49	24 ⎫ 51
Voted Labour	3 times	29 ⎭	27 ⎭	30 ⎭	25 ⎭	27 ⎭
Voted Liberal	3 times	2	2	2	3	6
Voted Other	3 times	–	–	–	–	1
Did not vote	3 times	3	3	1	3	3
Proportion whose vote was constant		62	59	59	54	60
Proportion whose vote changed		38	41	41	46	40
Total per cent		100%	100%	100%	100%	100%
Number of respondents		1,240	900	900	1,640	736

Note: Only those eligible in all three elections have been included. 'Constant vote' includes consistent non-voters; 'changed vote' includes movement to and from abstention. Unlike Table 2.15, the percentages in this and the next table are necessarily based on unweighted flow-of-the-vote data.

Data source: for 1959–64–66: Butler and Stokes' 1964–66 panel sample and respondents' recall, in 1964, of 1959 vote
1964–66–70: Butler and Stokes' 1964–66–70 panel sample
1966–70–Feb 74: BES 1970–Feb 1974 panel sample and respondents' recall, in 1970, of 1966 vote
1970–Feb 74–Oct 74: BES Feb 74–Oct 74 panel sample, and respondents' recall, in Feb 1974, of 1970 vote
Feb 74–Oct 74–1979: BES Feb 74–Oct 74–1979 panel sample

Table 2.18 *Constancy and instability of voting over the four elections from 1959 to 1970 and from 1970 to 1979*

		1959 – 1964 – 1966 – 1970	1970 – Feb 74 – Oct 74 – 1979
		%	%
Voted Conservative	4 times	25 ⎱ 48	23 ⎱ 47
Voted Labour	4 times	23 ⎰	24 ⎰
Voted Liberal	4 times	1	2
Voted Other	4 times	–	1
Did not vote	4 times	1	1
Proportion whose vote was constant		50	51
Proportion whose vote changed		50	49
Total per cent		100%	100%
Number of respondents		786	718

Note: Only those eligible to vote in all four elections have been included. 'Constant vote' includes consistent non-voters; 'changed vote' includes movement to and from abstention.
Data source: 1959–1970: Butler and Stokes' 1964–66–70 panel sample and respondents' recall in 1964 of 1959 vote
  1970–1979: See note to Table 2.9.

succession. This capacity is also reflected in the fact that the Conservative and Labour parties can only count on the unswerving support of a quarter of the electorate each. Their domination of the electorate has depended on their continuing ability to attract the support of an almost equal number of less committed electors.

One further feature of the electoral volatility of the 1970s requires comment. Not surprisingly, consistent voting across three and four elections was less common than across only two. Yet the difference was smaller than one might have expected. Had electoral instability been 'cumulative', that is, had the probability of electors switching votes between one pair of elections been independent of whether or not they switched at the previous pair, voting consistency over the longer term would have been considerably less prevalent than in fact it was. Figure 2.B presents the differences between a cumulative level of voting consistency and the actual level. It shows, for example, that the proportion of electors voting the same way twice running was 58 per cent in February 1974, 69 per cent in October 1974 and 62 per cent in 1979. On the assumption of cumulative change only 25 per cent of all eligible electors (i.e. 58% x 69% x 62%) would have cast the same vote at all four elections in the 1970s. The actual figure was 50 per cent.

A related phenomenon is revealed in Table 2.19. It shows that the proportion of electors who repeated their 1970 vote in 1979 was substantially higher than the observed rates of instability within shorter intervals would have led one to

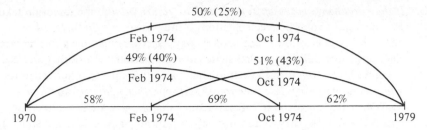

Note: Percentage of electors voting consistently (cumulative percentages in brackets).
Data source: See Tables 2.17 and 2.18.

Figure 2.B *Consistency of voting 1970 – February 1974 – October 1974 – 1979: the difference between observed and hypothetically cumulative levels*

Table 2.19 *The proportion of Conservative, Liberal and Labour voters in 1970 who repeated their vote in 1979: observed and hypothetically cumulative levels*

	Actual proportion	Proportion assuming cumulative change 1970 – Feb 1974 – Oct 1974 – 1979
% of Conservatives in 1970 who voted Conservative in 1979	70%	52%
% of Liberals in 1970 who voted Liberal in 1979	39%	18%
% of Labour voters in 1970 who voted Labour in 1979	60%	40%

Data source: See note to Table 2.9.

expect. If the changes that occurred in the three short inter-election periods had been cumulative only 52 per cent of Conservatives and 40 per cent of Labour voters in 1970 would have voted the same way nine years later; in fact 70 per cent and 60 per cent respectively did so.

How does this paradox of short-term flux but longer-term stability arise? In their study of the 1960s Butler and Stokes came across the same phenomenon.[25] Their explanation rested upon the particular form that vote switching over more than two elections often took. On the basis of their panel data they found that some three-stage movements were more frequent than others. Their main findings can be summarised in the following propositions:

1. *The propensity to switch votes is not uniform*: electors who change votes between one pair of elections are more likely than those who do not to change votes again between the following pair of elections. People with a history of switching their vote are more prone than others to go on switching their vote. Moreover –

2. *If they do change votes again they tend to 'return home'*: the direction taken
    by a change of votes between elections 2 and 3 is strongly influenced by
    party choice at election 1. Put another way, electors switching votes between
    elections 2 and 3, having earlier switched votes between elections 1 and 2,
    are more likely to return to their original party than to any other. Therefore –

3. *The Liberal party acts as a turn-round station rather than half-way house*:
    temporary defectors to the Liberals from a major party are more likely to
    regard the Liberal party as a refuge before returning home than as a stepping
    post on a journey to the other side.

The addition of panel data on the elections of 1974 and 1979 allows us to
examine these propositions in the light not simply of further time points, but of
an unusually widespread movement between the major parties and the smaller
parties and the smaller parties or abstention. Did these patterns recur in the
1970s? And if so, to the same extent? For example, was the advance and partial
retreat of the Liberals over the decade accompanied by an increase in 'homing'?
Or did the Liberal party manage to retain a higher proportion of its recruits
from the major parties in the 1970s than in the 1960s? Had the three-step journey
from one end of the party spectrum to another become a less unusual event?

The general truth of proposition 1 is confirmed in Table 2.20. In each of the
triads of consecutive elections between 1959 and 1979 changing voters were
considerably more likely than constant voters to change again at the following
election.[26] The extent to which they did so varied, but not in a way to suggest
a long-term trend. The source of variation appeared to be the differing time
intervals between pairs of elections. Between the closely-held elections of
1964 – 1966, and February 1974 – October 1974, only a minority of prior
movers again moved (39 per cent and 45 per cent respectively); between the
more normal intervals of 1966 – 1970, 1970 – February 1974 and October
1974 – 1979 a majority of prior vote switchers switched votes again. This
suggests that political memory counts for something; that it may take a normal
parliamentary term for the majority of vote changers to forget the party they
turned to and to forgive the party they left.

The impact of political 'memory' is further illustrated by the behaviour of
Conservative and Labour defectors (see Table 2.21). If Labour defectors changed
votes again at the following election they were more likely to return to their
prior Labour allegiance than to move elsewhere (except in 1970).[27] This was
even true in 1979, despite the strong Conservative tide that was then flowing.
Similarly, in the normal election intervals of 1966 – 1970, 1970 – February
1974 and October 1974 – 1979 the majority of prior Conservative defectors did
return home even when, as in October 1974, the national swing was towards
Labour. Only in the elections of 1966 and October 1974, separated by unusually
short intervals from the preceding election, did the majority of previous Conservative defectors stay with their party of adoption. In these two instances
conversion, albeit temporary, was more common than reversion.

Table 2.20 *Proportion changing vote between two elections by whether they changed votes at the preceding pair of elections, for each triad of consecutive elections 1959–1979*

	1959 – 1964 – 1966		1964 – 1966 – 1970		1966 – 1970 – Feb 74		1970 – Feb 74 – Oct 74		Feb 74 – Oct 74 – 1979	
	Constant vote 1959 – 1964	Changed vote 1959 – 1964	Constant vote 1964 – 1966	Changed vote 1964 – 1966	Constant vote 1966 – 1970	Changed vote 1966 – 1970	Constant vote 1970 – Feb 74	Changed vote 1970 – Feb 74	Constant vote Feb – Oct 74	Changed vote Feb – Oct 74
% changing vote between *second* pair of elections	16%	39%	25%	53%	18%	64%	17%	45%	24%	59%
Number of respondents	871	298	627	165	643	223	1,027	516	518	227

Note: Only those eligible in all three elections have been included. 'Constant vote' includes consistent non-voters; 'changed vote' includes movement to and from abstention.

Data source: for 1959–64–66: Butler and Stokes' 1964–66 panel sample and respondents' recall, in 1964, of 1959 vote
1964–66–70: Butler and Stokes' 1964–66–70 panel sample
1966–70–Feb 74: BES 1970–Feb 1974 panel sample and respondents' recall, in 1970, of 1966 vote
1970–Feb 74–Oct 74: BES Feb 74–Oct 74 panel sample, and respondents' recall, in 1970, of 1970 vote
Feb 74–Oct 74–1979: BES Feb 74–Oct 74–1979 panel sample

Table 2.21 *How major party defectors voted at the following election, for each triad of elections 1959–1979*

	Defected from major party between					
	1959 – 1964 and in 1966:	1964 – 1966 and in 1970:	1966 – 1970 and in Feb 1974:	1970 – Feb 1974 and in Oct 1974:	Feb 1974 – Oct 1974 and in 1979:	Average (mean) for 1959 – 79
	%	%	%	%	%	%
Conservative defectors at following election:						
Stayed with party of adoption	60	35	28	52	26	44
Changed again:						
reverted to Conservatives	26	56	54	22	60	40
but not to Conservatives	13	9	18	26	14	16
Total per cent	100%	100%	100%	100%	100%	100%
Number of respondents	57	37	50	168	73	
Labour defectors at following election:						
Stayed with party of adoption	41	49	36	48	39	36
Changed again:						
reverted to Labour	44	16	50	34	36	43
but not to Labour	15	35	15	18	25	22
Total per cent	100%	100%	100%	100%	100%	100%
Number of respondents	73	37	109	149	69	

Note: The percentage figures in the far right column are the mean of the percentages for each of the five triads of elections.
Data source: See Table 2.20.

Table 2.22 *How major party defectors to the Liberals voted at the subsequent election: 1959-1970 and 1970-1979*

	Switched from Conservative or Labour in 1959 to Liberal in 1964 and/or 1966 and in 1970:	Switched from Conservative or Labour in 1970 to Liberal in Feb 1974 and/or Oct 1974 and in 1979:
At following election:	%	%
Stayed Liberal	33	31
Changed again:		
Reverted to party of origin	43	46
To *other* major party	16	13
To non-voting or minor party	8	10
Total per cent	100%	100%
Number of respondents	75	177

Data source: 1959–70: Butler and Stokes' 1964–66–70 panel sample; vote in 1959 is based
               on recall in 1964
               1970–79: See note to Table 2.9.

Despite the stronger position of the Liberals at the end of the 1970s than of the 1960s, there is no evidence to suggest that major party defectors have become more willing to adhere to their party of adoption and less willing to return home. As Table 2.22 shows, of the Liberals' recruits from Conservative and Labour ranks in the mid 1960s only 33 per cent remained Liberal by 1970; but of their recruits in the mid 1970s the retention rate, at 31 per cent, was no better.[28] What left the Liberals in a stronger position in 1979 than 1970 was the fact that they advanced further into the major parties' territory in 1974 than they had in 1964, not that they retreated less. The increased volatility of Conservative and Labour supporters in the mid 1970s was not followed by a consolidation of their new party preferences but by further volatility which partially restored the *status quo ante*.

The pattern of constancy and change that we have traced for the 1970s reveals a marked degree of flux in the British electorate. When a third of the electorate switches vote between two elections, and up to half change vote at least once in the decade, we can no longer regard the 'floating voter' as confined to a small minority. Yet the pattern also suggests continuity and stability. It does not differ significantly between the 1970s and 1960s. Although the Liberals advanced further in the 1970s they did so by a similar route to that taken ten years earlier; and like the 1960s they retreated by the end of the decade, although not to as quite far back. Our examination discloses that built into the electorate are some still powerful stabilisers of support for the two major parties. In the next chapter we shall examine one such stabiliser, the social structure.

3

The lockgates on the vote

The previous chapter was devoted to the flow of the vote among parties and many of the forthcoming chapters will show how that flow was a response to the issues, events and leading political figures in the 1974 and 1979 election campaigns. This chapter deals with the lockgates that control the flow.[1] For in focusing on the fluidity of electoral choice we should not overlook its degree of stability. Throughout the 1970s half the eligible electorate never deviated in their party support, and from one election to the next a majority voted the same way; moreover, a substantial amount of vote switching consisted of temporary deserters returning to their normal party colours. For some electors a general election is an opportunity for making a fresh appraisal of the parties; but for many it is an occasion for reaffirming a long-standing party preference.

Where do these long-standing party preferences come from, and what sustains them over time? Early upbringing, a particular incident many years past, and sheer force of habit can all play a role. But these factors illustrate rather than define the foundation of long-term party preferences, which is the social structure. By this is meant the relatively enduring features of people's lives which, often at the prompting of the parties themselves, produce a sense of collective interest and instil a certain set of values. Region, race, nationality, language, religion, age, generation and sex have all, separately and in combination, provided the social basis of party preferences at other times and in other countries. But in Great Britain since the First World War 'class' is the primary, almost exclusive, social basis of party choice; 'all else is embellishment and detail'.[2]

3.1 The middle-class/working-class divide

The importance of social class arises partly from the absence of any competing social basis for the electorate's party loyalties. Language and culture are an alternative in rural Wales; national identity in Scotland; race and religion in a few major cities. But none of these can form a basis for party loyalties across

74

Great Britain as a whole. Moreover, the link between class and party in the electorate is reinforced by links at Westminster. The Labour party, as its name suggests, was established to represent the interest of workers, by electing working men to Parliament. To this day its finances and organisation, and some of its MPs, are formally tied to trade unions. Its political purpose – 'to secure for the workers by hand or by brain the full fruits of their industry and the most equitable distribution thereof' – is enshrined in its constitution. Nothing so formal ties the Conservative party to a particular social class; indeed, its principles and policies are rarely couched in terms of class interest. Yet the overwhelming majority of its MPs are drawn from the ranks of finance, business, land, and the professions, and it receives substantial contributions from private companies. Speaking in Parliament shortly after the 1918 election the Prime Minister, Lloyd George, said he felt he had the Trade Union Congress in front of him and the Association of Chambers of Commerce at his back.[3] Not many electors would depict the party system quite as starkly as that; nonetheless we shall see in the next chapter that for many it is as representatives of the middle and working classes that the two parties are seen and judged.

A few words of definition are necessary. The term 'social class' literally means no more than a category of society. The very generality of the phrase both reflects and encourages a wide range of meaning and measurement. We shall use 'social class' in its customary and everyday sense to refer to a segment of society which has a similar amount of money, status and power at its disposal. We recognise that the number of segments, their boundaries, their hierarchical ordering, the grounds for placing people in one rather than another, and the general theories of inequality from which these operational decisions derive are subject to rich variety. Any classification must select from the almost inexhaustible permutation of possibilities. We recognise too that the division of the entire electorate into only a few such segments cannot capture nuances. It provides no more than a rough and ready indication of our respondents' position on the ladder of inequality.

Occupational status and voting

For purposes of comparison we have adopted Butler and Stokes' 'social grades of occupation', which are closely related to those used by market research societies, as a summary indicator of social class. These occupational grades are described in Table 3.1. Married men and unmarried respondents were classified according to their own occupation; married women, even if in paid employment, were classified according to their husband's occupation. The retired and unemployed were classified according to their normal former occupation.[4] In turn these occupations are placed in one of six grades, on a mixture of grounds: whether the work is manual or non-manual; the skills and responsibilities demanded; whether employment or supervision of other workers is involved; the prestige of the job; and the normal level of pay. The six grades are ranked according to their general level of income,

Table 3.1 *The classification of occupations into status grades*

Market research designation	Our designation	Grade	Examples[1]
A	I	Higher managerial or professional	Doctors, dentists, university teachers, senior government officials, architects, surveyors, engineers with professional qualifications, clergymen, barristers, solicitors, scientists with professional qualifications, company directors, senior managers with more than 25 subordinates, self-employed builders with 10 or more employees, farmers with over 500 acres.
B	II	Lower managerial or administrative	Farmers with 100 to 500 acres, shop proprietors with 4–9 employees, senior managers with 10–25 subordinates, other managers with over 25 subordinates, qualified nurses and pharmacists, company secretaries without professional qualifications.
C1	III	Skilled or supervisory non-manual	Farmers with 30–90 acres, telegraph operators and radio operators, typists or secretaries with at least one subordinate, civil service executive officers, local authority officers without professional qualification, commercial travellers, manufacturers' agents, salesmen with at least one subordinate, shop proprietors with 3 or less employees, managers with less than 25 subordinates, draughtsmen, bank clerks.
C1	IV	Lower non-manual	Shop salesmen and assistants, policemen, caretakers, lodging-house keepers, street vendors, factory guards, waiters, telephone operators, non-supervisory clerks, inspectors (transport).
C2	V	Skilled manual	Coal miners (faceworkers and firemen), glass and ceramics makers, telephone installers and linesmen, furnace and foundry operatives, workers in electrical trades, fitters, instrument makers, wood workers, textile and clothing workers, food, drink, and tobacco workers, paper and printing workers, skilled construction workers, painters and decorators, firemen and guards, drivers of road goods vehicles.
D	VI	Semi-skilled and unskilled manual	Agricultural workers, gardeners and groundsmen, postal workers, quarrymen, miners (other than faceworkers and firemen), unskilled factory and process workers, laundry workers, dockworkers, warehousemen, porters, roundsmen, domestic workers, cleaners, messengers.
E[2]	VII	Residual, on pension or other state benefit	Persons not elsewhere classified (all were retired and supplied no evidence about their own or their spouses' previous occupations).

Notes

[1] The examples are taken from Michael Kahan, David Butler and Donald Stokes, 'On the Analytical Division of Social Class', *British Journal of Sociology*, XVII (1966), 122–32, pp 131–2. Butler and Stokes divided the middle class and working class between grades III and IV in the first edition of *Political Change in Britain* but between IV and V in the second edition. We have adopted the latter course.

[2] Category VII is not included in our tables on occupational grades.

status and power. The ranking is closely associated with many aspects of inequality which do not directly enter into the construction of the occupational
grade scale. Later in the chapter we shall explore whether some of these related
yet distinct facets of inequality have an independent bearing on party choice.

For a simple statistical summary of the strength of the class–party
relationship we shall use Alford's Index of Class Voting. The Index score
is the difference between Labour's percentage of the middle-class vote and
Labour's percentage of the working-class vote.[5] It should therefore be regarded
as a class index of Labour voting. The index requires a dichotomous conception
of social class. This is often the distinction between manual workers (occupational grades 5 and 6) and non-manual workers (grades 1 to 4), but it need
not be. By analogy we can use the same kind of index for comparisons between
other pairs of social groups, for example, members and non-members of trade
unions, or the self-employed as distinct from employees. Scores range from 0
to 100. A score of 0 can only occur when the two percentages are equal (as in
the left panel of Figure 3.A that follows) and means that there is no relationship. A score of 100 can only occur when nobody in the middle classes but
everybody in the working class votes Labour (or, even more improbably, vice
versa) and means that the class–party relationship is perfect.[6] The score can

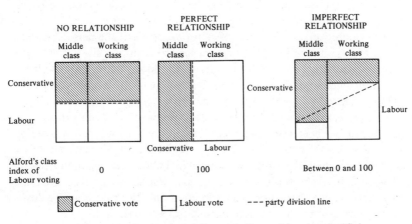

Note: By excluding the vote for Liberals and other minor parties these models are over-simplified,
but not misleading. The Liberal/Other vote could be incorporated by adding a horizontal band, varying
in width according to the size of Liberal vote, across each model. If this were done it would be strictly
incorrect to describe the middle model as a 'perfect' relationship.

Figure 3.A   *Relationships between class and party*

be regarded as the arithmetical equivalent of the slope of the party division
lines in Figure 3.A; the sharper the slope, the stronger the relationship.

Evidence on the connection between class and party is deceptively easy to
misinterpret. Before examining the data, therefore, we shall introduce readers
to the range of forms the connection can take and to the different ways in which
it can be expressed. Figure 3.A displays in an over-simplified way – it is confined
to the two major parties – three logical possibilities. We may imagine first a
situation in which there is no connection at all (see the left-hand panel). Among
the voting public the party division cuts squarely across the class division.
Looking *across* shows us the class support of the Conservative and Labour
parties. In this case it is identical. Since the majority of voters are working
class, both parties would have an equal claim to call themselves a 'party of
the working class'. Looking *down* shows us the party support of the two classes.
In this case it is again identical. To know an elector's social class therefore
provides no means of predicting his or her party choice.

But in Britain social class does offer a basis for prediction. How good a
basis? The central panel in Figure 3.A displays a situation in which knowledge
of the electorate's social class would allow us to predict its vote with unerring
accuracy. There is a perfect 'fit' between class and party. Divisions of class
and party are in perfect alignment rather than at right angles. Looking across
shows that the class support of the parties is exclusively different: all
Conservatives are middle class, all Labour voters working class. Looking down
shows that party support of the social classes is equally exclusive: all the
middle class vote Conservative and all the working class vote Labour. Since
the working class outnumber the middle class, a perfect connection between
class and party would ensure that Labour won every election.

Yet the Conservatives have held office for exactly half the period between
1945 and 1979, winning five of the eleven general elections. Even if the entire
middle-class vote was Conservative this result would have been impossible
without additional support from at least a minority of the working class.
An evenly balanced two-party system can only be sustained, therefore, by
a less than perfect relationship between class and party. A rough approximation
of what has in fact been the typical relationship since the war is displayed on
the right-hand side of Figure 3.A. The majority of the middle class has voted
Conservative, the majority of the working class Labour, leaving minorities of
class 'dissenters'. It is in this sense that one can describe social class as a major
basis of party choice, even though an imperfect one. But from looking down
the diagram we can see that the relationship has also been non-symmetrical.
For if the two parties' majority share of their respective social classes were
equal, the numerical preponderance of the working class would continue to
ensure recurrent Labour victories at the polls. For the Conservatives to win
an election the middle-class Conservative majority must outstrip the working-

class Labour majority. And there is a logical corollary: the working-class
Conservative minority must outnumber the middle-class Labour minority. Of the
two social classes, it must be the middle classes who engage in the more disciplined
class voting.

The right-hand side of Figure 3.A brings out one further point of importance.
Looking across rather than down reveals the crucial difference between the party
support of the classes and the class support of the parties. One cannot be inferred
from the other. The fact that the middle class is largely Conservative does not
mean that the Conservative vote is largely middle class; in fact only a small majority of it is. This is because a large slice of a small cake (the Conservative share
of the middle class) can be similar in size to a smaller slice of a larger cake (the
Conservative share of the working class). Similarly the fact that Labour voters
are over-whelmingly working class does not mean that the working class is over-
whelmingly Labour; in fact only a modest majority is.

Table 3.2 sets out the 1979 vote of the six occupational grades. We may note
first the absence of any relationship between occupational status and the Liberal
vote, which was drawn in equal proportions from each of the grades (except grade
I, where it was slightly higher).[7] But there is a clear division between manual and
non-manual workers in their support for the two major parties. Among the four
grades of non-manual workers the Conservatives secured a decisive majority over
Labour (60 per cent to 23 per cent); among the two grades of manual workers
Labour achieved a comfortable but less decisive majority over the Conservatives
(50 per cent to 35 per cent). Moreover, gradations of skill and prestige within
these two broad groups appeared to make little difference. Labour's advantage
among skilled manual workers was not discernibly different from that among their
less skilled counterparts. Similarly, the Conservatives' edge over Labour did not
increase steadily from lower to higher rungs on the occupational ladder; in fact
it was fractionally greater in grade III (skilled and supervisory manual workers)
than grade I (higher managerial and professional staff). For the purpose of constructing simple summaries of the class–party connection the clear distinction
between 'workers by hand' and 'workers by brain' offers a suitable basis.

The imperfect and non-symmetrical relationship between class and party is
brought out well in Table 3.2. In our 1979 sample manual workers out-numbered
non-manual workers by 56 per cent to 44 per cent. Had every non-manual worker
voted Conservative the Labour Government would still have been re-elected if it
could rely on the support of four out of five manual workers. Yet the Conservatives won handsomely. They were helped a little by the marginally higher turnout
rates of non-manual workers (88 per cent) than manual workers (83 per cent).
But their success is largely due to their customary ability to do better than Labour
not only at obtaining the support of their natural class 'allies' but also at winning
over support from their natural class 'opponents'. A clear majority (60 per cent)
of non-manual voters were Conservative; only a plurality of manual workers were

Table 3.2 *Vote by occupational grade in 1979*

| | Occupational grade | | | | | | |
| | Non-manual workers | | | | Manual workers | | All |
	I Higher managerial and professional	II Lower managerial and administrative	III Skilled or supervisory non-manual	IV Lower non-manual	V Skilled manual	VI Semi-skilled or unskilled manual	
Vote in 1979	%	%	%	%	%	%	%
Conservative	62	61	65	55	35	35	46
Liberal	18	14	16	13	13	14	14
Labour	17	24	17	30	50	51	38
Other	2	1	2	2	2	0	2
Total per cent	100%	100%	100%	100%	100%	100%	100%
Number of respondents (including non-voters)	142	227	166	197	650	289	1,671
Occupational grade as per cent of all respondents in table	8%	14%	10%	12%	39%	17%	100%
Per cent of each occupational grade who voted	93%	92%	87%	84%	83%	83%	86%
Conservative lead over Labour	+44	+37	+48	+25	-15	-16	+8

Table 3.2. (cont.)

Party support of the classes

Vote in 1979	Occupational grades	
	I–IV	V–VI
	%	%
Conservative	60	35
Liberal/Other	17	15
Labour	23	50
Total per cent	100%	100%
Number of respondents (excluding non-voters)	650	779

Class index of Labour voting = 27

Class support of the parties

Occupational grade	Vote in 1979		
	Conservative	Liberal/Other	Labour
	%	%	%
I–IV	59	49	27
V–VI	41	51	73
Total per cent	100%	100%	100%
Number of respondents (excluding non-voters)	663	539	227

Note: Married men and unmarried persons are classified according to their own occupations, while married women are classified according to their husbands' occupations as explained in note 4 page 366. A small number of students in full-time education as well as a residual category who could not be classified because of missing information are excluded from the occupational classification. Furthermore a small category of persons who refused to say whether they voted or which party they voted for are excluded from the table.

Data source: BES May 1979 Election Survey.

Labour. Over one in three manual workers 'crossed over' to the Conservatives whereas less than one in four non-manual workers 'crossed over' to Labour.

Class voting and electoral change

That social class had an important bearing on the vote in 1979 is not in doubt. But how important a bearing? Our index score for the class–party relationship in 1979 is twenty-seven. Whether that should be regarded as strong or weak depends on one's benchmark. How does it compare with the past? Or with other class-related bases of the vote? Our first comparison is with the October 1974 election. At this point it is important to distinguish between class as a basis of the vote at one election and class as a basis of a change in the vote between two elections. The one has almost no predictable connection with the other. The fact that social class was associated with the vote in 1979 does not mean that it was associated with the swing from Labour to Conservative between October 1974 and 1979. Even if it were, moreover, we could not infer that it was in the same direction. Because the middle class was the more likely to vote Conservative in 1979 it does not follow that they were also the more likely to have swung to the Conservatives since October 1974.

The Conservatives could have owed their victory in large measure to either of the two social classes, or in equal measures to both. The three possibilities are depicted in Figure 3.B. The first, shown on the left-hand side, is that the Conservatives won by 'class appeal', mobilising most of their additional vote from their home base in the middle class. Had this been the case the class–party relationship would have strengthened. There was much in the Conservatives'

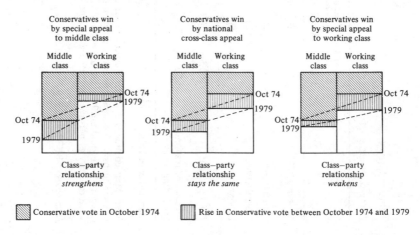

Figure 3.B *Changes in the class/party relationship and the increase in the Conservative vote, October 1974 – 1979*

campaign to make this likely. The promises of tax cuts and trade union reform, wrapped up by Mrs Thatcher's vigorous advocacy of free enterprise, indivdual-ism and self-help, looked a more attractive package for the middle class than the working class.

Yet the Conservatives do not deliberately seek to confine their appeal to what is a minority of the electorate. Their aim is a broad 'national appeal' that reaches across the social classes. Had this been the basis of the Conservative victory, their share of the middle-class and working-class vote would have risen by the same amount and the class–party relationship would have remained unchanged (see centre of Figure 3.B).

The third possibility is that the Conservatives made most of their electoral advances in the less favourable territory of the working class. Had this occurred the class–party relationship would have weakened (see right-hand side of Figure 3.B). This route to victory has always had its champions within the Conservative party, although views differ sharply on how to attract the working-class vote. Populist authoritarians wish to promote the party as defender of the established moral and social order; adherents of the One Nation tradition wish to promote it as the party of social reform and economic opportunity. Yet neither of these emphases appeared to play a major role in the Conservatives' 1979 campaign.

As Table 3.3 reveals, the class–party relationship did weaken between October 1974 and 1979, falling from thirty-two to twenty-seven. Among manual workers the swing to the Conservatives was 9 per cent; among non-manual workers 5.5 per cent.[8] Yet we should not immediately conclude that the Conservatives took the third path to victory. A close look at the figures shows that the class basis of their win was less neat and tidy than any one of the three possibilities outlined earlier. The larger swing to the Conservatives amongst manual workers owed more to changes in the Labour than the Conservative vote. The rise in the Conservative vote share was similar among non-manual workers (+9 per cent) and manual workers (+11 per cent). But among the former it was at the expense of the Liberals (–7 per cent) more than Labour (–2 per cent); among the latter at the almost equal expense of both (–5 per cent and –7 per cent respectively).

Similar grounds for caution are provided by a breakdown of the two social classes into six occupational grades (see Table 3.4). With one partial exception, the swing to the Conservatives was similar across the range of occupational grades, as was the increase in the Conservatives' share of the vote. What varied was whether this was more to the cost of Labour than of the Liberals and other minor parties. In grades I and II Conservative gains were at the net expense of the Liberals, not Labour. In grades III–VI they were at the expense of both, but of Labour more than of the Liberals. Among semi- and unskilled manual workers, the Liberals' vote share actually increased (+2 per cent) whereas Labour's fell by more than in any other grade (–9 per cent). The half-exception was grade I – the upper middle class of senior management

Table 3.3 *Party support of the classes and class support of the parties, October 1974*

Party support of the classes, October 1974

	Occupational grade	
	I–IV	V–VI
Vote in October 1974	%	%
Conservative	51	24
Liberal/Other	24	20
Labour	25	57
Total per cent	100%	100%
Number of respondents	834	1,010

Class support of the parties, October 1974

	Vote in October 1974		
	Conservative	Liberal/Other	Labour
Occupational grades	%	%	%
I–IV	64	50	27
V–VI	36	50	73
Total per cent	100%	100%	100%
Number of respondents	662	399	783

Class index of Labour voting = 32

Data source: BES October 1974 Election Survey.

Table 3.4 *Percentage point change in vote from October 1974 to 1979 within occupational grades*

	Occupational grade						
	Non-manual workers				Manual workers		
	I Higher managerial and professional	II Lower managerial and professional	III Skilled or supervisory non-manual	IV Lower non-manual	V Skilled manual	VI Semi-skilled or unskilled manual	All[1]
Conservative	+3%	+13%	+10%	+12%	+11%	+13%	+10%
Liberal	-9%	-10%	-3%	-3%	-5%	+2%	-4%
Labour	+7%	-1%	-6%	-7%	-5%	-9%	-5%
Other	-2%	-2%	-1%	-2%	-1%	-6%	-2%
Swing[2] to Conservative	-2%	+7%	+8%	+8.5%	+8%	+11%	+7.5%
Number of respondents[1] in 1979	132	208	145	165	540	239	1,429
in October 1974	135	191	284	224	673	337	1,844

Notes
[1] i.e respondents in the table. Non-voters and respondents from whom information about their vote was not obtained are excluded.
[2] Swing is the average of the percentage point increase in the Conservative vote and the percentage point decrease in the Labour vote.

Data source: BES October 1974 Election Survey; BES May 1979 Election Survey.

and the professions. Although a comfortable majority voted Conservative, as at all elections, they swung to Labour by 2 per cent in 1979. This 'swing' is only a technical one: the Conservative vote share actually increased (+3 per cent) but Labour's increased by even more (+7 per cent). But it does allow us to dismiss the suggestion that the Conservatives owed their victory to a specifically middle-class appeal. They drew their additional votes from across the social spectrum; indeed they possibly advanced slightly further among semi- and unskilled workers, where Labour appeared to retreat most, than elsewhere. How the Conservatives managed to attract and Labour to repel this crucial band of vote changers, especially among manual workers, is the subject of later chapters.

Class voting fell in 1979 because the popularity of the Conservatives rose while that of Labour dropped among manual workers. But that had happened before; perhaps class voting merely fluctuates around a steady level according to which party wins the election. Table 3.5 makes plain, however, that 1979 was only the latest instalment in a series of elections at which class voting has fitfully but gradually declined. The table sets out the Conservative, Labour and Liberal/Other division of the vote, among manual and non-manual workers, at each general election between 1959 and 1979. This is a convenient period of comparison, as it begins and ends with decisive Conservative victories[9] and is marked in the middle (1970) by another, although slightly less impressive, Conservative win. The table also sets out two indicators of class voting additional to the class index of Labour voting which we have already cited. One is the correlation (Somer's d) between class and vote.[10] The advantage of this statistic is its comprehensiveness: it incorporates the class index of both Conservative and Labour voting as well as any association that exists between class and a vote for one of the smaller parties. The other indicator is the sum of the manual Labour vote and non-manual Conservative vote as a proportion of all votes. Its advantage is that it treats all Liberal and minor party votes, as well as the Labour middle class and the Conservative working class, as evidence of the absence of class voting.

The three measures capture different facets of class voting but record the same story of its decline. The class index of Labour voting stood at forty in 1959, fell to thirty-three at the next Conservative win in 1970, and again by a similar amount to twenty-seven in 1979. The Somer's d correlation followed an exactly parallel path. The proportion of manual Labour + non-manual Conservative votes dropped from 65 per cent in 1959 to 55 per cent in 1974 and 1979. In this sense only a bare majority of voters have voted along class lines in the last three elections. There remains a class basis to the vote but clearly it is not as important as it once was. The trend since 1959 prompts one further reflection. The overall decline in class voting has arisen from what appear to be fairly even changes within both social classes. The Conservative share of the non-manual vote fell by 9 per cent; the Labour share of the manual vote by 12 per cent.

Table 3.5 *'Class-voting' 1959–1979: party division of the vote in non-manual and manual occupational strata*

Votes	1959 election Non-manual	1959 election Manual	1964 election Non-manual	1964 election Manual	1966 election Non-manual	1966 election Manual	1970 election Non-manual	1970 election Manual	February 1974 election Non-manual	February 1974 election Manual	October 1974 election Non-manual	October 1974 election Manual	1979 election Non-manual	1979 election Manual
	%	%	%	%	%	%	%	%	%	%	%	%	%	%
Conservative	69	34	62	28	60	25	64	33	53	24	51	24	60	35
Liberal or minor party	8	4	16	8	14	6	11	9	25	19	24	20	17	15
Labour	22	62	22	64	26	69	25	58	22	57	25	57	23	50
Total per cent	100%	100%	100%	100%	100%	100%	100%	100%	100%	100%	100%	100%	100%	100%
Number of respondents	526	792	595	914	595	945	392	577	893	1,060	834	1,010	650	779
Class index of Labour voting	40		42		43		33		35		32		27	
Somer's *d* for vote trichotomy in the table	0.40		0.43		0.43		0.35		0.39		0.36		0.25	
Non-manual Conservative + manual Labour voters as % of all voters	65%		63%		66%		60%		55%		54%		55%	

Data source: Butler and Stokes' Election Surveys 1964, 1966 and 1970, BES February 1974, October 1974 and May 1979 Election Surveys. Data on voting in 1959 were obtained from recall in the 1964 survey.

But this small difference may be more significant than it seems. For one thing it was class voting among manual workers that fell further, and from a lower point; never in the twenty-year period was it as low as in 1979. For another, the same period has seen the gradual replacement of manual labour by machinery, and of manufacturing industry by the service sector, with the result that the non-manual labour force has expanded and the manual work-force contracted. In our series of election surveys (which probably under-estimate the trend) the ratio of non-manual to manual voters moved from 40:60 to 45:55. By itself a change of this kind does not necessarily alter the strength of the class–party connection; the slope of the party division line can remain the same (see the hypothetical cases shown in Figure 3.C).

But what could be expected to alter is the *relative* amount of class voting within each class. From the recruitment of manual workers' children (and wives) into the non-manual labour force, especially the rapidly expanding lower grades, and from the resulting growth in white-collar trade unions, we would anticipate a gradual fall in the Conservative share of the non-manual vote. And as the manual workforce contracts, increasingly confined to those 'left behind', we might expect it to become more solidly Labour. Thus the twenty-year decline in the non-manual Conservative vote might have been foreseen; the decline in the manual Labour vote could not.

The class–party relationship has gradually weakened in a second sense. Not only have the party differences between the social classes narrowed; so too have the class differences between the parties. Class voting has diminished; so have 'voting classes'. Table 3.6 uses the same data as Table 3.5 but reverses perspective: it sets out the class make-up of Conservative, Labour and Liberal/ Other voters from 1959 to 1979. The essential differences between the parties have not altered much over the twenty years. The Labour vote is cast over-whelmingly by manual workers and is clearly the most 'class-specific', that is, the most dependent on a single class. This produces a paradox: by 1979 Labour could no longer be described as the party of the working class, but manual workers clearly remained the class of the Labour party. The class composition of the Conservative and Liberal/Other vote is more balanced. Non-manual workers form the majority of Conservative voters but not to the same degree as manual workers do among Labour voters. The class make-up of minor party voters (of whom at least 80 per cent are Liberals) is more balanced still, and nationally the most representative of all.

A simple measure of the class difference between Conservative and Labour voters is the difference between the percentage of the Conservative vote cast by manual workers and the percentage of the Labour vote cast by manual workers. Scores range from 0 to 100. A score of 0 means that the percentages are the same, and that there are no class differences in the vote (see left panel of Figure 3.A). A score of 100 means that the Conservative vote came entirely from one class, the Labour vote entirely from the other (see centre of Figure

3.A). The actual score has ranged between thirty-two and forty-one, falling in fits and starts from thirty-eight in 1959 and forty-one in 1964 to thirty-two in 1979. The main contributor to the downward drift has been the slow but steady rise in the proportion of Labour votes coming from non-manual workers: in 1959, 1964 and 1966 it was one in five, but since then one in four. Only part of the change can be attributed to the expansion of white-collar jobs, for over the period 1959–79 the proportion of the Labour vote

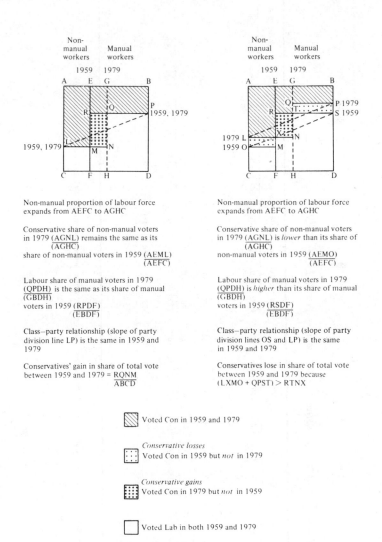

Non-manual proportion of labour force expands from AEFC to AGHC

Conservative share of non-manual voters in 1979 (AGNL) remains the same as its (AGHC)
share of non-manual voters in 1959 (AEML) (AEFC)

Labour share of manual voters in 1979 (QPDH) is the same as its share of manual (GBDH)
voters in 1959 (RPDF) (EBDF)

Class–party relationship (slope of party division line LP) is the same in 1959 and 1979

Conservatives' gain in share of total vote between 1959 and 1979 = RQNM
ABCD

Non-manual proportion of labour force expands from AEFC to AGHC

Conservative share of non-manual voters in 1979 (AGNL) is *lower* than its share of (AGHC)
non-manual voters in 1959 (AEMO) (AEFC)

Labour share of manual voters in 1979 (QPDH) is *higher* than its share of manual (GBDH)
voters in 1959 (RSDF) (EBDF)

Class–party relationship (slope of party division lines OS and LP) is the same in 1959 and 1979

Conservatives lose in share of total vote between 1959 and 1979 because (LXMO + QPST) > RTNX

Voted Con in 1959 and 1979

Conservative losses
Voted Con in 1959 but *not* in 1979

Conservative gains
Voted Con in 1979 but *not* in 1959

Voted Lab in both 1959 and 1979

Figure 3.C *Why a change in the ratio of non-manual to manual workers need not change the Class index of Labour voting.*

Table 3.6 *The class composition of the parties' voters 1959–1979*

Occupational grade	1959 election			1964 election			1966 election			1970 election			February 1974 election			October 1974 election			1979 election		
	Con	Lib/ Other	Lab	Con	Lib/ Other	Lab	Con	Lib/ Other	Lab	Con	Lib/ Other	Lab	Con	Lib/ Other	Lab	Con	Lib/ Other	Lab	Con	Lib/ Other	Lab
	%	%	%	%	%	%	%	%	%	%	%	%	%	%	%	%	%	%	%	%	%
I–IV: non-manual workers	57	57	19	59	57	18	60	59	19	57	45	23	65	53	25	64	50	27	59	49	27
V–VI: manual workers	43	43	81	41	43	82	40	41	81	43	55	77	35	47	75	36	50	73	41	51	73
Total per cent	100%	100%	100%	100%	100%	100%	100%	100%	100%	100%	100%	100%	100%	100%	100%	100%	100%	100%	100%	100%	100%
Number of respondents	634	609	75	625	716	168	593	807	140	441	433	95	728	801	424	662	399	783	663	227	539
Index of class polarisation of parties[1]	38			41			41			34			40			37			32		

Note:
[1] i.e. the difference between the percentage of the Conservative vote cast by manual workers and the percentage of the Labour vote cast by manual workers.

Data source: See Table 3.5.

cast by non-manual workers has risen by 8 per cent, whereas the proportion of
the workforce constituted by non-manual workers has risen by only 5 per cent.

The class gap between the parties' supporters has narrowed in another way. At
the beginning of the period the class composition of Liberal/Other voters was almost identical to that of Conservatives: in both cases the majority were non-
manual workers. There was therefore a clear division between Labour voters and
the rest of the voting electorate. By the end of the period the social make-up of
Liberal/Other voters had diverged from that of Conservatives, having become less
middle class (while still being slightly more middle class than voters as a whole).
In their class background they still resembled Conservative voters more than
Labour voters; but the class differences between the parties could no longer be
described as a simple dichotomy between Labour voters and the rest. Not only
had the class polarisation of the parties narrowed; it had also fragmented.

3.2 Beyond the two-class divide

If class voting is on the decline and has already reached modest levels, what – if
anything – has taken its place? Have some of the 'embellishments' on class – sex
or age perhaps – become more important? Or have completely new social divisions
emerged to rival the impact of social class? Our survey could reveal no serious
competitor.

Sex, age and voting

The vote of men and women was virtually identical. Women were fractionally the
more likely to vote Conservative, as customary, but the difference was probably
smaller than at any time since the war.[11] Age produced only the faintest of
imprints on the vote. The young were marginally less likely to vote Conservative,
marginally more likely to vote Labour (and Liberal). It would be more accurate,
however, to distinguish between the bulk of the electorate, aged 25–64, among
whom age had no discernible impact, from the very young (18–24) and the
retired (65+) whose party preferences did stand in some contrast. An Alford-style
'age index' of Labour voting, based on a division of voters into over 45 and under
45, produced a score of zero (as did a male/female index); and even between the
two polar age groups there was a mere 5 percentage point difference in the Labour
vote.

Earlier we found that social class had a much stronger bearing on party choice
in one election than on changes of vote between elections: it stood as a lockgate
through which the vote flowed. The reverse is true for age and sex, which form
a very weak basis of party choice but were possibly associated with the size of
the swing from 1974 to 1979. The swing to the Conservatives was stronger
among the young than the old. It ranged from 14 per cent in the 18–24 age
group – most of whom will have been new voters – to 3.5 per cent among the

Table 3.7 Sex, age and the vote in 1979

| | Men | | Women | | Age | | | | | | | | | | | |
| | | | | | 18–24 | | 25–34 | | 35–44 | | 45–54 | | 55–64 | | 65+ | |
	Vote in 1979	Oct 74–1979	Vote in 1979	Oct 74–1979	Vote in 1979	Oct 74–1979	Vote in 1979	Oct 74–1979	Vote in 1979	Oct 74–1979	Vote in 1979	Oct 74–1979	Vote in 1979	Oct 74–1979	Vote in 1979	Oct 74–1979
	%	%	%	%	%	%	%	%	%	%	%	%	%	%	%	%
Conservative	45	+10	48	+11	40	+16	45	+15	47	+12	44	+9	48	+6	55	+9
Liberal	15	0	13	– 7	19	– 1	16	– 6	14	– 5	15	– 3	12	– 3	9	– 5
Labour	38	– 7	38	– 2	40	– 12	37	– 3	38	– 5	39	– 6	39	– 1	35	– 3
Other	2	– 3	1	– 1	1	– 3	2	– 5	1	– 2	2	0	1	– 2	1	– 1
Total per cent	100%		100%		100%		100%		100%		100%		100%		100%	
Number of respondents (including non-voters)	877		935		173		415		321		338		251		326	
Category as a per cent of all respondents	48%		52%		9%		23%		18%		19%		14%		18%	
% of each category who voted	85%		85%		70%		81%		85%		91%		92%		88%	
Conservative lead over Labour	+7		+10		0		+8		+9		+5		+9		+20	
Swing to Conservatives	+8.5%		+6.5%		+14%		+9%		+8.5%		+7.5%		+3.5%		+6%	

Note:
The figures in the Oct 74–1979 columns are the percentage point changes between October 1974 and 1979 in the party's share of the vote of the population group.

Data source: See Table 3.4.

55-64 year olds and 6 per cent among the over 65s. This illustrates the well-known tendency for young voters to be the most fickle, old voters the most steadfast, irrespective of party. The 18-24 age group was the only one in 1979 where the Labour vote did not lag behind the Conservatives' (they were level pegging); but it was also the one where Labour lost most ground since October 1974. The difference in the swing between men (+8.5 per cent) and women (+6.5 per cent) was less marked, but is repeated in other large-scale surveys conducted at the time.[12] It allows us at least to assert that a woman leader did no obvious damage to her party's male vote.

The combined evidence on age, sex and social class suggests that the Conservatives made most ground where their support is customarily weakest – the very young, men, and semi-skilled and unskilled manual workers – and made least ground where it is normally strongest – the elderly, women, and the professional and managerial grades. Part of the Conservatives' achievement was to attract most of its additional votes from beyond its home base; and as a result the party divisions between the major social and demographic groups narrowed.

Variations on the class structure

In seeking alternative social bases of the vote it might be more fruitful to continue exploring economic divisions within British society. The conventional scale of occupational grades on which we have relied so far combines a mixture of aspects of social status, any one of which might prove to be a more power-ful correlate of the vote. For example, each grade includes both employees and employers – the crucial distinction in classical definitions of class. The useful-ness of the distinction is suggested in Table 3.8. The size of our sample precluded our making a further division between major employers of labour and those with no employees outside the family (for example, small shop-keepers),[13] but this appeared to make little difference: in 1979 the whole group of self-employed was overwhelmingly Conservative. Three out of four voted Conservative, to give the party a 60 per cent lead over Labour. Moreover, the self-employed status they shared overrode differences of occupational grade: self-employed manual workers such as plumbers and decorators were as likely to vote Conservative as independent professionals – and *more* likely to do so than professional employees.

A division of the electorate between employee and self-employed rather than manual and non-manual therefore has one benefit. The vote of the self-employed can be predicted with greater certainty than the vote of non-manual workers. But otherwise it offers no clear advantages. The class index of Labour voting based on employment status is no higher (twenty-six) than one based on occu-pational status (twenty-seven). Moreover, the self-employed form only a 10 per cent minority of the electorate. Among the remaining 90 per cent differences of

Table 3.8 Employment status and occupational grade by vote in 1979

	Self-employed								Employees							
	Occupational grades I-II		Occupational grades III-IV		Occupational grades V-VI		All self-employed		Occupational grades I-III		Occupational grades IV		Occupational grades V-VI		All employees	
	Vote in 1979	Oct 74 - 1979	Vote in 1979	Oct 74 - 1979	Vote in 1979	Oct 74 - 1979	Vote in 1979	Oct 74 - 1979	Vote in 1979	Oct 74 - 1979	Vote in 1979	Oct 74 - 1979	Vote in 1979	Oct 74 - 1979	Vote in 1979	Oct 74 - 1979
Vote in 1979	%		%		%		%		%		%		%		%	
Conservative	77	+12	71	-1	76	+28	75	+12	60	+12	54	+11	32	+10	43	+11
Liberal	11	-17	13	+1	6	-18	9	-11	16	-7	13	-4	14	-1	14	-3
Labour	11	+7	13	0	18	-6	15	+1	22	-3	31	-6	52	-7	41	-5
Other	0	-3	2	0	0	-5	1	-2	2	-2	2	-2	2	-2	2	-2
Total per cent	100%		100%		100%		100%		100%		100%		100%		100%	
Number of respondents (including non-voters)	50		63		59		172		431		188		880		1,499	
Category as a per cent of all respondents	3%		4%		4%		10%		26%		11%		53%		90%	
Per cent of each category who voted	88%		83%		83%		84%		92%		85%		83%		86%	
Conservative lead over Labour	+66		+58		+58		+60		+38		+23		-20		-9	
Swing to Conservatives	+2.5%		-0.5%		+17%		+5.5%		+7.5%		+8.5%		+8.5%		+8%	

Note:
See note 13 on p. 368 for an explanation of why the self-employed non-manual workers are divided between grades II and III whereas the non-manual employees are divided between grades III and IV.

Data source: BES October 1974 Election Survey; BES May 1979 Election Survey.

occupational grade are as important as in the electorate as a whole, and override the fact of common employee status. The class index among employees only is the same as that for all electors. Employment status is a necessary refinement to measures of social class derived from occupational status, and a useful addition to it as a social basis of the vote; but it is not a superior alternative.

A second production-related cleavage which needs to be considered separately from occupational grade is that between the private and public sector. Since the war, especially under Labour governments, the public sector has expanded: private industry has been nationalised, health and welfare services extended, higher education expanded, and the role of local and central government widened. The public sector's proportion of the labour force has grown commensurately.[14] At the same time the distinction between the two sectors has become more 'political'. The various incomes policies since the early 1960s have led public-sector workers to regard their ultimate paymaster, the government, as their real employer for the purpose of wage bargaining; the rapid growth in the size and militancy of public-sector trade unions has been one response. The private/public sector division has also become increasingly subject to party conflict. The Conservative party has for long had an instinctive sympathy for the private sector, Labour for the public sector. These sympathies have deep ideological roots, nurtured by the parties' selective recruitment of MPs and councillors from the two sectors.[15] But the alignment was particularly obvious in 1979. The Conservative campaign was widely regarded as a threat to the public sector. It made much of the need to curb the growth in public expenditure in order to free resources for private investment. Its insistence that this could be achieved by eliminating 'bureaucratic waste' rather than jobs did not necessarily convince all electors, but implied that the bureaucratic vices of large organisations were peculiar to the public sector. There were therefore persuasive grounds for thinking that voters might divide along sectoral lines. However, other prominent issues did not align themselves with the private/public sector division quite so neatly. The question of incomes policy was one. Low-paid workers are thought to be helped more by incomes policies than by free collective bargaining; and low-paid workers are concentrated in the public sector. On the other hand, the fiercest resistance to the Labour government's 5 per cent pay norm during the 'Winter of Discontent' came from the public-sector unions.

Perhaps this was one of the reasons why the division between private and public sector did not prove to be a major basis of the vote in 1979, or of the change in vote since October 1974 (see Table 3.9).[16] It is true that the data hint at a marginally stronger swing to the Conservatives among manual workers in the private sector (+10 per cent) than in the public sector (+5.5 per cent); but this is counter-balanced by the reverse difference among non-manual workers. The really striking feature of the data is the evenness of the Conservatives' advance across both sectors of the labour force. It is true, too, that the Conserva-

Table 3.9 *Vote in 1979 by occupational grade and whether employed in private or public sector (employees only)*

	Occupational grades I-IV				Occupational grades V-VI				All employees			
	Private sector		Public sector		Private sector		Public sector		Private sector		Public sector	
	Vote in 1979	Oct 74 – 1979	Vote in 1979	Oct 74 – 1979	Vote in 1979	Oct 74 – 1979	Vote in 1979	Oct 74 – 1979	Vote in 1979	Oct 74 – 1979	Vote in 1979	Oct 74 – 1979
Vote in 1979	%		%		%		%		%		%	
Conservative	62	+9	50	+12	34	+12	27	+7	45	+11	37	+9
Liberal	15	−4	18	−6	14	−2	12	−2	14	−3	15	−4
Labour	22	−3	28	−6	50	−8	58	−4	39	−6	44	−4
Other	1	−2	4	0	1	−3	3	−1	1	−3	3	−1
Total per cent	100%		100%		100%		100%		100%		100%	
Number of respondents (including non-voters)	338		236		548		282		886		518	
Category as a per cent of all respondents in the table	24%		17%		39%		20%		63%		37%	
Per cent of each category who voted	88%		92%		82%		86%		84%		89%	
Conservative lead over Labour	+40		+22		−16		−31		+6		−7	
Swing to Conservative	+6%		+9%		+10%		+5.5%		+8.5%		+6.5%	

Data source: See Table 3.4.

tive vote was lower and the Labour (and Liberal) vote higher among public-sector as opposed to private-sector workers, and that this was so irrespective of whether they did manual or non-manual jobs. But the difference between sectors was relatively small, falling well short of that made by the division between manual and non-manual workers. An Alford-style 'sector index' of Labour voting produced a score of only five. Used in conjunction with the manual/non-manual cleavage, the private-sector/public-sector distinction can define the social basis of party choice a little more sharply. But it is not a substitute.

The same might not be said, however, about yet another production-related division of the electorate – that between members and non-members of a trade union. There are obvious reasons why trade union membership should provide a powerful basis of partisanship. The Labour party and the trade unions are the political and industrial wings of the same movement, linked by ties of organisation, money, personnel and sentiment since the Labour party's foundation. At general elections both wings campaign for the interests of the other, although with fluctuating enthusiasm. The Conservative party is widely and traditionally regarded as 'anti-union', a view encouraged by the abortive attempt at trade union reform and the dispute with the miners under the Heath government, and by the Conservatives' revival of reform proposals in response to the series of strikes in the early part of 1979.

Trade union membership and occupational status are, of course, correlated: manual workers are more likely to belong than non-manual workers.[17] This raises the possibility that the manual/non-manual division of the vote reflects what is really a union member/non-member division of the vote. The correlation, however, is not perfect: there are significant minorities of working-class non-members and middle-class members. This raises the further possibility that trade union membership in fact provides a *stronger* basis of the vote than occupational status. Table 3.10 explores these possibilities by setting out the vote in 1979, and change of vote since October 1974, for three categories of trade union membership within separate groups of manual and non-manual workers. The three categories are (1) *direct membership*, i.e. the respondent belongs to a (TUC-affiliated) trade union, (2) *indirect membership*, i.e. the respondent does not belong, but someone else in the household does (e.g. the husband of a non-working wife), (3) *non-membership*, i.e. neither the respondent nor anyone else in the household belongs. (Table 3.10 excludes the self-employed who by definition will not belong.) The party preferences of indirect members lie in between those of members and non-members, being equidistant in the case of non-manual workers but much closer to direct members in the case of manual workers.

Table 3.10 suggests that trade union membership made little difference to the swing in 1979. The Conservatives increased their vote fractionally more among non-members than members, but Labour's vote fell further among members than non-members. The overall result was a similar swing across all categories. There was therefore little to suggest that the Conservative party's plain and vigorous

Table 3.10 *Vote in 1979 by occupational grade and whether member of a trade union (employees only)*

	Occupational grades I–IV (employees only)						Occupational grades V–VI (employees only)						All (including self-employed)					
	Member of trade union		Not member, but in trade union household		Not in trade union household		Member of trade union		Not member, but in trade union household		Not in trade union household		Member of trade union		Not member, but in trade union household		Not in trade union household	
	Vote in 1979	Oct 74 – 1979	Vote in 1979	Oct 74 – 1979	Vote in 1979	Oct 74 – 1979	Vote in 1979	Oct 74 – 1979	Vote in 1979	Oct 74 – 1979	Vote in 1979	Oct 74 – 1979	Vote in 1979	Oct 74 – 1979	Vote in 1979	Oct 74 – 1979	Vote in 1979	Oct 74 – 1979
Vote in 1979	%		%		%		%		%		%		%		%		%	
Conservative	44	+11	56	+17	67	+16	25	+11	31	+12	44	+15	32	+12	40	+14	56	+16
Liberal	17	−5	15	−8	15	−6	14	+4	12	−8	13	−5	16	+2	13	−8	13	−6
Labour	37	−5	25	−7	16	−8	58	−13	56	−3	43	−6	49	−12	45	−4	30	−7
Other	2	−1	4	−2	2	−2	3	−2	1	−1	0	−3	3	−2	2	−2	1	−2
Total per cent	100%		100%		100%		100%		100%		100%		100%		100%		100%	
Number of respondents (including non-voters)	192		101		327		351		183		346		546		325		800	
Category as per cent of all respondents[1]	11%		6%		20%		21%		11%		21%		33%		19%		48%	
Per cent of each category who voted	90%		91%		89%		84%		86%		80%		86%		88%		83%	
Conservative lead over Labour	+7		+31		+51		−33		−25		+1		−17		−5		+26	
Swing to Conservative	+8%		+12%		+12%		+12%		+7.5%		+10.5%		+12%		+9%		+11.5%	

Note:
[1] i.e including the self-employed. Three self-employed respondents were members of trade unions, and 41 belonged to a household containing a trade union member.

Data source: See Table 3.4.

disapproval of the public-service strikes, the closed shop and secondary picketing did it particular damage among trade unionists, including working-class trade unionists; nor that the Labour party's ties to the trade unions were of particular benefit.

However, the same evidence leaves little doubt that trade union membership formed an independent basis of party choice. Whether or not a manual worker, or a non-manual worker, belonged to a trade union made a marked difference to the vote. The Conservatives were 51 per cent ahead of Labour among the 'pure' middle class of non-manual non-members, but only 7 per cent ahead among the white-collar unionists, the non-manual members.[18] Labour was 33 per cent ahead in the 'pure' working class of manual trade union members, but 1 per cent behind among manual non-members. Yet the impact of the manual/non-manual distinction was not obliterated. For whether a trade union member, or non-member, was in a manual or non-manual job made even more difference to their vote. An index of Labour voting based on a dichotomy of the electorate into non-members (including the self-employed) and members (including indirect members) produces a score of twenty, more than that of any other alternative social basis explored so far, but still less than that based on the conventional manual/non-manual cleavage. If trade union membership forms an independent basis of party choice it is probably one that overlaps and reinforces rather than replaces it.

We are far from exhausting the range of possible social bases for the vote. But rather than seek a social basis in the sphere of production, it might be more rewarding to focus on the sphere of consumption. Inequality of possessions and attainments serve as visible boundaries and barriers between social classes, and are equally subject to party political conflict; they can be as formative an influence on political outlook as inequalities at work. Tables 3.11 to 3.13 break down the 1979 vote by two general indicators of consumption inequalities, income and standard of living, and by two specific indicators, education and housing. All four raise issues of conflict between the Conservative and Labour parties and make a plausible basis for the vote. The idea that the Conservatives are the 'party of the rich' and Labour is the 'party of the poor' is deeply rooted in the popular consciousness (as the next chapter shows). In 1979 such impressions will have been reinforced by the Conservatives' campaign pledge to reduce both the standard rate and highest rate of income tax, and by Labour's record on pensions and its counter-pledge to protect the real value of welfare benefits. The relation between party policy and educational divisions is a little less clear cut, because both parties would claim as their aim the raising of educational standards. But the Conservatives' emphasis is on protecting the standards of brighter children, through preserving the grammar schools; Labour's on raising the standards of the average child, by establishing comprehensive schools. In that sense the two parties align themselves with the interests of, respectively, the better and less well qualified. The relation between housing tenure and party conflict also has its ambiguities. In local politics Labour is the party of low council house rents, high rates, and more council house-

Table 3.11 *Vote in 1979 by income and standard of living*

	Annual income				Standard of living				
	£6,001+	£4,001–6,000	£2,501–4,000	–£2,500	High 4–5	3	2	1	Low 0
Vote in 1979	%	%	%	%	%	%	%	%	%
Conservative	65	45	39	40	75	64	46	40	31
Liberal	12	17	15	14	13	13	18	12	9
Labour	21	36	44	45	10	22	35	47	57
Other	2	2	2	1	2	1	1	1	3
Total per cent	100%	100%	100%	100%	100%	100%	100%	100%	100%
Number of respondents (including non-voters)	188	387	408	515	95	274	649	476	310
Category as per cent of all respondents in table	13%	26%	27%	34%	5%	15%	36%	26%	17%
Per cent of each category who voted	89%	88%	85%	82%	97%	89%	88%	82%	78%
Conservative lead over Labour	+43	+9	–5	–5	+65	+42	+11	–7	–26

Notes
[1] For *married persons*, the income classification pertains to husband's and wife's combined income. The annual income has been calculated on the basis of respondent's weekly or monthly income stated with reference to a scale of income categories, e.g. £34–38 per week; the conversion to annual income, therefore, involves a slight element of approximation at the boundaries between income categories.
[2] The standard of living classification is a simple index obtained by assigning a score of 1 to each of the following: (a) having the use of a car in the family, (b) having the use of a second car in the family, (c) having a private telephone, (d) having a medical insurance to pay for a private bed in hospital, (e) having paid help to clean the house.

Data source: BES May 1979 Election Survey.

building; the Conservatives the opposite. Moreover, council house estates and private owner-occupier estates form distinct, socially homogenous, communities in which Labour and Conservative sympathies are likely to be reinforced. However, the alignment between housing tenure and party preference was disturbed in 1979 by the Conservative party's commitment to oblige local authorities to offer council houses for sale at a discount to their tenants. Council house dwellers will have found themselves under an unaccustomed cross-pressure of conflicting personal interests.

The relationship between inequalities of consumption and the vote in 1979 followed the expected pattern. The Conservatives were the party of the 'haves', Labour the party of the 'have nots'. The better off and better educated were more likely to vote Conservative than the poor and poorly educated; owner-occupiers were more likely to vote Conservative than council house tenants. The Liberals drew their support evenly from across the social spectrum. But, once again, the relationship was neither perfect nor symmetrical. The Conservatives could count on more solid support from their home base than Labour could

Table 3.12 *Vote in 1979 educational attainment*

	University; professional qualification; GCE 'A' level and equivalent or higher	GCE 'O' level; CSE and equivalent	Vocational training; apprentice-ship and equivalent	Obligatory schooling; no additional qualifications
Vote in 1979	%	%	%	%
Conservative	58	53	47	41
Liberal	19	16	13	11
Labour	21	30	37	47
Other	2	1	3	1
Total per cent	100%	100%	100%	100%
Number of respondents (including non-voters)	322	291	331	885
Category as per cent of all respondents in table	18%	16%	18%	48%
Per cent of each category who voted	91%	84%	84%	84%
Conservative lead over Labour	+37	+23	+10	−6

Note:
Respondents are classified according to their highest educational qualification. It was not possible to calculate vote changes within educational categories between October 1974 and 1979 because comparable data on educational qualifications were not collected in the October 1974 survey.

Data source: May 1979 Election Survey.

from its own; and they attracted correspondingly more 'cross-over' votes from beyond their social base than Labour did from beyond its. A comparison of the richest and poorest voters makes the point. Among the richest one-fifth of voters (standard of living categories 3, 4 and 5) the Conservative lead over Labour was 50 per cent. More than two in three voted Conservative (68 per cent), whereas under one in five voted Labour (18 per cent). But among the poorest one-fifth of voters (standard of living category 0) Labour's lead was only half as much (26 per cent). Little more than half (57 per cent) voted Labour whereas almost one in three voted Conservative (31 per cent). This was the measure – repeated in so many social divisions of the electorate – of Labour failure and Conservative success at the election.

Table 3.13 *Vote in 1979, and change in vote since October 1974, by housing*

	Owner-occupied; owned outright		Owner-occupied; mortgage		Private rented[1]		Council house	
	Vote in 1979	Oct 74 – 1979	Vote in 1979	Oct 74 – 1979	Vote in 1979	Oct 74 – 1979	Vote in 1979	Oct 74 – 1979
Vote in 1979	%		%		%		%	
Conservative	61	+7	53	+12	48	+15	28	+10
Liberal	15	–3	16	–8	13	–5	11	–1
Labour	23	–4	29	–2	38	–5	59	–6
Other	1	0	2	–1	1	–4	2	–3
Total per cent	100%		100%		100%		100%	
Number of respondents (including non-voters)	402		611		251		552	
Category as per cent of all respondents in table	22%		34%		14%		30%	
Per cent of each category who voted	90%		89%		77%		82%	
Conservative lead over Labour	+38		+24		+10		–31	
Swing to Conservatives		+5.5%		+7%		+10%		+8%

Note:
[1] 'Private rented' includes other types of housing which were neither an owner-occupied house, nor a council house. Council house includes 'new town' corporation housing.

Data source: BES October 1974 Election Survey; BES May 1979 Election Survey.

None of the differences in consumption were as powerful a predictor of the vote as the manual/non-manual cleavage. There were groups whose Conservative vote exceeded that of non-manual workers (e.g. 75 per cent of the richest one-twentieth of our respondents voted Conservative) or whose Labour vote exceeded that of manual workers (e.g. 59 per cent of council house tenants voted Labour). But these groups were relatively small minorities at the very top or bottom of the scale. It was not possible to dichotomise the electorate according to their general standard of living, education or housing so as to produce a stronger basis of the vote than that provided by the conventional division between manual and non-manual workers. No index score of Labour voting could match the fairly modest twenty-seven produced by the manual/non-manual dichotomy; the nearest was twenty-one, between owner-occupiers (including mortgagees) and rent-payers (including private as well as council tenants).

Until now the impact of a series of social cleavages on the 1979 vote has been examined one by one. In some ways this provides too full a picture. For each of these cleavages represents a facet of what is a general and interconnected condition of inequality; to a greater or lesser extent each cleavage overlaps with the other. As a result we cannot easily tell in any one case how much of the apparent relationship with the vote in fact reflects that of another cleavage, and how much is independent of it. We know, for example, that trade union members and council tenants are more likely to vote Labour than Conservative; but we also know that trade union members are more likely than non-members to live in council houses. What we do not know is whether trade unionists vote Labour because they are council tenants, or the tenants vote Labour because they are trade unionists, or indeed whether both groups vote Labour because in the main they are manual workers. What is required is a method of ordering these cleavages into a hierarchy of importance. How this is done, and with what results, is the subject for the rest of this chapter.

3.3 The social bases of Conservative and Labour voting in 1979: a 'tree' analysis of the social determinants of voting

In the preceding sections of this chapter, we have examined the relationship between voting and social characteristics with the aid of several classifications intended to capture the individuals' social status or some aspect of their occupational roles. Already the simple two-class divide – with its distinction between occupation in non-manual or manual work – proved to remain an important concomitant of voters' party choice, albeit less important than in the past. The six-category occupational status classification threw light on variations in party strength among different strata within the two main classes. A picture even richer in nuances emerged, however, when we subdivided broader strata according to more specific features of the occupational roles of the individuals (or of the breadwinner in the household), for example, whether the person was self-employed or an employee, whether someone in the household was a member of a trade union, and whether the family lived in an owner-occupied house or in rented housing.

What we shall set out to do in this part of the enquiry is to use a computerised classification technique to summarise all this information about the social determinants of voting in the 1979 election. As a result we will obtain socio-economic category schemes which are at once more comprehensive and more

specific than the classifications we have examined earlier. The purpose is to
distinguish between social categories that were more and less likely to cast a
Conservative or a Labour vote in 1979. To that end, the category schemes will
consist of a number of combinations of social characteristics, which help to
identify the sources of strong Conservative and Labour support as well as the
sections of the electorate where the two major parties are more evenly balanced.
The computerised procedure carries out the required search for these combinations of social characteristics in such a way that it will arrive at the category
schemes that can best account for the party division of the vote. The technique
is known as 'tree' analysis, and why it has been given that name will soon become
apparent.[19] The purpose of a tree analysis is to find the combination of characteristics that can best account for some attribute or criterion. In the first of the
category schemes to be presented, that criterion will be whether the individual
voted Labour, or voted for one of the two other parties. (Minor parties' voters as
well as non-voters are excluded.) In the second analysis, the criterion is, instead,
whether the individuals voted for the Conservatives or for either Labour or the
Liberals.

All information about the individuals' characteristics on each of the
classifications is stored in the computer memory, and it is the computer that
actually carries out the procedure which we will now describe. The first step
is to divide all the individuals into two groups which differ with regard to
the criterion chosen (e.g. the percentage of Conservative voters). For each of
the classifications available, we will obtain a table with two rows (Conservatives
and others, respectively) and two columns, which divide all respondents into
two groups with regard to the relevant social characteristic. If the classification
contains more than two categories – as for example our occupational status
classification – then these categories will be combined into two groups: one
more and one less likely to vote Conservative.[20]

Of these many 'two-by-two' tables, the one will be chosen which shows
the strongest relationship between party choice and the social characteristic
concerned.[21] We have thus divided the sample into two groups which start
two 'trunks' in the tree. For each of the two groups thus obtained, the
procedure is repeated and it is divided into two sub-subgroups, 'branches
in the tree'. In the next step the same procedure is applied to each one of
the four groups created in the previous step and they are further divided, if
possible. The procedure continues in following steps, each one resulting in
a division of a group into two subgroups, 'twigs in the tree'. The further
splitting of a group comes to an end, when it is found that no additional
social characteristic 'makes any difference'; that is, when we cannot create
any two subgroups that differ significantly with regard to the Conservative
(or Labour) percentage of the vote. In other words: whilst some people vote
Conservative and others vote for another party within such 'final' a group, we
have exhausted our ability of 'explaining' why this is so.[22]

Not all the social characteristics which are known to bear some relationship to party choice will actually be used for the purpose of splitting off groups. And some social characteristics will appear early on in the formation of the 'tree', whilst others will appear only as means to define specific, perhaps small, sub-categories. To some extent, the way in which a classification is employed in the creation of the tree is a reflection of its 'importance' as a determinant of party choice. Caution is called for, however. Social characteristics are mostly correlated to each other, and some of the classifications we use incorporate important elements of others. Thus, for example, once we have divided a sample according to social status we have, implicitly, also taken education into account inasmuch as many high-status occupations require some form of higher education. The fact that a given classification does not appear in the definition of any of the groups in the tree, therefore, should not be taken as evidence that it bears no relationship to party choice. It may often only mean that it is correlated to one of the more 'powerful' predictors that already has been used to define group splits. For that reason, it cannot add significantly to the information we have already made use of. This property of the technique may be considered both as a strength and as a limitation. It is a strength inasmuch as it leads to parsimony. We can define the social categories with different voting patterns with the aid of a comparatively small number of characteristics, up to the point where 'nothing more can be explained'. It is a limitation in the sense that some relationships between party choice and characteristics that are concomitant to those actually used for group splitting will be missing from the tree categories, although they may be of substantive or theoretical interest from other points of view.[23] We will comment on some of these omissions in the following discussion of the two 'trees'.

The predictor classifications used in the tree analysis are essentially the same as the social and economic classifications introduced earlier in this chapter. They are listed in the form used in the tree analyses in Table 3.14 (at the end of this chapter).

One of these category schemes is an occupational status classification which differs somewhat from the commonly employed scale of social status or 'social grade' categories. The conventional scale attempts to grade occupations primarily according to the prestige associated with various types of work and the degree of responsibility or skill required to carry out the work; to some extent it also yields a stratification with regard to standard of living, but only imperfectly so. This classification does, however, not explicitly take into account one of the characteristics of a person's occupational role which is generally associated with the concept of class; the missing distinction is simply that between people who are employed by someone else and those who are self-employed. In order to bring this criterion into the classification, we have subdivided the 'social grade' categories into self-employed and employees. In some instances, this results in very small categories, however. We have therefore applied the employer/employee distinction to a somewhat compressed version of the conventional 'social grade' classification by merging status categories which show very similar divisions of the vote. The result is the seven-category classification shown in Table 3.14.

In this category scheme, married men and unmarried persons are classified according to their own occupations, whereas married women are classified according to the husband's occupation. Retired persons and unemployed are classified according to their normal occupations when they were economically active.[24] The same rules were applied in the private/public sector employment and the 'occupation type' classifications.

The tree classification applied

The results of the tree analyses just described are charted in Figures 3.D and 3.E for Labour and Conservative voting, respectively. As the two classifications are so similar – the Conservatives are strong in the groups where Labour is weak and vice versa – we will discuss the outcome of the two tree analyses together.

With regard to both Conservative and Labour voting, the first dividing line in the electorate is defined by occupational status. The voters are divided into one group which includes employees in all kinds of non-manual, white-collar work together with all proprietors of enterprises and other self-employed and a second group which comprises all employees in manual work. This division differs from the more common distinction between non-manual and manual work only with regard to its treatment of the self-employed. Employers and other self-employed who run their own businesses vote Conservative with large majorities – and are much less likely to vote Labour than virtually any other group – irrespective of the size of their firms, and independently of whether they manage an enterprise or do manual work as individual entrepreneurs. For the sake of brevity we will use the term *middle class* for the white-collar and self-employed trunk in the tree, and the term *working class* for the category of employees in manual work.

Once this division has been made, two classifications are almost equally efficient as predictors of voting within both middle class and working class: trade union membership and whether the individual lives in an owner-occupied house, in some privately rented accommodation or in a coucil house.

Interestingly housing proves to be a slightly better predictor of Labour voting than trade union membership (and therefore takes precedence as a splitting criterion in that tree), whilst the opposite is true for Conservative voting (compare Figures 3.D and 3.E). We have actually included the trade union classification in two different versions in these analyses. In the one version, the classification pertains only to membership in a TUC-affiliated union, whilst the other includes all unions. Both classifications distinguish between: persons who themselves are union members, those who are not members but have a union member in the

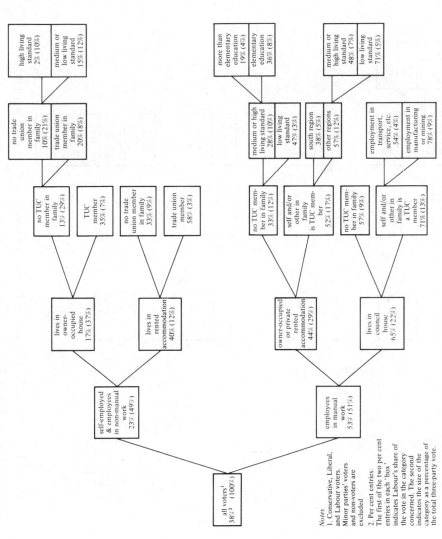

Figure 3.D *The social determinants of the Labour vote in the 1979 election*

Notes
1. Conservative, Liberal, and Labour voters. Minor parties' voters and non-voters are excluded

2. Per cent entries:
The first of the two per cent entries in each 'box' indicates Labour's share of the vote in the category concerned. The second indicates the size of the category as a percentage of the total three-party vote.

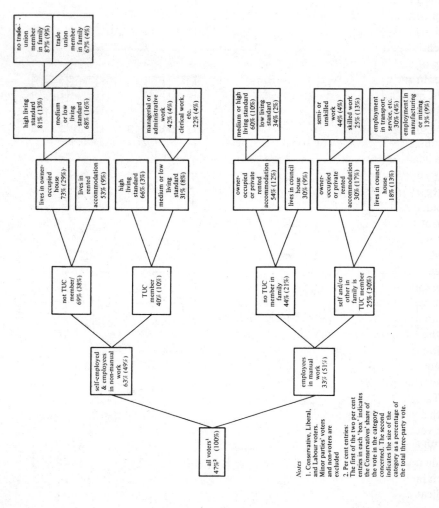

no trade-union member in family 87% (9%)

trade union member in family 67% (4%)

high living standard 81% (13%)

medium or low living standard 68% (16%)

managerial or administrative work 42% (4%)

clerical work, etc. 22% (4%)

medium or high living standard 60% (10%)

low living standard 34% (2%)

semi- or unskilled work 44% (4%)

skilled work 25% (13%)

employment in transport, service, etc. 30% (4%)

employment in manufacturing or mining 13% (9%)

lives in owner-occupied house 73% (29%)

lives in rented accommodation 53% (9%)

high living standard 66% (3%)

medium or low living standard 31% (8%)

owner-occupied or private rented accommodation 54% (12%)

lives in council house 30% (9%)

owner-occupied or private rented accommodation 30% (17%)

lives in council house 18% (13%)

not TUC member/ 69% (38%)

TUC member 40% (10%)

no TUC member in family 44% (21%)

self and/or other in family is TUC member 25% (30%)

self-employed & employees in non-manual work 63% (49%)

employees in manual work 33% (51%)

all voters[1] 47%[2] (100%)

Notes

1. Conservative, Liberal, and Labour voters. Minor parties' voters and non-voters are excluded

2. Per cent entries: The first of the two per cent entries in each 'box' indicates the Conservatives' share of the vote in the category concerned. The second indicates the size of the category as a percentage of the total three-party vote.

Figure 3.E *The social determinants of the Conservative vote in the 1979 election*

family and, finally, those whose families include nobody with a trade union membership. The two classifications are obviously overlapping to a large extent. In general, TUC membership is more closely related to voting than membership of other unions. In the middle class, however, where there are comparatively fewer TUC members, the alternative classification proves to be more efficient in a couple of instances. With a small margin, membership of the TUC (or perhaps rather *not* being a member of TUC) emerges as a more efficient criterion than home-owner-ship when it comes to 'predicting' Conservative voting both in the middle class and in the working class. It is interesting, though, that the criterion is slightly dif-ferently applied in the two classes: in the middle class it is the voter's own member-ship of a TUC union that distinctively reduces his likelihood of voting Conserva-tive. In the working class, it is sufficient that at least someone in the family is a TUC member. Likewise with a small margin, the second most important social characteristic to determine the propensity to vote Labour turns out to be the kind of housing accommodation in which the voters live. In the middle class the dividing line goes between those who live in owner-occupied houses and all who live in any kind of rented accommodation. In the working class, the split occurs instead between those who live in council houses and all others. Given that the category of persons who live in privately rented accommodation is comparatively small, and heterogeneous, the difference between the two splitting definitions is not of too much importance. The important contrast is between those who live in owner-occupied houses and the families on the council house estates.

At this stage, we have obtained four categories in both of the tree classi-fications, but the social classes are divided by different criteria in the two trees. The similarity is restored almost entirely, however, in the next step. Three of the four groups in the Conservative vote classification are now divided with regard to home owner-ship as well as trade union membership, and all the four groups in the Labour vote classification are split according to membership of a trade union as well as housing. The classification proceeds in both instances to make a few further splits, mostly with the aid of a 'standard of living' classification. Then the splitting comes to an end. The remaining social characteristics listed in Table 3.14 are not capable of distinguishing between any further subgroups with statistically significant differences with regard to the party divisions of the vote.

When taken together, the modified social class division, type of housing, trade union membership, and standard of living form a category scheme of such inclusiveness that it nearly exhausts the 'explanatory capacity' of other indicators of the individual's social position or social milieu. Adding further characteristics to the classification, and allowing further splitting into sub-groups, does indeed add only slightly to our ability to 'predict' whether a person will vote Conservative or Labour. We could therefore actually have terminated the splitting procedure already with the eight group classifications obtained at the third splitting stage in each of the trees. However, the further splits shown in the tree charts are still 'statistically significant' and yield some quite interesting further insights. The additional criteria concerned are, for example, employment in mining or manufacturing rather than other types of manual work, having administrative or managerial functions rather than clerical tasks in a white-collar job, and so on. These are all characteristics which are associated with a propensity to vote Conservative or Labour. They add, in effect, only a degree of further refinement to the same aspects of the social positions which are captured already by our four most efficient classifications.

The connection with vote of several of these characteristics can often be traced through many of the subgroups of the trees, even though the actual split is made on some other criterion. This is true, for example, of the *regional* difference between the South (excluding the Greater London region) and the rest of the country. In the tree chart, it shows up only in connection with Labour voting among non-unionised workers who do not live in council houses. Living in the South also reduces the likelihood of casting a Labour vote in several other groups in the tree, but only slightly so. For the most part, the contrast between the South and other regions, we must conclude, was the result of a concentration in the South of such factors which in general made for a strong Conservative and a weak Labour vote.

Whether a person is employed in the public sector or in the private sector was one of the characteristics included in the analysis. In fact that criterion was never used to define a group splitting. As is shown in Table 3.14 the Conservative share of the vote was noticeably smaller – and the Labour percentage higher – in the public sector than in the private sector. That difference actually survives in most of the subgroups created in the third splitting stage in the tree. It can even be traced, albeit in a weaker form, through some of the 'twigs' in the tree. But it is consistently overtaken by more powerful determinants of the party choice, and it adds too little to the overall predictive capability to generate any group split-ting when these have been taken into account. Yet, it is an interesting example of the type of further specification that could be made.

Of the remaining classifications in Table 3.14, *income* is omitted altogether from the tree; the 'standard of living' classification is clearly more efficient an indicator. *Age* and *sex* are likewise omitted from the tree classifications: both of these factors show only weak relationship to voting in the electorate as a whole, and they emerge only in the form of slight variations in the subgroups.

Conclusion: the social determinants of Conservative and Labour voting in 1979

The tree analyses created a modified class division in the search for the social determinants of voting. This divides the electorate into two sections of almost equal size. No other similar partitioning results in as sharp a contrast between two population groups as this class division. Even so, it again becomes apparent that neither of the two major parties is entirely predominant in either the middle class or the working class; and both of the two major parties draw a significant share of their voting support from outside the class which forms its social base. The Conservatives, it is true, attracted nearly two-thirds of the votes among white-collar employees and self-employed in 1979, but almost a quarter of the middle class, thus defined, voted Labour. In the working class, the significance of class is even less marked: Labour gained only a little more than a majority of the votes, and the Conservatives won the support of about a third. (Here, as well as in the following commentary all references to the electorate actually pertain to the votes cast for the three main parties.)

Inspection of the branches of the two trees reveals where the two parties have their strongest support within each of the two social classes. Within the middle class, the Conservatives won nearly three-quarters of the votes among voters who lived in owner-occupied houses and belonged to families in which nobody was a member of a TUC-affiliated trade union. That category comprises 29 per cent of the electorate. The Conservatives' share increases to nearly nine voters in ten if we add two further criteria: a high standard of living, and no member of a trade union of any description in the family. In that Conservative preserve the Labour vote is negligible, but it includes only about a tenth of the electorate (9 per cent).

Labour achieves a strong support – amounting to 71 per cent of the vote – in the working-class families who live in council houses and in which at least someone in the family is a member of a TUC-affiliated trade union. That category makes up only 13 per cent of the electorate, however. The Labour percentage increases to 78 per cent if we add the criterion that the voter (or her husband) is employed in manufacturing or mining rather than, for example, transport or service work. The 'final' groups in which Labour gets 57 per cent or more of the vote comprise 26 per cent of the electorate.

Both the importance and the limitation of the social bases of the two major parties is perhaps best illustrated by a slightly different way of adding up the percentages: The 'final' categories, where either the Conservatives or Labour won at least 70 per cent of the vote, form 23 per cent of the electorate. If we add together, instead, the 'final' middle-class groups where the Conservatives got at least 60 per cent and the working-class groups where Labour got 60 per cent or more of the vote, then these categories are found to include somewhat less than half of the electorate (46 per cent). The remainder is more evenly contested ground.

Which are the marginal groups? That is, which are the middle-class groups where the Conservatives are weak and Labour is strong, and which are the working-class categories where Labour is weak whereas the Conservative vote is comparatively strong? Again, the categories in the two trees give a quite clear indication.

The Conservatives have a weaker support among those middle-class voters who have some kind of trade union tie and/or do not live in owner-occupied houses. In the tree for Conservative voting, the group that consists of middle-class TUC members with a moderate or low standard of living gives even stronger support for Labour than for the Conservatives (the group comprises 8 per cent of the electorate). As is seen from the final branching of this group, the Conservatives are particularly weak among those with clerical (rather than managerial or administrative) jobs. A tiny middle-class group with a Labour majority is actually singled out in the tree for Labour voting: trade union members who do not live in an owner-occupied house.

The section of the working class where the Conservatives draw their strongest support, and the Labour party is at its weakest, consists of non-unionised workers who do not live in council houses. In that category – which comprises 12 per cent of the electorate – the Conservatives won a majority of 54 per cent of the vote. If we specify one step further, so as to single out the sub-category with at least a medium standard of living, the Conservative vote increases to 60 per cent and the Labour vote goes down to 28 per cent. As is seen from the tree for Labour voting, the Labour vote is also weak among unionised workers if they are not council house tenants and live in the South.

The Conservative vote in 1979 was quite strong, however, even in those working-class groups that were less marginal: it was only in the hard-core Labour group of council house tenants with a TUC-affiliation and employment in manufacturing or mining that the Conservatives obtained less than 25 per cent of the vote.

The class divide forms an important political cleavage, but only to the extent of defining two broad social categories of which one shows a substantial Conservative majority, whilst the Labour party obtains a comparatively large share of the vote in the other. The additional social concomitants of a Conservative or a Labour vote are diverse and cut across the class boundaries: life style (e.g. house-ownership and standard of living), membership of trade unions for both blue-collar or white-collar employees, and specific occupational roles or types of occupation. Even when all such social characteristics have been taken into account, however, a variety of sub categories show either a fairly even balance between the two major parties or do not differ much from the electorate as a whole; these comprise about half the total vote cast for the Conservatives, Liberals and Labour in the 1979 election. The social bases of a *very* strong support for either of the two main parties (say, at least 70 per cent of the vote) comprised, as we have seen, only about a quarter of the electorate.

It would be futile to treat the results of this specification of the social determinants of voting only as a means of defining 'intermediary strata', between the two major classes. The diversity of socio-economic factors which affect voting in both middle class and working class is too wide, and the section of the electorate where class differences are blurred is too large. It is the two-class conception of the parties' social bases that needs to be reconsidered.

In the next part of this book the enquiry will focus upon voters' opinions on parties and policies rather than on their occupations or social status. In the course of that enquiry we shall introduce a statistical measure of how accurately individuals' party choices can be predicted with the aid of explanatory factors of the one type or the other. For the sake of comparison it is worth noting, already at this stage, that the voters' opinions on policies and on the parties' performances in office 'explain' more than twice as much as all the social and economic characteristics taken together.[25]

Table 3.14 *Socio-economic predictors in the 'tree' analyses of voting in the 1979 analyses.*

As explained in the text, two versions of the tree analysis were carried out. In one version (Figure 3.E) the classification was done with regard to the Conservative share of the three-party vote in the categories created, whilst the Labour percentage was the criterion for the other version (Figure 3.D). The Conservative and Labour percentage share of the three-party vote is given for each category in the predictors. The E^2 statistic given for both the Conservative and the Labour vote is the 'explained proportion of the variance' obtained when the predictor concerned is used to divide all the three main parties' voters into two groups.

	Tree analysis for:				
	Conservative vote Conservative per cent of category	E^2	Labour vote Labour per cent of category	E^2	Per cent distribution for all respondents included in the tree analysis*
Occupational status		0.09		0.10	%
Proprietors of larger enterprises; self-employed professionals (I-II)	77%		11%		3
Proprietors of smaller enterprises; self-employed professionals (III-IV)	73%		14%		4
Self-employed in manual work	76%		18%		3
Employees: higher and middle status non-manual work (I-III)	61%		22%		28
Employees: lower status non-manual work (IV)	55%		31%		11
Employees: skilled manual work (V)	32%		54%		34
Employees: semi- or unskilled manual work (VI)	35%		51%		17
					100%
Membership of TUC-affiliated union		0.07		0.06	%
Respondent is a member	30%		54%		30
Someone in family is a member (but not respondent)	39%		47%		18
No one in family a member	60%		26%		52
					100%

*See footnote on page 115.

Table 3.14 (*cont.*)

	Tree analysis for:				
	Conservative vote Conservative per cent of category	E²	Labour vote Labour per cent of category	E²	Per cent distribution for all respondents included in the tree analysis*
Accommodation		0.06		0.08	%
Council house	28%		61%		28
Other rented, etc.	47%		40%		12
Owner-occupied – on mortgage	54%		30%		37
Owner-occupied – owned outright	61%		23%		23
					100%
Living standard		0.05		0.06	%
Low 0	31%		58%		14
1	39%		50%		25
2	47%		35%		39
3	65%		22%		17
4	73%		15%		4
High 5	91%		0%		1
Index based on use of services, car-ownership, etc.					100%
Trade union member- ship (whether TUC- affiliated or not)		0.06		0.05	%
Respondent is a member	33%		51%		32
Someone in family is a member (but not respondent)	41%		45%		20
No one in family is a member	60%		26%		48.
					100%
Occupation type		0.04		0.05	%
Farming, fishing	69%		23%		4
Mining, manufacturing	35%		51%		40
Transport, clerical, service	51%		33%		34
Administration and management	58%		24%		22
					100%
Note: This is a compressed version of the 'Occupation Order' classification used by OPCS					
Public/private sector		0.01		0.01	%
Public-sector work	39%		45%		32
Private-sector work	51%		35%		68
					100%

Table 3.14 (*cont.*)

		Tree analysis for:				
		Conservative vote Conservative per cent of category	E²	Labour vote Labour per cent of category	E²	Per cent distribution for all respondents included in the tree analysis*
Income			0.02		0.02	%
Low	1	40%		45%		24
	2	47%		40%		41
	3	46%		37%		24
High	4	67%		22%		11
						100%

Note: husband's and wife's combined income for married persons

Education			0.02		0.04	%
Low	1	40%		48%		46
	2	47%		38%		18
	3	53%		30%		17
High	4	59%		21%		19
						100%
Age			0.00		0.00	%
Youngest	1	39%		42%		5
	2	45%		38%		26
	3	47%		39%		40
Oldest	4	52%		37%		29
						100%
Sex			0.00		0.00	%
Men		46%		39%		51
Women		49%		37%		49
						100%
Region			0.01		0.03	%
The South (excluding Greater London)		56%		27%		32
Other regions		43%		44%		68
						100%

*The tree analysis includes only voters of the three main parties; moreover, a category of respondents who would not be assigned to any of the occupational status groups are excluded from the analysis. For the purpose of the tree analysis (and the above table) respondents with missing data on any of the other predictor classifications were included in the category deemed most appropriate or 'most likely'. Specifically all cases with missing data on income were included in group 2 of that classification.

Data source: BES 1979 Election Survey.

Part II

Issues, opinion and party choice in the 1979 election

4

Opinions on political issues and voting — the directions of the enquiry

4.1 The electorate's verdict – what did it mean?

The Conservative surge in the 1979 election brought the Conservatives back into power and increased their share of the vote by 8 per cent in comparison with the October 1974 election. The Conservatives had lost both of the elections of 1974 and the election results had opened the way for a Labour government. In that sense, Labour won in 1974; the October 1974 election even gave it a slender majority in the House of Commons. Yet, the size of Labour's electoral support makes it hard to describe either of the 1974 elections as victories for Labour. Even in the October 1974 election, Labour's share of the vote was well below the party's average for the elections in the post-war era. As the election period went on, the Labour government's majority crumbled, and it met the electorate in May 1979 as a minority government. In contrast, the May 1979 election returned a Conservative government with a comfortable majority. After the vagaries of the electorate in 1974, the pendulum had swung in the Conservatives' favour.

But was the voice of the electorate really so unequivocal? For the Conservative party, the 1979 election signalled a recovery from the decline in 1974 rather than an unqualified victory. The large Liberal vote in the 1974 elections meant the presence in 1979 of a large pool of disaffected former Conservative supporters who could be won back to defeat a Labour government. Yet, the Conservative share of the vote in 1979 was smaller than in 1970 when they had last won an election. Before 1974, no post-war government had taken office and won a majority in the House of Commons with an electoral support quite so far short of a majority of the votes. On the other hand, in no other election since 1945 had the winning party achieved as big a lead over its major opponent at the polls as did the Conservatives in 1979. What, then, were the causes of this election result?

Was it a verdict on the Labour government's managing of the economy in the last few years? If so, did it express disenchantment with the government's

119

attempts to implement an incomes policy, or did it reflect dismay about industrial unrest, concern about rising prices or worries caused by a growing level of unemployment? Or was it rather that a large portion of the electorate was attracted to the Conservatives' alternative economic programme? The Conservatives promised a return to a system with less government and more room for private enterprise. Moreover, they pledged to curb excessive trade union power, to put an end to state intervention in wage negotiations, to uphold law and safety in the streets of the cities and to lower the tax burden. Were the Conservatives' specific policy proposals the decisive factor in the election, or was it rather the general thrust in the party's approach to the problems in the country's economy that appealed to the electorate? Or, is the election result to be attributed to all of these things taken together?

In the following chapters we shall use interview survey data to draw a map of the divisions of opinion in the electorate over these and other issues in the 1979 election. The map will describe the public's views concerning the two major parties' ability to deal with the main problems the country was facing in 1979, as well as the public's views of the policy alternatives the parties were standing for. The map will also serve to highlight the issues that were salient in the campaign and it will show the extent to which the balance of opinion on these issues was weighted in favour of one or the other of the parties. In several instances, the state of public opinion in 1979 will be compared with the situation at the election in October 1974. Throughout this surveying of the state of opinion in the electorate, we shall explore the relationships between opinions and votes.

The purpose of the enquiry is twofold: first, we wish to account for the outcome of the 1979 election, to explain individuals' party choice in the light of their opinions on policies and parties. Secondly, we seek to gain insights into the process of political representation in democratic elections. Votes are cast for candidates and parties. Yet the parties offer the voters a choice between alternatives that stand for different policies, priorities and aims. Our survey data throw light on how the electors' opinions were expressed through their party choice and how the divisions of opinions in the electorate were reflected in the party division of the vote.

A survey carried out immediately after an election obviously cannot gauge the extent to which the opinions and expectations of the voters were in accordance with all the policies pursued by the government that came to power as the result of the election. But our mapping of opinions and votes can provide answers to such questions as: what kinds of policies did Conservative, Liberal and Labour voters actually seek to support? What differences did they think there were between the parties? What did they like and dislike about the three parties? How different were Conservative, Labour and Liberal voters when it came to things they thought the government should do or the goals they thought it should seek to realise? Surveying opinions at the time of an election, finally, yields empirical knowledge that will help to answer some crucial questions about the representative function of an election: what strength of support did the parties have for their policy commitments, among their own voters, and within the electorate as a whole? If voters gave the victorious party a mandate, what did they expect that party to deliver?

4.2 Examining relationships between opinions and voting

Strictly speaking, the 1979 survey was not a survey *at* the time of the May election. It would not have been feasible to conduct a survey of this scope on the election day: it involved nearly 1,900 interviews which on average lasted for about an hour and a quarter each. As we wanted to conduct the interviews at a time when individuals in the sample had heard all they wanted to hear of the arguments in the campaign, had made up their own minds and had come to their final voting decision, we chose to undertake the fieldwork during a period commencing immediately after the election day. The great majority of the interviews were completed within a month. The same design was used in the February and October 1974 election surveys. Obviously, there are methodological problems involved in employing data collected after the actual event to account for that event. In some instances we shall therefore find it necessary to note that the election result may itself have affected the data. But, in general, the division of opinion recorded by our survey is not likely to have altered appreciably between election day and the time of the interview.

The relationships between voters' opinions and their party choice form the main theme of the following chapters. Yet, none of the numerous tables will show so clearcut a division of opinions that, say, all Labour voters hold one view and all Conservatives another. What will emerge, instead, are more or less sharp relationships, with people holding one view more likely to vote Conservative, and people holding the opposite view more likely to vote Labour. When the answers to our interview questions have recorded a series of opinion positions that can be ordered from 'left' to 'right', the relationship takes the form of an increasing proportion of Conservative voters and a declining proportion of Labour voters from one end of the scale to the other. Likewise, the opinion distributions among Conservative voters will be found to differ, more or less distinctively, from those among Liberal and Labour voters. How strong such a relationship is will depend on which aspect of policies a particular interview question is concerned with. The strength of these relationships is one of the indicators we will employ to gauge the relative importance of different issues in the 1979 election.

The tables will obviously illuminate relationships between opinions and party choice. We will also frequently use correlation coefficients as summarising in-dicators of the strength of such relationships. The coefficient employed in

connection with many of the tables (Kendall's Tau-b) indicates the strength of
a relationship between two classifications in which the categories can be seen
as rank-ordered according to some criterion, e.g. from the most 'right-wing' to
the most 'left-wing' positions on a series of response alternatives.[1] When such
an opinion 'scale' is correlated with voting behaviour the parties are considered
as ordered from either right to left, i.e. Conservative, Liberal and Labour, or
from left to right, i.e. Labour, Liberal and Conservative. For the purpose of
calculating correlation coefficients, the party and opinion classifications concerned are always ordered in the same direction (which means that the original
ordering of the response alternatives sometimes are reversed), and all correlation
coefficients are therefore reported with a positive value. Using the three-party
classification means that the correlation coefficients will summarise both those
relationships where the sharpest dividing line appears to be between Labour
and the non-socialist parties and also those where the dividing line goes between
the Conservatives and other parties, while at the same time taking into account
that the division of opinions among the Liberals is in most instances more
evenly balanced than among Conservative and Labour supporters.

In order to assess the extent to which a set of issue opinions jointly can
account for individual voting, we will use more comprehensive models of
analysis (multiple regression and discriminant analysis). There will be no need
to enter into technical discussion of these complex analysis methods. Their
value lies in their capability of summarising a multitude of relationships and
patterns present in the data. Anyone who prefers the richness of detail in
the full picture should turn his or her attention to the tables showing straightforward opinion distributions, of which there are many.

4.3 Charting the chapter contents

Chapter 5 provides a backdrop for the more searching analyses that come in
the following chapters. It is mainly based on a series of questions – at the
very beginning of the interviews – in which those interviewed were asked to
say what they thought were the good and bad things about each of the
Conservative, Labour and Liberal parties. Thousands of favourable and unfavourable comments on the parties were elicited through these questions.
These comments are summarised in classifications which describe the voters'
images of their own and other parties and also to highlight the issues that
were foremost in the voters' minds at the time of the 1979 election.

The chapter begins by examining the role of the party leaders in the
voters' evaluations of the parties. It then goes on to outline the divisions
of opinions over the parties' performance within major areas of policy
making. In a subsequent part of the chapter we seek to portray the voters'
views of the important dividing lines between the Conservatives and Labour,
with regard to ideological aims as well as the interests of social classes. The

chapter concludes with a section in which 'free answer' data as well as several
other interview questions are used to describe the public's image – or, rather,
images – of the trade union movement and its role in British politics.

Chapters 6, 7 and 8 are concerned with changes in the state of opinion
between 1974 and 1979 as well as the relationships between opinions and party
preferences at the time of the 1979 election. The theme of Chapter 6 is the
voters' assessment of the ability of the Conservatives and Labour to handle three
major problems in the country's economy: strikes, unemployment and rising
prices.

Was the Conservative surge in the 1979 election an indication of a rightward
turn in popular responses to the cultural and social change that had occurred in
the last decades? This is one of the questions we attempt to answer (with the aid
of data from 1974 and 1979) in Chapter 7. The analysis is based on batteries of
questions that encompass aspects of cultural change in Britain as well as economic
and policy goals. Chapter 8 presents an analysis of a rightward shift in electoral
opinions from 1974 to 1979 on two traditional landmark issues in British
politics: nationalisation and social welfare policies.

Chapters 9, 10 and 11 focus on the main issues in the 1979 election which
involved a choice of policy alternatives for the next few years. Chapter 9 begins
by examining the first requirement that must be met before a question of policy
can become an electoral issue: that the political parties are seen to differ. The
chapter continues with a description of the divisions of opinions on each of the
issues concerned and with an analysis of the relationship between the opinions
of individuals and their party choice. We take into account the voters' perceptions of party stands on each issue and explore how the salience of the issues
affected the relationship between opinion positions and voting. Our analysis
will furthermore throw light on the two-way relationship between opinions on
political issues and party preferences: while voters' opinions on issues undoubtedly will influence their party preferences, there is also a tendency for
individuals' party preferences to colour their opinions both on the policies
advocated by their own party and the alternatives espoused by other parties.
Chapter 10 examines in greater detail the relationship between party choice
and opinions on three issues where there was room for uncertainty about the
aims or stands of the major parties: incomes policy, Britain's role in the EEC,
and the questions of race relations and immigration.

In Chapter 11 we shift the emphasis from individuals' voting decisions to the
impact of each of the issues on the party division of the vote. The first part of
the chapter examines the relationship between issue opinions and voting
change. In the second part of the chapter, a comprehensive statistical analysis
technique is used to assess how far issues opinions can account for party choice.
The chapter continues with a discussion of two essential aspects of the relationship between opinions in the electorate and the election result: the strength
of the relationship between the opinions of individuals and their party choice,

and the distribution of opinions in the electorate as a whole. Were opinions for and against the policies advocated by the Conservatives and Labour evenly balanced, or was the balance of opinions weighted in favour of one of the parties? The chapter concludes with a 'balance sheet' which illuminates the strength of the Conservative party's appeals on most of the issues.

Chapter 12 is concerned with the party system and the opinion bases of the parties in the electorate. First, we examine the opinion differentiation in the electorate with the aid of a scale of partisanship in issue opinions. Next, we explore the bond between voters and parties that may be described as party allegiance or, with a more technical term, 'party identification'. Much of the analysis in this chapter is concerned with the 'middle ground' in the electorate and with the role of the Liberal party in the party system. As will be seen, the number of voters who 'thought of' voting Liberal but did not do so is of the same magnitude as the Liberal party's actual voting support; on the other hand, that support included a very large portion of voters who voted Liberal in 1979 but still thought of themselves as Conservatives or Labour supporters. The middle ground is found to comprise a sizeable part of the electorate, which is shared among Conservatives, Labour and the Liberals, and where all the three parties compete for voting support. Chapter 12 concludes with an analysis of how the voters perceived the positions of the Conservative, Liberal and Labour parties relative to each other.

If the preceding chapter is concerned with more or less abiding structural features of the party system, Chapter 13 examines electoral change: wavering voting intentions during the campaign, the switching of party sympathies, and the changing of votes from one election to the next. The analytic tools introduced in Chapter 12 – partisanship in issue opinions and party identification – are also used in this analysis. But the purpose now is to describe the opinion characteristics of the voters whom the parties 'nearly lost' in the course of the campaign and of the electors who switched their votes between the October 1974 and the May 1979 election. We conclude Part II by revisiting the questions posted at the very outset: What were the causes of the Conservative surge and the Labour decline in the 1979 election?

5

Why the parties were liked and disliked

5.1 Voters speak their minds about the parties

Among the very first questions in the survey interviews was a series of queries in which we asked the persons in the sample to say what they liked and what they disliked about each of the three main parties. In the following hour or so the interviewer was to draw the respondent's attention to one after the other of the many issues in the campaign and ask specific questions about each subject. At the stage in the interview when the six questions about the parties' good and bad sides were asked, none of these matters had yet been raised. It was left to the person being interviewed to decide what he or she thought important. It was also left up to the respondent to decide whether to talk about the parties' ideologies, their leaders, their past records or their current positions on policy questions.[1]

The total mass of answers to these three pairs of questions contains views on a wide range of matters and comments on the parties from a variety of view-points. It does not record the opinions of all the individuals in the sample on each one of these matters. What we have recorded here are the things that were foremost in the voters' minds when they considered the parties' good and bad points; and most aspects of party politics were more salient to some people than to others.

Four questions about the 1979 election

We will use this record of the electorate's evaluation of the parties as the basis for an initial mapping of the issues – the word taken in a broad sense – in the 1979 election. We will attempt, in this chapter, to answer four questions about the 1979 election, using these 'free answer' data in conjunction with several complementary measurements of public opinion:

1. How important were the party leaders?
2. Which were the important issues in the campaign – and to what extent were

'salient opinions' on these issues balanced in favour of either the Conservatives or Labour?

3. What did Conservative and Labour voters think of as the important dividing lines in the party system?

4. What was the public's image of the trade unions – and how did it affect the electors' views of the political parties?

The response classification

Our six 'free answer' questions yielded several thousands of favourable and unfavourable comments on the parties. An overview of the subject matters and aspects of politics referred to is given in Tables 5.1A–C in one table for each of the three main parties. Many respondents gave more than one reason for liking or disliking a party, whereas others either offered no comment or replied in terms so vague that their responses could not be included in any of the contents categories, and the percentages in a column will not, therefore, add up to 100 per cent. (All the percentages are based on the total number of respondents included in the appropriate column.)[2] As can be seen from the tables, we have used the same contents classification for both positive and negative comments on the parties.[3] The first two categories in this classification comprise references to the party leader and to other politicians (including constituency candidates). The 'general features of the party' category contains mainly very general comments on qualities such as unity, experience and steadiness of purpose. In the case of the Liberal party, this category also includes comments on its position as a small and under-represented party, its espousal of proportional representation and its previous pact with the Labour party.

References to specific policies (such as taxation) or important economic and social problems (e.g. unemployment) are classified according to policy area and are grouped under two headings: 'foreign policy and defence' and 'domestic policy'. Comparatively few comments on policies were made in connection with the Liberal party and, for that reason, we have omitted most of the policy categories from the table for the Liberal party.

Ideological statements and general views on the economic system as a whole are classified under a common heading with one general category and another, special category for references to nationalisation. The nationalisation category is narrowly defined so as to include only explicit references to state ownership of industries. The general category comprises all other ideologically coloured statements covered by the common heading. (When appropriate an answer was included in both of these categories.) We have taken the concept of ideology in a broad sense and included in this category, for example, all answers containing any mention of 'left', 'centre' and 'right' as well as mentions of concepts like 'free enterprise' or 'equality'.

Many answers contained references to the social bases of the parties or comments on how parties represented the interests of social classes or other broad social strata. The words 'working class' (or 'workers') and 'middle class' were of course commonly used, but we have also included in this category a variety of related concepts which imply a differentiation with regard to income, wealth or social prestige. The category labelled 'class interests' comprises all statements of this kind.

The data

We have pointed out that the questions about the good and bad sides of the parties will primarily record the views that were the most salient elements in voters' images of the parties. The data obtained through these questions will not necessarily describe how the electorate as a whole was divided over any particular issue or aspect of politics. For example, the percentage of respondents mentioning taxation in one of their answers cannot be taken as a measure of the proportion of the electorate that had an opinion about taxation. To take another example, many more than those who mentioned nationalisation in response to these questions turned out to have a view on that matter when they were asked specifically about nationalisation later in the interview. Further, as we have also noted, some respondents focused their answers on the ideological or social dividing lines in the party system, whereas others chose to comment on the particular policies they agreed with or disliked. Many respondents' answers, on the other hand, contained elements of both types. It does not follow, of course, that the respondents who gave answers of the first type had no opinions on policy matters, or that those who referred explicitly only to specific policies were unaware of any ideological differences between the parties. People answered our questions in different ways because they looked at politics from different viewpoints. The things that were prominent in some individuals' minds were less salient to others.

What is recorded in Tables 5.1A–C is rather like a composite of a series of pictures of different but overlapping sections of the electorate. Each section is represented in the sample by those individuals who referred to a particular policy area or aspect of politics when stating what they liked or disliked about each party. These were the voters to whom that aspect mattered the most, or at least it mattered more than the things they did not mention at all. The sections overlap because most voters expressed opinions on more than one subject. Some sections were larger than others, because some aspects of politics attracted more attention – were more important in the 1979 election – than others.

For each of the subject matter categories, the percentages of positive and negative comments will thus indicate how a party was evaluated with regard to one aspect of politics and by voters in one segment of the electorate. The frequencies of such comments are expressed as percentages of the total number of respondents included in the table column – either the number of respondents

Table 5.1A *Reasons for liking and disliking the Conservative party, May 1979 election*

	Conservative voters		Liberal voters		Labour voters		All respondents	
	Likes	Dislikes	Likes	Dislikes	Likes	Dislikes	Likes	Dislikes
	%	%	%	%	%	%	%	%
Leading politicians								
Mrs Thatcher	13	8	6	15	3	20	8	13
Other politicians	3	2	1	3	2	2	3	2
General features								
of party	23	9	13	10	6	11	14	9
Foreign policy								
and defence								
EEC	3	3	1	3	1	2	2	2
Other foreign								
policy and defence	6	1	5	3	1	3	4	2
Domestic policies								
Taxation	18	3	13	9	8	10	13	7
Prices	2	5	2	10	1	12	1	8
Unemployment								
policies	3	0	1	1	2	2	2	1
Economic policy								
in general	11	3	6	7	3	9	7	5
Social services;								
pensions; education	19	3	11	6	10	13	13	7
Housing	7	1	3	5	4	5	5	3
Trade unions;								
industrial relations	19	3	11	7	4	4	11	4
Immigration; race;								
law and order	16	4.	13	3	12	4	14	3
Northern Ireland	0	0	1	0	0	0	0	0
Other domestic								
policy	2	1	1	.5	1	1	1	1
Views on the								
economic system and								
ideology								
Socialism, Liberalism,								
Conservatism, free								
enterprise vs. state								
economic control and								
related concepts	46	7	25	12	11	16	29	11
Nationalisation of								
industries	9	1	6	4	1	4	5	2
Class and group								
interests	8	8	2	30	1	40	4	23
Number of respondents	732	732	215	215	586	586	1,893	1,893

Note: The percentage entries in Tables 5.1A–C are based on the number of respondents given in the bottom row of each column. The percentages in a column do not add to 100 per cent, because some respondents' answers were included in more than one contents category; while other respondents gave answers containing no classifiable contents.
Data source: BES May 1979 Election Survey.

Table 5.1B *Reasons for liking and disliking the Labour party, May 1979 election*

	Conservative voters		Liberal voters		Labour voters		All respondents	
	Likes	Dislikes	Likes	Dislikes	Likes	Dislikes	Likes	Dislikes
	%	%	%	%	%	%	%	%
Leading politicians								
Mr Callaghan	7	4	7	2	7	2	7	3
Other politicians	2	5	2	3	3	2	2	3
General features								
of party	7	11	9	10	19	5	12	9
Foreign policy								
and defence								
EEC	1	2	3	1	3	1	2	2
Other foreign								
policy and defence	1	3	1	1	1	1	1	2
Domestic policies								
Taxation	1	8	1	5	3	3	1	5
Prices	4	2	7	2	14	1	8	2
Unemployment								
policies	1	2	4	1	7	0	4	1
Economic policy								
in general	3	8	11	6	12	5	7	6
Social services;								
pensions; education	13	20	22	18	25	11	19	15
Housing	0	1	3	0	4	1	2	0
Trade unions;								
industrial relations	4	39	8	35	11	14	7	28
Immigration; race;								
law and order	0	3	2	3	1	4	1	3
Northern Ireland	0	0	0	0	0	0	0	0
Other domestic								
policy	1	2	2	2	2	1	2	1
Views on the								
economic system and								
ideology								
Socialism, Liberalism,								
Conservatism, free								
enterprise vs. state								
economic control and								
related concepts	11	40	13	31	20	18	14	29
Nationalisation of								
industries	0	25	2	18	4	6	2	15
Class and group								
interests	9	4	23	2	49	2	25	3
Number of respondents	732	732	215	215	586	586	1,893	1,893

Data source: BES May 1979 Election Survey

Table 5.1C *Reasons for liking and disliking the Liberal party, May 1979 election*

	Conservative voters		Liberal voters		Labour voters		All respondents	
	Likes	Dislikes	Likes	Dislikes	Likes	Dislikes	Likes	Dislikes
	%	%	%	%	%	%	%	%
Leading politicians								
Mr Steel	17	2	21	3	14	2	15	2
Other politicians	7	12	8	10	4	7	5	10
General features								
of party	18	42	40	32	20	29	21	34
Domestic policies								
Taxation	2	0	7	0	2	1	3	0
Economic policy								
in general	4	0	6	0	2	0	3	0
Views on the								
economic system and								
ideology								
Socialism, Liberalism,								
Conservatism, free								
enterprise vs. state								
economic control and								
related concepts	27	5	46	2	21	10	26	6
Class and group								
interests	2	1	10	1	4	1	4	1
Number of respondents	732	732	215	215	586	586	1,893	1,893

who voted for a party or the entire sample. When the sample is divided according to the respondents' party vote, one will find, in general, that the balance of
opinions on any aspect of politics is most favourable for the voters' own party.
But this is not invariably the case. Moreover, the strength of the support voters
give to their own party, as well as the strength of their disapproval of other
parties, varies substantially among the various aspects of politics. The parties
gain more salient support – both among their own voters and in the electorate
at large – for some of their aims and policies than for others. The 'all respondents' column in each table gives an overall account of the strength of salient
support and disapproval that a party received with regard to each of the aspects
of politics that are defined by the categories in our classification.

5.2 The party leaders

All the three party leaders were leading their parties for the first time in a
general election campaign. Mr Callaghan had the advantage of being well-known,
and there is ample evidence in the opinion polls that his performance as a Prime
Minister was well regarded. Mrs Thatcher was the first woman to become the
leader of a British party. Whether because of her political profile, her person-
ality, or her sex – perhaps it was a mixture of all these things – her ratings in
the polls trailed behind Mr Callaghan's (with the exception of a temporary
reversal during February – March 1979). During the last month of the election
campaign, Mr Callaghan consistently had a lead over Mrs Thatcher as the party
leader who 'would make the best Prime Minister'.[4] It was generally acknowl-

edged that Mr Steel came across as sympathetic and sincere. The Liberal party may, on the other hand, have been damaged by the calamities of its previous leader (this is the subject of most of the negative comments on 'other politicians' in Table 5.1C).

As can be seen from Tables 5.1A–C, more favourable comments were made about Mr Steel than about any of the other party leaders. Critical comments were made more frequently about Mrs Thatcher than about Mr Steel or Mr Callaghan. Indeed, it was only about Mrs Thatcher that disapproving comments outnumbered approving.

How important was the personal appeal – or lack of appeal – of any one of the party leaders in the 1979 elections? The leaders played a prominent, if not predominant, role in the mass media during the campaign. One of them was to become the country's next Prime Minister. Given that, it is perhaps surprising that only a small minority of the electors in our sample volunteered any comments on the party leaders when asked what they liked or disliked about the parties. As we have pointed out, however, this type of data serves primarily to highlight a range of salient matters, whereas it is less reliable as a measure of the spread of opinions on any particular matter in the electorate at large. To obtain a more inclusive picture of how the party leaders were rated, we shall go beyond the 'free answer' data material and employ a more comprehensive measure of opinions.

For the party leaders to have an independent, personal impact on the vote, they need to be judged separately and differently from their parties. Even so, their personal standing may neither enhance nor diminish the number of votes cast for their parties. There is obviously no certainty that voters will cast their votes for the party whose leader they like best, in fact they often do not. But on balance a highly regarded party leader must be more of an asset for his or her party than one less highly regarded. Our measure consists of a series of questions in which respondents were asked to indicate their feelings about parties as well as leading politicians in the form of a 'mark out of ten' for each party and person. The average marks awarded to the three main parties and their leaders are given in Table 5.2.

In these ratings Mr Callaghan emerges as the best-liked of the party leaders. Both Mr Callaghan and Mr Steel received, on average, higher ratings than their parties. On the other hand, Mrs Thatcher was about as highly rated by her own supporters as Mr Callaghan and Mr Steel by theirs, and if her popularity did not exceed that of her party's, she did not do worse. Mrs Thatcher undoubtedly attracted more hostile comments – even among Conservative voters – than most party leaders, but the people who reacted that way were, after all, a small minority. What were the views of the party changers? A more detailed analysis (not shown in the table) revealed that amongst those who switched to the Conservatives in the 1979 election, the marks for Mrs Thatcher were higher than for any other party leader and nearly as high as their marks for the Conservative

Table 5.2 *The voters' ratings of the parties and
their leaders*

Respondents were asked to rate each party and party leader on
a scale from 0 to 10 to indicate how much or how little they
liked them. ('Marks out of ten', where 10 is the highest mark.)

Entries in this table are arithmetic *mean* values.

Parties and party leaders	Average marks given by:		
	The party's own voters	Other parties' voters	All respondents
Conservative party	8.2	4.9	6.2
Mrs Thatcher	8.0	5.0	6.2
Liberal party	7.5	5.1	5.4
Mr Steel	8.1	6.0	6.3
Labour party	8.1	5.1	6.1
Mr Callaghan	8.1	6.0	6.7

Data source: BES May 1979 Election Survey.

party. And those who switched from the Conservatives gave low marks *both* to
the party and its leader.

Mr Callaghan (like Mr Steel) was somewhat more popular outside his own
party than was Mrs Thatcher. But this was after all a popularity that was not
converted into votes. Had Mr Callaghan's personal appeal played any independent
and significant role in mitigating Labour's defeat at the polls, one would have
expected him to be more popular than his party among Labour voters and, perhaps, more highly rated by his own voters than Mrs Thatcher was by Conservative
voters. On neither count is there any evidence in the data that Mr Callaghan
had any such independent impact. This is not to say that Mr Callaghan's style of
leadership or his public stance was of no importance; it is only to say that his
leadership affected his party's fortunes only to the extent that it helped to shape
the voters' overall impressions of the party. The same goes for Mrs Thatcher.
Only in the case of the Liberals is there some indication that a party was helped
by its leader's coat-tails.

Is being a woman a liability for a politician? A little, it seems, but not much.
In response to a question whether it made any difference if an MP was a man or
a woman, 85 per cent said it made 'absolutely no difference', while only 11 per
cent thought a woman was not as good as a man. When the same question was
asked about the office of Prime Minister, 72 per cent thought it made no difference. The proportion who would prefer a man was 20 per cent, a bit more than
in the case of MPs. There is no appreciable difference between men's and women's
views on a female Prime Minister. As one might expect, perhaps, Liberal and
Labour voters said somewhat more often than Conservative voters that a woman
is not as good as Prime Minister (Conservatives 11, Liberals 19, and Labour voters

28 per cent). Again, there was no real difference between opinions of women and men.[5]

If the fact that the Conservative leader was a woman had any impact on voting, one would have expected that those who switched from the Conservative to another party in 1979 should have been particularly negative towards the idea of a female Prime Minister. But that was not the case. Of the former Conservatives who switched to another party, 80 per cent said that the sex of the Prime Minister made 'absolutely no difference', whereas 79 per cent of those who switched from another party to the Conservatives held the same view. In fact, party changers in both directions were slightly more positive to a woman as a Prime Minister than the electorate as a whole. Admittedly, it is still not conclusively proven that the prospect of a female Prime Minister may not have deterred some voters from switching to the Conservative party. But it seems far more plausible that the party difference we observed at first was mainly due to a partisan colouring of Labour and Liberal voters' comments on the leader of another party. The suggestion that a woman Prime Minister was less good than a man may well have been made by many Labour and Liberal supporters who would not have thought of voting Conservative in any case. There is no real evidence in the data that Mrs Thatcher's being a woman should have had any appreciable net effect on the vote. She was less popular than Mr Callaghan. But we have no real indication in the data that Mrs Thatcher as a party leader cost her party any votes; probably, she did not gain it many either. In the final account, the 1979 election was decided by issues rather than by leaders. The prospective Prime Minister's sex was not one of the important issues.

5.3 Parties and policies

At first glance, the percentages for references to *foreign* and *domestic policy* issues in Tables 5.1A–C may convey an impression of a scattering of concerns, with only tiny minorities mentioning any one of the subjects that were in the foreground in the mass media in the campaign. This is partly a result of the question technique. The persons we interviewed were not asked to compose lists of important issues. They were asked to give reasons for liking or disliking parties, and if they answered at all in terms of specific policies, they would normally mention one, two, or three things that they felt particularly strongly about.

The important feature of the picture that results is not dispersal but rather a concentration on matters which are all, in a broad sense, aspects of economic and social policy. This is the content of politics, as far as most voters are concerned. Within that general field, social welfare stands out as the area for which Labour gained most credit – but also much criticism. The Conservatives had a strong standing on taxation, social policy and the trade union issue. In contrast to Labour, however, the Conservatives gained approval in the social policy field mostly because they were seen as the party that would prevent the abuse of social benefits. Disapproval of the Conservative party's social policies – which was also comparatively frequent – was often given for the opposite reason, that the party showed lack of generosity and lack of compassion.

If we take into account all the like-and-dislike answers about the Conservative and Labour parties, it turns out that 40 per cent of all our respondents mentioned social welfare policies in their comments on one or both of the parties – as a ground for either approval or disapproval.

Many answers contained comments on rising prices, unemployment, housing and economic policy in general. Mostly, these answers gave vent to concern about the country's economic difficulties and the parties' ability to manage the economy. Economic policy issues and taxation were mentioned by 50 per cent of the respondents in at least one of their answers about the Conservative and Labour parties.[6] Concern about the country's economy also formed the background for frequent comments on the activities of the trade unions and the strikes for which the unions were blamed. But the Labour party was blamed too: the balance of negative and positive comments on trade unions and strikes was more decidedly unfavourable for the Labour party than on any other domestic policy issue. The public's views on the trade unions will be examined further in the following two sections in this chapter.

There is one exception to this predominant concern with the impact of politics on the material standard of living. This consists of a cluster of worries about immigration, race relations and 'law and order' which often were intertwined in the voters' minds. It was mentioned only by a minority. If importance is measured by the sheer number of mentions, then it is overshadowed by the amount of attention paid to economic and social welfare problems. Nevertheless, the Conservative party gained approval for its stance on immigration and 'law and order' issues about as often as for, say, its views on taxation; and the balance of positive to negative comments was decidedly in its favour (14 per cent liked and 3 per cent disliked the Conservative party's views on immigration and law and order). Immigration does not account for all of this, but there is little doubt that it was at the heart of the matter.

The world outside England, Scotland and Wales may not be unimportant to the British public, but it hardly affects the public's opinions about the political parties. Northern Ireland, it is worth noting, was virtually never mentioned by our respondents. In comparison with domestic politics, foreign policy and defence, as well as Britain's relations with the EEC, were also of negligible importance.

We have summarised the positive and negative comments on the Conservative and Labour parties in Table 5.3. The purpose of this table is to provide an overall indication of the extent to which support and disapproval were balanced to either party's advantage in each of the main policy areas.

Obviously, the things that voters liked about the one party were generally the reverse of the things they disliked about the other, although the respondent may have chosen to state his views on a particular policy area in only one of his answers. As a source of information about individuals' policy opinions the answers to our questions about the good and the bad sides of the parties are complementary. On the assumption that any individual's overall appreciation of a party was affected both by his approval of its policies and by his dislike of the policies of its major opponent, we have created two response categories for each major policy area. The one includes pro-Conservative and anti-Labour statements, whilst the other comprises pro-Labour and anti-Conservative comments.

The two categories thus comprise expressions of opinions with opposing political tendencies, and include all respondents who mentioned the policy area concerned in at least one of the answers to the two relevant questions. In the table, they are labelled 'Pro-Conservative/Anti-Labour comments' and 'Pro-Labour/Anti-Conservative comments', respectively. We have calculated the percentages of respondents included in each of these categories. The *difference* between the two percentages (also given in the table) indicates how strongly the balance of opinion was tilted towards one party or the other. A positive sign indicates a Conservative advantage, a minus sign a Labour advantage.[7]

It was possible, of course, for an individual to make appreciative comments on the policies of both the Conservative and Labour parties in a particular area. It was also possible (and occurred somewhat more frequently) for someone to make critical comments on both parties with reference to the same policy area. These respondents are included in both of the appropriate tendency categories in the table, but their two responses cancel out each other when differences between the percentages are taken. The percentage difference will thus always indicate a net advantage for one of the parties. The policy area classification in Table 5.3 is largely the same as in the previous tables except that references to economic policies and problems and taxation are included in a single category. Likewise, there is only one subject category for foreign policy, defence and Britain's relations with the EEC.

No one will be surprised to see from the table that opinions among Conservative and Labour voters were in general distinctively balanced in favour of the party they voted for. It is all the more noteworthy, therefore, that the Conservative party had an advantage even among Labour voters in two areas: trade unions, and the issues involving immigration, race relations and law and order. In the electorate as a whole, the balance was to the Conservatives' advantage in all policy areas but one. The exception being social welfare, where favourable and unfavourable comments on the two parties were evenly divided.

Trade unions and strikes was the issue that gave the Conservatives their strongest advantage, as measured by our index of the balance between positive and negative comments on the two major parties. As we saw from our earlier tables, this was partly because many voters looked with sympathy at the Con-

Table 5.3 *The partisan tendency of comments on*
Conservative and Labour party policies

Percentage entries are the percentages of the respondents in each column
who made the specified type of comment in each of the policy areas. The
Difference entry is the Pro-Conservative/Anti-Labour percentage *minus* the
Pro-Labour/Anti-Conservative percentage.

Policy area and tendency of comments	Conservative voters	Labour voters	All respondents
Foreign policy and defence			
Pro-Conservative/Anti-Labour	11%	4%	7%
Pro-Labour/Anti-Conservative	4%	7%	5%
Difference	+7	−3	+2
Economic policy and taxation			
Pro-Conservative/Anti-Labour	41%	23%	32%
Pro-Labour/Anti-Conservative	17%	43%	28%
Difference	+24	−20	+4
Social services; pensions; education			
Pro-Conservative/Anti-Labour	31%	17%	23%
Pro-Labour/Anti-Conservative	16%	32%	23%
Difference	+15	−15	0
Trade unions; industrial relations			
Pro-Conservative/Anti-Labour	47%	16%	33%
Pro-Labour/Anti-Conservative	6%	14%	10%
Difference	+41	+2	+23
Immigration; race; law and order			
Pro-Conservative/Anti-Labour	18%	14%	15%
Pro-Labour/Anti-Conservative	4%	4%	4%
Difference	+14	+10	+11

Data source: BES May 1979 Election Survey.

servatives' position on trade union matters, but it was even more because a still
larger number expressed distrust of the Labour party. Other data, to be examined later, indicate, however, that there was more doubt about the Conservatives' ability to deal with the trade unions than is expressed in these answers.
The advantage that the Conservative party could derive from the trade union
issue was perhaps not quite as great as the relative size of the percentage difference may suggest. Nevertheless, all our data suggest that the Conservatives
gained from the issue while Labour was hurt.

The overall balance of opinions in the answers that referred to specific economic policies and problems (excluding the trade union issue) was only slightly
to the Conservative party's advantage. It would have been much more so if we
had taken into account the many general statements in favour of private enter-

prise, which are included in our category of ideological statements. As will be seen in the following section, it was in such terms that a large proportion of our respondents spoke when stating what they liked about the Conservative party.

5.4 The dividing lines – as seen by the voters

The two sections in Tables 5.1A-C labelled 'Views on the economic system and ideology' and 'Class and group interests' comprise a large proportion of the answers to our questions about the parties' good and bad features. Mostly, these answers contain statements of generalised beliefs about the parties, their aims and the interests they represent. It was the dividing lines between the parties, rather than the specific policies they pursue, that these voters were thinking of.

Generalised beliefs are the stuff from which popular images of the parties are formed. Such images, as has often been observed, have a longer life than campaign issues.[8] An image of a party is not necessarily accepted in its entirety by friends and foes alike, but it contains a meaning that is widely thought to be true. The differences between the British parties, as depicted in common knowledge, are well known: Labour stands for social welfare, socialism and the interests of ordinary, working people. The Conservatives defend private enterprise, stand up for the nation and traditional values – and look after the interests of those who are better off. When people use different words to describe such images, it is often because the same trait is regarded as a virtue by some, as a flaw by others. What we aim to capture in the response categories discussed in this section are the components of party images that bear upon ideologies and social class interests.

The image of an object may take on different appearances depending on the observer's viewpoint. That phenomenon comes to mind when one compares Conservative and Labour voters' views of the ideological features and the social class connections of the parties.

Labour voters define both their own party and the other parties, first and foremost, in terms of social class differences (the 'class interest' response category); 49 per cent of the Labour voters gave class interests as the grounds for liking the Labour party, and 40 per cent gave the same kind of reason for disliking the Conservative party. References to ideology or views on the economic system were much less frequent. When they occurred as grounds for supporting the Labour party, they tended to be couched in terms of general values such as equality and compassion as opposed to selfishness. Remarkably, ideological notions appeared almost as often in the Labour voters' critical comments about their party as in the reasons they gave for liking it. Mostly – but not exclusively – it is 'leftist' tendencies that are the object of disapproval. Only a small fraction of the Labour voters even mentioned nationalisation, and if they did it was more often than not because it was something they did not like about their party.

The dividing line between the two major parties foremost in the Conservative voters' minds was that between the free enterprise system and state control of the economy. This was the predominant substantive theme in the ideological reasons that a large proportion of the Conservative voters gave for liking their own party and disliking Labour. In this context, values were typically stated in terms referring to the individual rather than to social groups: freedom for the individual and the importance of rewarding individual achievement.

Conservative voters were much less likely than Labour voters to focus their answers on the different social class bases of the parties. This is not to say that Conservative voters were unconcerned with economic group interests. For example, a businessman who said he liked the Conservatives because they were in favour of private enterprise would presumably not only be expressing his support for an economic philosophy; he would also have his own interests in mind.[9] But even when no immediate self-interest was involved, Conservative voters still tended to state their political views in terms of support for the free enterprise system.

In our classification, the general ideology and the nationalisation categories are somewhat overlapping (i.e. some individuals gave answers that fell into both categories). If we take both response categories into account, well over 50 per cent of the Conservative voters prove to have given ideological reasons for liking their party, and around 60 per cent said they disliked the Labour party on ideological grounds. In their answers to all four questions concerning the Conservative and Labour parties, it is worth noting, 28 per cent of the Conservatives referred explicitly to nationalisation, whereas only 13 per cent of Labour voters did so. Labour's socialist creed is apparently more salient to its opponents than to its supporters.

There is one departure from the rule that Labour voters speak mostly about social groups, while Conservative voters speak about the economic system. Although the Conservatives seldom mentioned social classes as such, we have noted in the previous section that they frequently involved their views on the trade unions when stating their grounds for liking the Conservative party or disliking Labour. Talking about the unions might be taken as just another way of talking about conflicting class interests. If so, the connection was mostly left implicit. Conservative voters voiced their opinions on the unions by expressing dismay about strikes and excessive trade union power, and by criticising Labour for its dependence on the unions. Labour voters were much less likely than Conservative voters to mention the unions at all. When they did mention the trade unions in connection with their own party, it was more often than not as a cause of dissatisfaction with the party (see Table 5.1B). It is interesting to note that those Labour voters who described either their own party or the Conservative party in social class terms did not differ from other Labour voters with regard to the unions; they were neither more nor less likely to comment on the trade unions and not more likely than others to express approval of the trade unions.

The extent to which the trade unions, as a political issue, had become separated from conceptions of class interests is indeed remarkable, and we shall look further at this phenomenon in the next section.

The differences between Conservative and Labour voters' views on the economic system, ideological principles and class interests are apparent in their answers to all the four like-and-dislike questions about their own party as well as the major opposing party. As before, therefore, we have constructed two sets of comprehensive catagories comprising all references to party ideologies and the class bases of the parties. One category comprises such references in reasons given for liking the Conservative party or disliking the Labour party, whereas the other comprises approving statements about the Labour party together with critical comments on the Conservative party.

These comprehensive classifications are employed in the summarising display below. The percentage entries show the percentages of each party's voters who referred to ideological and class differences, respectively, in at least one of the two relevant answers. In this instance, mentions of nationalisation are included in the 'economic system and ideology' category.

	Conservative voters	Labour voters
Views on the economic system and ideology		
Pro-Conservative and Anti-Labour comments	68%	29%
Pro-Labour and Anti-Conservative comments	16%	34%
Class interests		
Pro-Conservative and Anti-Labour comments	11%	4%
Pro-Labour and Anti-Conservative comments	4%	62%

Entries are the percentages of each party's voters whose answers contained each type of comment.

Two perspectives on party differences – almost two languages in which to describe the meaning of the choice between the Conservative and Labour parties – emerge from this summary of the data. That associated with support for the Conservative party amounts to an endorsement of private enterprise as an economic system, often in ideological terms, and a rejection of socialist ideas about the economy. A large majority of the Conservative voters (68 per cent) gave reasons of this kind for liking the Conservative party or disliking the Labour party. Whilst the importance of creating a favourable climate for private enterprise was often stressed explicitly, the possibility of any conflict of interest between the social classes was much less often touched upon. The trade unions came to the fore of this perspective primarily as a cause of disturbances in the economy – and as a problem that socialist Labour could not and would not tackle properly.

From the quite different perspective of Labour voters, the aims of parties are most readily described in terms of the social groups whose interests they protect and whose support they rely on. Of the Labour voters, 62 per cent considered class interests as a ground for supporting their own party or disapproving of the Conservatives. Moreover, as we have already noted, Labour voters were thinking of egalitarian goals rather than fundamental changes in the economic system when they expressed ideological support for their party. We have also noted that they showed little enthusiasm for nationalisation. When one reads through Labour voters' answers to these questions, it is indeed only rarely that one comes across articulated support for any major structural change in the economic system. There is nothing like the manifest ideological cohesiveness of the Conservatives to be found within Labour's electoral base. Only a minority (34 per cent) of Labour supporters referred to ideological differences between the parties as their grounds for liking Labour or disliking the Conservatives. And it is important to note that almost as many (29 per cent) were disenchanted with some ideological tendency within Labour, or found something in the ideas of the Conservative party that they agreed with.

What do Labour voters have in mind when they speak of Labour as the party of the working class, or distrust the Conservative party because it stands for the interests of the employers and the well-off? To answer that question one has to look at the whole range of demands that Labour voters make on the political system. These involve matters such as full employment, the workers' standards of living, public services and benefits for those who need it. Implicitly, these demands require that government should remedy the shortcomings and inequities in the economic system. Would a Conservative government not do that, too? Perhaps, but Labour voters are clearly confident that a Labour government can and will manage the economy to the advantage of 'ordinary working people'. That expectation is at least implicitly ideological, inasmuch as it presupposes that the state should intervene actively in the economic system in order to promote socially desirable goals. This is perhaps where the real dividing line lies, although it is seen in different perspectives by Conservative and Labour voters.

5.5 The images of the unions

Voting support for Labour amongst manual workers may have shown a steady decline in the 1970s, but the allegiance of a large part of the working class was still Labour's single most important electoral asset at the end of the decade. Yet, as an issue in the 1979 election, the vexed questions about the proper role of the (largely working-class-based) unions became an electoral liability rather than an asset for Labour. As we have seen in the preceding section, feelings about the trade unions were mixed, even among those Labour voters who thought of their party as the party of the working class. Moreover, the impact of the trade union issue was certainly not simply a matter of Labour losing middle-class support because of the unions' unpopularity. Indeed, Labour's electoral support held up better in the middle class than in the working class.

How, in fact, were the trade unions seen by the public? If there was dissatisfaction, how widespread was it? What did the public think of the relations between the political parties and the trade unions? The Callaghan government's last year in office had been a time of troubled relations with the trade union movement. Was Labour nevertheless seen to be too close to the trade unions? And what was the public's view of the Conservative party's attitude towards the unions? The truth is, of course, that there was not *one* public opinion on any of these matters; opinions were divided. Here we will describe these divisions in broad outline. In the following chapters we shall explore further the relationships between voting in the 1979 election and opinions on the issues that involved the trade unions: strikes, incomes policy, and proposals to curb what some considered excesses and abuses of trade union power.

So what was the public's image of the trade unions? In a most striking fashion, the survey data suggest that the answer depends on whether one is thinking of the trade unions as organisations representing the interest of their membership or, alternatively, as a national economic and political pressure group. The one view is favourable and sympathetic. The other is critical, not to say hostile. Both views are shared by large majorities of the electorate.

Thus, when asked how good a job the trade unions were doing for their members, nearly seven out of ten electors (68 per cent) said the unions were doing a 'very good' or 'fairly good' job.[10] Almost as big a majority (61 per cent) among trade unionists thought their own union was doing a 'very good' or 'fairly good' job for themselves and their families. Since the previous winter's strikes were the cause of such widespread discontent, it is interesting to note that only a small minority of the union members thought their own union was too militant. Only 16 per cent thought their union branch was 'far too ready' or 'a little too ready' to take industrial action. On the other hand, there was no strong support for militancy either; a minority of 27 per cent took the view that their local union was 'not quite' or 'not nearly' ready enough to take industrial action. The bulk of the membership (52 per cent) thought their union branch had got it 'about right'. It is interesting to note that this proportion was almost exactly the same, independently of which party the trade union members voted for in 1979.

A sharply different picture emerges, however, from the voters' answers to questions about the consequences for the country as a whole of trade union activities and about the power of the trade unions. Nearly six voters out of ten (58 per cent) thought the trade unions were doing a 'not very good' or 'no good at all' job for the country. Nearly eight out of ten (79 per cent) felt that the trade unions had too much power.[11]

To a remarkable extent, such misgivings about the role of trade unions in the national context were shared also by the trade union members. Among the union members, 52 per cent thought the unions were doing a 'very good' or 'fairly good' job for the country, while 47 per cent said the unions were doing a 'not very good' or 'no good at all' job in that regard. As in the general public, a large majority of trade unionists (68 per cent) felt the unions had too much power. The proportion of trade union members who thought that big business had too much power was actually slightly smaller (63 per cent).

Our data are summarised in Table 5.4 for each of the three parties' voters. As would be expected, Conservative voters were most hostile towards the unions. But even among Labour voters, 61 per cent thought the unions had too much power, and one out of three Labour voters had a low opinion of the job that the trade unions were doing for the country as a whole.

It is not a new phenomenon, it should be noted, for a large proportion of the British public to feel that the trade unions have too much power. But the breadth of the support for that view has increased dramatically over the last decades.[12] At the time of the 1964 election, 54 per cent felt that the unions had too much power. By 1970 that portion of the electorate had risen to 66 per cent. By 1979 the situation was as one of near consensus.

When voters were critical of trade union power, this was to some extent an expression of a more general distrust in organisational and corporate power. When asked whether they felt that 'big business' had too much power, more than half of our sample said yes, they did.[13] The percentages of each of the main

Table 5.4 *How good a job are trade unions doing for the country?*
Do trade unions and big business have too much power?

Views on trade unions				
Per cent of all respondents in each category of voters	Conservative voters	Liberal voters	Labour voters	All respondents
Thinks that the job trade unions are doing for the country as a whole is 'not very good' or 'no good at all'	79%	57%	34%	58%
Thinks trade unions have too much power	95%	84%	61%	79%
Views on big business				
Thinks big business has too much power	42%	62%	66%	55%

Data source: BES May 1979 Election Survey.

parties' voters holding that opinion are set out in the bottom row of Table 5.4. As is seen from these percentages, Labour voters were the most likely to think that big business had too much power, but substantial proportions of Conservative and Liberal voters shared the same view.

More than four voters out of ten in the electorate took the view that both big business and trade unions wield too much power. As can be seen from Table 5.4 and the data displayed below, this combination of opinions was held by the largest part of the voters for all the three main parties. The second biggest category (36 per cent) consists of those who thought trade unions had too much power, whereas big business did not. The opposite view could, perhaps, be considered the radical view of power relations in the British society; it is shared by only a tenth of the voters. Surprisingly, there is no correlation between the two opinions; that is, those who think big business has too much power are neither less nor more likely than others to consider the trade unions too powerful.

As we saw in Table 5.4, opinions both on the power of big business and on trade union power were associated with the voters' party choice in the 1979 election. The substance of this relationship is that those who thought trade unions had too much power were *less* likely than others to vote Labour, whereas those who thought big business had too much power were *more* likely to vote

Percentage entries within circles show the size of each opinion category as a percentage of the total number of respondents voting for one of the three main parties.

Deviation of Labour vote is the difference between Labour share of the three-party vote in the entire sample (38 percent) and Labour's share of the vote in each of the opinion categories. A + sign indicates that Labour's support in the category is stronger; a − sign indicates that it is weaker.

		BIG BUSINESS	
		Not too much power	Too much power
TRADE	Too much power	Deviation of Labour vote: −19%	Deviation of Labour vote: −1%
		36%	44%
UNIONS	Not too much power	Deviation of Labour vote: +25%	Deviation of Labour vote: +48%
		9%	10%

Labour. It is noteworthy that this relationship is markedly stronger in the case of unions than in the case of big business.[14] In the data set out above, the relationship of both opinions to the Labour voting is indicated by the *deviation* from Labour's share of the three-party vote in the sample as a whole within each of the four opinion combinations. It emerges that Labour support was strong in the two categories of voters who did not agree that the unions had too much power. In particular the support for Labour is strong among those who thought that big business had too much power, whilst the trade unions did not. That category, however, comprises only one-tenth of the three-party vote, and the two categories taken together include only one-fifth of the three-party vote. In the much larger category of voters – one-third of the three-party vote – who took the view that only the unions had too much power, support for Labour is very weak.

Thus there are significant differences between opinions on trade unions and opinions on big business. Dislike of trade union power is much more widespread than dislike of big business power and is more strongly correlated with voting. Furthermore, distrust of the power of big business, unlike distrust of trade union power, shows no tendency to increase over time. In the early 1960s, the percentages of voters who thought trade unions and big business had too much power were about equal, 54 per cent in both cases (1964). With regard to big business no real change has occurred.[15] The British public has become much more distrusting of the trade unions than of big business in the 1970s.

We have described here two apparently conflicting images of the trade unions, both held by majorities in the electorate. How can they be reconciled? Indeed, they can, if it is understood that our interview questions elicited responses pertaining to the trade unions in two different roles. It was generally recognised that the unions, as labour market organisations, should and do perform a legitimate and effective role in representing their members' interests. The other role is that of a sectional interest group, powerful enough to challenge – or even frustrate – a government's economic policy. In that alternative role, the unions were widely seen – justifiably or not – as doing a poor job for the country. After 'the winter of discontent' many voters may also have felt that the unions were able to further their own memberships' interests with too little regard for the general public.

If trade unions were seen to be too powerful, what was the public's view of the relationship between Labour and the unions? Was Labour seen to yield too much to union demands? Or had the previous winter's clash between a Labour government and the unions rather created the opposite impression? Was the Conservative party seen to be too aloof from trade union interests, or did the public think the Conservatives had got it about right, despite the Heath government's confrontation with the unions? And how responsive were the parties believed to be towards business and industry interests?

Our respondents' views of that aspect of interest group influence were elicited by means of a separate series of questions concerning the two major parties.[16] In each question, respondents were asked how willing the party in question was to 'listen to the views of' a particular economic group: too willing, about right, or not willing enough. Questions were asked about the trade unions, business and industry, and 'self-employed people'. The third of these categories is, of course, different from the other two. The term 'self-employed people' would normally be taken to mean small businessmen and hardly evokes any notion of organisational power.

The response distributions for all the three questions about the Conservative and Labour parties are set out in Tables 5.5A–B. It is readily apparent that voters' party preferences colour their impressions of interest group influences. The modal view among both Conservative and Labour voters is that their own party gives due recognition to the opinions of both sides of industry whereas the opposing major party pays too much regard to one side and too little to the other.

There are variations in this pattern, however. Over a third of the Labour voters think their own party is too willing to listen to the unions, and an even larger proportion think it pays too little attention to self-employed people. Among Conservative voters, it is notable that as many as one voter in five thought their party was not willing enough to listen to the trade unions. On the other hand, Conservative voters are much more critical of Labour's dependence on the trade unions, than Labour voters are of the Conservatives' closeness to business and industry. The data hardly suggest that the recent clash between the Callaghan government and the unions over incomes policy had led many Labour voters – or others – to conclude that the Labour party was unwilling to take the unions' views into account: even among Labour voters it was much more common to think that the party erred in the opposite direction.

To summarise the opinions in the electorate as a whole, we have calculated an 'index of attention bias' for each of the two parties' relations with each of the groups. The index is, simply, the percentage thinking the party is 'too willing' to listen to a group *minus* the percentage thinking it is 'not willing enough' to listen. (The percentages pertain to the sample as a whole.) A positive index value indicates that a party is paying too much regard to a particular group, whereas a negative value means it is not paying enough attention. The index values are displayed below:

	Index of attention bias		
	Trade Unions	Business and industry	Self-employed people
Conservative party	−37	+22	+ 3
Labour party	+58	−27	−63

If one sums the index values, disregarding signs, an overall index of attention bias is obtained for each of the two parties: 62 for the Conservatives, 148 for

Table 5.5 A *How willing is the Conservative party to listen to the views of trade unions, business and industry, and self-employed people?*

How willing is the Conservative party to listen?	Conservative voters			Liberal voters			Labour voters			All respondents		
	Trade unions	Business and industry	Self-employed	Trade unions	Business and industry	Self-employed	Trade unions	Business and industry	Self-employed	Trade unions	Business and industry	Self-employed
	%	%	%	%	%	%	%	%	%	%	%	%
Too willing	5	18	12	5	35	17	4	42	25	5	29	18
About right	68	72	73	42	54	61	23	40	48	46	56	59
Not willing enough	21	5	10	46	3	17	68	10	18	42	7	15
Don't know	6	5	5	7	8	5	5	8	9	7	8	8
Total per cent	100%	100%	100%	100%	100%	100%	100%	100%	100%	100%	100%	100%
Number of respondents	723	720	721	213	213	213	578	577	577	1854	1848	1850

Data source: BES May 1979 Election Survey

Table 5.5B *How willing is the Labour party to listen to the views of trade unions, business and industry, and self-employed people?*

How willing is the Labour party to listen?	Conservative voters			Liberal voters			Labour voters			All respondents		
	Trade unions	Business and industry	Self-employed	Trade unions	Business and industry	Self-employed	Trade unions	Business and industry	Self-employed	Trade unions	Business and industry	Self-employed
	%	%	%	%	%	%	%	%	%	%	%	%
Too willing	88	8	8	69	7	2	36	12	5	64	10	3
About right	8	28	9	24	51	22	53	70	46	27	46	24
Not willing enough	3	58	86	5	36	71	9	13	41	6	37	66
Don't know	1	6	3	2	6	5	2	5	8	3	7	7
Total per cent	100%	100%	100%	100%	100%	100%	100%	100%	100%	100%	100%	100%
Number of respondents	724	724	723	214	214	214	580	579	578	1858	1856	1855

Data source: BES May 1979 Election Survey.

Labour. Labour is far more often considered too attentive to trade union interests than the Conservatives are considered too unfriendly towards the unions. Moreover, Labour's bias against business, in particular small business, is also observed far more often than the Conservatives' bias against the unions. The result is that Labour is more firmly identified with one particular group interest than the Conservative party – and that group interest, the unions, was already considered too powerful. If the trade union issue became a liability for Labour in the 1979 election, it was because of this combination of the voters' negative image of the power of the trade union movement and their perception of Labour's closeness to the unions.

Yet, we also have evidence that voters were worried about the Conservative party's attitude towards the trade unions. The most interesting sector in the electorate, from this point of view, consists of the voters who thought the Labour party was too willing to listen to the trade unions. Would they nevertheless consider the Labour party the lesser of two evils, if they thought the Conservatives went too far in the opposite direction?

In Table 5.6 we have classified the voters in this particular sector of the electorate with regard to their views of the Conservative party's relations with the unions. The three-party division of the vote is calculated for each of the three sub-categories thus obtained.

Most of the voters who thought Labour leaned too far towards the unions were of the opinion that the Conservative party had got it about right (60 per cent). Among these voters, the Conservative majority in the election was massive,

Table 5.6 *The relation of party vote to perceptions of the Conservative party's attitude towards the trade unions among voters who thought the Labour party was too willing to listen to the unions.*

Three-party vote	Opinions on the Conservative party's relation to the trade unions		
	Too willing to listen	About right	Not willing enough to listen
	%	%	%
Conservative	68	78	39
Liberals	6	12	20
Labour	26	10	41
Total per cent	100%	100%	100%
Number of respondents	46	566	326

Data source: BES May 1979 Election Survey.

as the table shows. It was almost as large in the small minority (see the left-hand column) who took the view that both Conservatives and Labour were too friendly with the unions. But about one-third of those who thought that Labour was too willing to listen to the unions felt at the same time that the Conservatives had gone too far in the opposite direction. The division of the vote within this sub-category (which includes about one-fifth of the total three-party vote) is strikingly different. Liberal support is particularly strong, and the remainder is about equally divided between Conservatives and Labour.

The overall effect of the trade union issues was thus to drain away support from the Labour party. But Labour's handicap would have been even greater if one part of the electorate had not felt uneasy about the Conservative party's attitude towards the trade unions. The presence of such countervailing opinion forces in the electorate will become even more apparent through the more detailed enquiry into the relationship between the issue opinions and voting in the following chapters.

6

Managing the economy – the Labour government's record and the Conservative alternative

6.1 Matters of concern: strikes, prices, unemployment

The state of Britain's economy dominated the scene in the election campaign, and the previous winter's outburst of industrial unrest formed the backdrop.[1] The Labour government's responsibility for rising prices, economic decline, increasing unemployment, deteriorating public services, recalcitrant trade union practices, a misconceived incomes policy, and above all heavy taxation for businesses and ordinary people alike: all came together as one main theme in the Conservatives' campaign message. The remedy, asserted the Conservatives, was an entirely new economic strategy in which lower taxes for everybody would be an essential ingredient.

The Labour government defended its record, of course: inflation had been brought down to a 'single-figure' level, unemployment was to be dealt with in the next phase of the government's economic strategy, a new compact had been hammered out with the trade unions, the balance of payments was healthy. An even more prominent theme in the Labour campaign, however, consisted of attacks on the Conservatives' remedies. The policies advocated by the Opposition, argued Labour's spokesmen, would lay Britain's industry waste rather than rejuvenate it; the Conservative alternative would lead to a new era of confrontation with the unions, neglect of the weaker members of the society and worsened unemployment; and the promised tax reduction would only be possible through damaging cuts in the National Health Service, education and other government services.

The parties were addressing a worried public. Asked how they felt about the state of the country, 'all in all', two out of three voters said they thought that the country was 'in poor shape' or that 'something is very wrong'; fewer than a third thought the country was in 'fairly good shape' and only a tiny fraction said it was in 'very good shape'. Nearly half of the electorate thought that the country's economy had got worse in the previous year or so, and more than a fourth thought that it would get worse in the ensuing year (Table 6.1).

150

Table 6.1 *Views in 1979 and 1974 on Britain's Economy in 'The Last Year' and in 'The Next Years', by Party Vote*

Views on the economy	Conservatives		Liberals		Labour		All respondents	
	May 1979 election	Oct 1974 election	May 1979 election	Oct 1974 election	May 1979 election	Oct 1974 election	May 1979 election	Oct 1974 election
Britain's economy in the last year or so:	%	%	%	%	%	%	%	%
Has got better	14	4	24	5	33	13	22	8
Has stayed about the same	24	13	29	25	32	32	28	23
Has got worse	59	80	47	66	32	49	47	64
Don't know	3	3	0	4	3	6	3	5
Total per cent	100%	100%	100%	100%	100%	100%	100%	100%
Britain's economy in the next few years:								
Will get better	57	18	34	30	20	51	38	32
Will stay about the same	21	19	26	26	20	16	22	19
Will get worse	14	54	28	35	48	23	29	38
Don't know	8	9	12	9	12	10	11	11
Total per cent	100%	100%	100%	100%	100%	100%	100%	100%
Number of respondents	726	704	214	352	582	830	1863	2349

Data source: BES May 1979 Election Survey and BES October 1974 Election Survey.

A substantial majority felt that their income had fallen behind prices in the last year, and almost as many expected the same in the coming year.[2]

Worry about the state of the economy is nothing new and, as Table 6.1 shows, the picture looked much the same after the October 1974 election.[3] If anything, 'the last year' looked a little less bleak in 1979 than it had after the October 1974 election; and expectations for 'the next few years' were a little less downcast in 1979. A closer look at this table reveals, furthermore, that appraisal of the economic situation is, to some extent, coloured by partisanship: Conservatives are more prone to say things have become worse than were Labour voters both in October 1974 and in 1979. Such partisan colouring becomes even more apparent in expectations about the years to come. After the October 1974 election, the Conservatives were the most pessimistic, while after the election in 1979 it was the Labour voters' turn to make the most bleak predictions. Such factors aside, the prevailing mood in 1979 was one of discontent with the past year and not much optimism about the future. The fact that things looked much the same at the time of the previous election cannot have given much comfort, especially not for those who had looked forward to a change for the better.

The effect of rising prices was felt by everyone, but an increasing number of people were also affected by other consequences of the economic crisis. In 1979, 18 per cent said that either they themselves or someone in their family had been unemployed or had had great difficulty in finding a job in the last year or so; in 1974 the figure was 10 per cent. When asked whether they personally had been affected as a result of a strike in the last year, about one in four said they had.[4] More than a third of the electorate (37 per cent) felt that they had been affected by either or both of these privations.

It was against this background that the electorate assessed the Labour government's record. We have already seen in the previous chapter that questions about the state of the country's economy over-shadowed most other concerns in the electorate in 1979. The Labour government's record in office was there to behold; the Conservatives' alternative was set out in the campaign. In addition, although not necessarily to the Conservatives' advantage, most voters presumably had the party's last term in office in relatively fresh memory. For a great many voters the question must have been: which of the two parties will be better able to manage the country's economy? The answer to that question would depend on the prospects that Conservatives and Labour seemed to promise. It would also depend on past experience. The voters' views on the Labour government's record in office would enter that kind of judgement, but so would opinions about whether a Conservative government would have done better or worse.

If the performance – or expected performance – of the two parties was weighed one against the other, how did the scales turn? And what impact did the electorate's collective assessment have on the overall result of the election? These are the questions we shall attempt to answer in this chapter.

The election survey included a set of questions which was specifically designed for this purpose. Three questions asked for the voter's assessment of the Labour government's handling of each of the three main problems in the economy: rising prices, strikes, and unemployment. By means of questions in the same format, those interviewed were further asked how well they thought the Conservatives would have handled the same problems if they had been in office at the time.[5] The scale of assessment used in all of these six questions consisted of four response alternatives: 'very well', 'fairly well', 'not very well', 'not at all well'.

A similar set of questions was asked in the October 1974 election survey. We will use these data as a baseline from which to gauge changes in the voters' assessment of the two major parties as well as the impact of such changes on the partisan division of the vote.

6.2 Labour's record or the Conservative alternative? The voters' assessment

What were the voters' views in 1979 on Labour's and the Conservatives' ability to deal with strikes, rising prices and unemployment? The distributions of opinions recorded by each of our six interview questions are shown in Tables 6.2–4.

If we look first at the electorate as a whole, it becomes clear that judgements on the Labour government's economic record were by no means altogether negative. A clear majority of the electors (61 per cent) thought that the problem of rising prices had been handled 'very well' or 'fairly well', and nearly half the electorate (49 per cent) held the same view of Labour's record on unemployment. Labour came out markedly better than the Conservatives with regard to inflation and only marginally worse than the Conservatives with regard to unemployment.[6] Where the voters felt that the Labour government had failed was in its handling of strikes; nearly two voters out of three thought its performance in that respect had been 'not very good' or 'not at all good'. On the other hand, the voters' rating of the Conservative party's ability to handle strikes was only slightly more favourable.

The tables show how the Conservatives and Labour were assessed by the voters for each of the three main parties. In the first place, these response distributions make plain that – not unsurprisingly – the voters' ratings were markedly partisan: Conservative and Labour voters alike gave their own party better marks than their opponents. However, at least as noteworthy a feature in the data is that neither of the two parties' voters were anything like unequivocal about the performance of their own party. On these economic questions, around a fifth to a third of the voters gave a mark of 'not very well' or worse to the party they voted for; and only small proportions thought their own party handled any of

Table 6.2 Labour and Conservatives: handling the problem of strikes

Handling of strikes	Conservative voters' views on:		Liberal voters' views on:		Labour voters' views on:		All respondents' views on:	
	Conservative party	Labour party	Conservative party	Labour party	Conservative party	Labour party	Conservative party	Labour party
	%	%	%	%	%	%	%	%
Very well	10	1	4	7	2	15	6	7
Fairly well	53	16	27	33	16	50	33	30
Not very well	25	47	38	41	48	28	36	40
Not at all well	5	36	26	18	31	7	18	22
Don't know	7	0	5	1	3	0	7	1
Total per cent	100%	100%	100%	100%	100%	100%	100%	100%
Number of respondents	728	729	214	214	582	581	1873	1875

Data source: BES May 1979 Election Survey.

Table 6.3 Labour and Conservatives: ability to handle the problem of rising prices

Handling of rising prices	Conservative voters' views on:		Liberal voters' views on:		Labour voters' views on:		All respondents' views on:	
	Conservative party	Labour party	Conservative party	Labour party	Conservative party	Labour party	Conservative party	Labour party
	%	%	%	%	%	%	%	%
Very well	7	5	1	12	2	26	4	13
Fairly well	62	39	32	53	18	59	40	48
Not very well	21	40	45	25	53	12	37	28
Not at all well	4	16	16	9	24	3	13	10
Don't know	6	0	6	1	3	0	6	1
Total per cent	100%	100%	100%	100%	100%	100%	100%	100%
Number of respondents	729	729	214	214	583	582	1876	1874

Data source: BES May 1979 Election Survey.

Table 6.4 *Labour and Conservatives: ability to handle unemployment*

Handling of unemployment	Conservative voters' views on:		Liberal voters' views on:		Labour voters' views on:		All respondents' views on:	
	Conservative party	Labour party	Conservative party	Labour party	Conservative party	Labour party	Conservative party	Labour party
	%	%	%	%	%	%	%	%
Very well	8	2	1	4	4	18	5	8
Fairly well	66	27	42	43	26	57	46	41
Not very well	16	48	39	43	49	22	32	37
Not at all well	3	20	9	6	16	2	9	11
Don't know	7	3	9	3	5	1	8	3
Total per cent	100%	100%	100%	100%	100%	100%	100%	100%
Number of respondents	729	729	214	213	581	580	1873	1871

Data source: BES May 1979 Election Survey.

the problems concerned 'very well'. Indeed, confidence in one's own party's ability to deal with the country's economic difficulties was tellingly qualified.

Liberal voters gave roughly the same marks to both of the major parties. This is not, it deserves to be noted, because Liberals necessarily took the view that both of the major parties were equally bad. Although the proportion distrusting both parties' ability was somewhat higher among Liberal voters, the overall balance is mainly the result of a division of opinion among Liberal voters; the Liberal vote comprises two components, one of which is leaning towards the Conservatives whilst the other is leaning towards Labour.[7]

Whether qualified or not, a voter's judgement on the performance of either of the two major parties is bound to be weighed against his expectations about the alternative party. We have attempted to capture both elements of that comparative assessment by combining the questions about the two parties into one classification for each of the three issues.[8] The result is displayed in Table 6.5A.

As we want to account for the causes of the Conservative surge in 1979, it becomes important to establish whether any change in the voters' assessment of the two major parties had occurred since the time of the last election in October 1974. To facilitate such a comparison, we have constructed the same type of classifications based on data drawn from the October 1974 survey; these are shown in Table 6.5B.

At first sight the per cent distributions in Table 6.5A – relating to the 1979 electorate – do not appear to suggest that Labour lost any electoral support because of its economic policies. Opinions are very nearly evenly balanced in the voters' assessments of the two parties' ability to deal with unemployment and strikes, while, when it comes to handling inflation, the balance is decidedly in Labour's favour.

A comparison with Table 6.5B reveals, however, that the foregoing observations about the 1979 opinion distributions tell less than half the truth. As can be seen from Table 6.5B, the distribution of opinions on strikes has actually shifted from a decidedly pro-Labour profile in 1974 to the slightly pro-Conservative profile of 1979. In the case of unemployment, there is a clear shift from a pro-Labour balance in 1974 to an even balance in 1979.[9] Only on the question of inflation is there an exception. At both elections the balance of assessments favoured the Labour party – if anything more so in 1979 than five years earlier.

It thus appears that the Callaghan government did succeed in convincing the electorate that bringing down the inflation rate to 'single figures' was no mean achievement. But the rating of Labour's ability to deal with strikes and unemployment fell off badly between 1974 and 1979. And, as the following summary shows, the shift of the balance of opinions against Labour on these two issues was substantially more pronounced than the improvement in its rating with regard to keeping inflation in check.

THE CHANGE IN ASSESSMENT

OF LABOUR AND CONSERVATIVES

A + sign indicates a change in the Conservatives'
favour; a − sign indicates a change in Labour's
favour.

STRIKES	+24
UNEMPLOYMENT	+19
PRICES	− 6

Entries based on the 'balance' figures in Tables 6.5A–B:
1979 balance minus 1974 balance

Table 6.5A *Voters' comparison of Labour's and Conservatives' ability to handle the country's problems, 1979*

Rating of Labour and Conservatives	Strikes	Rising prices	Unemployment
	%	%	%
Strong pro-Labour	11	14	8
Moderate pro-Labour	13	19	14
Weak pro-Labour	2	5	5
Marginal pro-Labour	6	2	2
Marginal pro-Conservative	5	2	2
Weak pro-Conservative	1	1	2
Moderate pro-Conservative	14	12	18
Strong pro-Conservative	14	7	8
'Trust' in both parties	9	21	20
'Distrust' in both parties	23	15	17
Don't know	2	2	4
Total per cent	100%	100%	100%
Number of respondents	1,893	1,893	1,893
Balance: pro-Conservative % *minus* pro-Labour %	+2	−18	+1

Data source: BES May 1979 Election Survey.

Table 6.5B *Voters' comparison of Labour's and Conservatives' ability to handle the country's problems, October 1974*

Rating of Labour and Conservatives	Strikes	Rising prices	Unemployment
	%	%	%
Strong pro-Labour	21	10	12
Moderate pro-Labour	21	18	28
Weak pro-Labour	2	2	*
Marginal pro-Labour	4	5	*
Marginal pro-Conservative	4	3	*
Weak pro-Conservative	1	1	*
Moderate pro-Conservative	10	11	16
Strong pro-Conservative	11	8	6
'Trust' in both parties	8	15	34
'Distrust' in both parties	15	24	*
Don't know	3	3	4
Total per cent	100%	100%	100%
Number of respondents	2,365	2,365	2,365
Balance: pro- Conservative % *minus* Pro-Labour %	-22	-12	-18

* This question was asked in a different format in 1974. The question was phrased: 'Now, using one of the statements on this card, could you say which describes how you feel the parties handled the problem of unemployment: 1. The Conservative party is much better; 2. The Conservative party is somewhat better; 3. There is no real difference between the parties; 4. The Labour party is somewhat better; 5. The Labour party is much better. In the table, response alternatives 1 and 5 are placed in the row for 'strong' party support; alternatives 2 and 4 are similarly put in the rows for 'moderate' party support. Response alternative 3 and DK answers are put in the row for 'both parties'.

Data source: BES October 1974 Election Survey.

6.3 The impact on the election result

When Conservative and Labour voters prove to have diverging views on how well the two major parties handle the country's economy, it is safe to assume that their judgements were coloured to some extent by their party sympathies. But undoubtedly the relationship is to an even greater extent attributable to individuals voting for the party they deem best able to govern the country. Party sympathies are shaped by individuals' experiences and by the views they have acquired about the matters on which the parties differ. The more confidence an individual has in a party's intentions and the more he agrees with the policies he thinks it stands for on a range of issues, the more likely he will be to cast his vote for that party. We look at the relationship between opinions and voting from that viewpoint in Table 6.6. In this table the interview questions asked in 1979 about strikes, prices and unemployment are combined so as to form a 'scale' or 'index' of opinions, ranging from a strongly pro-Labour to a strongly pro-Conservative pole; the mid category on the scale comprises individuals whose views are not discernibly more favourable to the one party than to the other.[10]

The relationship brought out by the table is very clear. The Conservative share of the vote gradually increases and the Labour share gradually decreases, as one moves from left to right on the scale. The vote is nearly unanimously Labour at the one end of the scale and nearly unanimously Conservative at the other. It is worth noting that the Conservatives got a much larger share of the vote than Labour in the category at the middle of the scale. It is not inconceivable that some voters in this category in fact had a slightly more favourable view of the Conservative party than of the Labour party, although it was not registered through our interview questions. It is more likely, however, that the explanation lies in the obvious fact that opinions on matters other than those included in this index – including other aspects of economic policy – also bore upon the individuals' voting decisions. If so, the data suggest that the balance of opinions on those 'other things' was weighed in favour of the Conservatives. What these 'other things' were, we shall consider in following chapters.

For a comparison with the state of opinion at the time of the October 1974 election, we have constructed the same handling-of-the-economy index with the aid of data drawn from our survey of that election. The relationship between index positions and voting in the October 1974 election are shown in Table 6.7. As can be seen from the table, the per cent distributions of the vote within each of the table columns are very nearly identical to those obtained from the 1979 data. (This applies also to the greater Conservative share of the vote in the mid category of the scale.)

It follows from all this that in both 1974 and 1979 there was a substantial degree of correlation between the voters' party choice and their overall assessment of the parties' ability to manage the economy. This is true also for each of the three component measures, taken separately:

	Correlation with party vote	
	1979	1974
Index of assessment	*0.59*	*0.64*
Strikes	0.52	0.56
Unemployment	0.51	0.57
Prices	0.52	0.56

The correlation coefficient is Kendall's Tau-b with vote treated as an ordinal scale comprising Labour, Liberals and Conservatives, in that order

The strength of the relationships between opinions and voting are very nearly the same in the data from the two elections (although the coefficients for the 1974 data are a little higher). This is of course in line with what one could observe from the per cent distributions in Tables 6.6 and 6.7.[11]

Nevertheless, a shift in opinion did occur between 1974 and 1979. As we observed in the previous section, the balance of opinions on strikes and unemployment became decidedly less favourable to Labour, whilst there was a smaller shift in the opposite direction with regard to the inflation issue. Since the opinion distributions on all three issues are aggregated in our index, the distributions of individuals across the seven categories will summarise the overall movement between the two elections. A glance at the bottom rows in Tables 6.6 and 6.7 shows that a substantial movement occurred out of the pro-Labour categories, to the left, and into the pro-Conservative categories on the right.

The impact of opinion change

How far was the election result in 1979 affected by the changes that occurred in opinion on each of the three economic problems we are concerned with here: strikes, unemployment and rising prices?

The question of how far opinion change on any single issue has contributed to a swing in the vote from one election to the next is notoriously intractable. In an ideal world, the task in this instance would be to assess how the party division of the vote in 1979 would have been affected if the balance of opinion on the Conservatives' and Labour's ability to handle each of the three problems in the country's economy had not changed between 1974 and 1979, everything else being equal. But everything else is most unlikely to be equal. Individuals' views on different aspects of politics are often interconnected, and a change of opinion on one issue is likely to occur in conjunction with changes of opinions on other issues. Moreover, when an alteration in an individual's outlook is also bound up with a change of party preference, this, too, may cause him to look at the parties' past and future performance in a new light.

For all of these reasons our calculation of the effects of opinion change with respect to the three economic issues must be accompanied by the reservation that it cannot take into account how voters' opinions on other issues would

Table 6.6 *Relation of voting in the 1979 election to overall assessment of Labour's and Conservatives' handling of economic problems*

Party voted for	Index of assessment						
	Strongly pro-Labour 1	2	3	4	5	6	Strongly pro-Conservative 7
	%	%	%	%	%	%	%
Conservatives	3	7	27	54	76	85	93
Liberals	13	16	19	17	15	10	6
Labour	84	77	54	29	9	5	1
Total per cent	100%	100%	100%	100%	100%	100%	100%
Number of respondents	199	256	210	271	207	215	175
Per cent distribution across categories	13	17	14	18	13	14	11 = 100%

Notes
The Index of assessment of Labour's and Conservative's handling of the economy is based on the three questions concerning prices, strikes and unemployment.
 The table comprises only Conservative, Liberal and Labour voters.
 The respondents' assessment of the Conservatives is the least favourable (and the assessment of Labour the most favourable) at score 1 on the scale; the balance shifts gradually in favour of the Conservatives for each step from the left to right on the scale.

Data source: BES 1979 Election Survey.

Table 6.7 *Relation of voting in the 1974 election to overall assessment of Labour's and Conservatives' handling of economic problems*

	Index of assessment						
	Strongly pro-Labour						Strongly pro-Conservative
Party voted for	1	2	3	4	5	6	7
	%	%	%	%	%	%	%
Conservatives	1	5	22	47	71	86	91
Liberals	7	19	25	29	24	13	8
Labour	92	76	53	24	5	1	1
Total per cent	100%	100%	100%	100%	100%	100%	100%
Number of respondents	314	404	266	332	190	240	139
Per cent distribution across categories	17	21	14	18	10	13	7 = 100

The table comprises only Conservative, Liberal and Labour voters.

Data source: BES October 1974 Election Survey.

have been affected if, say, their opinions on the problem of strikes had not changed between 1974 and 1979. Furthermore, we will have to make one rather strong assumption about the data: that is, we will not make any allowance for the possibility that individuals' general party preferences influenced the opinions they expressed on political issues. (Or, more precisely, when we compare the effects of opinions on the three problems in the economy, we will assume that none of them was influenced more than the others by general party preferences.)

The first step in our calculation is to obtain a measure of the 'net effect' of opinions on each of the three economic issues on voting in the 1979 election. For this purpose we use a technique known as multiple regression. The technique, to be discussed in a later chapter, explores the relationship between a whole set of 'causes' and some criterion which is presumed to be dependent on these causes. Here we treat individuals' opinions on political issue in 1979 as the causes, and it is the effect of each of them on voting that is assessed through the multiple regression. Individuals' opinions on political issues are thus used to 'explain' or 'predict' their way of voting. What is predicted in this case (the 'dependent variable') is whether the person cast his vote for the Conservatives or for some other party in 1979. (Non-voters are excluded from the analysis.)

We include in this analysis the individuals' opinions on strikes, unemployment and rising prices, and also all of the other opinion measures in the entire questionnaire that showed any appreciable correlation with voting. For purposes of the multiple regression analysis, all opinion measures were converted into numerical variables (see Chapter 11). The multiple regression analysis then yielded measures of the 'net effect' on voting of individuals' opinion positions on our three economic issues over and above the effect of their opinions on all other issues. The result of the regression analysis can be presented in the form of the following equation:

$$\bar{Y} = a + b_1\bar{X}_1 + b_2\bar{X}_2 + b_3\bar{X}_3 \ldots$$

In this instance, the $\bar{Y}$ stands for the Conservative proportion of the vote in 1979; a is a constant and the b's are coefficients which indicate the 'net effect' of each of the opinions that have been measured. The $\bar{X}$'s are the mean values on these opinion measures in 1979.

In the second step of our analysis, we calculated what the Conservative vote would have been if the mean value of opinions on strikes were changed to the value it had in 1974, whereas all other elements in the equation remained the same. Similarly, we then calculated how the Conservative share of the vote would have been affected if the mean values for opinions on unemployment and prices had been held at their values in October 1974.

In effect, we have thus calculated what the Conservative share of the vote in 1979 would have been if the 'average opinion' on each of the three economic questions in 1979 had remained the same as in 1974, everything else being equal to the situation in 1979. If the Conservative share of the vote would have been smaller than its actual value, then the difference indicates how much the party 'gained' because of the change of opinions on the issue concerned. Conversely, if the Conservative share would have been larger, then the difference indicates that the party lost ground as a result of the opinion change.[12]

The main purpose of these calculations, to repeat, is to obtain a base for comparing the effects of opinion changes on the three issues concerned. The result is set out below in the form of a gain or a loss in the Conservative percentage of the vote for each of these issues. As can be seen from these figures, the result of our analysis suggests that the Conservative party's substantial gains on the strikes and unemployment issues clearly outweighed what little benefit that Labour derived from its record on fighting inflation.[13]

	Calculated Gain (+) and Loss (−) in the Conservative per cent share of the vote
Strikes	+3.2%
Unemployment	+1.8%
Prices	−0.2%

The sum total of these three effects on the Conservative vote cannot be taken as a precise measure of how much they jointly contributed to the increase in the Conservative share of the vote. But obviously the result suggests that the Conservative party benefited considerably from the decline in the electorate's confidence in Labour's ability to manage the economy that had occurred since 1974.

It was not – and this deserves to be stressed again – that the electorate in 1979 had much more confidence in the Conservatives than in Labour, when it came to dealing with such problems in the economy as strikes, unemployment and inflation. The balance of opinions was only marginally in the Conservatives' favour on two of these issues and was actually in Labour's favour on the third. But back in 1974, the greater confidence in Labour's approach to such problems had been one of the party's electoral assets. By the 1979 election Labour had lost that asset.

It is worth noting that these findings are in line with the observations made in our review of the voters' reasons for liking and disliking the major parties. As we saw there, it was primarily the Conservatives' overall economic programme that was being endorsed, and it was the more ideological elements in Labour's approach to the economy (such as nationalisation) that were being rejected. It is true that the trade union issues, including Labour's dependence on the unions, emerged much more clearly as a liability for Labour in the voters' free-answer comments on the parties, whereas our questions about how a Labour and a Conservative government handles the problem of strikes rather registered a distinctive decline of confidence in the Labour party – to the point where Conservatives were marginally preferred. On the other hand, we observed also in the likes-and-dislikes data that the balance was unfavourable to Labour more because of expressions of dissatisfaction with Labour's performance than because of positive support for the Conservatives. Both measurements thus point in the same direction inasmuch as they both record a sense of disappointment in the electorate which damaged Labour's electoral fortunes.

Voting decisions are influenced by views on many aspects of politics, only one of which we have been concerned with in this chapter. We can think of an election outcome as the net effect of a number of opinion forces. Some of them favoured Labour in 1979, some favoured the Conservatives, and some yielded a net advantage to neither party because opinions in the electorate were evenly balanced. A change in the party division of the vote is the result of changes in these opinion forces. The implication of our findings in this chapter is that one major opinion force that worked to Labour's advantage in October 1974 – confidence in the Labour government's handling of the economy – had become nearly neutralised in 1979, thus contributing to shift the overall balance of forces in favour of the Conservative party.[14]

7

Responses to social and cultural change

7.1 The climate of opinion

As societies change, so the prevailing mood also changes. The 1950s are remembered as an era of modestly affluent acquiescence. The mid 1960s were years of cultural change: the values of the permissive society became embodied in new, liberal legislation, new educational opportunities were opened up, and traditional deference to authority gave way to a more assertive mood. These were also the years when the public sector was not only allowed but positively expected to grow, in response to optimistic planning as well as to new demands for higher-standard public services. To be sure, there was impatience with the performance of the economy, but few really doubted that wealth could be made to grow; it was a matter of devising the right strategy.

The years since then have been different. The 1970s were years of economic decline and diminishing expectations. Economic crises caused governments to make vast but apparently ineffectual commitments to sustain ailing industries. As a consequence of the resulting claims on governmental expenditure, retrenchment became the signal for the public services. The climate of opinion in the 1970s was one in which governments, in this country as in others and irrespective of political complexion, were on the defensive: there were more short-comings and frustration to be held accountable for than there were successes to claim credit for.

In Britain, the Conservatives offered an alternative economic strategy in 1979 and won the election. But was the shift in the vote that brought the Conservatives into power entirely due to a shift of opinion in the economic sphere? Was the Conservative surge in the 1979 election not also an indication of a rightward turn in the popular mood, and a reaction to the cultural and social change of the previous decades?

We will attempt to answer these questions by examining the broad range of divisions of opinions and opinion trends; some are easily recognisable examples of the economic and social welfare issues that divide left from right in British politics, whilst others pertain to various aspects of cultural change. The latter include changes in moral standards and in attitudes towards deviant behaviour in the 'permissive' society, new developments in education and the relatively new experience of large-scale immigration.

The data were obtained by means of two batteries of questions which were asked in our survey at the October 1974 election as well as in the 1979 election survey.[1] One of the batteries is explicitly concerned with 'the general changes that have been taking place in Britain over the last few years', and respondents were asked whether they felt change had gone too far or not. In the other battery, the questions were couched in terms of what the government should, or should not, do – but the purpose was still to elicit the respondents' views on changes and trends in society.

Three features of these opinion distributions are of interest. Firstly, we want to establish whether the prevailing attitude in 1979 was conservative or radical, whether in a party-political or a cultural sense. Secondly, we want to know whether public opinion shifted, in either direction, between 1974 and 1979. And, thirdly, we want to determine whether – and how strongly – voters' views on social and cultural change were related to their party choice in 1979. In the following sections, we will examine the entire array of opinion questions in the two batteries from these points of view.

7.2 A review of opinions on political issues and cultural change

The distributions of opinions recorded by our two batteries of questions are presented in full in Tables 7.1 and 7.2. The first of these sets out the questions asking those interviewed whether they felt change had gone too far or not far enough in a number of areas. The eight questions are ordered according to the proportion feeling that change had gone too far, with the highest proportion at the top of the table. The correlation coefficients in the right-hand column indicate the strength of the relationship between opinions and party vote. The higher the correlation coefficient, the stronger the tendency for opinions to differ: the Conservatives thinking 'change has gone too far', whilst Labour voters think it 'has not gone far enough'.[2]

The distribution of opinion for the sixteen questions on what the government should or should not do are presented in Table 7.2 From the top row of the table and downwards, the questions are ordered according to the percentage of the electorate in favour of each goal or policy proposal. An asterisk after a question text indicates that Labour voters tend to be more in favour and Conservative voters more opposed to the policy in question. Otherwise the direction of the relationship is reversed: Conservative voters are more likely than Labour voters to support the policy mentioned in the question. The strength of each relationship is indicated by the correlation coefficient.[3]

Table 7.1 *Has change gone too far − or not far enough?*
Per cent distributions of opinions in 1974 and 1979. Correlations to party vote

How do you feel about . . .		Gone much too far	Gone a little too far	Is about right	Not gone quite far enough	Not gone nearly far enough	Total per cent	Correlation of opinion and party vote
1	the right to show nudity and sex in films and magazines?	1979	38	28	29	3	2	100%	0.04
		1974	39	25	30	4	2	100%	0.07
†2	people challenging authority?	1979	32	33	21	10	3	100%	0.18
		1974	49	33	10	5	3	100%	0.13
3	the reduction of Britain's military strength?	1979	33	29	25	8	5	100%	0.22
		1974	22	26	36	11	5	100%	0.25
†4	change towards modern methods in teaching children at school nowadays?	1979	29	25	32	9	5	100%	0.22
		1974	18	24	43	11	4	100%	0.18
5	availability of abortion on the National Health Service?	1979	26	18	44	8	4	100%	0.02
		1974	24	19	42	11	4	100%	0.07
6	the welfare benefits that are available to people today?	1979	21	29	33	13	4	100%	0.29
		1974	12	22	42	18	6	100%	0.26
7	attempts to ensure equality for coloured people?	1979	12	18	41	21	8	100%	0.13
		1974	11	16	44	22	7	100%	0.09
8	attempts to ensure equality for women?	1979	9	14	48	22	7	100%	0.08
		1974	7	12	46	26	9	100%	0.07

Interview
question: 'Now we would like to ask your views on some of the general changes that have been taking place in Britain over the last few years. Thinking first about . . .'
Respondents were asked to choose one of the response alternatives (shown on a printed card at the interview) for each one of the statements about change in this table (the phrasing of statements with an † was slightly different in the 1974 study). The order in which the statements appear in the table is not the same as in the interview.

Data source: BES May 1979 Election Survey and BES October 1974 Election Survey. The percentage base is the total number of interviewed respondents in each of the surveys, excluding only respondents who gave 'Don't know' answers or whose opinions were inadvertently not recorded. The correlation coefficient is Kendall's Tau-b; these coefficients pertain to voting for the three main parties taken in the order: Conservatives, Liberals, Labour.

Table 7.2 *What the government ought – ought not – to do*
Per cent distributions of opinions in 1974 and 1979 on policy proposals.
Correlations to party vote.

Policy		Very important that the govern- ment *should do*	Fairly important that the govern- ment *should do*	It doesn't matter either way (or don't know)	Fairly important that the govern- ment *should not do*	Very important that the govern- ment *should not do*	Total per cent	Correlation of opinion and party vote
1	Giving stiffer sentences to people who break the law	1979	67	24	6	2	1	100%	0.07
2	Taking tougher measures to prevent Communist influence in Britain	1979	53	20	14	6	7	100%	0.14
		1974	60	16	15	4	5	100%	0.20
3	Putting more money into the National Health Service*	1979	52	35	6	5	2	100%	0.14
		1974	47	37	8	6	2	100%	0.14
4	Making more efforts to protect the countryside and our finest buildings	1979	47	40	10	2	1	100%	0.05
		1974	43	42	11	3	1	100%	0.06
5	Spending more money to get rid of poverty in Britain*	1979	46	34	12	6	2	100%	0.17
		1974	50	34	9	4	2	100%	0.21
6	Bring back the death penalty	1979	44	25	8	10	13	100%	0.08
7	Giving council house tenants the right to buy their houses	1979	37	36	14	8	5	100%	0.20
8	Withdrawing troops from Northern Ireland immediately*	1979	31	16	13	21	19	100%	0.11
9	Redistributing income and wealth in favour of ordinary working people*	1979	25	27	22	16	10	100%	0.36
		1974	23	31	19	17	10	100%	0.42
10	Giving workers more say in the running of the place where they work*	1979	17	38	15	21	9	100%	0.23
		1974	17	41	16	17	9	100%	0.26
11	Going ahead with further expansion of the nuclear power industry	1979	16	30	25	15	14	100%	0.09
12	Sending coloured immigrants back to their own country	1979	14	15	21	27	23	100%	0.05
		1974	16	19	28	24	13	100%	0.05
13	Establishing comprehensive schools in place of grammar schools throughout the country*	1979	12	18	24	21	25	100%	0.39
		1974	15	24	25	18	18	100%	0.34
14	Increasing state control of land for building*	1979	12	18	29	22	19	100%	0.31
		1974	24	33	16	17	10	100%	0.35
15	Reducing the powers of the House of Lords*	1979	11	13	46	18	12	100%	0.29
16	Giving more aid to poorer countries in Africa and Asia*	1979	8	28	17	26	21	100%	0.11
		1974	9	30	15	26	20	100%	0.08

Interview question: 'I am going to read out a list of things that some people believe a Government should do. For each one you can say whether you feel it is . . .'
(response alternatives in table headings). The order in which the statements appear in the table is not the same as in the interview.
Data source: BES May 1979 Election Survey and BES October 1974 Election Survey. The percentage bases are the total number of respondents for each survey with slight variations in the number depending on small numbers of inadvertently 'not ascertained' responses. The correlation coefficient is Kendall's Tau-b; these coefficients pertain to voting for the three main parties. An asterisk indicates that parties are taken in the order: Labour, Liberal, Conservative; otherwise the order is in the reverse.

All of the matters covered in our questions are, in some sense, 'political', but this is not to say that they are necessarily seen as issues in party politics or bear upon the citizens' electoral choice. Indeed, the correlation coefficients reveal that many of these issues have very little effect on the party division of the vote. In several instances, it is clear that one way of looking at a social or cultural trend is so predominant in the electorate that the state of public opinion on the issue very nearly amounts to a consensus.

As can be seen, this is in general true of attitudes towards societal changes connected with the coming of the permissive or liberal society. Thus, large majorities in the electorate remain unconvinced by novel ideas about the *treatment of law-breakers*: the prevailing view is that stiffer sentences on criminals are required and nearly seven out of ten voters would wish to see capital punishment reinstated. Not quite as many, but a substantial majority (66 per cent), think that the permissiveness towards *pornography* has gone too far. Opinions are more divided on the question of *abortion*. The view that current legislation has gone too far falls short of a majority, but it has much stronger support than the view that change has not gone far enough. Opinions on none of these issues, however, show more than a trace of relationship to the voters' party vote.

There is no consensus in public opinion about *children's schooling*, but the balance is tilted somewhat in favour of a conservative view on teaching methods and also on comprehensive schools. Moreover, there is a very substantial correlation between opinions and voting in the case of comprehensive schools.

Feelings about the changing *style of politics* are apparently mixed. On the one hand, there is widespread disenchantment with the tendency to challenge authority (admittedly, respondents were probably not only thinking of 'political' activities in this context). But the public is, on the other hand, mildly in favour of participation when it takes the form of giving workers more say at their place of work. On these questions there is a discernible but not very strong correlation between opinions and party preferences: Conservatives are more dismayed about lack of respect for authority and more wary of allowing workers more influence at their places of work.

Political extremism of the left, in the form of Communist activities, is roundly rejected, and nearly three voters out of four (73 per cent) would wish to see tougher measures being taken against Communist influence in Britain. This near-consensus means that in this case there is only a weak correlation between opinions and party preferences.

Questions concerning *the environment* may be intrinsically important, but they do not affect election outcomes. Public opinion is clearly divided on the wisdom of expanding the nuclear power industry any further, but this is scarcely reflected in the way people vote. Even less partisan is the near unanimous approval of government measures to protect the countryside and historic buildings.

Equality is a notoriously protean concept. Equality for women is perhaps the meaning most obviously connected with contemporary cultural trends. The changes that have already occurred in that direction meet with the approval of a substantial majority; but it is noteworthy that only about a third of the electorate thinks that they have not gone far enough. We find the same ambiguity with regard to equality for coloured people; in fact, the two distributions are remarkably similar. Confronted with the concrete proposal that coloured immigrants should be sent back to their countries of origin, those opposed outnumbered those in favour by five to three; yet more than one in four were in favour of the proposal. As on many other matters, only minorities support the more extreme view: the prevailing mood emerging as moderately conservative rather than liberal or radical. On neither of these aspects of equality, however, is there registered more than the barest indication of a relationship to party choice.

Equality in the sense of a more equal distribution of income and wealth strikes a more familiar chord in ideology-laden attitudes and there is actually more support for equality in this sense. In this instance there is also a conspicuously strong correlation between opinions and vote. On the other hand, if valuing equality arises out of a sense of solidarity with the less well-off, then such feelings are not easily extended beyond the boundaries of one's own country. More voters were opposed to than in favour of increasing aid to poor countries in Africa and Asia; and we find only a feeble indication of any link to party-political views in the correlation coefficient.

The picture that emerges of public feelings about *the welfare state* is intriguingly ambiguous. There was wide support for the view that social welfare benefits had 'gone too far' in 1979, and the proportion agreeing with that view had increased significantly since 1974. On the other hand, most people thought more money should be put into the National Health Service, and a very large majority thought that more money should be spent on 'getting rid of poverty' in Britain. But whereas the voters' views on social benefits showed a substantial correlation with voting, one finds only a very mild relationship of that kind for views on the health service and poverty. Apparently, there is a partisan division of opinion and a conservative mood in the electorate over the social benefits in general; but there also exists a broad, almost non-partisan, consensus in favour of what are seen to be 'deserving' causes in the social policy field.

Among the *current policy issues* on which opinions were appreciably related to party preferences were proposals such as allowing council house tenants to buy their own homes, increasing state control over land designated for building, and the fear that the reduction in Britain's military strength had gone too far. On all of these issues the Conservatives' approach was more widely supported than Labour's. On one other current issue – the proposal to reduce the power of the House of Lords – the preponderant view among voters was apparently that 'it doesn't matter either way', but fewer were in favour than against.

Finally, the question of *Northern Ireland*. Given the bi-partisan truce on the matter it is perhaps surprising that no consensus was to be found on whether the troops should be withdrawn from Northern Ireland. In contrast to official government policy, as many as 47 per cent of the voters wanted the troops to be withdrawn immediately, while 40 per cent were against.

7.3 Dimensions of attitudes towards social and cultural change

When opinions on many different issues are measured it can sometimes be shown that several opinions are all related to one underlying, more general attitude. When one thinks of an attitude as a continuum, or a scale on which positions can range from, for example, a strongly conservative to a strongly radical extreme, it is often referred to as an attitude dimension. For the purpose of our analysis, we need to establish now whether the opinions on different aspects of change are all rooted in one or more general attitude towards societal change. If more than one attitude dimension with regard to change exists, we want to determine how much each of them bears upon the voters' party choice.

We have employed an analysis technique, factor analysis, which is devised precisely for this purpose. The analysis reveals whether the observed opinions are related to one or more underlying dimensions or 'factors'. If there is more than one dimension, the analysis shows which cluster of opinions most clearly reflects individuals' positions on each of these dimensions.

The result of our analysis was, firstly, that there is no single, comprehensive attitude toward all aspects of societal change. In fact, our analysis yielded five separate attitude dimensions. Two of these have a substantial partisan content. One of them comprises primarily opinions on social welfare and workers' partici-pation, whereas the other encompasses views on state economic control, for example, land ownership, the other classic left/right issues such as the House of Lords and the country's military strength. Interestingly, opinions on the distri-bution of wealth are strongly associated with both of these attitude dimensions. Opinion on comprehensive schools is related to the second of these dimensions – evidence as good as any that this is now seen as an issue in party politics. We will refer to these dimensions as the social welfare attitude dimension and the left/right attitude dimension, respectively. The two are correlated to each other; that is, individuals who are on the conservative side on one tend also to be on the con-servative side on the other. The party choices of individuals are clearly related to both of these attitude dimensions, most strongly so to the left/right one.

Opinions on the treatment of law-breakers, capital punishment, and whether Communism in Britain should be curbed form a third attitude dimension. A fourth cluster of opinions is formed by opinions on racial equality, immigration and (more marginally) aid to developing countries. We will refer to these dimen-sions as the 'law and order' and 'ethnocentrism' attitudes respectively. The 'law and order' attitude shows substantial correlations with the left/right dimension and ethnocentrism. Interestingly, however, party voting shows only a mild associ-ation with the 'law and order' dimension. The 'ethnocentrism' dimension has a substantial correlation with the 'law and order' dimension as well as a somewhat weaker correlation with social welfare attitudes. But there is virtually no association between party preference, as expressed in voting, and ethnocentrism. Finally, there is a 'moral' dimension, comprising opinions on pornography, deference towards authority, and abortion. This attitude shows some relationship to the ethnocentrism dimension, but not to any other attitude dimension or to party choice.[4]

Although these attitude dimensions show some degree of inter-correlation, they emerge as distinctly separable orientations to different types of change and cannot be seen as merely parts of a common, general attitude. The social welfare and left/right attitudes stand apart from the others; not only are they correlated with each other, but they are also the only dimensions that show a substantial relationship to voting.

In one sense, what could have been expected has been confirmed by this analysis. What counts when it comes to casting the votes are the things that form part of the traditional left/right and social welfare cleavages in the British party system: state control of the economy, the distribution of wealth, military defence, and social policies. We might even have expected that partisanship in Britain should encompass two different, but correlated, attitude dimensions.

Aside from education, which did prove to be a salient political issue, views on changes in cultural standards and immigration showed only flimsy or no indications of having any bearing on party choice. Moreover, there was no consistent shift in a conservative direction between 1974 and 1979 in these non-partisan opinions on cultural change, as can be confirmed by inspection of Tables 7.1–2.

Our analysis, so far, may seem to lead to the conclusion that attitudes towards cultural change are irrelevant to British party politics. Yet, is this in fact the case? Looking back at the opinion distributions in Tables 7.1–2, one gains the overall impression that most of the developments we are concerned with have been met with no more than an uneasy welcome. Sizeable sections of the population – in some instances approaching or reaching majorities – seem to regard some of the new features of society with feelings ranging from apprehension to revulsion. One reason why attitudes of this nature do appear not to bear on the voters' party choice may well be that they involve the kind of questions on which parties avoid taking a stand. Capital punishment and abortion are good examples of issues on which governments are happy to allow a free vote in Parliament. Nonetheless, these divisions of opinions exist in the electorate and are articulated in public debate. The differences of opinions are certainly sensed by party strategists. The prevailing views on such issues are therefore likely to impose constraints on what proposals the parties find it prudent to put on the agenda for policy making. If so the influence of public opinion on policy making would in general be conservative rather than radical or reformist.

7.4 Law and order

Given that the voters so frequently mentioned the Conservative party's stands on law and order as well as immigration as things they liked about the party (see Chapter 5), it is noteworthy that we have not observed any strong relationship in the present analysis between opinions on related issues and party choice. In the case of the law and order issues included in the batteries of questions discussed so far, this is partly the result of the fact that such large majorities were actually found to hold conservative, with a small 'c', opinions. Many voters who held a conservative view on these matters must, in fact, have voted for the Labour party for other reasons. To take just one example, 76 per cent of Conservative voters thought the death penalty should be brought back, but 64 per cent of Liberal voters and 62 per cent of Labour voters also held the same view. Opinions on such matters apparently have only a slight impact on voting decisions.

This does not mean, however, that the Conservative party's profile is not recognised or that the party is not given credit for its views, when people are asked what they like about it.[5] The Conservative party was indeed seen to have a better record in office than Labour on handling the questions of law and order. This was shown by the results of two questions in which respondents were asked how well the Labour government had handled such matters and how well the Conservatives would have dealt with them if they had been in office. (The format of these questions is the same as that used in the questions about how well the parties handle economic problems; see Chapter 6.)[6]

The response distributions to these questions, by vote in the 1979 election, are shown in Table 7.3. As is seen in the table, 80 per cent of the electors thought that the Conservatives handle law and order questions 'very well' or 'fairly well', whereas only 51 per cent thought this could be said of the Labour government. Approval of what is seen as the firmer Conservative attitude towards law-breakers is, of course, most wholehearted among voters who cast their votes for that party in any event. But on the questions of law and order even Labour voters were comparatively favourably disposed to the Conservatives; in fact, 28 per cent of the Labour voters thought that law and order questions had been handled 'not very well' or 'not at all well' by the Labour government, whereas a slightly smaller proportion (23 per cent) thought this would have been true if the Conservatives had been in power.

By combining respondents' answers to both of these questions we obtained a measure of their overall assessment of the Conservatives' and Labour's performance in office with regard to law and order. (The combined classification of the answers was constructed in the same way as the measures of voters' assessments of the parties' handling of economic problems.) The resulting 'balance of opinions' is heavily in favour of the Conservative party among those who thought there was any difference between the parties. However, nearly half the electorate gave the same marks – high or low – to both parties (45 per cent and an ad-

Table 7.3 *Labour and Conservatives: upholding law and order, 1979*

Handling of law and order	Conservative voters' views on:		Liberal voters' views on:		Labour voters' views on:		All respondents' views on:	
	Conservative party	Labour party	Conservative party	Labour party	Conservative party	Labour party	Conservative party	Labour party
	%	%	%	%	%	%	%	%
Very well	27	6	13	7	17	16	20	9
Fairly well	64	29	71	44	55	54	60	42
Not very well	5	40	10	38	19	22	11	32
Not at all well	0	24	1	10	4	6	3	15
Don't know	4	1	5	1	5	2	6	2
Total per cent	100%	100%	100%	100%	100%	100%	100%	100%
Number of respondents	728	727	213	213	581	579	1872	1867

Interview question: 'How well do you think the recent Labour government managed to uphold law and order – very well, fairly well, not very well, or not at all well?' – 'If the Conservative party had been in power, how well do you think they would have managed to uphold law and order . . .?' (Same response alternatives.)

Data source: BES May 1979 Election Survey.

ditional 3 per cent who had no opinion on the matter). In the other half of the electorate, 43 per cent rated the Conservatives' performance more highly than Labour's, whereas only 9 per cent thought Labour had the best record on up-holding law and order. This classification, furthermore, shows a substantial relationship to party choice in the 1979 election (the Tau-b coefficient is 0.39), although it is much weaker than those we found for the voters' assessment of the parties' handling of the economy (see Chapter 6).

That the Conservative party is good at maintaining law and order is clearly part of its party image. One can think of circumstances in which this could have a decisive impact on an election. But in 1979, the law and order issue was over-shadowed by the problems in the economy. We shall find further evidence for this conclusion in Chapter 11, when we construct a 'balance sheet' for the impact of the issues. However, the Conservative stance on law and order was appreciated by many voters who did not vote Conservative. When a party has a positive appeal of this kind it may be thought of as a 'dormant asset' which could be activated if circumstances were to change.

Why are the Conservatives seen to have a better record than Labour on law and order? At least a part of the answer to that question can actually be found in the results of our enquiry into the public's more general attitudes towards social changes in Britain. It is true that the general attitudes to moral issues and law and order emerged as more or less 'non-partisan' in the sense that they showed little or no relationship to voting in 1979. Nevertheless, the distribution of opinions that we recorded clearly indicates that the prevailing sentiments on many law and order issues were in tune with the kind of policies that the Conservatives – rather than Labour – would be associated with. One can safely assume that it was this difference between the parties' approaches that was being recognised in the voters' appraisals of their ability to maintain law and order.

7.5 Opinions on change and party vote

We have noted that opinions on some of the issues discussed in this chapter were clearly correlated with the way people voted. The relationship indicated by a cor-relation coefficient obviously means that the party division of the vote differs, from category to category, along the scale of opinion positions. We expect, for example, the Labour share of the vote to be largest in the leftmost category and then decline gradually at each step towards the right on the scale.

Tables 7.4–5 will serve to illuminate 'how much difference' there was between the opinion categories with regard to the party division of the vote. The tables include only questions on which there was a substantial relationship between opinions and voting (a correlation coefficient of at least 0.2). The opinions that showed the strongest association with voting are at the top of the tables.

The tables contain two sets of entries. One entry for each opinion category is the 'Conservative–Labour balance' in the vote; that is, the Conservative percent-

Table 7.4 *Relation of views on changes in society to vote in the May 1979 election*

Entries with plus and minus signs are the Conservative per cent of the vote minus the Labour per cent of the three-party vote in each category. Entries followed by a % sign are the Labour per cent of the vote in each category.

Change	Gone much too far	Gone a little too far	Is about right	Not gone quite far enough	Not gone nearly far enough
The welfare benefits that are available to people today					
Conserv. – Labour balance	+49	+30	−13	−34	−37
Labour %	19%	27%	49%	61%	63%
The reduction of Britain's military strength					
Conserv. – Labour balance	+39	+14	−16	−17	−21
Labour %	25%	35%	51%	51%	56%
Changes towards modern methods in teaching children at school nowadays					
Conserv. – Labour balance	+38	+29	−9	−19	−27
Labour %	24%	27%	48%	53%	59%

Data source: BES May 1971 Election Survey.

age of the three-party vote minus the Labour percentage. A plus sign indicates that the Conservatives are strongest and a minus sign indicates that Labour is strongest among the voters in an opinion category.[7] In addition, the 'Labour %' gives Labour's percentage of the three-party vote.

The tables confirm that there is a pattern of differences among the opinion categories of the kind we would expect. The stronger the correlation, the steeper the gradient both in the 'Conservative–Labour balance' and in the Labour share of the vote across a range of opinion categories. In some instances, the differences between the extreme categories are very sharp indeed. These extreme categories, on the other hand, mostly include only small proportions of the total electorate. The tables furthermore show very clearly that there is no neat one-to-one relationship between opinions and voting on any one issue. It is by no means the case that all voters on one side of the midpoint of these scales are Conservative

Table 7.5 *Relation of views on what the government should – or should not – do to vote in the May 1979 election*

Entries with plus and minus signs are the Conservative percent of the vote minus the Labour per cent of the vote in each opinion category (Conservative–Labour balance). Only Conservative, Liberal and Labour voters are included in this analysis. Entries followed by a % sign are the Labour per cent of the vote in each category.

Policy	Very important that the government *should do*	Fairly important that the government *should do*	It doesn't matter either way (or don't know)	Fairly important that the government *should not do*	Very important that the government *should not do*
Redistributing income and wealth in favour of ordinary people					
Conserv.–Labour balance	–43	–6	+21	+52	+72
Labour %	66%	46%	29%	18%	10%
Establishing comprehensive schools in place of grammar schools throughout the country					
Conserv.–Labour balance	–55	–32	–10	+37	+61
Labour %	72%	60%	46%	24%	13%
Increasing state control over land for building					
Conserv.–Labour balance	–36	–23	–7	+32	+63
Labour %	64%	53%	47%	25%	13%
Reducing the power of the House of Lords					
Conserv.–Labour balance	–36	–26	+5	+38	+61
Labour %	61%	54%	40%	25%	15%
Giving workers more say in the running of their place of work					
Conserv.–Labour balance	–29	+1	+1	+40	+51
Labour %	58%	42%	41%	24%	20%
Giving council house tenants the right to buy their houses					
Conserv.–Labour balance	+28	+20	–17	–27	–51
Labour %	29%	32%	51%	55%	68%

Data source: BES 1979 Election Survey.

(or Liberal) or that all those on the other side vote Labour. It is only the probabilities of voting Conservative, Liberal or Labour that change, albeit markedly in some instances, along the opinion scales.

Tables 7.6 and 7.7 throw light on the same set of relationships from another angle. These tables show the divisions of opinions *within* parties. Even when there is a fairly substantial connection between the opinions that people hold and their party preferences, there can be a very considerable spread of opinions among voters who supported the same party. Conservative voters, for example, are quite divided on the question whether income and wealth should be more evenly distributed and on workers' participation. Labour voters are very divided in their views on modern teaching methods in the schools and on whether social welfare benefits have gone too far. On two other issues – reduction of Britain's

Table 7.6 *Views on changes in society by party vote in the May 1979 election*

The table shows, for the voters of each of the three main parties, the percentage thinking that change had gone too far ('much too far' or 'a little too far') as well as the percentage thinking that change had not gone far enough ('not quite' or 'not nearly far enough'). The remainder to 100% consists of the percentage who either thought the change had been 'about right' or 'didn't know'.

Change	Party voted for in 1979		
	Conservatives	Liberals	Labour
The welfare benefits that are available to people today			
Gone too far	66%	51%	32%
Not gone far enough	9%	14%	25%
The reduction of Britain's military strength			
Gone too far	71%	61%	46%
Not gone far enough	8%	10%	15%
Changes towards modern methods in teaching children at school nowadays			
Gone too far	58%	52%	31%
Not gone far enough	8%	9%	17%

Data source: BES May 1979 Election Survey.

military strength and the selling of council houses – opinions among Labour voters were very decidedly balanced in favour of the Conservative party.

The division of opinion on most issues among Liberal voters is, in general, somewhere 'in between' those for Conservative and Labour voters. All voters tend to agree with the Conservatives on some issues and with Labour on others, but the Liberals clearly attract support from among those voters who find the pros and cons of the two major parties particularly evenly balanced.

As we have seen, individual voters' opinions are not necessarily constrained by any sharp ideological demarcation lines between the parties. A great many voters hold views that we would not expect them to hold if a British election were wholly a matter of a choice between competing party ideologies by people committed to such ideologies. Yet, Labour voters are consistently somewhat more likely than others to express broadly social-democratic views, and Conservative voters are equally consistently somewhat more likely than others to take issue with what they see as misguided egalitarianism or threats to private enterprise. The mass of such individual differences accumulate so as to form two distinctively different opinion profiles for the two major parties' electoral bases.

The nine questions we have examined in this section are mainly related to the left/right and social welfare cleavages; they are all cases of well-known party

Table 7.7 *Opinions on what the government should – or should not – do by party vote in the May 1979 election*

The table shows, for the voters of each of three main parties, the percentage in favour of as well as the percentage opposed to the policies listed below. The remainder to 100% consists of voters who either thought 'it doesn't matter either way' or 'didn't know'.

Policy	Party voted for in 1979		
	Conservatives	Liberals	Labour
	%	%	%
Redistributing income and wealth in favour of ordinary people			
In favour	34	47	73
Opposed	44	22	11
Establishing comprehensive schools in place of grammar schools throughout the country			
In favour	15	24	51
Opposed	68	48	22
Increasing state control over land for building			
In favour	19	29	45
Opposed	54	45	22
Reducing the power of the House of Lords			
In favour	14	29	37
Opposed	45	24	17
Giving workers more say in the running of their place of work			
In favour	44	56	66
Opposed	44	26	19
Giving council house tenants the right to buy their houses			
In favour	84	70	61
Opposed	6	15	20
Number of respondents	726	214	583

Note: The actual percentage bases vary slightly from question to question from the number given above because of small variations in the numbers of 'not ascertained'.

Data source: BES May 1979 Election Survey.

differences in current politics. Do the opinion distributions on such issues help to account for the Conservative victory in 1979? Was there any rightward shift in opinions between October 1974 and 1979? We cannot, of course, claim that these nine questions form a representative sample of all the issues that affected the voters' party choice in 1979. But it throws some light on the weakness of Labour's tactical situation, that on seven of these questions there was more support for opinion positions on the 'rightist' side of the scale than for those on the 'left' (that is, if one compares the size of the categories that are politically to the right of the status quo, or midpoint category, with those to the left, see Tables 7.1 and 7.2). Furthermore, we find that amongst the seven of these questions for which we have comparable measurements from 1974, five show opinion shifts towards the right. None showed a shift to the left.

We have cast our net widely in this chapter in order not to leave out any division of opinion that could have contributed to the Conservative victory at the polls. We did the same in Chapter 5 where the analysis relied mainly on the respondents' comments on what they liked and disliked about the political parties. In both of these parts of our enquiry, the results have pointed in the same direction: it was the problems in the economy in conjunction with well-known differences between the Conservatives' and Labour's ideological profiles that mattered most in 1979. It was on such matters that we have found the strongest correlations between opinions and voting; it was also on questions related to these aspects of politics that opinions were found to have shifted in favour of the Conservatives between 1974 and 1979.

8

Nationalisation and social welfare policies – a rightward shift in electoral opinion 1974 – 1979

8.1 Two landmarks

Apart from their association with the two main social classes, no features of the Conservative and Labour parties are more generally recognised than their differences on state ownership of industry and social welfare policy. The parties' stands are not eternally fixed, however. Conservative governments have been known to take private companies into state ownership, and after three years of expenditure cuts, the Labour government's standing as the champion of the social services may have looked a little dishevelled in 1979. Yet, most people would agree that if one wants either or both nationalisation and an ambitious social policy, then this would be a reason to vote for the Labour party. Equally, if one wants less of either – or at least thinks it is time to hold back – then this would be a reasonable ground for voting Conservative.

If social welfare and nationalisation are the traditional landmarks in British politics, what stands were the Conservatives and Labour actually seen to be taking by the electorate in the 1970s? How far were the parties seen to differ? And what difference did these issues make to the voters' party choice?

To answer these questions, we need to explore both how the party positions were perceived by the electors and the state of opinion in the electorate. We will do so with the aid of a series of questions about the two issues asked in our surveys of both the October 1974 and 1979 elections. The question technique employed was to present those interviewed with four statements which formed a scale of differing opinion positions. The four statements of nationalisation are shown in Tables 8.1A–B, and the statements on social welfare policies are given in Tables 8.2A–B. As is seen in the tables, the questions were phrased so as to present statements ordered from a 'most left' to a 'most right' position on nationalisation, while the statements on social welfare policies were presented in the reverse order.

Table 8.1A *Voters' perceptions of the Conservative party's stand on nationalisation 1974 and 1979* (By party vote at elections in October 1974 and May 1979)

Conservative party's view is closest to:	Conservative voters		Liberal voters		Labour voters		All respondents		Change 1974 – 1979*
	1974	1979	1974	1979	1974	1979	1974	1979	
	%	%	%	%	%	%	%	%	
A lot more industries should be nationalised	1	2	3	4	6	7	4	5	+1
Only a few more industries should be nationalised	4	3	7	2	4	3	5	3	–2
No more industries should be nationalised, but industries that are now nationalised should stay nationalised	57	18	49	14	33	12	44	15	–29
Some industries that are now nationalised should become private companies	34	71	37	73	47	69	39	68	+29
Don't know	4	6	4	7	10	9	8	9	
Total per cent	100%	100%	100%	100%	100%	100%	100%	100%	
Number of respondents	693	728	348	214	806	583	2305	1873	

Table 8.1B *Voters' perceptions of the Labour party's stand on nationalisation 1974 and 1979* (By party vote at elections in October 1974 and May 1979)

Labour party's view is closest to:	Conservative voters		Liberal voters		Labour voters		All respondents		Change 1974– 1979*
	1974	1979	1974	1979	1974	1979	1974	1979	
	%	%	%	%	%	%	%	%	
A lot more industries should be nationalised	87	72	77	48	59	39	72	54	–18
Only a few more industries should be nationalised	7	18	15	40	27	37	17	28	+11
No more industries should be nationalised, but industries that are now nationalised should stay nationalised	2	4	3	6	6	14	4	8	+4
Some industries that are now nationalised should become private companies	1	1	1	0	1	1	1	2	+1
Don't know	3	5	4	6	7	9	6	8	
Total per cent	100%	100%	100%	100%	100%	100%	100%	100%	
Number of respondents	693	727	348	214	805	582	2304	1871	

Notes

*Entries in the Change column are the difference between the percentages for 'All respondents' in the appropriate row (1979 percentage *minus* 1974 percentage).

Interview questions: '. . . which statement do you think comes closest to the view of the Conservative party?' – 'And which statement do you think comes closest to the view of the Labour party?'

Data source: BES October 1974 Election Survey and BES May 1979 Election Survey.

On both issues, respondents were asked which of the statements came closest to their own view. They were then asked, first, which statement they thought came closest to the Conservative party's view and, secondly, which one they considered closest to the Labour party's position.[1]

The party positions – as seen by the voters

We will begin by examining how the voters perceived the setting in party politics at the time of the October 1974 election and at the May 1979 election. Tables 8.1A–B display the data on voters' perceptions of the stances taken by the Conservatives and Labour on the issue of nationalisation; Tables 8.2A–B contain the same kind of data concerning the parties' views on social services and benefits.

That the Conservatives and Labour aim in different directions with regard to state ownership of industries is widely recognised by the electorate. A large majority believe that Labour would like to nationalise at least 'a few more' industries, while an equally large majority think that the Conservatives are opposed to further nationalisation. As always with survey questions, small proportions of voters 'did not know' about one or both of the parties, or clearly have 'got it wrong'. But if we combine the answers to both questions, it is found that more than eight voters out of ten (82 per cent) in 1979 placed Labour to the left of the Conservatives on the scale formed by the four policy alternatives in our interview question.[2] The difference between the parties' views on social services and benefits does not emerge quite as distinctively. It was quite common in 1974 to think that the Conservatives wanted to preserve the existing standard of social services, whilst the same view was about as commonly held about Labour in 1979. As seen by the voters, the parties' positions on social welfare were more sharply differentiated in 1979 than at the preceding election. In 1974, 62 per cent placed Labour 'to the left' of the Conservatives on our scale, the remainder mostly placing the parties at the same point or proving unable to locate at least one of the parties (but a small proportion placed the parties in the reverse order). At the 1979 election, nearly eight voters out of ten (77 per cent) thought that Labour was more positive towards social services than the Conservatives.

Whilst at both elections most voters placed Labour to the left of the Conservatives with regard to both social welfare and nationalisation, the voters' perceptions of the parties' actual positions changed quite markedly between 1974 and 1979. The Conservatives in 1979 were seen by most people, 68 per cent, to aim at denationalisation. In 1974, only a minority, 39 per cent, had that impression, and a slightly larger proportion thought that, while opposing nationalisation, the Conservatives intended to keep already nationalised industries in state ownership (44 per cent). The Labour party was much less often thought to want 'a lot more' nationalisation in 1979 than in 1974 (54 per cent in 1979 as compared with 72 per cent in 1974). There is a similar shift to the right in the voters' perceptions of party positions on social services and benefits. The modal view of the Conserva-

Table 8.2A *Voters' perceptions of the Conservative party's stand on social services and benefits 1974 and 1979* (By party vote at elections in October 1974 and May 1979)

Conservative party's view is closest to:	Conservative voters		Liberal voters		Labour voters		All respondents		Change 1974–1979*
	1974 %	1979 %	1974 %	1979 %	1974 %	1979 %	1974 %	1979 %	%
Social services and benefits have gone much too far and should be cut back a lot	7	24	8	37	20	46	13	33	+20
Social services and benefits have gone somewhat too far and should be cut back a bit	21	50	25	40	26	31	24	40	+16
Social services and benefits should stay much as they are	48	15	40	12	34	13	39	14	−25
More social services and benefits are needed	15	7	13	6	9	5	12	7	−5
Don't know	9	4	14	5	11	5	12	6	
Total per cent	100%	100%	100%	100%	100%	100%	100%	100%	
Number of respondents	691	729	348	214	805	581	2302	1874	

Table 8.2B *Voters' perceptions of the Labour party's stand on social services and benefits 1974 and 1979* (By party vote at elections in October 1974 and May 1979)

Labour party's view is closest to:	Conservative voters		Liberal voters		Labour voters		All respondents		Change 1974 – 1979*
	1974	1979	1974	1979	1974	1979	1974	1979	
	%	%	%	%	%	%	%	%	%
Social services and benefits have gone much too far and should be cut back a lot	3	2	2	0	2	1	2	2	0
Social services and benefits have gone somewhat too far and should be cut back a bit	3	4	2	6	4	10	4	6	+2
Social services and benefits should stay much as they are	13	32	18	42	27	43	20	38	+18
More social services and benefits are needed	73	57	69	49	61	42	66	49	–17
Don't know	8	5	9	3	6	4	8	5	
Total per cent	100%	100%	100%	100%	100%	100%	100%	100%	
Number of respondents	691	729	348	213	805	581	2302	1873	

Notes

*Entries in the Change column are the difference between the percentages for 'All respondents' in the appropriate row ((1979 percentage *minus* 1974 percentage)

Interview questions: '. . . which statement do you think comes closest to the view of the Conservative party?' – 'And which statement do you think comes closest to the view of the Labour party?'

Data source: BES October 1974 Election Survey and BES May 1979 Election Survey.

tives in 1974 was that of a party wanting to keep social services as they were; the proportion that thought the Conservatives wanted to cut back on social welfare then increased from 37 per cent in 1974 to 73 per cent in 1979. Perceptions of Labour's position changed less, but the proportion who thought the party wanted to expand social services declined from 66 per cent in 1974 to 49 per cent in 1979. (The entries in the 'Change 1974–79' columns in the tables summarise all these shifts.)

The data from the two elections convey an impression of a revolving stage moving towards the right while the two actors on the scene keep their distance from each other. The scene looks a little different, it is true, depending on the observer's viewpoint. More Labour voters than Conservative voters saw the Conservative party occupying the position farthest to the right with regard to social welfare. More Conservative voters than Labour voters believed the Labour party was aiming at 'a lot more' nationalisation as well as more social services and benefits. In many voters' perceptions, the stand of the party they have rejected is pushed towards the extreme end of the scale. Yet, the rightward movement in both parties' positions is registered independently of the voters' partisan sympathies.

8.2 Opinions in the electorate 1974–1979

As far as the voters are concerned, the stands that the parties are seen to take on nationalisation and social welfare policy are the policy alternatives on these issues that they are confronted with in an election. We have found that there was a fair amount of variation in the voters' perceptions of the parties' positions, but we have also seen that most voters held the same general view of how the parties stood relative to each other. We will now go on to compare these perceived choice alternatives with the voters' own policy preferences.[3]

The distributions of responses to the questions about the voters' own preferences are given in Table 8.3 for nationalisation and in Table 8.4 for social services and benefits.

The modal view on nationalised industries in the electorate was that the status quo should be maintained: no new industries should be nationalised but those already under state ownership should remain that way. In 1979, most voters believed that the Conservatives wanted to denationalise some industries and were opposed by a Labour party that wanted to go ahead with further nationalisation; but in the electorate there was only minority support for change in either direction. Opinions on social services and benefits in 1979 were clearly balanced in favour of cutting back rather than expanding. Nearly one voter in two, 49 per cent, wanted at least some cutting back, while only 26 per cent thought the current standard should be maintained. Only 20 per cent wanted more social services or benefits.

Opinion shifted towards the right between 1974 and 1979 on nationalisation

Table 8.3 *Views on nationalisation 1974 and 1979*
(By party vote at elections in October 1974 and May 1979)

	Conservative voters		Liberal voters		Labour voters		All respondents		Change 1974– 1979
	1974	1979	1974	1979	1974	1979	1974	1979	
	%	%	%	%	%	%	%	%	%
A lot more industries should be nationalised	0	1	4	1	18	11	9	6	−3
Only a few more industries should be nationalised	5	3	18	7	36	19	21	10	−11
No more industries should be nationalised, but industries that are now nationalised should stay nationalised	55	33	51	53	30	48	42	41	−1
Some of the industries that are now nationalised should become private companies	36	61	23	34	5	14	20	37	+17
Don't know	4	2	4	5	11	8	8	6	
Total per cent	100%	100%	100%	100%	100%	100%	100%	100%	
Number of respondents	687	726	347	213	798	577	2290	1863	

Interview question: 'There has been a lot of talk recently about nationalisation, that is the government owning and running industries like steel and electricity. Which of these statements comes closest to what you yourself feel should be done?' (Response alternatives shown on printed card.)

Data source: BES October 1974 Election Survey and May 1979 Election Survey.

Table 8.4 *Views on social services 1974 and 1979*
(By party vote at elections in October 1974 and May 1979)

	Conservative voters		Liberal voters		Labour voters		All respondents		
	1974	1979	1974	1979	1974	1979	1974	1979	Change 1974–1979
	%	%	%	%	%	%	%	%	%
Social services and benefits have gone much too far and should be cut back a lot	22	27	10	22	6	10	13	20	+7
Social services and benefits have gone somewhat too far and should be cut back a bit	32	39	30	29	16	22	25	29	+4
Social services and benefits should stay much as they are	29	19	33	25	37	35	32	26	–6
More social services and benefits are needed	15	11	24	19	38	28	27	20	–7
Don't know	2	4	3	5	3	5	3	2	
Total per cent	100%	100%	100%	100%	100%	100%	100%	100%	
Number of respondents	685	725	346	214	797	582	2284	1871	

Interview question: 'Now we would like to ask what you think about social services and benefits. Which of these statements do you feel comes closest to your own views?' (Response alternatives shown on printed card.)

Data source: BES October 1974 Election Survey and May 1979 Election Survey.

as well as on social welfare. The proportion of the electorate in favour of cutting back the social services increased from 38 per cent in 1974 to 49 per cent in 1979. Those wanting some state industries to be denationalised nearly doubled in number, with an increase in the percentages from 20 to 37 per cent.[4]

These opinion shifts undoubtedly contributed to an increase in the Conservative vote, as we shall see in a moment. But when the centre of gravity of public opinion moves in a given direction, then the resulting waves are often wider than the changes in the party division of the vote would suggest. In this instance it is evident that a broad change had occurred by 1979. Opinions on nationalisation and social welfare policies had become less favourable within the electoral bases of all of the three main parties. We have calculated (from the data in the tables) measures of the balance of opinion in 1974 and 1979 which serve to summarise all of these changes:

	Party vote			
	Conservative	Liberal	Labour	All respondents
Per cent wanting *more* social services and benefits *minus* per cent wanting *less*				
October 1974	−39	−16	+16	−11
1979	−55	−32	− 4	−29
Per cent wanting *more* nationalisation *minus* per cent wanting denationalisation				
October 1974	−31	− 1	+49	+10
1979	−57	−26	+16	−21

Opinions on nationalisation and social welfare and perceptions of the parties' current aims evidently changed in tandem during the four years between the elections of October 1974 and 1979. So did, in fact, the parties' messages to the electorate. Since 1974 some industries had indeed been nationalised, but the Labour manifesto for the May 1979 election contained no hard commitments to any further nationalisation. Likewise, there had been some improvements in social services since 1974, but during its last years in office the Labour government had made determined efforts to curb the rising trend in public expenditure, and the 1979 Labour manifesto did not pledge the party to any major new social policy developments. The Conservatives, under Thatcher's leadership, were meanwhile propounding the doctrines of economic liberalism more stridently than at any other time since the war. The opinion shift in the electorate was, to some degree, a response to changing signals from both of the major parties.

8.3 The impact on the vote

How much difference do an elector's opinions on nationalisation or social welfare make to the likelihood of his casting his vote for the Conservatives, the Liberals, or Labour?

To answer that question we need to look at the party division of the vote at each point on the scales of policy preferences formed by our interview questions. The percentage distributions for the three major parties, at the elections in October 1974 and May 1979, are given in Table 8.5 for nationalisation and in Table 8.6 for social services and benefits.

The pattern appearing in both tables reflects a substantial relationship between opinions and voting. The Conservative share of the three-party vote increases quite steeply from left to right on the scales, whereas the Labour vote declines. At both elections, opinions on nationalisation 'make more difference' to the party division of the vote than do opinions on social welfare policies. The strength of these relationships is indicated by the correlation coefficients given below:[5]

Correlation of issue opinions to three-party vote (Kendall's Tau-b coefficient)		
Election	Nationalisation	Social services
October 1974	0.49	0.28
1979	0.45	0.28

Table 8.5 *Relation of opinions on nationalisation to vote in October 1974 and May 1979*

Vote in October 1974 and May 1979 respectively	Opinion on nationalisation							
	'A lot more'		'A few more'		'No more'		'Some should be denationalised'	
	1974	1979	1974	1979	1974	1979	1974	1979
	%	%	%	%	%	%	%	%
Conservative	2	10	8	16	48	38	68	74
Liberal	7	4	17	11	22	18	22	12
Labour	91	86	75	73	30	44	10	14
Total per cent	100%	100%	100%	100%	100%	100%	100%	100%
Number of respondents	162	77	385	147	795	624	363	594

Note: The table includes only respondents who voted Conservative, Liberal or Labour.
Data source: BES 1979 Election Survey and BES October 1974 Election Survey.

Since the tables show that the party vote is most polarised in the categories at the two ends of the policy scales, it is important to bear in mind that the modal views on both nationalisation and social welfare policies are nearer to a preference for the status quo. In that opinion range, the party division of the vote is more evenly balanced and voting decisions are presumably to a large extent determined by other considerations.

In fact, none of the parties would have even a remote chance of achieving an electoral majority if they were to rely only on voters faithful to a staunchly partisan outlook. At the 1974 election those in favour of both more nationalis-ation ('a lot more' or 'a few more') and expanded social services comprised only 12 per cent of the electorate. By 1979 that proportion had shrunk to 6 per cent. At the other end of the ideological spectrum, voters who wanted to see both the social services cut back ('a bit' or 'a lot') and wanted some state industries to be turned into private companies made up only 11 per cent in the electorate in 1974. That firmly conservative combination of views had gained much more support in 1979, but it was still held by only 25 per cent of the total electorate.

As we have stressed before, many different issues are likely to affect a voter's party choice, and opinions on no single issue have a uniform impact on all individ-ual voting decisions. It might be added that voters switch their votes for many different reasons. The Conservative surge in 1979 caused some voters to change parties irrespective of their views on, for example, nationalisation or social wel-fare. As a result, it can be observed that the Conservative vote increased somewhat in most of the opinion categories in the tables, whereas the Labour vote declined. All the same, the strength and the shape of the relationships between opinions on both issues and voting were strikingly similar in 1974 and 1979; the correlation

Table 8.6 *Relation of opinions on social services to vote in October 1974 and in May 1979*

Vote in October 1974 and May 1979 respectively	Opinion on social services							
	'More needed'		'Stay much as they are'		'Cut back a bit'		'Cut back a lot'	
	1974	1979	1974	1979	1974	1979	1974	1979
	%	%	%	%	%	%	%	%
Conservative	21	28	33	34	48	60	64	65
Liberal	17	14	18	14	23	13	15	16
Labour	62	58	49	52	29	27	21	19
Total per cent	100%	100%	100%	100%	100%	100%	100%	100%
Number of respondents	491	283	604	395	454	472	231	303

Note: The table includes only respondents who voted Conservative, Liberal or Labour.
Data source: BES May 1979 Election Survey and BES October 1974 Election Survey.

coefficients were very nearly of the same value and the 'steepness' of the increase in the Conservative share of the vote also remains very much the same, as can be seen if one compares the categories from left to right across each scale.[6]

What did change, however, as we saw a moment ago, were the proportions of the electorate comprising each of the opinion categories along our scales of policy preferences. As we observed in the preceding section, opinions on nationalisation as well as on social welfare policies in the electorate shifted towards the right from 1974 to 1979. At the 1979 election, therefore, a larger proportion of the electorate was on the side of the opinion spectrum where there was a strong likelihood of Conservative votes being cast.

Although the move to the right in public opinion on these issues evidently contributed to the Conservative victory in 1979, it coincided with similar opinion changes on other issues. Individuals' opinions on many aspects of politics tend to be interdependent, and changes of opinion on one issue are often related to changes of opinion on other issues. It is, therefore, no simple matter to gauge the impact of opinion change on any one issue. Nevertheless, we shall employ basically the same technique as in Chapter 6 to try to establish a baseline from which to compare the relative impact of the nationalisation and social welfare issues. As in Chapter 6, we have calculated the effect on the Conservative vote of the change that occurred between 1974 and 1979 in the distributions of opinions on the issues concerned. We have constructed a prediction equation for voting in 1979, in which the predictors are the voters' opinions on nationalisation and social welfare and, in addition, their assessment of the parties' ability to handle some of the major problems the country was facing. The latter measures were included in order to establish the 'net effect' of the two issue opinions over and above the impact of the voters' more general assessment of the parties at the time of the 1979 election. We have then calculated what the Conservative proportion of the vote would have been if the 'average' opinion on nationalisation and social welfare policies, respectively, had not changed since 1974, whilst 'everything else' had been equal to the situation in 1979.[7] The result is an estimated 'gain' to the Conservative party as a result of the change in the distributions of opinions on these two issues between 1974 and 1979. It has to be stressed that the precise result of this calculation is useful only for the purpose of comparing the impact of the two issues and, also, that the gains calculated here cannot be added to those calculated in Chapter 6 because the underlying equations are not identical. With these caveats the results are those given below:

	Conservative gain as a result of opinion disribution change October 1974 – 1979
Nationalisation	+3.5%
Social services	+0.9%

The results reflect the fact that opinions on nationalisation showed both a more marked change towards the right and a stronger relationship to voting behaviour than opinions on social welfare. The nationalisation issue, therefore, had a stronger impact on the change of party division of the vote.

Needless to say, these two issues did not alone decide the outcome of the 1979 election. But the evidence weighs decidedly in support of one inference: it was the Conservatives' espousal of private enterprise more than the shift in opinion on social services than won the election for the Conservatives; and it was faltering confidence in state control of the economy more than declining support for the welfare state that weakened Labour's appeal to the electorate.

It is interesting to note that our analysis of the voters' comments on the good and bad sides of the parties (Chapter 5) led to the same general conclusion about the relative importance of opinions on private enterprise and nationalisation in comparison with opinions on social welfare policies. There was no strong support for any further nationalisation in 1974 either, of course. Many voters always vote Labour even though they are not in favour of any extension of state ownership of industry. Yet, the shift to the right meant that one of the opinion forces had become even more unfavourable to Labour in 1979. Nationalisation, a handicap to Labour in 1974, was an even greater handicap in 1979.

9

Policy alternatives and party choice in the 1979 election

9.1 Policy alternatives in the 1979 election

As the election campaign unfolded, the exchange of arguments over the country's economy centred increasingly upon policy choice in four fields: taxes, jobs, wages, and the proper role of trade unions. In all of these four debates within the debate, policies were proposed and consequences were assessed in a Labour perspective as well as in a Conservative perspective. The choice between them was to some extent a choice between priorities, but – as both Conservatives and Labour impressed upon the electorate – it was more than that. Two different ways of looking at Britain's economic problems were set forth, two different frameworks of expectations and two different sets of values. At least this was the way in which the choice was presented by the two major parties.

Thus, when the Conservatives promised to cut taxes, Labour countered by emphasising the importance of the public services that would be endangered; whereupon the Conservatives retorted that they were, indeed, the only party that could achieve a sound economic basis for such public services as were really essential. The Conservatives promised to create a better climate for private enterprise and vigorous competition. That was the only way, they claimed, to create 'real jobs', whereas state intervention and job creation schemes under Labour had signally failed to prevent unemployment rising. Labour, in turn, countered by warning that a massive increase of unemployment in already depressed areas would be the inevitable result, if the Labour government's industrial policies were to be dismantled. The winter of discontent provided ammunition for both sides. The Conservatives took it as evidence of both the illusory nature of the Labour government's incomes policy and the need to legislate against abuse of trade union power. Labour argued that it demonstrated the anarchy that must be the result of the Conservatives' 'free for all' recipe; only Labour could reach the kind of understanding with the unions that could forestall confrontation in the future.

In the Liberal campaign, the goal of ending the 'dead-lock' created by the two-party system and the need for electoral reform were the central themes. The

Liberal party had its own profile on some issues – for example, incomes policy (where it was alone in proposing a policy 'enforced by law'). Otherwise it steered a middle course between the Conservatives and Labour on industrial and economic policy. It followed, from the political geometry so favoured by centre parties, that a strong Liberal 'wedge' in the next Parliament would insert a moderating influence on the big battalions to the left and to the right.

We obviously recorded some of the impact of the debate during the campaign in Chapter 6 when we explored the voters' opinions on how the country's problems had been handled by the Labour government – and on how well they could have been handled by a Conservative government. Similarly with our investigation of the voters' opinions on nationalisation and social welfare in the previous chapter. Although Labour said little about nationalisation, the issue was kept alive in the Conservative campaign. In a sense, the nationalisation issue always serves to epitomise the differences between the two parties' views on the proper role of the state in the economy. Party differences on social welfare, on the other hand, were left largely implicit in the Conservatives' campaign but were forced into the open through Labour's attacks on the Conservatives' pledge to cut taxes.

If these were perennial issues, then in 1979 – as in all elections – there were also some prominent issues which were defined by the positions the parties had taken in current policy proposals. These issues were also in an immediate sense concerned with policy making and policy choices in the next few years. Four of the issues we shall be concerned with here have to do with the economic and industrial debate that we have just referred to. These are the questions about taxation, the right approach for tackling unemployment, incomes policy, and the appropriate legal framework for regulating trade union activities. We shall also explore the divisions of opinions on two questions that were less prominent in the 1979 campaign but are of special interest for other reasons: Britain's relations with the EEC, and the problems of immigration and race relations in Britain. Britain's role in the EEC obviously involves economic policy questions, but its implications are much wider. In the 1979 election, the issue with regard to the EEC was no longer Britain's actual membership.[1] It was rather the Conservative criticism of the Labour government for its lack of wholehearted commitment to Europe and, more specifically, for its pursuit of Britain's interests in a manner that was so abrasive as to be counter-productive. The Conservatives, it was stressed, would achieve better results by conducting negotiations in a more European spirit, with more co-operativeness and trust. Immigration, as such, played a much smaller part in the campaign than many had expected (or feared). But it was inexorably (albeit often implicitly) linked to the problems of race relations in Britain and also the problems of law and order. And law and order was to some extent an issue in the 1979 election.

This chapter and the next explore how opinions on these issues were related to the voters' party choice in the 1979 election. The focus is on individuals' voting decisions. In Chapter 11 we shall examine the relative importance of each of these issues for the overall election result. The focus of our enquiry will be redirected in Chapters 12 and 13. Our concern in these chapters will be the electoral process. We shall continue to base our enquiry on data concerning individuals' opinions and perceptions of politics – but the aim is to throw light on the nature of the opinion bases of the parties, the preconditions for party strategies, and the relationship between such overall characteristics of the electorate and the voting changes that led to the Conservative victory in 1979.

The measures of issue opinions

Our survey measures of voters' opinions on the policy alternatives in the 1979 election consist of a series of interview questions devised to record both the voters' own policy preferences and their perceptions of what the two major parties actually stood for. It was intended, in these questions, to create a choice situation that was as realistic as possible in terms of the current party-political debate. To that end, each of the interview questions contained two statements which comprised different policy alternatives and in some instances also suggested different ways of looking at a given issue:

Tax reduction vs. government services

1. 'Taxes should be cut even if it means some reduction in government services such as health, education and welfare.'

2. 'Government services such as health, education and welfare should be kept up even if it means that taxes cannot be reduced.'

Best way to tackle unemployment

1. 'The best way to tackle unemployment is to allow private companies to keep more of their profits to create more jobs.'

2. 'It is mainly up to the Government to tackle unemployment by using tax money to create more jobs.'

How wages and salaries should be settled

1. 'The government should set firm guidelines for wages and salaries.'

2. 'The government should leave it to employers and trade unions to negotiate wages and salaries alone.'

Trade union legislation

1. 'There should be stricter laws to regulate the activities of trade unions.'

2. 'There is no call for stricter laws to regulate the activities of trade unions.'

EEC

1. 'Britain should be more willing to go along with the economic policies of other countries in the Common Market.'

2. 'Britain should be readier to oppose Common Market economic policies.'

Immigration and race relations

1. 'The first thing to do about race relations is to put a stop to all further immigration.'

2. 'The first thing to do about race relations is to tackle the problems of jobs and housing in the large cities.'

For most issues, it was possible to formulate statements that could easily be identified with either a Conservative or a Labour point of view. However, for reasons to be discussed later, quite as clearcut alternatives could not always be contrived. A third statement expressing lack of concern – 'it doesn't matter much either way', 'there is no need for a change', or a phrase of similar meaning – was also always included. The respondents were asked which one of the three statements came closest to their views. Respondents who agreed with one of the policy alternatives were asked: 'How strongly are you in favour of this statement: 1. very strongly, 2. fairly strongly, or 3. mildly in favour?' (The statements as well as response alternatives were also shown on a printed card.) This question format makes it possible to array respondents on a seven point scale of the kind shown below.

In favour of statement 1			It doesn't matter much either way		*In favour of statement 2*	
Very strongly	Fairly strongly	Mildly		Mildly	Fairly strongly	Very strongly

Having recorded the respondent's own opinion, the interviewer continued: 'And now we would like you to think about where the parties stand on this issue.' With the same question format, the respondent was then asked what the views of the Conservative and Labour parties were on the matter concerned. Using these responses we are thus able to locate each respondent's perceptions of the stands of the two major parties on the seven-point scale for each issue.[2]

It is to be expected that the more importance a person attaches to a policy choice, the more weight will his opinion on the issue carry for his voting decision. We therefore included in each of these series of questions an item asking those interviewed to tell us how important they considered the issue to be when they decided how to vote in the election.[3] We also asked whether they preferred any of the parties with regard to the issue concerned and, if so, which party that was. As we shall see, the answers to this question reflected not only individuals' 'objective' opinion positions, but also their general partisan sympathies.

The steps in the enquiry

(1) For a matter to become an issue in an election, it is a first requirement that the parties' policies are seen to differ. Starting from there, we begin with an exposition of the voters' views of what the parties stood for in 1979.

(2) In the next step of the enquiry, we will review the divisions of opinions on the main issues in the electorate and explore the relationships between the voters' policy preferences and their party choice. The tables in this section serve to outline how much support each of the two major parties had for the policies they advocated – in the electorate as a whole as well as among their own voters.

(3) From the voter's point of view, the choice in the election must often have been a matter of supporting the one of the parties whose stands on the issues appeared closest to his own views. On some of the issues, a voter might well have felt that he did not agree entirely with either of the parties but nevertheless was more in agreement with one of them. In the third step of the analysis we therefore make use of our data both on the individual policy preferences and on the perceptions of the positions of the parties on the issues. Voters' opinions on the issue are then defined in terms of the 'distances' between their own opinion positions and their perceptions of the parties' positions. We will thus be looking at the relationships between opinions and party choice from the individual voter's own point of view and in terms of his own appraisal of the choice situation.

(4) All issues are not of equal importance to all the voters, and some issues are regarded as important by larger portions of the electorate than others. In the concluding part of this chapter, we shall explore how the salience and the importance of the issues to the individuals operate as weighting factors in the making of voting decisions.

Our enquiry into the importance and impact of the policy alternatives will be continued in Chapters 10 and 11. What happens when parties change their positions or when the parties' positions on the issues are ambiguous? Chapter 10 explores further three issues on which there was room for both real uncertainty and different views on what policies the Conservatives and Labour were actually aiming to pursue: incomes policy, Britain's role in the EEC, and the questions of race relations and immigration. Chapter 11 goes on to a comprehensive analysis of the impact of issue opinions on voting change and party choice in the electorate as a whole. The chapter concludes with a summarising 'balance sheet', which will allow us to examine at once all of the opinion forces that contributed to the Conservative surge in the 1979 election. Our purpose is to answer two questions. Which were the issues that 'made the most difference' when people decided which party to vote for? On which issues was the balance of opinions in the electorate most decidedly weighted in favour of the Conservatives?

9.2 The electoral choice – as seen by the voters

What did the parties stand for in the 1979 election? An election offers the voters a choice between political parties rather than an opportunity to express their views on all the issues in the campaign. To the extent that a vote cast in an election means anything beyond an expression of trust in a party or an endorsement of a party's general aims, it is bound to be a vote for a package of policies. As we shall see, few voters actually cast a vote of deliberate support for the policies of their chosen party on all the issues; on some issues they had no firm opinions, and on others they disagreed outright with the party they voted for. It is part of the democratic process that it is for the individual to decide whether his or her opinion on a particular policy issue should count for much or little when deciding which party to support in the election. Yet, the extent to which voters hold realistic views of the meaning of the choice alternatives is an essential property of an election as a collective decision. The following mapping of the choice situation, as it was understood by the voters, therefore describes one important aspect of the representational function of the 1979 election. For our enquiry into the impact of the issues this mapping also serves another purpose: the proportion of the voters who were aware of any differences between the parties on each of the issues, and were informed about the nature of these differences, can be taken as one indicator (although not the only one) of the salience of the matter within the electorate.

As explained in the preceding section, the interview questions were designed with a view to set out the alternatives on the main policy issues in the 1979 election. In some instances we have perhaps made the choice situation more unambiguous than it might have appeared when the Conservative and Labour parties each presented their case in the campaign; to take just one example, both Labour and the Conservatives promised to reduce income tax, and both parties stressed that essential public services must be maintained. But the priorities were different. This is what we have endeavoured to capture in the two statements about tax reductions as well as in the other pairs of statements.

The data are set out in Table 9.1. In this instance, it is the voters' perceptions of the directions in which the two parties wanted to steer the country that is essential. For the sake of clarity, the table shows only the percentages of the voters who identified the parties with either side of the argument. With regard to three of the four economic policy choices, there was a near consensus in the electorate about the nature of the differences between the parties. More than seven voters in ten (72 per cent) believed that Labour would give priority to maintaining the standard of public services rather than cutting taxes, and nearly as many, 68 per cent, believed that the Conservatives were of the opposite view. Large majorities of around 80 per cent or more likewise believed that the Conservatives would rely on private industry to create more jobs and intended to enact stricter laws to regulate trade union activities. Almost as strong majorities thought that the Labour party took the view that the government must intervene to tackle unemployment and that Labour was opposed to further legal constraints on the rights of the unions.

There was much less agreement about where the parties stood on incomes policy, one may say for good reasons. Labour had come to power in the wake of the collapse of the Heath government's statutory incomes policy. But the Labour government's incomes policy had stopped only just short of being a return to the statutory model. After the failure of the social compact of 1974, it had endeavoured to steer the economy with the aid of government guidelines for wage settlements. Yet, although this was the strategy of the Labour government, it failed to win the confidence of the Labour party conference, and within the trade union movement the urge to restore 'free collective bargaining' was strong. The Conservatives, on the other hand, had gradually come around to Labour's position of 1974 (and, for that matter, to their own position back in 1970). The Conservatives now promised to put an end to state intervention in wage bargaining. There may be room for doubt as to whether the truth was revealed to any of the parties in the progress of these years, but they were certainly trekking in different directions. The result was the uncertainty about the parties' current positions which is reflected in our data: 58 per cent thought Labour was for government guidelines and 22 per cent thought the party was against; 48 per cent thought the Conservative party wanted to leave wage negotiations to employers and unions, while 34 per cent thought the party favoured firm governmental guidelines. It is therefore with some qualms that we have labelled the government-guidelines policy the 'Labour alternative' in the following discussion.

We find a similar lack of agreement about the Conservatives' and Labour's attitudes towards the economic policies of the EEC. The prevailing view amongst those who saw any difference between the parties was that the Conservatives wanted Britain to participate in the EEC in a more co-operative manner, whereas

Table 9.1 *What do the parties stand for?*
Voters' perceptions of the Conservative party's and Labour party's views on policy alternatives in the May 1979 election

Entries are the percentages of voters who thought that the views of the Conservative party and the Labour party, respectively, were closest to each of the two statements for each issue. The remainder up to 100% consists of respondents who didn't think the party favoured any of the alternatives or 'didn't know' what view the party had. Percentages are given separately for Conservative, Liberal and Labour voters as well as for all respondents.

Policy alternatives	Conservative voters		Liberal voters		Labour voters		All respondents	
	Conserv. party view	Labour party view	Conserv. party view	Labour party view	Conserv. party view	Labour party view	Conserv. party view	Labour party view
Tax cuts vs. government services								
Cut taxes	66%	11%	76%	8%	72%	12%	68%	12%
Keep up government services	25%	71%	16%	80%	15%	76%	20%	72%
Tackling unemployment								
Allow companies to keep profits to create more jobs	86%	4%	83%	6%	73%	13%	78%	8%
For government to use tax money to create jobs	7%	81%	9%	82%	11%	72%	9%	75%
How wages and salaries should be settled								
Firm government guidelines	39%	59%	30%	69%	35%	60%	34%	58%
Leave it to employers and unions to settle	52%	22%	54%	22%	47%	22%	48%	22%
Stricter laws to regulate trade union activities								
For stricter laws	92%	9%	86%	12%	83%	22%	86%	15%
Against stricter laws	1%	79%	4%	71%	4%	60%	4%	69%
EEC economic policies								
Britain should be more willing to go along with EEC economic policies	44%	21%	52%	22%	53%	21%	48%	21%
Britain should be readier to oppose EEC economic policies	33%	49%	29%	49%	23%	55%	28%	49%
Best way to improve race relations								
Stop further immigration	64%	7%	66%	7%	64%	13%	63%	10%
Tackle the problems of jobs and housing	19%	45%	13%	46%	13%	53%	16%	46%
Number of respondents	728	728	212	212	583	583	1871	1871

Data source: BES 1979 Election Survey.

Labour would be readier to be critical. That view was held by nearly half of our sample. But substantial minorities had the opposite impressions of the parties' positions (28 per cent in the case of the Conservative party, and 21 per cent in the case of Labour).

Our question about race relations in Britain is, at the same time, a question about immigration. The wording was designed to contrast two ways of looking at the presence of ethnic minorities in the community. One statement suggests that bad race relations are, primarily, the result of social inequities and proposes social reforms in urban areas as the best way to resolve them. The alternative statement points instead to immigration as the root cause of the problem; it suggests implicitly that no policies will work if the immigrant population is allowed to continue to grow.

Obviously, the policies of the two major parties cannot be summed up completely in two statements of this kind. The Labour government, for example, had already endeavoured to reduce the numbers of new immigrants, when the Conservatives were arguing for further restrictions. Nevertheless, the alternatives in the question would seem to capture the general tenor of the messages that the Conservatives and Labour were conveying.

As can be seen from the table, 63 per cent thought the Conservative party's view was closest to the 'stop immigration' alternative, whereas only 16 per cent identified the party with the contrary view. There was more uncertainty about Labour's stand. But 46 per cent felt that Labour would tackle the race relations problem by providing for jobs and housing in the cities, as against 10 per cent who thought that Labour would choose to stop immigration.

It has become apparent from this review that the differences between the parties did not stand out with equal clarity on all issues; there is always more or less room for different perceptions of party positions, and some voters simply do not know what one or both of the major parties stand for. This is not surprising, given that party positions are more ambiguous on some issues than on others, and that some issues attract more public attention than others. All the same, the parties did have easily recognised profiles on many of the most important policy issues, and on other issues there emerges at least a distinctive tendency for the two major parties to be associated with opposing policies.

9.3 The voters' views

What kinds of policies did the voters who cast their votes for the Conservatives, the Liberals or Labour actually want the next government to pursue? Which side of the argument on each of these issues had most support in the electorate? We already know that there was less – and, in some instances, much less – than full agreement in the electorate about what policy alternatives the two major parties actually were standing for. Hence, we could not expect to find any perfect correlations between voting and policy preferences, even if all voters had voted for

a party they believed they supported on all issues. And of course they did not.
Some voters supported a party in the election despite, rather than because of, its
policy in a particular area; others did not know what their chosen party stood
for, sometimes they may well not have thought much about the matter before
being asked about it in our interview. Yet, the following review of the relationships between opinions on policy alternatives and the voters' party choice
obviously describes a central element in the representative system of government.

The basic data are given in Table 9.2 which sets out the distribution of
opinions on each of the six policy issues within the electoral bases of the three
main parties as well as in the electorate as a whole. The overall pattern in this
table suggests that Conservative and Labour voters alike sided with their own
party's stand more often than did the supporters of other parties – but not over-
whelmingly so and with noteworthy exceptions. There were strong electoral
majorities in support of the Conservative view on the best ways of tackling unemployment and creating more jobs, and also on the need for stricter trade union
legislation. On these issues Conservative voters endorsed their party's view with
near unanimity. Labour voters were fairly evenly divided on both issues, but a
slight plurality actually came out in favour of the Conservatives' policies. When it
came to choosing between tax reduction or government services, on the other
hand, the majority of the electorate gave priority to public services. On that issue
it was the Labour voters who showed very strong support for their party's viewpoint, and even among Conservative voters the balance of opinion was in favour
of public services rather than tax reduction.

As we shall see later, these findings do not necessarily mean that Conservative
voters preferred Labour's policy on taxation. The situation in the campaign was
more ambiguous than that. After all, the Conservative party pledged that taxes
could be cut without any harm being done to public services. Yet, it is still noteworthy that most Conservative voters thought their party would cut taxes even
at the expense of public services, whilst they themselves indicated a different
personal preference.

On incomes policy, the EEC, and race relations, the electorate was clearly
divided, but not along the expected party lines. A bare majority of both Conservative and Labour voters were opposed to government control of wage settlements, but within both parties roughly one voter in three was in favour. Only
among Liberal voters were the two views about evenly balanced. As regards the
EEC, there was an all-party consensus that Britain should take a tougher line.
On race relations, about half the electorate, independently of party preference,
thought that putting an end to further immigration was the solution to the problem, whilst about one voter in three believed an effort to improve employment
and housing for coloured people was a better approach.

Table 9.3 is more elaborate. It shows the 'balance' of the two-party vote as
well as the Labour share of the vote within each of the categories on the seven-
point scales. The categories in the issue 'scales' are ordered so that the 'Labour'

Table 9.2 *Voters' views on policy alternatives at the May 1979 election*

This table presents, in a compact form, the division of opinions on the six policy issues. The table shows, for each interview question, the percentage in favour of each of the alternatives offered; the balance to 100% consists of respondents who have no preference for or do not support either alternative, or have given a 'don't know' answer. Percentages are given for each of the three major parties' voters separately as well as for all respondents.

Policy alternatives	Conservative voters	Liberal voters	Labour voters	All respondents
Tax cuts vs. government services				
Cut taxes	36%	20%	13%	25%
Keep up government services	51%	69%	77%	62%
Tackling unemployment				
Allow companies to keep profits and to create more jobs	81%	66%	41%	63%
Government to use tax money to create jobs	11%	13%	37%	22%
How wages and salaries should be settled				
Firm government guidelines	36%	45%	37%	37%
Leave it to employer and unions to settle	53%	41%	51%	50%
Stricter laws to regulate trade unions				
For stricter laws	90%	71%	47%	70%
Against stricter laws	5%	15%	32%	17%
EEC economic policies				
Britain should be more willing to go along with the economic policies of other countries in EEC	26%	17%	15%	20%
Britain should be readier to oppose EEC economic policies	58%	65%	66%	60%
Best way to improve race relations				
Stop further immigration	55%	50%	49%	51%
Tackle problems of jobs and housing	33%	38%	39%	36%

Data source: BES May 1979 Election Survey.

Table 9.3 *Relation of opinions on policy alternatives to vote in the May 1979 election*

Entries with plus or minus signs are the Conservative percentage of the vote minus the Labour percentage of the vote in each opinion category (Conserv.-Lab. balance). Entries followed by a % sign are the Labour percentage of the vote in each category (Labour %). Only Conservative, Liberal and Labour voters were included in these percentage calculations. The bottom row in the section for each issue gives the percentage distribution of responses for all the three main parties' voters. ('Doesn't matter' includes 'Don't know'.)

Policy alternatives	'Labour alternative'			'Doesn't matter'	'Conservative alternative'			
	1 Very strongly	2 Fairly strongly	3 Mildly	4	5 Mildly	6 Fairly strongly	7 Very strongly	
Tax cuts vs. government services								
Conserv.-Lab. balance	-26	-5	+17	+19	+61	+46	+49	
Labour %	56%	44%	33%	34%	15%	20%	21%	
Per cent distribution of opinions	23	29	11	12	5	10	10	100%
Tackling unemployment								
Conserv.-Lab. balance	-45	-44	-40	-27	+ 3	+30	+50	
Labour %	68%	68%	66%	54%	38%	27%	19%	
Per cent distribution of opinions	6	10	5	15	7	26	31	100%
*How wages & salaries should be settled**								
Conserv.-Lab. balance	- 4	+16	+11	+ 6	+36	+12	- 4	
Labour %	45%	33%	32%	39%	27%	38%	47%	
Per cent distribution of opinions	15	17	6	11	10	26	15	100%
Stricter laws to regulate trade unions								
Conserv.-Lab. balance	-81	-66	-30	-43	- 2	+20	+52	
Labour %	86%	76%	57%	64%	41%	32%	19%	
Per cent distribution of opinions	5	7	4	13	8	24	39	100%
*EEC economic policies***								
Conserv.-Lab. balance	- 7	+ 5	+26	+ 4	+31	+35	+26	
Labour %	46%	41%	28%	41%	27%	27%	33%	
Per cent distribution of opinions	26	26	10	17	6	10	5	100%
*Best way to improve race relations****								
Conserv.-Lab. balance	-22	+10	+27	+ 7	+35	+ 6	+15	
Labour %	54%	36%	31%	41%	24%	41%	36%	
Per cent distribution of opinions	30	15	7	11	7	17	13	100%

Notes
  *'Labour alternative': firm Government guidelines
 **'Labour alternative': Britain should be readier to oppose EEC economic policies
***'Labour alternative': tackle problems of jobs and housing

Data source: BES May 1979 Election Survey.

alternative is always in the columns to the left. When there is a systematic relationship between opinions and voting, this will thus appear in the form of an
increasingly pro-Conservative balance in the party division of the vote from left
to right within each row of the table.

In fact, such a relationship emerges with any clarity on only three issues: tax
reduction vs. public services, the best way to tackle unemployment and create
new jobs, and trade union legislation. We have seen already, in the previous
section, that these are also the issues on which there existed a generally accepted
view in the electorate of how the Conservative and Labour parties differed from
each other. No relationship appears in the case of incomes policy, only a slight
trickling in the case of the EEC, and almost none with regard to the best way of
handling race relations.

We have summarised these data, below, in correlation coefficients that indicate
the strength of the relationship between voting for the three main parties and the
voters' positions on the six seven-point scales of opinions on policy issues.[4] For
comparison we have included also the two policy issues discussed in the last
chapter, nationalisation and social services (marked with asterisks). As can be
seen from these coefficients, opinions on trade union legislation are nearly as
strongly correlated with voting as are the voters' opinions on nationalisation. The
questions concerning social services and benefits, the best way to create more
jobs, and tax reductions form a second group: the correlations with voting are,
by comparison, only moderately strong. For the three remaining issues (EEC,
race relations and incomes policy), only weak relationships, or none at all, can
be discerned. In the next section, we will investigate how these relationships are
affected when voters' perceptions of the parties' positions and the degree of
saliency of the issues are taken into account.

Issue	Correlations between voting and voters' issue opinions (7-point scales) (Kendall's Tau-b coefficient)
*1. Nationalisation	0.45
2. Stricter laws to regulate trade unions	0.41
3. Tackling unemployment and creating jobs	0.35
*4. Social services and benefits	0.28
5. Tax cuts vs. government services	0.25
6. EEC economic policies	0.11
7. Best way to improve race relations	0.07
8. How wages and salaries should be settled	0.00

9.4 Voters' opinions, perceptions of party positions and party choice

The data just described show how the divisions of opinions on political issues in the electorate were related to the party division of the vote. As we have stressed already, this is an essential relationship to explore from one point of view: it tells us something about the representation of opinions through voting for parties in a parliamentary election. But if we shift the emphasis of our enquiry to the complementary purpose of accounting for the way people vote in an election, it becomes clear that one important intermediary link is missing. We need to look at the voters' opinions in relation to their own perceptions of what the parties actually stood for.

The voter who can see no difference between the major parties on a particular issue is obviously not facing the same choice as a voter who thinks that their policies differ. Likewise, two voters who both wish to support the same policy may have different perceptions of which party is in favour of that policy and therefore come to support different parties. On the other hand, voters with very different policy preferences may end up supporting the same party, if they are acting under different impressions of that party's policy aims.

As will be recalled, our measures of opinions and perceptions of the parties' positions are such that the individual has indicated both his own view and the position he thinks the two major parties occupy on seven-point scales. We have made use of this property of the measurement tool for two analytical purposes. Firstly, we have constructed a classification which represents the individuals' perceptions of the parties' positions relative to each other. On the issue scales we can distinguish between a pro-Labour and a pro-Conservative side in terms of the parties' official policies. For simplicity's sake we will refer to the two sides of the scales as the one 'to the left' and the opposite, 'to the right', although this usage may be questionable in some instances (e.g. the EEC issue). This is not necessarily the way in which party positions are perceived by the voter, however, and obviously the meaning of the choice alternatives in the election looks very different if the voter's own picture is turned the other way round. The classification was constructed so as to distinguish between voters who placed the Labour 'to the left' of the Conservatives and those who placed Labour 'to the right' of the Conservatives on the scale. A third category consists of voters who saw no difference between the parties (placed them in the same point) or could not tell what view either or both of the parties had. The three response patterns represented by these categories are illustrated in Figure 9.A.

Our second classification pertains to the degree of proximity between an individual's own view and the position on the scale which he has given to each of the parties. For each of the issues, we obtain one category of voters who have placed themselves closest to Labour on the scale and another who placed themselves closest to the Conservatives. There will naturally be a third category, consisting of persons who are at the same distance from both parties, and there will also be a category of people who were unable to place one or both of the parties.

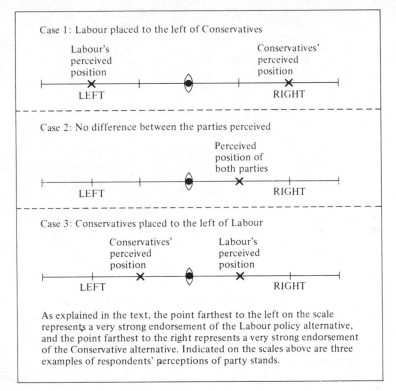

Figure 9.A

(The two last-mentioned groups are combined into one category in many of the analyses reported here.) We assume that, given the choice, the individual will prefer the party policy that he perceives to be closest to his own view on the relevant scale.[5] Figure 9.B illustrates how this classification was done. The classification is based entirely on the individual's own understanding of the choice he faces: if he is in favour of stricter regulation of trade unions and thinks the Labour party wants the same, whereas the Conservatives are against, then he is 'closest to Labour' in this classification. He may objectively be wrong, but in his own world it would be rational for him to vote for Labour if there were no other considerations involved.

The two classifications are combined in Table 9.4. We have included in this table and in the following analysis also the questions about nationalisation and 'social services and benefits' which were asked in a similar form (see Chapter 8). On most issues, as can be seen from the table, a substantial majority of voters did locate both of the parties and perceived their relative positioning in the way one would expect. The two notable exceptions are incomes policy and Britain's relationship with the EEC. Less than half the electorate, 48 per cent, had the

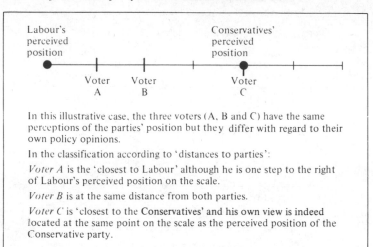

In this illustrative case, the three voters (A, B and C) have the same perceptions of the parties' position but they differ with regard to their own policy opinions.

In the classification according to 'distances to parties':

Voter A is the 'closest to Labour' although he is one step to the right of Labour's perceived position on the scale.

Voter B is at the same distance from both parties.

Voter C is 'closest to the Conservatives' and his own view is indeed located at the same point on the scale as the perceived position of the Conservative party.

Figure 9.B

impression that Labour was more in favour of government guidelines for wage settlements than were the Conservatives. Similarly, less than half, 47 per cent, had the impression that Labour was the more critical of the two parties towards the EEC. On both issues, a sizeable portion of the electorate had a 'reversed' view of the parties' standpoints. In addition a comparatively large portion of the electorate was unable to identify the parties' positions or saw no difference between them. The race relations issue is a borderline case: a majority of 61 per cent identified the Conservatives with a 'stop immigration' policy and Labour with a social reformist approach, but the proportion who either believed it was the other way round, or did not know where the parties stood, was substantial.

On the questions concerning the creation of jobs, trade unions, social services, and nationalisation, around 75 per cent or more of the voters placed the parties in the expected left and right positions, while 68 per cent did so in the case of the tax vs. public services issue. Although these majorities are quite large, it remains true that around a fifth of the electorate apparently have a poor grasp of the relationship between parties and policies, even with regard to prominent issues in a campaign.

Table 9.5 shows how Conservative, Liberal and Labour voters perceived the distances between their own opinion positions and the stands of the two major parties.[6] It is instructive to compare this table with the opinion distributions in Table 9.2. We found in Table 9.2 that, on most issues, there were substantial proportions of Conservative and Labour voters whose views differed from their parties' official policies. Table 9.5 not only confirms this but also demonstrates that many voters clearly recognised that they did not wholly agree with the policies of their parties. (The respondents were shown a card setting out the

Table 9.4 *Voters' perceptions of party positions relative to their own views on policy alternatives*

The column totals are not equal to 100%. The remainder to 100 consists of respondents who failed to locate both of the parties or placed them in the same position.

Perception of party positions and own position relative to parties	Tax cuts vs. govt. services	Tackling unemployment	How wages and salaries should be settled	Stricter laws to regulate trade unions	EEC economic policies	Best way to improve race relations	Social services*	Nationalis-ation*
	%	%	%	%	%	%	%	%
Respondents placing Labour 'to the left' of Conservatives on the scale: of whom:								
Own position closest to Labour	68	75	48	79	47	61	77	82
Same distance to both parties	42	18	16	19	29	22	25	13
Own position closest to Conservatives	5	6	2	5	4	4	11	13
	21	51	30	55	14	35	41	56
Respondents placing Labour 'to the right' of Conservatives on the scale: of whom:								
Own position closest to Labour	12	7	25	4	19	9	6	6
Same distance to both parties	3	4	11	2	3	4	2	4
Own position closest to Conservatives	1	1	2	1	3	1	1	1
	8	2	12	1	13	4	3	1
Total per cent	80%	82%	73%	83%	66%	70%	83%	88%

*See Chapter 8.
Data source: BES May 1979 Election Survey.

Table 9.5 *Party vote and perceived distance to party positions on policy alternatives*

This table comprises only voters who voted for one of the three main parties. The table shows, for each party, the percentage of voters who placed themselves closest to the perceived positions of the Labour Party and the Conservative Party, respectively, on each of the 'policy scales'. The remainder to 100% for the issue concerned consists of voters who could not place both of the parties, or were at the same distance to both parties, or had no opinion on the issue.

Policy issue	Party voted for in 1979		
	Conservatives	Liberals	Labour
Tax cuts vs. government services			
Closest to Labour	29%	54%	65%
Closest to Conservatives	44%	27%	11%
Tackling unemployment			
Closest to Labour	8%	18%	40%
Closest to Conservatives	77%	55%	29%
How wages and salaries should be settled			
Closest to Labour	14%	30%	42%
Closest to Conservatives	60%	41%	26%
Stricter laws to regulate trade union activities			
Closest to Labour	5%	21%	41%
Closest to Conservatives	82%	59%	28%
EEC economic policies			
Closest to Labour	22%	37%	45%
Closest to Conservatives	38%	29%	15%
Best way to improve race relations			
Closest to Labour	18%	30%	35%
Closest to Conservatives	49%	38%	31%
*Social services and benefits			
Closest to Labour	11%	28%	46%
Closest to Conservatives	65%	45%	22%
*Nationalisation			
Closest to Labour	3%	13%	34%
Closest to Conservatives	83%	54%	30%

*See Chapter 8.
Data source: BES May 1979 Election Study

response alternatives in such a way that any difference between their own opinion and that of their party actually became visually apparent.)

In some instances the picture changes significantly when the voters' perceptions of party positions are taken into account. These changes have mainly to do with divisions of opinions among Labour voters. Thus we now find that Labour voters were definitely more likely to be closer to the Labour party than to the Conservative party with regard to the best way of tackling unemployment, incomes policy and trade union legislation. In Table 9.2 the opposite appeared to be the case. To some extent, and notably in the case of incomes policy, the explanation is that some voters had actually reversed the parties' positions in their own perceptions. A less drastic but also important factor is that some Labour voters have placed themselves and their party at or near the midpoint of the seven-point scale, whilst projecting the Conservatives' position towards the extreme right on the scale. They did not exactly endorse their party's view, but were nevertheless nearer to Labour than to the Conservatives, or equidistant from the two.

The Conservatives had, in general, much stronger electoral support than Labour on the policy issues in the campaign. This emerges with great clarity also when the data are analysed in the 'closeness to parties' format, and especially so among the voters who saw the Labour party as occupying a position to the left of the Conservatives. As is shown by Table 9.4, the Conservatives had the edge over Labour on six of the eight issues in the table – indeed, on all but tax cuts vs. government services and the EEC.

Furthermore, on most of the policy issues Conservative voters sided more often with their party's view than Labour voters did with theirs. We have summarised the data by calculating the average proportion of respondents who were closest to the Conservative and Labour parties, respectively, on all of the eight issues taken together. On average, as is shown below, nearly two out of three (62 per cent) of Conservative voters sided with their own party, whereas this was true for only 44 per cent of Labour voters. We do not have entirely comparable data for the Liberal voters (because we did not record the perceived positions of the Liberal party), but it is interesting to note that Liberal voters sided with the Conservatives significantly more often than with Labour. In the electorate as a

Average percentages of voters who were closest to the Conservative and Labour parties on eight policy issues

Voters' policy opinions	Conservative voters	Liberal voters	Labour voters	All respondents
Closest to Conservatives	62%	44%	24%	43%
Closest to Labour	14%	29%	44%	27%

whole, an average of 43 per cent were closest to the Conservatives' positions, whereas 27 per cent were closest to Labour's. The difference is as good an indicator as any of the strength of the Conservatives' appeal in the 1979 election.

The relationship to voting

Measures of perceived 'distances to parties' yield stronger relationships to voting behaviour than the respondents' actual opinion positions. This comes as no surprise since the 'distance measures' were intended to record more precisely the choice situation perceived by the individual. The effect is summarised in Table 9.6. The table gives three sets of correlation coefficients for the relationship between issue opinions and voting for either of the three main parties. The first two columns comprise the entire sample and contain the coefficients for opinions measured by scale positions and opinions measured by distances to parties, respectively. The third column includes only those respondents who placed the Labour party 'to the left' of the Conservatives on the issue concerned.[7]

As the table shows, all relationships are strengthened when opinions are measured by distances to parties rather than by the original scales of opinion positions. The effect is striking in the case of opinions on incomes policy, which shows no relationship at all to voting until the data were converted into distance format. Fairly substantial correlations with voting also come to light for opinions on the EEC and race relations.

Among voters who perceived Labour as occupying a position 'to the left' of the Conservatives on a policy issue, the strength of the relationship between opinions and voting is consistently stronger, as is shown by the third column in the table. In most instances, the apparent explanation is that these are the voters with the best grasp of the policy issue concerned. We have, in effect, excluded a category of persons many of whom had little knowledge about the political context of the issue and possibly little interest in the matter.

There are two exceptions to this pattern. One is the race relations question and the other is incomes policy. In the case of race relations, the correlation with voting shown in the table is not very strong among those who placed Labour 'to the left' of the Conservatives (0.23) and it is, in fact, of the same magnitude among the small minority of voters who thought Labour was taking a tougher line than the Conservatives on immigration. Incomes policy is the more interesting case, given that as much as one fourth of the electorate believed that the Conservatives were the champions of government control over wage settlements. As we will see from the further analysis in Chapter 10, this was an issue on which the relationship to voting actually was stronger among the voters who had 'got it wrong' about the two major parties' current policy positions.

With the exception of incomes policy, the rank ordering of the issues with regard to the correlation coefficients comes out as almost exactly the same, irrespective of how the relationship between opinions and voting is measured. If we

Table 9.6 *The relation of opinions on policy issues to voting for the three main parties*

Entries are correlation coefficients (Kendall's Tau-b) calculated with reference to voting as explained in the text.

Policy issue	Correlation coefficients		
	Opinion positions	Distances to parties	Left/right perceptions of parties: Distances to parties:*
1. Nationalisation†	0.45	0.48	0.52
2. Stricter laws to regulate trade unions	0.41	0.47	0.52
3. Tackling unemployment/ creating jobs	0.35	0.42	0.46
4. Social services and benefits†	0.28	0.39	0.44
5. Tax cuts vs. government services	0.25	0.33	0.40
6. How wages and salaries should be settled	0.00	0.32	0.34
7. EEC economic policies	0.11	0.24	0.33
8. Best way to improve race relations	0.07	0.19	0.23

*As explained in the text, this column includes only respondents who placed Labour 'to the left' of the Conservatives on the appropriate policy scale; see Table 9.4.
†See Chapter 8.

Data source: BES May 1979 Election Survey.

take this connection between individuals' opinions and their voting as our criterion on which to judge the relative importance of the issues in the election, these data yield therefore a distinctive rank-ordering of the issues. Nationalisation and stricter laws to regulate the trade unions emerge again as the issues most strongly connected with party choice in 1979. A second group is formed by the questions about the best strategy to tackle unemployment and create new jobs, social services, and the choice between tax reductions and maintaining the standard of government services. Opinions on incomes policy and the EEC show comparatively weaker correlations to voting even when opinions are measured by 'distances to parties'. Finally, race relations and immigration come at the bottom of the list in this rank-ordering.

The influence of party sympathy: looking at the issues through tinted glasses

There is an alternative way of exploring how voters' party choices are linked to their opinions on policies. It may even look like a more direct approach at first sight. That is, those interviewed can be asked which party, if any, they prefer when it comes to dealing with the various policy problems that have become issues in the election campaign. As mentioned before, questions of that kind concluded each of our eight question series about current policy alternatives.

The response distributions, by party vote in the 1979 election, are presented in Table 9.7. Answers to questions of this type are likely to be quite distinctively coloured by the individual's general party sympathy at the moment. It is one thing to express a view which is at variance with a policy proffered by the party one votes for; it is quite another to admit that one actually prefers the policy of another party. The first observation one must make when inspecting the table is that the data bear out this expectation with regard to Conservative and Labour voters but, interestingly, not with regard to Liberal voters. Liberal voters did indeed say that they preferred the Liberal party more often than did the Conservative or Labour voters. Yet, Liberal voters mentioned one or other of the major parties more often than their own. One reason may be that many Liberal voters have taken only temporary shelter in the Liberal fold because of dissatisfaction with the party they normally vote for. Another, and perhaps more important, reason may be that the predominance of the two major parties is such that even Liberal voters often found it natural to think of Conservative and Labour policies as the real alternatives. A third reason why the Liberals were mentioned so infrequently may simply be that the party's policy stands were not well known.[8]

Among Conservative and Labour voters, large majorities of those who expressed any preference at all are found, on every single issue, to prefer the party they voted for. Even if those who had no preference are taken into account, the predominance of preferences for the voters' own party is clearly more marked than one would have expected on the basis of our measures of distances to perceived party positions. In some instances, the increase in explicit support for the voter's own party is quite drastic, as may be found by comparing Table 9.7 with Table 9.5. For example, 72 per cent of Conservative voters said they preferred the Conservatives on taxes, whilst only 44 per cent were 'closest to the Conservatives' on the policy scale. Likewise, 63 per cent of Labour voters said they preferred Labour when it came to dealing with unemployment and creating jobs, while only 40 per

Table 9.7 *Voters' preferred party on policy issues 1979*

Issue and preferred party on each issue	Conservative voters	Liberal voters	Labour voters	All respondents
Tax cuts vs. government services				
PREFER:	%	%	%	%
Conservatives	72	22	8	38
Liberals	1	20	1	4
Labour	4	26	65	30
No preference*	23	32	26	28
Total per cent	100%	100%	100%	100%
Tackling unemployment				
PREFER:	%	%	%	%
Conservatives	74	28	9	40
Liberals	1	16	1	3
Labour	3	21	63	28
No preference*	22	35	27	29
Total per cent	100%	100%	100%	100%
How wages and salaries should be settled				
PREFER:	%	%	%	%
Conservatives	69	22	9	37
Liberals	1	17	1	3
Labour	4	20	55	25
No preference*	26	41	35	35
Total per cent	100%	100%	100%	100%
Stricter laws to regulate trade union activities				
PREFER:	%	%	%	%
Conservatives	84	38	14	49
Liberals	1	18	1	3
Labour	1	13	54	22
No preference*	14	31	31	26
Total per cent	100%	100%	100%	100%
EEC economic policies				
PREFER:	%	%	%	%
Conservatives	52	15	9	29
Liberals	1	20	1	4
Labour	7	23	49	25
No preference*	40	42	41	42
Total per cent	100%	100%	100%	100%
Best way to improve race relations				
PREFER:	%	%	%	%
Conservatives	56	30	19	37
Liberals	1	14	1	3
Labour	3	13	32	16
No preference*	40	43	48	44
Total per cent	100%	100%	100%	100%
***Social services and benefits*				
PREFER:	%	%	%	%
Conservatives	56	20	8	31
Liberals	2	21	1	4
Labour	6	22	60	29
No preference*	36	37	30	36
Total per cent	100%	100%	100%	100%
***Nationalisation*				
PREFER:	%	%	%	%
Conservatives	81	37	12	46
Liberals	1	19	3	4
Labour	1	15	52	21
No preference*	17	29	33	29
Total per cent	100%	100%	100%	100%

*The 'no preference' category includes a small proportion who mentioned a minor party.
**See Chapter 8.

Interview question: 'And when it comes to the question of . . . do you prefer any of the parties?' (If yes:) 'Which party?'.

Data source: BES May 1979 Election Survey.

cent were 'closest to Labour' on the 'distance' measurement. Most of the discrepancies are smaller, but still substantial. The average increase in support for one's own party is 7 percentage units, and the average decrease in support for the opposite party is 9 percentage units.

It is as though individuals were looking at the issues and the parties' policies through tinted spectacles with the effect of making the party one sympathises with look a bit better and the opposite party a bit worse.[9] When there was a conscious conflict between individuals' policy opinions and their party sympathies (or antipathies), they apparently sometimes resolved it by stating that they preferred none of the parties. It is all the more noteworthy that the proportions of all Conservative and Labour voters preferring their own party were fairly moderate on some issues. Not much more than half of the Conservative voters said they preferred their own party on social services (56 per cent), the EEC (52 per cent), or race relations (56 per cent). Among Labour voters the proportion preferring the Labour party was less than 60 per cent on five of the eight issues; the exceptions being social services and benefits, priority for public services over tax cuts, and tackling unemployment through government intervention.

Not having a party preference on an issue may mean that one does not know what the parties stand for, or that one can see no difference between them, or even that one simply does not care. Whatever the reasons some voters may have for not preferring the policy of any party, the proportion of individuals in the electorate who do prefer one party over the others can be taken as *one* indicator of an issue's electoral importance (although not the only one). That is, the larger the proportion of the voters who prefer one of the party's policies on an issue, the larger the number of voting decisions that can be affected by such preferences. Britain's role in the EEC and race relations stand out as the two least important issues in 1979 if we apply this criterion. More than 40 per cent of the voters said they preferred none of the parties on these questions.

One conclusion that can be drawn from our analysis of party preferences is that these responses are less useful than the 'distance to parties' measures, when the purpose is to gauge how public opinion is divided on the substance of the issues. This is so because the distance measures are less influenced by the voters' general partisanship. Our analysis of party preferences on issues is of interest, rather, because of the light it throws on the cognitive processes that reduce the likelihood that the individual will, subjectively, experience any incongruity between his policy opinions and his voting intention. For the individual, such processes serve to strengthen his sense of having made the right choice among the parties. The tendency for issue preferences to be coloured by partisanship will thus, by itself, help to sustain partisanship.

The main difference between the results obtained from the party preference questions and from the 'distance' measures is that the divisions of opinions will look more partisan within parties. In other respects the two types of measurements lead to much the same inferences. This is brought out quite clearly when one calculates the average percentages of voters who preferred the Conservatives and Labour on all of the eight issues, as we have done below. The *differences* between the two percentages are especially informative when compared with the corresponding differences for the average on the distance measures.

As is shown below, both types of measures indicate that the Conservative voters supported their own party's policy positions much more consistently than did the Labour voters. The overall balance in the electorate as a whole comes out as almost the same with both types of measures (the partisan tendencies in response to party preference questions cancel out each other). Both types of data indicate that the Conservatives' policy alternatives had a broader support than Labour's in the electorate.

Our mapping of the balance of opinions on each of the issues in this and the preceding chapters has provided us with a foundation on which we shall build further in Chapters 11 to 13. One aspect of individuals' voting decisions remains to be explored, however. So far, we have examined the role of voters' perceptions of party standpoints as a connecting link between their opinions and their way of voting. Now, we shall be concerned with the voters' rating of the importance of the issues.

Average support for the parties on eight policy issues

Voters' policy opinions	Conservative voters	Liberal voters	Labour voters	All respondents
Average per cent preferring the Conservatives	68%	27%	11%	38%
Average per cent preferring Labour	4%	19%	54%	25%
Difference	+64	+ 8	−43	+13
*Distance measures: Average percentages**				
'Closest to Conservatives' *minus* 'Closest to Labour'	+48	+15	−20	+16

*Based on data on p. 215.

A + sign in the difference rows indicates stronger support
for the Conservatives; a − sign indicates stronger support for Labour.

9.5 The voters' views on the importance of the issues

All issues are not equally important to all voters. Individuals do their own weight-ing of the matters that bear upon their voting decisions. No analysis model could replicate all the variations in these individual voting decisions. What we can do, however, is to specify conditions that are likely to affect the strength of the relationship between the individual's opinions on political matters and his party choice. If voters' ratings of the importance of the various questions on the politi-cal agenda affect their voting decisions, one would expect a stronger relationship between issue opinions and voting among those who consider a given issue important than among those who are less concerned.

The voters' views on the importance of the issues in the campaign were re-corded through a question asked towards the end of the series of questions about each of the issues. Those interviewed were asked how important they rated the matter at the time when they 'were deciding about voting'. Table 9.8A shows the percentages of voters who rated each of the policy issues as 'extremely important' and also the percentages who considered it either 'extremely' or 'fairly import-ant'. (The remainder to 100 per cent are those who said it was 'not very import-ant' or 'did not know'.) The table bears out our previous observations about two of the issues: Britain's relationship with the EEC and race relations. We have noted already that opinions on these questions showed only weak correlations to voting and also that the number of voters who said they did not prefer any of the parties were especially large on these issues. Likewise, when we asked about party positions on issues, Britain's relations with the EEC was the one that showed the largest percentage of voters seeing no difference between the parties or unable to tell what policy each stood for. As Table 9.8A shows, these two issues were rated as 'extremely' or 'fairly important' less often than the others. In general, however, there is only a feeble relationship between the proportion rating an issue as 'extremely important' and the strength of the correlation be-tween opinions and voting. The issues are ordered in the table according to the strength of that correlation, and it is readily apparent that a rank ordering with regard to ratings of importance would look quite different.[10] For example, the nationalisation issue, which showed a strong correlation with party choice, is rated as 'extremely important' by only 19 per cent of the voters.

It is all the more noteworthy that individuals' ratings of the importance of an issue emerge as a powerful mediating (or intervening) factor when we look at the relationships between opinions and voting for each policy issue separately.[11] As can be seen from the columns on the left side of Table 9.8A, the strength of the correlations between opinions and voting increases regularly with increases in the importance rating for all of the issues but one. In most instances the in-crease is quite sharp. Opinions on nationalisation, for example, show a rise from 0.38 to 0.60 from the lowest to the highest level of importance ratings, and for opinions on tax reduction there is an increase from 0.25 to 0.44. Among the

Table 9.8A *Opinions on policy issues, rating of the importance of issues, and party vote*

Issues	Correlation of issue opinion to vote				Per cent considering the issue 'extremely' important	Per cent considering the issue either 'extremely' or 'fairly' important
	Issue rated as:					
	Extremely important	Fairly important	Not very important	All respondents		
Policy alternatives						
1. Nationalisation	0.60	0.55	0.38	0.48	19%	51%
2. Stricter laws to regulate trade union activities	0.62	0.47	0.38	0.47	23%	63%
3. Tackling unemployment	0.46*	0.41*	0.46*	0.42*	33%*	71%*
4. Social services	0.51	0.41	0.36	0.39	23%	63%
5. Tax cuts vs. government services	0.44	0.33	0.25	0.33	33%	78%
6. How wages and salaries should be settled	0.42	0.37	0.28	0.32	25%	69%
7. EEC economic policies	0.47	0.31	0.11	0.24	17%	52%
8. Best way to improve race relations	0.36	0.24	0.14	0.19	14%	46%

Notes:
Correlation coefficients are (Kendall's Tau-b) calculated with reference to three-party vote. Opinion measures are in 'distance to parties' format.
*The importance question was asked in connection with the questions about the parties' handling of the problem of unemployment.
Interview question: 'When you were deciding about voting, how important was this question . . . (issue) – extremely important, fairly important, or not very important?'
Data source: BES May 1979 Election Survey.

Table 9.8B *The parties' handling of major problems: rating of importance and party vote*

Voters' assessments of Conservatives' and Labour's handling of:	Correlation of issue opinion to vote*				Per cent considering the issue 'extremely' important	Per cent considering the issue either 'extremely' or 'fairly' important
	Issue rated as:					
	Extremely important	Fairly important	Not very important	All respondents		
Prices	0.60	0.48	0.41	0.52	41%	79%
Strikes	0.53	0.52	0.43	0.51	38%	74%
Unemployment	0.56	0.56	0.39	0.51	33%	71%
Law and order	0.44	0.34	0.25	0.39	42%	77%

Note:
*The opinion measures are the 'rating' classifications described in Chapter 6. Correlations are calculated with reference to three-party vote (Kendall's Tau-b).
Data source: BES May 1979 Election Survey.

voters who rate an issue as extremely important, we find substantial correlations in all instances. It is especially notable that the correlation of voting with opinions on the EEC rises to 0.47 among those who consider it 'extremely important', whereas it is only 0.11 amongst those who consider the matter 'not very import-ant'.

The issues we have discussed so far have all posed choices between policy alternatives. In Chapter 6 we reviewed a series of opinion questions which instead were focused upon the voters' assessment of the Conservatives' and Labour's ability to handle some of the major problems the country was facing. These questions were stated in broad terms so that there could hardly be any disagree-ment about the desirability of the goals. Presumably almost everyone must agree, for example, that any government should strive to bring down inflation and maintain law and order. The question is rather: which party is more capable of achieving the goals?[12] Table 9.8B shows how such assessments of the parties were affected by the individuals' rating of the importance of the issues. Since we are now concerned with voters' evaluations of each party's record, it comes as no surprise that the responses show quite high correlations with party choice. (We have observed this already in Chapter 6.) It is not surprising, either, that quite large numbers of voters rated problems such as rising prices, strikes, unemploy-ment and upholding law and order as important.[13] However, as can be seen from the table, there is virtually no relationship between the percentages of voters who rated each of these issues as 'extremely important' and the strength of the cor-relations between opinions and voting. Law and order, for example, was con-sidered extremely important a little more often than the other problems, but opinions on that issue show the weakest correlation to voting. Yet, in the same way as we have observed before, individuals' views on the importance of each of these four problems affect the strength of the relationship between voting and assessments of the parties, although the tendency is somewhat weaker than in our battery of position-issue questions.

We have thus found that the correlation between voting and opinions on a political issue, almost without exception, increases with increasing rating of the importance of that issue. Yet, when comparing correlations and importance ratings in the entire sample for several issues, we found only a slight tendency for issues with high importance ratings to show comparatively high correlations be-tween voting and opinions. Why is that? Apparently, the correlation between voting and opinions on an issue is not *only* dependent on the importance of the issue in the sense that importance is measured by our interview question. It is likely that individuals, when they answered the importance rating questions, were often thinking of how much attention a particular issue attracted during the campaign or how heated the debate between the parties had been. We have thus measured 'importance' in the sense of *saliency*. But a party's position on an issue can also be more or less important in the sense that it is seen as a more or less *decisive reason* for voting or not voting for it, independently of whether the issue was seen to play a prominent role in the campaign. To take nationalisation as an example, no major nationalisation proposal was put forward in the election campaign, and this may be the reason why not many voters thought it was a very important issue at the time when they made their voting decisions. But someone who was strongly opposed to nationalisation would, nevertheless, be comparatively unlikely to consider voting for Labour, and we will therefore find a strong correlation between issue opinions and voting at all levels of salience rating. The degree of 'decisiveness' will be different for different issues. The salience of an issue to individuals will then have the function of a weight factor: it will amplify the correlation between opinions and voting among the voters for whom the issue is salient.[14] When the level of salience for a particular issue is high in the electorate as a whole, the correlation between opinions and voting with regard to that particular issue will thus become higher *than it otherwise would have been* for that issue – but not necessarily higher than the correlation for a less salient issue; this would depend on the relative 'decisiveness' of the issues concerned. Hence, we did not find any simple rank-order relationship between the percentages of voters to whom the various issues appeared 'extremely important' (i.e. salient) and the correlations between voting and opinions.

9.6 Campaign strategies and the salience of the issues

The effect of salience on the relationship between opinions and voting has interesting implications for changes over time. In each election there will be some new issues, and some old ones will appear in a new light because of alterations in the circumstances. The salient issues will not be the same from one election to the next. The whole question of the legal regulation of trade union activities, for example, is certainly not a new issue but it took on much more significance in the late 1970s than in the 1950s or mid 1960s. The degree of importance that individuals attach to social and economic problems – such as inflation, unemployment, or race relations – will likewise vary, even though the problems in some sense have been and will be with us for a long time. For any given issue, the strength of the correlation between voting and opinions will increase if the overall salience of the issue increases from one election to the next; likewise the correlation will decrease when the perceived importance of the issue declines.

The issues that come to the fore in an election campaign are likely to acquire more importance as determinants of voting behaviour than they would have had under other circumstances. It follows that it is advantageous for a party (as politicians have, of course, always known) to try to focus the attention in a campaign on the issues on which the underlying 'balance of opinions' is favourable. If it succeeds, the strategy will give more people reasons for casting their votes for the party. The strategy can be frustrated, however, if the balance of opinions changes when more people take more interest in a policy question. There is some indication in the data that this is what happened to the Conservative party with regard to the inflation issue and to the Labour party with regard to the unemployment issue in the 1979 campaign. Rising prices would normally be held against the party in office but, as we have seen, Labour seems to have been comparatively successful in defending its record. On the other hand, in the past it has always been assumed that unemployment is a good issue for the Labour party to emphasise *vis-à-vis* the Conservatives. But in 1979 trust in the Labour party's ability to maintain full employment had declined, and the party evidently failed to persuade the electorate that its policies held better prospects for the future than the Conservatives' strategy of cutting taxes and encouraging private enterprise.

Despite the voters' willingness to give Labour credit for its efforts to keep inflation down, the general picture that emerges from the data is one of a campaign in which the Conservatives had more support than Labour on almost all the issues that involved a choice between policy alternatives. Indeed the Conservatives did not only have the edge over Labour in the electorate as a whole; as we have seen, they also had more support for their policies among Conservative voters than Labour had for its policy positions among Labour voters.

On three of these issues, comparatively large proportions of the electorate seem to have had difficulty in finding their bearings – incomes policy, Britain's role in the EEC, and race relations. The positions of the parties were apparently less easily recognisable on the incomes policy and EEC issues than on other issues. The EEC and race relations were considered important issues by comparatively small proportions of the electorate. And a large proportion of the voters did not think there was much to choose between the parties with regard to race relations. As a result, different parts of the electorate responded distinctly differently to these issues; the strength of the relationship between opinions and voting depended on perceptions of party positions, or the salience of the issue, or a combination of these factors. In the next chapter we will explore each of these three special cases in more depth.

10

Ambiguity and change in party positions: three special cases

In this chapter we return to a question posed when we outlined the steps of our enquiry in Chapter 9: what happens to the linkage between opinions on an issue and voting behaviour, when parties change their positions, or when the parties' stands on the issue are ambiguous or not readily distinguishable?

We have seen already that an individual's opinions on political issues, his perceptions of what the parties stand for and his overall party preference (as expressed in his way of voting) are all more or less interdependent elements in his political outlook. That interdependence is especially clearly illustrated by the incomes policy issue in the 1979 campaign. In the case of Britain's role in the EEC, we found that the relationships between party choice and opinions differed markedly among voters with different degree of interest in the issue. On the question of race relations, finally, many were uncertain about the policies of the parties or saw no difference, and a large portion of the voters did not feel that they preferred any of the parties' handling of that question. We shall now take a closer look at the state of opinion on each of these three issues.

10.1 Incomes policy

Nearly half of the electorate, as we have seen, thought that Labour was more in favour of government guidelines for wage settlements than were the Conservatives (see Table 9.4). We found a marked tendency, within that part of the electorate, for voters to vote for the party whose policy they took to be closest to their own view; the correlation coefficient was 0.34. However, one voter in four had the opposite impression of the parties' stands on incomes policy; these voters believed it was the Conservatives, rather than Labour, who were the advocates of an incomes policy imposed by the government. In that part of the electorate, there was actually an even stronger tendency for voters to cast their votes for the party whose policy they felt closest to; the correlation between opinions on the issue and voting was 0.45. This is as far as we went in the preceding chapter. We shall now examine in more depth the relationship between opinions on policies and party choice in the two sectors of the electorate which held such opposing views as to the positions of the two main parties on incomes policy.

Firstly, the voters' own policy preferences and their impressions of their own party's view on incomes policy were interdependent to some degree. One way of describing this relationship is to say that Conservative voters who themselves were in favour of incomes policy were more likely than others to believe that this was indeed the Conservative party's position on the matter, and those who were against were also particularly likely to believe that this was what the Conservative party stood for. The same relationship holds true (but somewhat less markedly) for Labour voters' opinions and impressions of the Labour party's stand on the issue.[1] When looked at from another angle, this relationship also means that the voters' opinions on incomes policy was – to some degree – dependent on what they thought their own party was standing for. In all probability this is a two-way relationship: individuals' policy preferences affect their beliefs about the policy of the party they support but, equally, the stand taken by their own party influences their policy opinions to some extent. Bearing this interdependence in mind helps to understand the pattern that emerges in Tables 10.1A–B which presents the relevant data in two different perspectives.

In Table 10.1A the three main parties' voters are divided into two sub-categories: those who thought Labour was most in favour of government guidelines for wage settlements and those who rather thought it was the Conservatives (the columns in the table). The table shows how each of the six categories thus obtained were divided with regard to the distances between the voters' own positions and the perceived stands of the Labour party and the Conservative party. We now find that a large majority of the Conservative voters held opinions that were closest to the Conservative party's stand as they perceived it irrespective of whether the Conservatives were seen to be for or against government guidelines (although the majority is a little stronger among those who thought their party was against).

The underlying mood in the electorate was marked by disenchantment with the last year's incomes policy. This shows up very clearly in the data for Labour voters. Labour voters who believed that the Conservative party was the one most in favour of government guidelines gave a strong support for free collective bargaining which they took to be the Labour view on the matter. Most Labour voters, however, had a more accurate perception of the current party positions; among these voters only a bare majority supported what they took to be the party line.

Among Liberal voters, perceptions of the two major parties' standpoints appear to make little difference. This may be reasonable enough, but there is

Table 10.1A *Relation of opinion on incomes policy to voters' party choice in the election and perceptions of party positions on the issue*

Party voted for	Voted Conservative		Voted Liberal		Voted Labour	
Perception of party positions	Party considered most in favour of government guidelines		Party considered most in favour of government guidelines		Party considered most in favour of government guidelines	
	Labour party	Conservative party	Labour party	Conservative party	Labour party	Conservative party
	%	%	%	%	%	%
Own view on incomes policy						
Closest to Labour	15	23	41	35	51	73
Same distance to both parties	4	8	7	5	5	6
Closest to Conservatives	81	69	52	60	44	21
Total per cent	100%	100%	100%	100%	100%	100%
Number of respondents	387	181	121	40	276	141

Data source: BES May 1979 Election Survey.

Table 10.1B *Relation of voting to perceptions of party positions and the voters' opinions on incomes policy*.

Perceptions of party positions	Labour seen to be more in favour of government guidelines than the Conservatives			Conservatives seen to be more in favour of government guidelines than the Labour party		
Voters' position	Closest to perceived Labour stand	Same distance to both parties*	Closest to perceived Conservative stand	Closest to perceived Conservative stand	Same distance to both parties*	Closest to perceived Labour stand
	%	%	%	%	%	%
Party voted for:						
Conservatives	24	42	63	70	56	26
Liberals	20	22	12	14	8	9
Labour	56	36	25	16	36	65
Total per cent	100%	100%	100%	100%	100%	100%
Number of respondents	250	36	498	179	25	158

*This category includes also respondents who expressed no personal view ('Don't know') on the issue.

Data source: BES May 1979 Election Survey.

on the other hand no indication that the Liberal party's pleading for a statutory incomes policy had any appreciable impact.

Table 10.1B displays the same data from a different angle. The left-hand section of the table comprises voters who thought the Labour party was more in favour of a government incomes policy than the Conservative party. The right-hand table section comprises the voters who had perceived the reversed picture of party standpoints. There is a substantial (though not very strong) relationship between perceived distances to parties and voting within both of the table sections. Irrespective of which picture of the parties' standpoints the voters beheld, those who thought they were closest to the Conservatives were most likely to vote Conservative, and those who believe they were closest to Labour were most likely to cast their votes for Labour. But cognitions of the real world in the two parts of the table are mirror images of each other; what is 'to the left' in one picture is 'to the right' in the other.

A comparison between the two parts of the table shows that the tendency to vote for the party seen to be closest to the voters' own views is slightly more marked among those who thought of incomes policy as a Conservative policy; this is why the correlation coefficient for the relationship between opinions and voting was stronger for those voters. These voters responded, in effect, to a world in which Mr Heath's government was still in office with Labour calling for an end to incomes policy, in opposition.

The incomes policy issue is also a good example to illustrate in more detail how the voters' general party sympathies colour their judgements on which party's policy they actually prefer. The data are given in Table 10.2.

The top section of the table displays the relationship between distance to parties and party preferences on incomes policies for everyone who voted for one of the three main parties. As is seen from these percentage distributions, there is a fair proportion who do not actually prefer any of the parties and, as one would expect, that proportion is particualarly large among those whose own views are 'at the same distance' from both of the major parties. For voters who do have a party preference on the issue, we find a reassuringly strong relationship between the two measurements.[2]

The import of the voter's overall party sympathy, on the other hand, is clearly brought out in the separate sections of the table for Conservative and Labour voters. If their own views on the policy issues were closest to the perceived position of the party they voted for, then, naturally, a very large majority supported that party on the issue preference question. But even when the 'distance' measure indicates that voters actually disagreed with their party, a quite large proportion still stated that they preferred the policy of the party they voted for. Only a minority would say that they preferred the other major party; instead they tended to say that they did not prefer any party. Conservative and Labour voters who were 'at the same distance' from both parties are, as one would expect, particularly likely to say they did not prefer any party on the

Table 10.2 *Opinions on how wages and salaries should be settled: relation of 'Distance to Parties' to issue party preference by vote*

Vote and party preference on the issue	Relation of respondent's view to perceived party positions		
	Closest to Labour	Same distance to both parties	Closest to Conservatives
All three-party voters			
PREFER:	%	%	%
Conservatives	13	20	62
Liberals	5	4	2
Labour	54	24	11
No preference*	28	52	25
Total per cent	100%	100%	100%
Voted Conservative			
PREFER:	%	%	%
Conservatives	44	50	81
Liberals	1	0	1
Labour	20	6	0
No preference*	35	44	18
Total per cent	100%	100%	100%
Voted Liberal			
PREFER:	%	%	%
Conservatives	4	12	45
Liberal	27	15	11
Labour	42	14	9
No preference*	27	59	35
Total per cent	100%	100%	100%
Voted Labour			
PREFER:	%	%	%
Conservatives	4	4	24
Liberals	1	1	1
Labour	74	44	44
No per cent	21	51	31
Total per cent	100%	100%	100%

*'No preference' category includes a small number of respondents who mentioned a minor party.

Data source: BES May 1979 Election Survey.

incomes policy issue; but there was also a strong tendency to express a preference for the party one had voted for.

Liberal voters, however, are strikingly different. As we have noted earlier,
Liberal voters show no strong propensity to prefer the Liberal party on any
given issue, although, of course, they prefer the Liberal party more often than
do Conservative and Labour voters. The real difference is, however, that Liberal
voters' response distributions are not affected by any predominant sense of
loyalty to either of the two major parties. To the extent that they state a preference for either of the two major parties on incomes policy, therefore, their
responses reflect quite closely their perceived distances to these two parties.
This is the kind of relationship we would have expected to find also among
Conservative and Labour voters, had they not looked at the issues through
the tinted glasses of their party sympathies.

Since the time of the Heath government positions of the two major parties
on incomes policy had been reversed. What we have observed here, in the case
of Conservative and Labour votes, can best be understood as the joint effect
of the new signals from the parties and the voters' experiences of previous
attempts to pursue an incomes policy. When asked about their own positions,
a majority of both Conservative and Labour voters who had a view on the
matter were against a government-run incomes policy, while minorities of
about a third of the Conservative and Labour voters were in favour (see Table
9.2). We have seen that voters of both parties who were informed about the
parties' current standpoints were more inclined to side with their own party.
Still, only a bare majority of these well-informed Labour voters supported an
incomes policy (Table 10.1A). Among both Conservative and Labour voters,
party loyalty helped to increase the number of voters who felt they preferred
their own party's view on incomes policy. But party loyalty has its limits.
Some voters switched to another party.

If opinions on incomes policy contributed to party switching in 1979, one
would expect the defection rate among each party's voters in October 1974
to be higher among voters who disagreed with their 1974 party's current policy.
To establish whether this was the case we have undertaken an analysis of the
relationship between voting change 1974 – 1979 and opinions on incomes
policy in 1979. Since very few voters in our sample switched from Conservative
voting in October 1974 to Labour in May 1979, we have included in this
detailed analysis only the 1974 Labour voters. The result of this analysis is
shown in Table 10.3. These voters are divided, firstly, according to their perceptions of the parties' current policy positions and, secondly, according to
their own opinion positions (as defined by their perceptions of the parties'
positions). As a result we obtain the four categories in the columns of the
table. The column furthest to the left, for example, comprises 1974 Labour
voters who thought that Labour was more in favour of incomes policy in
1979 than were the Conservatives and were also themselves closest to Labour's

perceived position. For each of these categories, the table gives the percentage distribution of the three-party vote in 1979. There are two categories of voters in the table whose own opinions were closest to the Labour party stand *as they saw it*. These are the categories where the percentage of party changes in 1979 (the defection rate) was the smallest. Interestingly, the percentage of stable Labour votes was biggest in the sub-category who thought, wrongly, that Labour was *less* in favour of incomes policy than the Conservatives, and were closest to Labour on that ground (91 per cent as compared with 82 per cent among those who agreed with the party line and knew what it was). The defection rates (i.e. the percentages voting Conservative or Liberal in 1979) were clearly larger among the 1974 Labour voters who disagreed with their party's incomes policy *as they saw it* in 1979. It is intriguing, though, that the defection rate was even higher among the small minority who were closest to the Conservatives because they thought the Conservative party was in favour of an incomes policy (43 per cent) than among those who disagreed with Labour for the opposite, and more realistic, reason (30 per cent). Undoubtedly, Labour lost more support among voters who disagreed with the party's stand on incomes policy, whether for well-founded or for ill-founded reasons. But as we have observed before, no single issue can account for more than part of the change that occurs from one election to the next: Labour lost 18 per cent of its 1974 voters even among those who wanted an incomes policy and recognised that Labour advocated the same view. And a majority of the 1974 Labour voters who disagreed with their party on incomes policy still continued to vote Labour in 1979.

Being associated with incomes policy appears, on balance, to have been a liability for a political party in the 1979 election. It is an intriguing question how this finding is to be reconciled with the result of several opinion polls which indicated that there was quite widespread support, both in the spring of 1979 and earlier, for the general principle that the government should aim to 'restrict wage claims' or 'limit wage increases'. (Such interview questions were asked, for example, in polls conducted by Gallup and NOP.) The most likely explanation is simply that the public was indeed unfavourably disposed towards excessive wage increases but – at the same time – had become disillusioned about a government-run incomes policy as a means to achieve that end. It would appear, therefore, that our survey and the opinion polls actually recorded different aspects of public opinion. The opinion poll questions to which we have just referred were actually phrased so as to couple support for wage restraint with support for government intervention and did (explicitly or implicitly) set this combination of goal and means as an alternative to free collective bargaining. Respondents who wanted to express the opinion that wage increases ought to be restrained were thus invited to endorse a government-run incomes policy at the same time. The question wording used in our survey, on the other hand, focused on the choice between the two methods for settling

Table 10.3 *Labour voters in 1974: party choice in 1979 by perceptions of party positions and own views on incomes policy*

Perceptions of party positions:	Party perceived to be *most in favour* of government guidelines for wages and salaries:			
	Labour party		*Conservative party*	
Respondent's own view	Closest to Labour party's	Closest to Conservative party's	Closest to Conservative party's	Closest to Labour party's
	%	%	%	%
Vote in 1979				
Labour	82	70	57	91
Liberals	9	9	14	4
Conservatives	9	21	29	5
Total per cent	100%	100%	100%	100%
Number of respondents	133	141	42	94

The table comprises only Labour voters in 1974 who voted for one of the three main parties in 1979. Respondents who had no view on the position of either the Conservatives or Labour or had no personal view on the issue are excluded from the table.

Data source: BES May 1979 Election Survey.

wages without explicitly mentioning the aim of avoiding excessive wage increases. Moreover, we asked that question after a campaign in which the Conservatives had argued that there was a better way than an incomes policy imposed by the government to achieve realistic wage settlements. Incidentally, this was – albeit on different grounds – also the view espoused by the trade unions throughout the winter of discontent. It is the balance of opinion on that issue – the unpopularity of a government-run incomes policy in 1979 – that is recorded in our survey. The Conservatives seemed to offer a better alternative – and a large proportion of the electorate were willing to give it a try.

10.2 Britain's role in the EEC

On all our criteria, the question of Britain's role in the EEC proved to be one of the least prominent of the issues in the 1979 election. Yet, Britain's membership has been a highly controversial matter in the recent past and it is still a latent issue which could come to the fore again. The question in 1979 was whether Britain should change its attitude towards policy making in the EEC, becoming either more co-operative or more ready to take a stand against EEC economic policies. As we have seen, the public wanted the latter rather than the former: 60 per cent said Britain should be readier to oppose EEC economic policies, whereas only 20 per cent thought that Britain should be more willing to go along with the policies that other member states in the EEC wanted to pursue (see Table 9.2). The relationship between voting and opinions on the matter was weak. Yet, when we controlled for the individual's rating of its importance, the correlation increased to a comparatively high level among the voters who did think it was an important issue (see Table 9.8A). Britain's role in the EEC is an interesting example of an issue that was virtually out of sight for half of the electorate but clearly had some political significance for the other half. It is worth examining the underlying state of opinion in some more detail.

The public's view of the consequences for Britain of having joined the European Community was rather gloomy, and had become more so since the October 1974 election (see Table 10.4). In 1974 those who thought Britain would be better off by staying in the EEC out-numbered those who thought Britain would be worse off, albeit with a slight margin. By 1979, nearly four voters in ten (39 per cent) believed that Britain would be worse off in the next few years because of its Common Market membership, whilst only one in five (21 per cent) believed it would be better off. The salience of the EEC as a political issue had declined, however. At the October 1974 election, 30 per cent thought the matter was 'not very important'. At that time, of course, the question was whether Britain should withdraw unless improved terms could be negotiated. In 1979 that percentage had risen to 48 per cent. In 1974, 71 per cent of the voters said they preferred one of the three major parties' stands on the EEC issue, whilst in 1979 the percentage had gone down to 58.

In the case of the EEC issue, the voters' views on the importance of the question were not unrelated to their own opinions on what course Britain ought to follow or to their party sympathies. There was a tendency, as is shown in Table 10.5, for those who considered the EEC question important also to be more critical of EEC policies. This holds true for Conservative, Labour and Liberal voters alike, but the Labour share of the vote was notably stronger among those who considered the EEC an 'extremely important' matter in the election: in that category 52 per cent voted Labour as compared to 35 per cent in the remaining (and of course much larger) part of the electorate.

The percentages in Table 10.6 demonstrates how the party division of the vote varied in relation to issue opinions and between different levels of importance ratings. The top row in each section of the table shows the Labour percentage of the vote when the sample has been divided according both to the voters' views on the importance of the EEC issue and their own opinions relative to the perceived positions of the two major parties.

Among the voters who consider the EEC issue 'extremely important', individuals' opinions on the EEC made a sharp difference: 70 per cent of

Table 10.4 *Views on the consequences of Britain's membership of the EEC in 1974 and 1979*

Interview question: 1979: 'Do you think being a member of the Common Market will make Britain better off, worse off, or will things stay about the same in the next few years?' 1974: 'Would staying in the Common Market make Britain better off, or worse off, or would things stay about the same in the next few years?'

Consequences of EEC membership for Britain in the next few years	Conservative voters		Liberal voters		Labour voters		All respondents	
	1979	1974	1979	1974	1979	1974	1979	1974
	%	%	%	%	%	%	%	%
Will make Britain better off	31	40	17	26	15	24	21	30
Will stay the same	35	36	41	40	29	34	33	35
Will make Britain worse off	28	16	37	26	50	33	39	27
Don't know	6	8	5	8	6	9	7	8
Total per cent	100%	100%	100%	100%	100%	100%	100%	100%
Number of respondents	727	693	213	348	583	805	1868	2305

*Including non-voters, etc.

Data source: BES May 1979 Election Survey and BES October 1974 Election Survey.

Table 10.5 *Relation of opinion on Britain's role in the EEC to opinion on the importance of the EEC issue*

Opinion on EEC policies	Importance of the issue		
	Extremely important	Fairly important	Not very important
	%	%	%
Britain should be more willing to go along with EEC economic policies	16	25	19
No change is needed*	5	10	28
Britain should be readier to oppose EEC economic policies	79	65	53
Total per cent	100%	100%	100%
Number of respondents	264	544	710

*Including 'Don't know' answers.

Data source: BES May 1979 Election Survey.

those whose views on the issue were closest to Labour voted for that party, whilst only 18 per cent voted Labour among those who were closest to the Conservative stand. The difference is 52 percentage points. At the lowest level of salience, the relationship between opinions and voting is considerably milder: 41 per cent voted Labour of the voters whose opinions were closest to Labour's perceived position, as compared to 27 per cent of those who were closest to the Conservatives, a difference of only 14 percentage points.

Our opinion classification defines the voters' positions in relation to what each individual thought were the stands of the two major parties.[3] All voters did not hold the same view of the parties' positions, however. The second and the third lines in each section of the table allow us to trace the relationship between voting and opinions within the two parts of the electorate who had diametrically opposed views of the situation. The largest part consisted of voters who thought that Labour was the more critical towards the EEC of the two major parties, 47 per cent of the electorate. A much smaller but still significant part, 19 per cent, believed it was rather the Conservatives who would be most ready to oppose EEC economic policies (see Table 9.4). The splitting up

Table 10.6 *Relation of voting to opinions on Britain's role in the EEC, by rating of the importance of the issue and perceptions of party stands*

The EEC opinion classification is in distance format. The table includes respondents who voted for one of the three main parties.

The top row in each of the three main sections of the table includes all respondents at the indicated level of importance rating. The voters in each row are further subdivided into: (A) those who thought Labour was most critical of the EEC (Labour 'to the left of' the Conservatives), and (B) those who thought the Conservatives were most critical of the EEC.

(The top row in each section also includes respondents who held neither of these views.)

Rating of importance/ perception of party stands	Voters' opinion in relation to perceived party positions			All respondents in the row
	Closest to Labour	Same $ distance	Closest to Conservatives	
	Per cent Labour of each category			
Extremely important	*70%*	*56%*	*18%*	*52%*
AMONG WHOM:				
(A) Thought Labour most critical of EEC	70%	*	13%	60%
(B) Thought Conservatives most critical of EEC	*	*	21%	29%
Fairly important	*51%*	*39%*	*17%*	*36%*
AMONG WHOM:				
(A) Thought Labour most critical of EEC	52%	29%	17%	39%
(B) Thought Conservatives most critical of EEC	41%	*	18%	25%
Not very important	*41%*	*34%*	*27%*	*34%*
AMONG WHOM:				
(A) Thought Labour most critical of the EEC	41%	29%	24%	34%
(B) Thought Conservatives most critical of EEC	40%	27%	31%	32%
TOTAL				
(A) Thought Labour most critical of EEC	53%	33%	19%	41%
(B) Thought Conservatives most critical of EEC	44%	37%	23%	28%

*Less than 20 respondents; percentages not given.

$Including voters who did not know the positions of parties or had no opinion on the issue.

Data source: BES May 1979 Election Survey.

of the sample yields very small sub-categories in some instances, but the overall pattern is clear. The relationship between voting and perceived party positions is the same, irrespective of whether the voter thinks it is the Conservatives or Labour who are most critical of the EEC. There is a strong tendency to vote for the party perceived as closest to one's own position among those who consider the EEC issue important, but only a weak tendency among voters who think it is 'not very important'.

However, there is also another tendency in the table: at each importance level Labour gets a bigger share of the vote when it is seen to be more critical of the EEC than the Conservatives (see the 'All respondents in the row' column in the table). Among those least interested in the EEC questions, the difference is marginal, but it increases to 14 percentage points in the 'fairly important' category and to 31 percentage points among those who thought the issue 'extremely important'. As can be seen from the two bottom rows of the table, Labour got 41 per cent of the vote among those who thought it was the party most ready to oppose EEC economic policies, as compared to 28 per cent in the category of voters who had the opposite impression. The prevailing opinion in the electorate was critical of the EEC, and as a consequence Labour evidently attracted support among the voters who recognised its position on the issue and, furthermore, considered the issue important.

As in the case of incomes policy, we seem to be observing a situation in which general party sympathy as expressed in voting, opinion on an issue, and perceptions of party standpoints, are interdependent, all being involved in two-way causal relationships with the other two elements. Firstly, voters who find that their own views on the issue concerned are closest to one of the parties, are more likely than others to cast their votes for that party. (In this case, the relationship was a mild one, with the exception of those who considered the EEC issue important.) At the same time, as we have observed, an individual's general party sympathy tends to influence his opinion: the mere fact that the party one normally trusts espouses a view on a political matter is often in itself a reason for thinking that this must be the right view. Finally, these data confirm that there is a tendency for the individual to interpret the political situation in accordance with his own view.[4] That is, if the situation is at all ambiguous, voters who have formed an opinion on a policy question will tend to associate the party they normally support as closely as possible with the policy they like; the opposing party will (if possible) be identified with a disliked policy position.

If we look at the data from the latter viewpoint, we can divide both Conservative and Labour voters into those who were critical of the EEC and those who thought Britain should become more co-operative within the EEC; we can examine the perceptions of party standpoints within each group. The percentages given below serve that purpose.

Party vote and own opinion on the EEC	Percentage in each row category who believed that their own party was more critical towards the EEC than the other major party*	
Conservative voters		
Pro-EEC	13%	(174)
Critical of EEC	48%	(264)
All	34%	(438)
Labour voters		
Pro-EEC	66%	(65)
Critical of EEC	84%	(291)
All	80%	(356)

*The number of respondents in each group is given within parentheses.

Note:
Only voters who had an opinion on the issue and had some view
on the positions of both parties are included.

As the figures show, a very large majority of both Conservative voters who
were pro-EEC and Labour voters who were critical of the EEC agreed on at least
one thing: the Labour party was more negative than the Conservative party towards the European Community (87 per cent and 84 per cent, respectively). The
deviant categories are the small category of Labour voters who were pro-EEC
and the much larger category of Conservative voters who were critical of the
EEC. About one-third of the voters in the first category and nearly half of the
second had 'reversed the picture' of the parties' stands: they thought Labour
was most willing to go along with the EEC and the Conservatives most ready
to oppose EEC economic policies.

The more visible party standpoints on a policy question become, the less
room will there be for such conflicting pictures of what the parties stand for.
A high degree of visibility may be the result of the parties taking unchangeable
positions on an issue over a long period of time (e.g. nationalisation). Visibility
may also increase because of developments in party politics that make an issue
more controversial and therefore more salient. The visibility of the parties' views
on the EEC as well as the salience of the question are factors that could conceivably change in a future election. It is an interesting matter of conjecture
what the consequences might be. If nothing else changed in comparison in 1979,
Labour would apparently stand to gain from a heightened level of salience for
the EEC issue. On the other hand, it seems unlikely that a change in saliency
would occur unless there is also a change in the nature of the issue – for example,
if the whole question of Britain's membership were to be revived.

10.3 Race relations and immigration

The question of race relations, like the EEC question, was one of the issues least often rated 'extremely important' when individuals made their decisions about voting. As in the case of the EEC issue, there was only a weak relationship between voting and the division of opinions in the electorate as a whole. These were, furthermore, the two issues on which more than 40 per cent of the electorate felt that no party had a better policy than the others. The race relations and EEC issues differed, however, in one respect. It was much less common for the voters to 'reverse' the parties' stands on race relations. A majority (61 per cent) thought the Conservatives would be 'tougher' than Labour, whilst only 9 per cent had the opposite impression. Yet, in comparison with several other policy issues, party positions were only fairly widely recognised. The ambiguity of the choice for many voters shows up in the large proportion (30 per cent) who did not know of any policy disagreement between the parties.

Our survey questions really involve three different but connected social and political questions: whether the large-scale immigration into Britain had been undesirable or not, whether it was now time to curb any further immigration and, finally, whether stopping immigration in itself would be the best method of dealing with Britain's race relations problems.

As to the first of these questions, it is abundantly clear from the data that the British public would prefer the question had never arisen; that is, the prevailing feeling was that the country should not have let in so many immigrants in the first place. When asked a straight question about the matter, 83 per cent of respondents expressed that view and only 13 per cent held the opposite view.[5] So far, there is a near consensus: Conservative voters thought somewhat more often than Liberal and Labour voters that too many immigrants had been allowed to settle in Britain, but that view was shared by large majorities of all the three main parties' voters (Conservatives, 90 per cent; Liberals, 79 per cent; and Labour, 77 per cent). Moreover, the data indicate that immigration was a matter of more than fleeting concern to many voters: as many as 42 per cent said they felt 'very strongly' and 39 per cent said they felt 'fairly strongly' about it.

In general the public's feelings about immigration must be understood as a negative response to an unwanted societal change rather than as a reaction to actual contacts with the immigrant population. When we asked in the survey whether there was any 'problem' with immigrants in the respondent's neighbourhood, only 12 per cent said there was. Those who felt they lived in an area with an immigrant 'problem' were somewhat more likely than others to feel 'very strongly' about immigration (59 per cent as compared to 40 per cent). They were also somewhat more inclined than others to consider race relations an 'extremely important' issue in the election (28 per cent as compared to 12 per cent). But personal experience of an immigrant problem accounts for only a small fraction of the variation in attitudes towards immigration among the general public.[6]

More voters believed that Conservative party policy on immigration would be different from Labour's: 61 per cent of all voters thought the Conservatives were 'more likely to keep immigrants out', whereas only 2 per cent thought that of Labour. The remaining 37 per cent thought there was 'not much difference between' the parties or did not know.[7] Again, this is a matter on which there is little disagreement in the electorate: 67 per cent of the Conservative voters thought the Conservative party would be most likely to curb immigration, but so did 64 per cent of Liberal voters and 54 per cent of Labour voters. Only 4 per cent of the Labour voters thought this could be said of their own party. To sum up: the presence of a fairly large immigrant population is a matter on which most voters had a firm (and mostly negative) view, and in 1979 – as in the case of race relations – it was fairly widely recognised that there was a difference between Conservative and Labour policies. All the same, there was only a weak relationship between the voters' views on immigration and their party choice.

This is consistent with our analysis of attitudes towards social and cultural change in Chapter 7. We found that individuals' responses to societal change were linked, not to one but to several different attitude dimensions, of which one comprised opinions on the immigrant population. This 'ethnocentrism' dimension proved to be of very little relevance to voting. The interview questions we examined in that context bear upon the current race relations situation in Britain. As will be recalled (see Table 7.1), respondents were asked whether efforts to ensure equality for coloured immigrants had gone too far: 30 per cent thought they had, but the same proportion thought that such efforts had not gone far enough, while 41 per cent thought the current situation was 'about right'. Although the public may not be happy about the presence of an immigrant population, only a minority of the voters thus thought that immigrants had been treated too generously. On the other hand, there was also only a minority who felt that more should be done to protect the interests of the immigrants. The more extreme proposal that coloured immigrants should be sent back to their own country was endorsed by 29 per cent, whilst 50 per cent rejected the idea.

The division of opinion on how Britain should tackle the race relations problem should be seen in the light of the more general attitudes towards immigration we have examined here. To stop further immigration was a policy that most voters anyhow thought desirable; 51 per cent believed it was also the most important thing to do in order to improve the relations between the immigrants and the wider community. In a sense, it is even more noteworthy that as many as 36 per cent (most of whom deplored the fact that so many immigrants had been allowed in) took the view that priority should be given to social policy measures.[8] (See Table 9.2.)

It is obvious that a large majority wished that large-scale immigration had never occurred, and that this did influence the public's views on race relations.[9] The race relations question was seen, nevertheless, as a separate social problem by a significant part of the electorate. In general, though, it was not seen as one of the really important issues in the election. More than four voters in ten said they felt very strongly about the fact that too many immigrants had been let in, but only one in seven thought of race relations as an extremely important issue when they decided how to vote. Yet, as is shown in Table 10.7, the more important the voter thought the race relations issue was, the more likely he was to think that stopping immigration was the best way to deal with the problem.[10]

Among those who considered the race relations issue 'extremely important' in the election, most voters voted Conservative, if they had an opinion on the issue and also thought there was any difference between the parties.[11] In this category one finds a quite substantial relationship between opinions on race relations and party choice. But this was a small minority in the electorate. As can be seen from Table 10.8, the relationship is more modest among voters who considered the matter only 'fairly important' and even weaker among those who thought

Table 10.7 *Relation of opinion on immigration and race relations to opinion on the importance of the issue*

Opinion on immigration and race relations	Importance of the issue		
	Extremely important	Fairly important	Not very important
	%	%	%
'People have different views about how to improve race relations in this country:'			
The first thing to do about race relations is to put a stop to all further immigration	72	58	44
Things should be left as they are*	4	7	16
The first thing to do about race relations is to tackle the problems of jobs and housing in the large cities	24	35	40
Total per cent	100%	100%	100%
Number of respondents	208	477	819

*Including 'Don't know' answers.

Data source: BES May 1979 Election Survey.

Table 10.8 *Relation of voting to opinion on immigration and race relations by opinion on the importance of the issue*

Entries in the table are the *Conservative* percentage of the three-party vote in each of the categories in the table. The classification of opinions on the race relations issue is in the distance to parties format. The number of respondents in each category is given within parentheses.

Importance of the issue	Opinions relative to perceived party positions:			All respondents in the row
	Closest to Labour	Same distance	Closest to Conservatives	
Extremely important	19% (43)	53% (49)	65% (118)	53%
Fairly important	30% (136)	49% (123)	59% (227)	49%
Not very important	36% (232)	47% (318)	53% (268)	46%

Data source: BES May 1979 Election Survey.

it was 'not very important'. In particular, it is noteworthy (in all the three importance categories) that there is comparatively little difference with regard to the party division of the vote between those who were closest to the Conservatives and those who had no opinion on the issue or thought there was no difference between the parties. It is the small category of voters who were closest to Labour on this issue that differs most markedly from others by giving the Conservatives a much smaller share of their votes.[12]

The views on immigration and race relations that had the strongest support in the electorate were evidently more in tune with Conservative policies than with Labour. This is not to say, however, that immigration and race relations became major vote-winning issues for the Conservatives. Opinions on race relations yielded additional support for the Conservatives mainly among the minority of very concerned voters; and that effect was partly offset by a negative impact on the Conservative vote within the minority of voters who disagreed with the party's policy. Like the question about law and order, race relations was one of the issues on which it was apparently quite possible for Labour and Liberal voters to appreciate the Conservative party's views without feeling that this was a sufficient reason to cast their vote for the Conservatives. Although we are not able to gauge the precise effect on the party division of the vote, the Conservatives probably gained a small amount as a result of the party's stands on immigration and race relations. But they gained much less than the bare distributions of popular opinions on these issues might suggest. Opinions were not very effectively translated into preferences for the policy of any of the major parties, or into votes.[13] In the final reckoning, the public's feelings about immigration and race relations in 1979 was a 'dormant', rather than an active, electoral asset for the Conservatives in the 1979 election. We shall find further evidence for this conclusion in the next chapter.

11

The impact of the issues – an overall account

We have surveyed the divisions of opinions in the electorate over a broad range of questions about the governance of Britain. Our review has encompassed the Conservatives' and Labour's records on managing the country's economy, the directions of change in British society, and the main issues in the 1979 election that involved more or less clearcut choices between policy alternatives. Although it cannot be claimed that our enquiry exhausts all the matters that conceivably could have borne upon voters' choice of party, our interview questions covered virtually all the issues and policies that emerged from the voters' own 'free answer' comments on what they liked and disliked about the two major parties. Indeed that inventory of the electorate's views on parties and policies can hardly differ much from what most observers of British politics would include in any listing of the issues that achieved some degree of prominence in the election campaign.

In a few instances, no statistical association between voter opinions and party choice could be discerned, and in some instances only mild relationships came to light. Most of our questions about how Britain should be governed, however, proved to touch on electoral issues in the sense that the voters' choice of sides showed a substantial relationship to their voting.

How far, then, can this mapping of opinions on political issues account for individual voting decisions or for the overall outcome of the election: the surge towards voting for the Conservatives and the decline in the support for Labour and the Liberals? In this chapter, we will first explore the relationships between issue opinions and voting change between the October 1974 and the May 1979 election. We will go on to employ a statistical analysis technique which allows us to assess both how far the entire array of opinion measurements can 'explain' individuals' voting decisions and also to select the issue opinions that carried most weight in those decisions. Using the results of that analysis, we will then return to the question: which were the issues that mattered most?

11.1 Political issues and voting change

We have found abundant evidence that voters rarely agree wholeheartedly with their chosen party on all the issues. Obviously, with at most three or four parties to choose from – and many would probably count only the two major parties as real alternatives – voting decisions have to be based on judgements about which of the parties is closest to one's own views rather than a matter of looking for a perfect match. Even so, on any given policy question, a sizeable portion of the voters must have cast their votes in the 1979 election for a party in spite of, rather than because of, the course of action their party advocated. When there is a statistical relationship between opinions on an issue and party choice, those who did side with one of the parties on the issue were certainly more likely than others to vote for that party. But some voters cast their votes differently, and some simply did not side with either of the parties on that particular issue. We have seen, of course, that the strength of relationships between opinions and voting depends to some extent on contingent factors, such as the salience of the issue and the individuals' understanding of the links between parties and policy alternatives. Some issues count more than others to the individual who is making his voting decision, and some issues count more than others in the electorate as a whole because they affect the voting decisions of a larger proportion of the electorate.

We can think of the individual's voting decision as resulting from an overall judgement on which party best represents his own views on how the country should be governed, or best looks after the interests he shares. If he feels closest to, say, the Conservatives in some respects and Labour in others, he will need to weigh the importance of his different concerns against each other and decide whether the Conservatives or Labour 'on balance' offer the better deal. Many voters saw the 1979 election as effectively a straight choice between the two major parties. Others made their overall judgements with regard also to the Liberals or one of the nationalist parties. If so, in making their final voting decisions they would have considered whether it was worth while voting for one of the smaller parties. Actually, we can think of that consideration as yet another issue in the election, important to some, of little consequence to others.

To use a simplistic model, we could describe the individual's voting decision as the result of a summation of the good and bad points of each of the parties, taking the importance of each point into account as a weighting factor in the summing up. So far the choice situation may not appear too different from the one experienced by, say, a prospective holiday-maker confronted with a selection of package tours at the travel agent's office. To make the comparison hold, however, we need to think of a large number of holiday-makers, many of whom have travelled to the same place many times before and are attached to it for a variety of reasons, both rational and affective. Someone who is used to taking his holiday in Devon may well accept that Majorca offers more sunshine – which is a good thing – but the beaches are not the same and the people he will meet there are not the same. It may take a lot to change his mind, even if the previous summer in Devon was rainy. Yet, one year he may indeed find that – taking everything into account – Majorca is the better choice. If a large number of people make the same decision – and a much smaller number switch from Majorca to Devon – then Majorca will enjoy a tourist boom and Devon will suffer a loss of popularity. The overall, net change would be the result of many individual decisions which could be made for many different reasons. In order to account for the causes of the collective outcome one needs to establish two things: first, how much weight each of these reasons for change carried in individual decisions; and second, the number of persons who would have been affected by each of the causes of change.

Two measures of the impact of the issues on vote switching

We know already from Chapter 2 that more than a fifth of the voters who voted in both of the elections switched in 1979 to a party other than the one they supported in October 1974. What we now aim to do is assess the impact of the issues in the 1979 campaign on this switching of votes. To that end, we shall examine the relationship between opinions on the issues and voting in the two elections. In fact, we shall look at some of these relationships from two angles – by assessing the impact of issue opinions on voters' propensity to switch parties, and by comparing issue opinions among the parties' stable supporters with the distributions of opinions among the party switchers.

The rationale for the first of these paths should be obvious. Among October 1974 Conservative, Liberal and Labour voters alike, we would expect those who disagreed with their parties' stands in 1979 to be more likely than others to switch their votes. One measure of the impact of a given issue on a party's voting support can, therefore, be obtained by simply comparing the rate of party change between 1974 and 1979 among those of its 1974 voters who were disenchanted with its policy on a given issue with the rate of change among the rest of its 1974 voting support. The greater the difference between such 'defection rates', the more difference it would have made whether the voter liked or disliked the party's record on the issue concerned in 1979.

Before we accept this difference between defection rates as an indicator of the impact of an issue on individuals' voting decisions, however, one qualification is required. It is not necessarily the case that, for example, a 1974 Labour voter, who switched to the Conservatives in 1979 and at that time agreed with the Conservatives on social welfare, actually thought of that particular issue as the one that tilted the balance in favour of the Conservatives when he made his voting decision in 1979. He may well have disliked Labour's social welfare policies already in 1974. What we can infer is that social welfare was one of the things that counted in the Conservatives' favour when he made up his mind to switch.

Similarly, if we find a large difference between defection rates for a given issue, this should not be taken to mean that that particular issue was the most decisive one for all those who decided to switch parties; but it does mean that the disagreement with one's previous party on that issue – perhaps in conjunction with other causes of dissatisfaction – was associated with a marked increase in the propensity to switch to another party.

So far, we have been concerned only with the effect of issue opinions on individuals' propensity to switch. The question whether an issue had an impact on vote switching that changed the party division of the vote is a somewhat different matter. In order to assess the impact of an issue on the party division of the vote, we need to take into account also the distribution of opinions, both among its 1974 supporters and among the 1974 supporters of other parties. The more dissatisfaction a party encountered among its previous supporters, the larger was the proportion of its 1974 voting support that was 'at risk' in the 1979 election. Similarly, the larger the number of other parties' previous supporters who were attracted by a party's stand on an issue, the larger the potential gain. Both the numbers involved and the effect on individual voters' propensity to switch will combine to determine the number of voters who actually switched. Thus, in 1979 a party could perhaps lose a large proportion of those of its 1974 voters who now disagreed with it on some issue, but this might still cause only a marginal loss, if the number of such disaffected voters was small. Everything else being equal, the loss would obviously be more damaging if there had been widespread dissatisfaction with the party's stand on the issue among voters who supported it in the last election. Likewise, the gain a party could make from other parties would depend both on the defection rates among the voters concerned and on their absolute number.

The joint effect of both of these factors can be captured by comparing the distributions of opinions among each of the three main parties' stable voters with the distributions of opinions among the voters each of them lost to one or the other of the other main parties. These comparisons will thus comprise three categories of voters who supported the same party in October 1974 and in 1979 and six categories of voters who switched in different directions between Conservatives, Liberals and Labour.

If the state of opinion on one of the issues contributed to vote switching from a party in 1979, then this will come to light when we compare the distribution of opinions on that issue among the party's stable supporters with the distribution of opinions among those previous supporters who switched to another party in 1979. We will often find that the proportion dissatisfied with the party's current stand on the issue was larger among the vote switchers than among the stable supporters. And the more two such opinion distributions differ, the more important was that particular issue as a concomitant of vote switching. We will therefore take this *difference* as our main measure of the impact of issue opinions on vote switching. This measure will be dependent both on the

extent to which there was disagreement with a party's stand in 1979 on the issue
concerned among its 1974 supporters and on the effect of such disagreement on
voters' propensity to switch parties. If disagreement was widespread and the
issue had a strong impact on voters' propensity to switch, then the opinion distributions will look very different. The two factors could obviously combine in a
variety of ways that would produce more modest or small differences. There
could, for example, be little disagreement but a distinctive effect on the propensity to switch among the few who did disagree, just as there could be widespread disagreement but only a slight effect on the defection rate.

One party's loss of voting support through vote switching is bound to become another party's gain. And if a party lost votes because of its stand on a
given issue, it might well have gained votes on the same score from other parties.
We will obviously need to take this into account when we assess the net impact
of the issues on vote switching.

Issue opinions and propensity to switch

We shall begin our examination of the data with the first of the two measures
of issue impact discussed above: the relationship between individuals' opinions
on the issues and their propensity to switch parties in 1979. As explained above,
we will do this by examining the defection rates among voters with different
opinions within the 1974 voting support of each of the three main
parties. The relevant data are set out in Table 11.1.[1] The table comprises three
policy alternative issues (nationalisation, ways of tackling unemployment, and
social services), together with a question about comprehensive schools (which was
included in our battery of questions about societal change), and also the voters'
judgements on the Conservatives' and Labour's records on handling strikes.

For each of these issues, we have divided the voters into three opinion categories: those who were closest to the Conservative party, those who held an
opinion 'in the middle' or had no opinion and finally those who were on the
Labour side. In the rows of the table, the voters are divided according to how
they voted in October 1974. The entries in the table show the defection rate for
each party's 1974 voters within each of the opinion categories. Thus we find,
for example, that while only 7 per cent of the 1974 Labour voters who were
closest to Labour on the nationalisation issue switched to the Conservatives or
Liberals in 1979, fully 34 per cent of those who sided with the Conservatives
on the nationalisation issue deserted Labour in 1979.

All of the questions in the table were among the ones on which we found
strong relationships between opinions and voting in 1979. Now, we also find
quite distinctive differences between the defection rates for voters who supported the policies of their 1974 party and those who did not. (See the column
farthest to the right of the table.) For the Conservatives' and Labour's 1974
supporters, the tendency is very clear: those who sided with the other major

party on an issue in 1979 were the most likely to change their votes; those whose 1979 opinions were in line with their 1974 party choice were the least likely to change. The only deviation from this pattern is found in the case of comprehensive schools. Whilst disapproval of a complete transition to comprehensive schools was associated with a markedly increased propensity to switch to the right among both Labour and Liberal voters, only a slight effect can be discerned amongst the few Conservative voters in favour of comprehensive schools.

In the case of the 1974 Liberals, the table gives two defection rates, one for switches to the Conservatives and one for switches to Labour; 1974 Liberal voters could switch both towards the right and towards the left, and we know from Chapter 2 that a large portion of the Liberals' 1974 vote was in fact lost to the two major parties in 1979. In almost every instance, the defection rates show that these voters' opinions on the issues markedly affected the direction of their change. The two issues most clearly associated with switches to the Conservatives were nationalisation and the problem of strikes.

The Conservatives and Labour lost much smaller proportions of their October 1974 voters than did the Liberals, as was shown by the analysis of the flow of the vote in Chapter 2. In fact, as Table 11.1 also reveals, both the Conservatives and Labour were able to keep the support of the great majority even of those 1974 voters who disliked their policy on any given issue in 1979. As will be recalled, we made the same observation in a special analysis of the impact of the incomes policy issue in Chapter 10.

People's party sympathies are generally embedded in broader views of the parties than the specific opinions we record by means of an interview question on a particular issue. Disagreement with the party one has voted for in the past on an issue is indeed associated with a higher probability of voting change. When a voter actually changes, the change is likely to be related to several issues and some more general sense of dissatisfaction. Many of the respondents in our sample who disagreed with their party on any one issue will nevertheless on balance still have found it preferable to any other party. This appears even to be true of matters that might be thought central elements in a party's ideology.

Labour voters' opinions on nationalisation is a case in point. As will be recalled from Chapter 8, there was no strong support for further nationalisation among Labour voters in 1974 and even less in 1979. We have found that those 1974 Labour voters who were closest to the Conservatives' view on nationalisation were more likely than others to switch their votes in 1979. Yet, most of them in fact remained loyal to their old party. In Table 11.2 we have taken our mapping of opinions on the nationalisation issue among Labour voters one step further by relating voting change not only to voting in 1974 and 1979 but also to *opinion change* between 1974 and 1979. (In order to obtain data on opinions on nationalisation in 1974, this analysis is based on the *panel* sample of respondents interviewed at both elections; the number of cases is, therefore, smaller than in other tables.)

Table 11.1 *Opinions on political issues and voting change 1974-1979*

In each row, the *entries* are the percentage of party changers within each of the three opinion categories. Voters are categorised (in the rows) according to their vote in the October 1974 election. The table includes only 1974 Conservative, Liberal and Labour voters who participated in the 1979 election and voted for one of the three main parties.

Political issue/ voter category	Opinion on issue			Difference between % party switch in 'Closest to Conservatives' and 'Closest to Labour' categories
	Closest to Labour	Same distance/ ambivalent	Closest to Conservatives	
Nationalisation[1]				
1974 Labour voters: per cent switch to Conservatives or Liberals in 1979	7%	22%	34%	27
1974 Conservative voters: per cent switch to Labour or Liberals in 1979	41%	17%	6%	35
1974 Liberals: per cent switch to				
(a) Conservatives in 1979	1%	6%	46%	45
(b) Labour in 1979	16%	26%	8%	8
Tackling unemployment (private enterprise or the government)[1]				
1974 Labour voters: per cent switch to Conservatives or Liberals in 1979	11%	22%	34%	23
1974 Conservative voters: per cent switch to Labour or Liberals in 1979	21%	8%	7%	14
1974 Liberals: per cent switch to				
(a) Conservatives in 1979	21%	26%	45%	24
(b) Labour in 1979	35%	14%	7%	28
Social services and benefits[1]				
1974 Labour voters: per cent switch to Conservatives or Liberals in 1979	13%	19%	40%	27
1974 Conservative voters: per cent switch to Labour or Liberals in 1979	18%	11%	6%	12
1974 Liberals: per cent switch to				
(a) Conservatives in 1979	17%	37%	46%	29
(b) Labour in 1979	20%	13%	9%	11
Should comprehensive schools be established throughout the country?[2]				
1974 Labour voters: per cent switch to Conservatives or Liberals in 1979	13%	20%	38%	25
1974 Conservative voters: per cent switch to Labour or Liberals in 1979	13%	16%	6%	7
1974 Liberals: per cent switch to				
(a) Conservatives in 1979	24%	34%	45%	21
(b) Labour in 1979	27%	11%	7%	20
Labour's & the Conservatives' ability to handle the problem of strikes[3]				
1974 Labour voters: per cent switch to Conservatives or Liberals in 1979	13%	20%	38%	25
1974 Conservative voters: per cent switch to Labour or Liberals in 1979	30%	10%	4%	26
1974 Liberals: per cent switch to				
(a) Conservatives in 1979	13%	39%	53%	40
(b) Labour in 1979	23%	12%	7%	16

Notes:
[1] Questions on policy alternatives, taken in 'distance to parties' format: see Table 9.5.
[2] For the purpose of the above table, the response alternatives in the original question have been combined so as to form three alternatives: Closest to Labour = 1 and 2; Ambivalent = 3; Closest to Conservatives = 4 and 5. See Table 7.5.
[3] The opinion measure is a compressed version of the classification in Table 6.5A.

Data source: BES May 1979 Election Survey. This and those of the following tables in which respondents are classified according to both 1974 and 1979 vote are based on the 1979 cross-section sample. However, we have made use of information about voting in 1974 given in interviews in the 1974 survey for respondents who were included also in that survey sample (the panel). Respondents in the 1979 survey who had not been interviewed in 1974 were asked to recall how they voted in the October 1974 election.

Table 11.2 *Labour voters 1974: stability in opinion on nationalisation and party vote 1974–1979*

Opinion on nationalisation 1974 – 1979	Per cent	Per cent who changed to another party in 1979
Stable opinion: *More* nationalisation or opinion shift to the *left*	28	4%
Stable opinion: *No more* nationalisation	16	12%
Opinion shift to the *right*	51	20%
Stable opinion: *less* nationalisation	5	64%
Total per cent	100%	
Number of respondents	243	

Note: The table includes only respondents in the panel sample who voted Labour in October 1974 and for one of the three main parties in May 1979.

Data source: BES October 1974 – May 1979 panel survey sample.

As is shown in the table, the stability of party sympathies was very high indeed among the voters who were in favour of further nationalisation at both elections, or changed their opinions towards the left; only 4 per cent switched parties in 1979. The defection was higher among those who wanted to preserve the status quo with regard to state ownership, and higher still among those who had switched towards the right on the issue (12 and 20 per cent, respectively). In the small category of October 1974 Labour voters who consistently were so hostile to nationalisation that they wanted some companies to be turned into private ownership, more than half (64 per cent) finally defected in 1979. One reason why the defection rate was not even higher among those whose opinions had shifted towards the right was perhaps that Labour's position was also seen as having shifted towards the right in many voters' views (see Chapter 8). That would not explain, however, why so many voters, both in 1974 and 1979, knew that they were much less in favour of nationalisation than the Labour party and, yet, still voted Labour. It appears that a large proportion of the Labour voters are prepared to live with the fact that the party has a programmatic commitment to nationalisation which they do not support. They continue to support the party for other reasons, such as its record on social welfare policies or its standing as the party of the working class. Nevertheless, when the reasons for dissatisfaction with the Labour party accumulated and led some previous Labour voters to change, the nationalisation issue was one of the things that contributed to tilting the balance for many of these voters, as we will see even more clearly from the next part of this enquiry.

Issue opinions among party changers and stable voters

Our second way of gauging the impact of issue opinions on vote switching involves comparisons of the divisions of opinions among party switchers and stable voters. The data are set out in Tables 11.3-5. The voters are categorised with regard to their party choice in both of the elections of October 1974 and May 1979. The tables show the balances of opinions across the entire array of issues for each of these nine categories of voters. Some of the voter categories in these tables comprise very small numbers; not many respondents in the sample, for example, switched from the Conservatives to Labour. The percentages given for such groups are obviously not very reliable as statistical estimates, when taken separately. It is the overall pattern in the table, therefore, rather than the precise percentage for smaller sub-categories, that is of substantive interest. The 'balance of opinions' within the nine voter categories serves as an indicator of the extent to which the distribution of opinions on each of the issues was skewed in favour of the Conservatives or Labour.[2]

Some distinctive differences between the nine categories emerge across all the issues in these tables:

1. The division of opinions is mostly decidedly partisan among the *stable Conservative* and *stable Labour* voters.

2. Because of the nature of the issues in the election (and partly, of course, because of the way the questions were designed), one cannot observe the same kind of staunch partisanship among the *stable Liberals*. The characteristic feature of the stable Liberal vote is, instead, that the balances of opinions lie 'in between' those for stable Conservative and stable Labour voters. Yet, it is also noticeable that on most of the issues there is more support among the stable Liberal voters for the Conservative than for the Labour view. It is moreover noteworthy that the Liberal party's stands on incomes policy and the EEC appear to obtain no more than limited support, even among its stable supporters.

3. The balance of opinions on almost all issues among voters who switched away from the Conservative and Labour parties differed distinctively from the opinions of the remaining supporters of the party they switched from; and the farther they switched, the more they differed. Thus, for example, Conservatives who changed to Liberal were clearly less in favour of their party's stand on the issues than were the stable voters; but those who changed to Labour were even less likely to support Conservative policies and even more likely to side with Labour.

4. The Liberals lost people with predominantly pro-Conservative views to the Conservative party and people with pro-Labour views to the Labour party.

5. The balance of opinions among voters who switched between two parties was, in general, about halfway between the balance of opinions among the stable supporters of the party they switched to and the stable supporters

Table 11.3 *Stable voters and party changers: comparisons of Labour's and Conservatives' ability to handle the country's problems, 1979*

This table is based on the 'ratings of parties classifications'. *Entry* is the *balance*, obtained by subtracting the per cent of voters in each category of voters who preferred the Labour Party from the per cent of voters who preferred the Conservative Party. *Entries in the columns for stable voters are printed in italics.*

Balance of ratings of parties' performance: pro-Conserv. *minus* pro-Labour	Conservative 1974			Liberal 1974			Labour 1974		
	Conserv. 1979	Liberal 1979	Labour 1979	Conserv. 1979	Liberal 1979	Labour 1979	Conserv. 1979	Liberal 1979	Labour 1979
Strikes	*+55*	+19	-40	+39	-3	-28	+49	-46	*-57*
Unemployment	*+55*	+27	-27	+47	*0*	-48	+15	-35	*-52*
Prices	*+37*	0	-60	+15	*-34*	-64	-3	-58	*-72*
Law and order	*+69*	+39	+27	+46	*+37*	+20	+53	+25	*+3*
Number of respondents	452	26	15	74	98	25	79	48	451

Table 11.4 *Stable voters and party changers: responses to change*

Entry in this table is the percentage, in each category of voters who expressed a Conservative opinion *minus* the percentage who expressed a Labour opinion.*

Issue	Conservative 1974			Liberal 1974			Labour 1974		
	Conserv. 1979	Liberal 1979	Labour 1979	Conserv. 1979	Liberal 1979	Labour 1979	Conserv. 1979	Liberal 1979	Labour 1979
	%	%	%	%	%	%	%	%	%
Change has gone too far/not far enough: *									
Welfare benefits that are available to people today	+62	+50	+48	+45	+42	+20	+44	+33	+8
Reduction of Britain's military strength	+72	+62	+40	+55	+52	+48	+42	+38	+28
Change towards modern methods in teaching children at school	+55	+38	+27	+51	+45	+20	+29	+44	+15
What the Government should/should not do: *									
Redistributing income and wealth in favour of ordinary people	+17	+31	−33	+4	−17	−42	−13	−57	−66
Establishing comprehensive schools in place of grammar schools throughout the country	+63	+62	−13	+50	+31	−21	+32	−2	−30
Increasing state control over land for building	+49	+42	+7	+36	+29	−1	+11	−25	−27
Reducing the powers of the House of Lords	+39	+31	−13	+39	+2	−4	+3	−34	−21
Giving workers more say in the running of their place of work	+7	−11	−13	−20	−30	−33	−23	−40	−50
Giving council house tenants the right to buy their houses	+79	+62	+93	+69	+60	+42	+73	+43	+38
Number of respondents	452	26	15	74	98	25	79	48	451

Notes: The number of respondents in each category of voters given above actually differ slightly from the percentage bases for the various questions because of a small and varying number of 'not ascertained' cases. For comparison, see Tables 7.6–7.
*The interview questions comprise five response alternatives: alternatives 1 and 2 or 4 and 5 were treated as pro-Conservative answers, depending on the phrasing of the question. Alternative 3 was treated as an ambivalent answer, and the remaining two alternatives as a pro-Labour answer. The per cent distributions on which the balance entries are based include also the 'ambivalent' alternative.

Data source: BES May 1979 Election Survey.

Table 11.5 *Stable voters and party changers: voters' opinions relative to perceived party positions on policy issues*

Percentage entries for each issue are the percentages, in each category of voting, who were closest to Labour and Conservatives, respectively. The remainder up to 100%, for each issue, is made up of voters whose opinions were at the same distance to both parties' positions, and voters who saw no difference between the parties or could not place both of them. All questions contain a 'scale' of opinion positions.

Balance entry for each category of voters and issue is the percentage 'Closest to Conservatives' *minus* the percentage 'Closest to Labour'.

Policy issue	Conservative 1974			Liberal 1974			Labour 1974		
	Conservative 1979	Liberal 1979	Labour 1979	Conservative 1979	Liberal 1979	Labour 1979	Conservative 1979	Liberal 1979	Labour 1979
*Nationalisation**									
Closest to Labour	2%	8%	33%	4%	13%	12%	6%	17%	36%
Closest to Conservative	87%	73%	33%	81%	62%	40%	70%	35%	18%
Balance:	+85	+65	0	+77	+49	+28	+64	+18	−18
Stricter laws to regulate trade union activities									
Closest to Labour	2%	8%	27%	8%	13%	36%	13%	42%	44%
Closest to Conservatives	86%	77%	53%	84%	66%	36%	68%	37%	27%
Balance:	+84	+69	+26	+76	+53	0	+55	−5	−17
Tackling unemployment									
Closest to Labour	7%	8%	40%	8%	13%	40%	14%	25%	42%
Closest to Conservatives	81%	85%	40%	77%	61%	36%	62%	37%	29%
Balance:	+74	+77	0	+69	+48	−4	+48	+12	−13
*Social services**									
Closest to Labour	8%	11%	33%	10%	25%	32%	20%	35%	48%
Closest to Conservatives	69%	65%	20%	61%	44%	36%	51%	46%	21%
Balance:	+61	+54	−13	+51	+19	+4	+31	+11	−27
Tax cuts vs. government services									
Closest to Labour	27%	35%	53%	32%	48%	60%	43%	75%	65%
Closest to Conservatives	48%	46%	27%	42%	31%	16%	21%	10%	11%
Balance:	+21	+11	−26	+10	−17	−44	−22	−65	−54
How wages and salaries should be settled									
Closest to Labour	12%	27%	33%	15%	28%	36%	21%	33%	43%
Closest to Conservatives	62%	54%	13%	57%	43%	28%	52%	40%	27%
Balance:	+50	+27	−20	+42	+15	−8	+31	+7	−16
EEC economic policies									
Closest to Labour	20%	27%	47%	23%	38%	20%	30%	50%	48%
Closest to Conservatives	40%	35%	27%	34%	29%	32%	35%	21%	14%
Balance:	+20	+8	−20	+11	−9	+12	+5	−29	−34
Best way to improve race relations									
Closest to Labour	16%	15%	27%	20%	32%	32%	25%	31%	36%
Closest to Conservatives	50%	54%	47%	53%	38%	36%	53%	44%	31%
Balance:	+34	+39	+20	+33	+6	+4	+28	+13	−5
Number of respondents	452	26	15	74	98	25	79	48	451

Notes: For comparison, see Table 9.5.
*See Chapter 8.

Data source: BES May 1979 Election Survey.

of the party they left. Those involved in the exchange of voters between the Conservatives and Labour or in the circulation of the Liberals' voting support were (as one would have expected) not people with either a consistently Conservative or a consistently Labour outlook. They changed parties because they disliked some of the previous party's stands or policies but they would often still share some of the views of the party they left.

6. As a result, those switching from the Liberals to one of the major parties often did not differ very much in their views on a particular issue from those who switched in the opposite direction. Those who switched between the Conservatives and Labour in opposite directions show more different divisions of opinions on several of the issues. Even in that exchange, however, the differences between the two categories of party changers are in general much milder than the differences between the two parties' stable supporters.

7. One group of issues, however, shows a different picture of voting change in the 1979 election. This consists of the voters' opinions on the Convervatives' and Labour's ability to handle problems in the country's economy (see Table 11.3). Firstly, on these issues the prevailing opinion among stable Liberals was pro-Labour rather than pro-Conservative. Presumably, this was an important reason why they resisted the move towards the Conservatives in the 1979 election. Secondly, on these issues the categories of voters who changed in opposite directions did differ quite sharply. Conservative defectors as well as Labour defectors were apparently people who had lost faith in their previous party, and this shows in their assessments of the two parties. Likewise, there is a clear difference between those who shifted from the Conservatives to the Liberals and those who changed in the opposite direction. This is most evident in the case of opinions on Conservatives' and Labour's ability to handle *strikes*.

A summary of the evidence

The election wind in the 1979 election was blowing the electorate towards the right. For this reason the categories of voters who changed towards the left (from Conservative to Liberal or Labour, or from Liberal to Labour) are numerically small. Our summing up of the findings will therefore be based on the characteristics of the flows of the vote that went from left to right in the party system: from Labour to the Conservatives and Liberals, and from the Liberals to the Conservatives.

A summary of the data in the previous tables is presented in Table 11.6. The entries in this table have been obtained by calculating the *differences* between the balance of opinions on each issue among changers and among stable supporters of the party they left. Such difference values are given for three categ-

Table 11.6 *Opinion differences on political issues between party changers and stable voters*

Entries for each issue is the *difference* between the balance of opinions for the party changers and the stable supporters of the party they changed from (see Tables 11.3–5). In all instances except one (marked with an asterisk)
the balance of opinions is *more in favour of the Conservatives* among the changers than among the stable voters.

Political issues	Difference between balances of opinions for:		
	Stable *Labour* and changers from Labour to Conservatives 1974–1979	Stable *Labour* and changers from Labour to Liberals 1974–1979	Stable *Liberals* and changers from Liberals to Conservatives 1974–1979
Assessments of the parties' ability to handle:			
Strikes	106	11	42
Rising prices	69	14	49
Unemployment	67	17	47
Law and order	50	22	9
Opinions on policy alternatives and social changes			
Nationalisation	82	36	28
Stricter laws to regulate trade unions	72	12	23
Should comprehensive schools be established throughout the country?	62	28	19
Tackling unemployment (private enterprise or government)	61	25	21
Social services	58	38	32
Should income and wealth be redistributed?	53	9	21
How wages and salaries should be settled	47	23	27
EEC economic policies	39	5	20
Should the state control land for building developments?	38	2	7
Have social welfare benefits gone too far?	36	25	3
Should council house tenants have the right to buy their homes?	35	5	9
Best way to improve race relations	33	18	27
Tax cuts vs. government services	32	9	27
Should workers have more say at their place of work?	27	10	10
Should the powers of the House of Lords be reduced?	24	*	37
Have modern teaching methods gone too far?	14	29	6
Has reduction of Britain's military strength gone too far?	14	10	3

Data source: BES, May 1979 Election Survey.

ories: switchers from Labour to the Conservatives, switchers from Labour to Liberals, and switchers from the Liberals to the Conservatives. One example may illustrate the meaning of the difference index used in the table. The balance of opinions on nationalisation among stable Labour voters was −18 (i.e. pro-Labour), whilst the balance of opinions among changers from Labour to Conservative on the same issue was +64 (i.e. pro-Conservative). These balance values can be taken as indicators of the average opinion positions in the two groups. The difference between them is 82, which is the value given as a summary indicator in Table 11.6.

The upper section of the table comprises the voters' assessments of the Conservatives' and Labour's ability to handle some of the most important problems the country was facing (see Table 11.3).[3] The lower part of the table includes all the opinion questions about policy alternatives and the various aspects of past and prospective changes in British society (Tables 11.4–5). Within both sections the issues are ordered according to the apparent impact of opinions on voting change, in particular with reference to switches from Labour to the Conservatives.

Let us look, first, at the upper section of the table – the voters' views of the two major parties' performance in office. It is very clear that the voters who switched from Labour voting to the Conservatives were people who had lost confidence in Labour as a governing party and, in particular, in its capability of coping with strikes. In sharp contrast, those who switched from Labour to the Liberals still decidedly had more trust in Labour than in the Conservatives when it came to handling strikes, unemployment and rising prices (see also Table 11.3). When the Liberals who switched to the Conservatives are compared with stable Liberal voters, the differences are bound to be smaller. However, it is evident that the 1974 Liberal voters who switched to the Conservatives were those who definitely preferred the Conservatives' way of managing the country's economy to Labour's. In 1974, many of these voters had probably voted Liberal as a means of expressing dissatisfaction with both of the major parties. By 1979, they had come to the conclusion that the Conservative, after all, were definitely preferable to Labour; hence they voted for a change in government.

As we saw in Chapter 6, the distributions of opinions on the two major parties' performance in office indicate both the strength and the limits of the Conservative surge in 1979. Evaluations of the two major parties had shifted distinctly in favour of the Conservatives between 1974 and 1979 – but only to the extent that Labour had lost most of the advantage it had had in 1974. The Conservatives were able to recapture a considerable proportion of the voters they had lost to the Liberals. But we have also found that the flow of former Conservatives to the Liberals – albeit much smaller than the flow in the opposite direction – consisted of people who lacked confidence in the Conservatives' ability to manage the economy. Likewise, many of the Liberals who resisted the surge to the Conservatives were evidently still not convinced that a Conservative government could do a better job than Labour.

The lower section of the table allows us to examine the opinion differences between party changers and stable voters across most of the issues in current politics that bear upon policy choices and the directions of change in British society. Most of our issue questions are focused upon the differences between the Conservative and Labour parties. It is not only for that reason, however, that the most noticeable differences between changers and stable voters appear in the column pertaining to switches from Labour to the Conservatives. These were also the changers who moved the farthest. It is therefore only to be expected that their views would diverge most sharply from the opinions of the stable supporters of the party they had left. The characteristics of this category are, moreover, of special significance inasmuch as the exchange between the Conservatives and Labour resulted in a net flow of votes to the Conservatives that was apparently even bigger than the net flow from the Liberals to the Conservatives.

Two issues stand out as the most important in the flow of the votes *from Labour to the Conservatives*: nationalisation and stricter trade union legislation. Although most of the 1974 Labour voters who had doubts about their party's views on the virtues of state ownership went on voting Labour, those who did change were nearly all people who sided with the Conservatives on that issue. The questions about strikes and trade unions were matters of even more immediate concern in the 1979 election; there can be little doubt that they precipitated many 1974 Labour voters' decisions to switch to the Conservatives.

A second range of issues of intermediate importance (the range between 47 and 62 in terms of difference values) includes questions on several aspects of economic policy, incomes policy and social services. Interestingly, one entirely non-economic issue, the question about comprehensive schools, also ranks among the issues with a relatively strong impact on voting change.

A third category of issues – on which the difference between changers and stable voters was less marked – includes some specific policy questions (e.g. state control over land for building developments) as well as matters not prominent in the election (e.g. reducing the powers of the House of Lords). The question about council house tenants' right to buy their homes falls into this category. This was not, it is interesting to note, because of any lack of support for the Conservative party's proposal. Even a majority of the stable Labour supporters supported the Conservatives on that issue. Had all the October 1974 Labour voters who liked the idea of selling council houses changed their votes, the result would have been a veritable landslide to the Conservatives; but so important a matter it was not. Views on welfare benefits are low on the list because even many stable Labour voters felt that change had gone too far. Interestingly, taxation – which *was* a prominent issue – together with race relations are also on a low rung.

Labour voters who switched to the Liberals differ much less from the stable Labour voters, for the reasons discussed above. Aside from the nationalisation issue, it appears that dissatisfaction with social welfare costs were among the most common grounds for this kind of change. There is nothing in the data to suggest that the change to the Liberals had much to do with any of the policy issues on which the Liberal party had a profile of its own, for example, the EEC, incomes policy, or workers' participation in the running of enterprises.

Vote switching *from the Liberals to the Conservatives* was associated – as is seen from the column furthest to the right in the table – with being more likely than stable Liberal voters to hold a pro-Conservative opinion across the entire spectrum of issues. None of the questions about policies emerges as definitely more important than any other in this respect. The Liberal shift to the Conservatives was broadly made up of voters who were favourable to many or most of the Conservative party's stands and, in addition, had a much stronger confidence than most stable Liberals in the Conservatives' ability to tackle the problems in the economy: strikes, unemployment and rising prices.

11.2 Opinions on the issues and party choice – the overall account

An opinion distribution is obtained by summing up responses to an interview question across individuals. When this is done for each party's voters separately, the result is the cross-tabulation of an opinion classification by a voting classification – and there are frequent examples given in the tables in this book. The question naturally arises whether one could not account more accurately for individuals' voting decisions by somehow summing each individual's views across the entire array of opinion measures. Rather than looking at the relation between opinions and voting on each issue taken separately, we would then be in a position to determine the strength of the relationship between voting and the individual's opinions on all of the issues taken together.

If we do this, we would in a sense replicate the overall judgement made by the voter when he made his voting decision. Of course, we cannot observe directly how the individual was summing up his reasons for liking and disliking each of the parties. What we can do is sum up the opinions he has expressed on the many political issues which are known to bear upon many voters' party choices and then establish (using some 'counting rule') whether he is most likely to vote Conservative, Liberal or Labour. Needless to say, it cannot be assumed that all individuals actually carry out such calculations for themselves as a deliberate thought exercise. For one thing, many individuals' 'overall judgements' are the result of accumulated experience over the years. They know which party they have most confidence in and do not need to reconsider the matter afresh at every election. Nevertheless, if they did not actually reconsider their party choices, this is not to say that they did not have reasons for voting as they did in 1979. Whilst it would be unrealistic to imagine that individuals in general decide their party choices in the style of calculating machines, it would be a great deal more unrealistic to assume that they thoughtlessly repeat their party choices from election to election, without any regard to their experiences of governmental actions or the arguments in the political arena. By and large it is sensible to assume that people choose parties on grounds that make sense. To 'explain' voting decisions is then to gain insight into the ways in which such grounds combine to form the bases for decisions. Many voters will know from past experience what to think about some of the important differences between the parties – whether state ownership is good or bad, or whether keeping taxes low should be a government's first priority – and they will have answered our questions accordingly. Other opinions will express reactions to current events. The range of answers given by an individual forms a balance sheet of pros and cons that we can sum up for the purpose of our enquiry even though the individual does not always need to do the sums for each election in order to know how he or she is going to vote.

The analysis model

The statistical technique we will employ in this chapter is known as multiple regression.[4] The essence of our multiple regression model is that it 'predicts' individuals' party choices by summing up their responses to a number of interview questions which are treated as 'predicting' measures of opinions.[5] The summation obviously requires that numerical values be assigned to the responses. Furthermore, each interview question is weighted (in the regression analysis) with regard to its net usefulness as a predictor, when opinions on all the other issues are taken into account. As will be explained later we are actually using a version of multiple regression which selects the most efficient set of predictors and deletes those which prove not to yield any net addition to our ability to predict voting. (The use of the term 'prediction' in this context, incidentally, is purely conventional. In fact, we are relating individuals' opinions to voting after the event, so 'postdiction' would actually be a more appropriate term.) The accuracy of our prediction can be assessed since we know (from the interviews) how the individuals voted; it is indicated by the multiple correlation coefficient (R). The coefficient takes values between 0.0 and 1.0 according to the strength of the overall relationship between voting and the predictors.

The underlying summation model is bound to be based on the 'average effect' of each of the issue opinions in determining individuals' decisions. It does not portray the entire variety of 'counting rules' that individuals would apply if they were to sum up their position across a number of issues through analogous, individual calculations; individual variations could emerge only as 'errors' in our prediction. As a further caveat, the model presumes what we know is only partially true: namely, that issue opinions are the causes and the individuals' party choices are the result.

Our analysis model also requires that voting, like the opinion measures, be treated as a scale of numerical values for Conservative, Liberal and Labour voting, in that order.[6] We are, in effect, presuming that individuals perceived the three parties as being positioned on a scale, with the main adversaries – the Conservatives and Labour – at a long distance from each other and with the Liberals halfway between them. In the logic of the analysis model, individuals will be predicted to vote Liberal if they have neither strongly Conservative nor strongly Labour opinions on many issues, or if they combine pro-Conservative views on some issues with pro-Labour views on about as many other issues.

The main justification for this model is really that this is the way the world of the voter looked when we examined a large number of opinion distributions over the three main parties' voters: as will be recalled the division of opinions for Liberal voters was almost invariably balanced somewhere half-way between those for Conservative and Labour voters. One reason why this should be so is that most of the issues in our analysis were ones on which the Conservatives and Labour do advocate contrary views, whilst the Liberals either take an intermediate stand or else side with the Conservatives on some issues and with Labour on others. The opinion measures which involve assessments of the Conservatives' and Labour's performance in office obviously present the same kind of choice situation. Not all political issues fit this pattern, however, although the ones we have included as predictors seem to do so. To take just one contrary example, had we asked questions about proportional representation, the Liberals would have been placed on one side of the divide with both the Conservatives and Labour on the other. Moreover, not all voters' views of the choice situation in an election is entirely in accordance with our model: even when other requirements of the model are fulfilled, some of the voters whose opinions locate them somewhere half-way between the Conservatives and Labour will not seriously consider voting for a third, minor, party. Not a few of these voters may be reluctant to vote for a party with little chance of getting into office; voting for one of the two major parties one dislikes the least may then appear a more rational choice. Finally, recognising the Liberals as the party in the middle need not be a sufficient reason for voting Liberal even for voters who agree with the Conservatives on some issues and Labour on others, unless the voter feels that the Liberal party indeed represents the particular mix of policies he would want to support.

Unavoidably, these limitations will entail some diminution of the 'explanatory power' of the model, and the effect must be some reduction of the overall correlation between opinions and voting. In Chapter 12, we will employ a different analysis technique which does not require any assumption about the parties' positions relative to each other. The fact that this second analysis technique also locates the three parties along a single dimension, with the Liberals in the middle, may be taken as a further validation of the assumptions made for the present regression model. The regression model, in short, does not match the real world exactly, but it is close enough to be fully adequate for our analysis.

The model applied

As will be recalled from the earlier chapters, our enquiry comprises three broad groups of opinion measurements: one is concerned with the voters' views on the Conservatives' and Labour's performance in office when it comes to handling the economic problems the country is facing; the second was intended to record electoral responses to societal change, and the third was concerned with the main policy alternatives that the parties offered in the 1979 election. The interview questions in these groups are different with regard to format but to some extent the groups are overlapping in the sense that questions in different groups elicit opinions on the same issues from different viewpoints. How strong is the joint relationship between the political opinions recorded in each of these groups and party choice? And how far can all of these measurements, when taken together, account for voting in that election? The answers are given in the form of multiple correlation coefficients in Table 11.7.

The bottom row of the table shows that the entire array of opinion measures has a multiple correlation of 0.77 with party choice.[7] This constitutes a far greater 'explanatory power' than could have been achieved by using any single opinion measure. It is also greater than the multiple correlations for each of the three groups of questions taken separately, as is shown by the table.

Before we can evaluate this result, however, we need to look at the other statistic given in the table: 'the explained proportion of the variance'. This is actually the squared value of the multiple correlation coefficient. As was explained, we have transformed voting for the three main parties into a numerical scale. Individuals obviously have different score values on that scale, and for all individuals the spread around the mean value is summarised by the 'variance' statistic. The squared correlation coefficient indicates how large a proportion of that

Table 11.7 *Multiple correlations between groups of opinion measures and voting in the 1979 election*

Group of opinion measures	Multiple correlation (R) between voting and each group of opinion	Explained proportion of the variance (R^2)
Assessment of the Conservatives' and Labour's ability to handle economic problems: strikes, unemployment, prices*	0.69	0.48
Responses to change: 'Left/right' and 'social welfare' attitude dimensions**	0.57	0.32
Policy alternatives in the 1979 election***	0.68	0.46
All opinion measures	0.77	0.59

*See Chapter 6.
**See Chapter 7.
***All the eight policy alternative issues discussed in Chapters 8–9.

Data source: BES May 1979 Election Survey.

variance that the predictors jointly account for. If it were nothing, the value would be zero; if it were the entire variance, the value would be 1.0.[8] The same statistic is given for each of the three groups of predictors.

We have included 'explained proportion of the variance' in the table in order to make one important point. The sum of the explained proportions for the three groups is considerably larger than the proportion they account for together, which is 0.59 (or 59 per cent of the variance). Partly this is because the contents of the questions in the three groups overlap, by containing opinion measures that relate to the same issues. If we know a person's opinion on, for example, Labour's ability to deal with strikes, this helps us to 'predict' how he will vote. If we also know whether he is for or against stricter laws to regulate trade union activities, we are able to 'predict' his vote even more accurately. The two questions can both be thought of as indicators of the different elements in the individual's views on how a government should deal with industrial relations. If one uses both together, the overall result is a better measurement. But clearly the two measures to some extent duplicate each other. The proportion of the variance these measures account for jointly is, therefore, larger than either of them can achieve alone but smaller than the sum of the two proportions they account for when taken on their own.

Interestingly, the same also applies to opinion measurements that do not obviously pertain to the same issue. Individuals' opinions on political issues are not unrelated to each other. People who are conservative on one issue are more likely than others to be conservative also on other issues. Radical opinions tend to go together in the same fashion. For example, if we already know that a person is strongly in favour of more nationalisation, more social services, and a more equal distribution of income and wealth, then we know that he is very likely to vote Labour. We add a little, but not much, to the certainty of our prediction by ascertaining that he is also in favour of, say, state control over land to be used for building development. Actually, we could predict fairly safely his answer to the last question, given his answers to the previous ones. In general, the more we know about a person's opinions on political matters, the better can we predict his vote. But because opinions are interdependent, diminishing returns will be obtained when we add on more and more opinion measurements as predictors of party choice.

It is for these reasons that we find in Table 11.7 that two groups of opinion measures each could account for the main part of the explanatory power of the entire set. The one of these groups comprises voters' assessments of the Conservatives' and Labour's ability to deal effectively with economic problems. The other includes the set of opinions on policy alternatives in the 1979 election.[9] The remaining group consists of measures drawn from our battery of questions about social and cultural change. Among these, we have included only opinions associated with the two partisan attitude dimensions that emerged in the factor analysis in Chapter 7. The content of the questions in this set is actually not much different from that covered by the policy alternative questions, although the questions are put in a different format. The single most effective predictor was the question about comprehensive schools.[10] If we combine the second and third groups of opinion measures in the table, the multiple correlation coefficient rises to 0.71 which is not much less than the maximum value we can achieve (which was 0.77).

These opinion measurements did in fact ask the respondents to make two different types of judgement. One is concerned with the well-known problems in today's Britain which any government must encounter. Almost everyone agrees that much depends on how successfully a government manages the economy. There is hardly any disagreement about the goals: most people want stable prices, full employment, and peaceful industrial relations. The question is, which party is best equipped to deal with these problems, or, at least, not make them worse? Our measures of the voters' assessments of the parties' performance in office have essentially recorded some of the judgements that individuals would have made when they answered that question. The other type of question is focused upon the goals and means of policy making: do the parties propose policies or approaches that are likely to lead to desirable results? In order to map individuals' views on such matters, we needed to employ a larger number of opinion measures. The number of measurements required is not excessively large, though. In fact, the data in Table 11.7 demonstrate that information about individuals' opinions on, say, eight or nine policy questions allows us to 'explain' their party choice as well or better than we could do by relying on their simple evaluations of the parties' performance in office.

In reality, of course, voters make both kinds of judgements, and the one kind of judgement is likely to be dependent on the other. If a voter believes that a party's economic policies are all wrong, he is not very likely to have much trust in its ability to cope with the country's economy either. And if a voter has come to believe that the country is better governed when one of the parties is in office, it is likely that he will have more confidence in the specific policies that that party is advocating (at least to the extent that he knows what the party proposes to do). The two types of interview questions are thus complementary for the purpose of explaining voting behaviour, because the answers reflect both of these aspects of the individual's choice situation.

Even when all the opinion measures are used, it is obvious that our multiple regression model falls short of explaining why all of the voters voted the way they did. We do not feel apologetic about this for the simple reason that a 'full explanation' in that sense is always an elusive goal for research into human behaviour. Although we can claim that the scope of the total set of opinion questions includes most of the things that were important to the large majority in the electorate, the variety of reasons that individuals can have for voting for a party is even larger. For one thing, all the questions in this part of the enquiry are concerned with what parties do, or propose to do. If someone casts his vote for a party mainly on the grounds that all his family and friends think it is the best, then his reason would not be recorded through any of the interview questions employed here. Moreover, as we have pointed out, the analysis model has its limitations and, finally, all survey data are vulnerable to measurement errors. Yet, if the experience gained from other and similar survey studies is taken as the standard, a multiple correlation of 0.77 for the relationship between a set of opinion measures and voting behaviour is undoubtedly very reassuring.

This lends credence to the two basic assumptions in this analysis: that voting decisions can be realistically described by a model that summarises individuals' opinions across several aspects of politics, and that the matters which bear upon most individuals' overall judgements of the parties can be adequately represented by a parsimonious set of interview questions about the current issues in party politics. In short, the model has done very well.

11.3 The issues that mattered most

Political opinions and the party division of the vote – the two sides of the relationship

One obvious way of appraising how differing opinions on a political issue are related to party choice is to examine a table of a type that has appeared frequently in the preceding chapters: individuals are divided into categories according to their opinions on the matter and the party division of the vote is given in per cent for each category in the columns of the table. If the opinion categories are ordered from, say, the one with the most strongly pro-Labour opinion at the one end to the most pro-Conservative at the other, with intermediate opinion positions in between, then one usually finds that the Labour share of the vote declines and the Conservative share increases as one reads off the percentages across the columns in the table. (Table 8.5 might serve as an example, illustrating the relationship between opinions on nationalisation and party choice.) The more the opinion categories differ with regard to the party division of the vote (for example, the more sharply the Conservative percentage increases from category to category), the more difference must opinions on that particular issue have made to individuals' voting decisions. In fact, in this chapter we shall not look at tables of that kind (such tables were discussed, e.g. in Chapter 9). Instead we will make further use of our regression analysis to determine 'how much difference' opinions on each of the issues made. This allows us to include all the issues in one comprehensive analysis and obtain a 'net weight' for each of the issues when the individuals' opinions on all the other issues are taken into account.

However – just as we noted in the preceding analysis of the impact of the issues on vote switching – the impact of an issue on the overall election result depends also on another side of the state of opinion in the electorate: the *distribution of opinions* for and against the stands taken by the parties. It is this distribution of opinions that reveals how the electorate at large has responded to the issue. For example, if there is a Conservative and a Labour policy alternative to choose between, we may find that opinions are about equally balanced, or that the balance of opinions is more or less strongly weighted in favour of the stand taken by one of the parties. The percentage distributions in the columns in the kind of table described above would not capture that side of the impact of the issue on the electorate; instead one would need to look at the number of individuals in each of the opinion eategories.

Obviously, not all the voters who support a party's view on a particular issue will actually vote for that party. But if a voter shares the views of one of the parties, this is likely to have been one of the things that at least counts in its favour when he considers the good and bad points about the parties. The impact of an issue on the party division of the vote will depend both on 'how much difference it makes' to individuals' voting decisions and the distribution of opinions in the electorate as a whole. If it 'makes a great difference' to individuals' propensity to vote Conservative or Labour whether they take the one view or the other on a given issue, then the effect on the party division of the vote will still be dependent upon the size of the portion of the electorate that agrees with each of the parties. If that division of opinions is about equally balanced, then even if the issue had a strong influence on individuals' voting decisions, the impact on the party division of the vote could well be neutral. That is, the number of voters 'pulled' towards each of the parties could cancel out, leaving none of the parties with any net advantage. In general, an issue will clearly have the most impact on the party division of the vote when two conditions are fulfilled: when opinions on the issue 'make a great deal of difference' to individuals and at the same time the distribution of opinions in the electorate as a whole is weighted in favour of one of the parties. In the extreme opposite case – when the relationship between individuals' opinions on the issue and their party choice is weak, and the balance of opinions in the electorate is even – the impact on the party division of the vote would be insignificant.

In the following examination of the data we will use a simple indicator of the *balance of opinions* on each of the issues. This is based on the percentage distribution of pro-Conservative, ambiguous or neutral, and pro-Labour opinions on the issue concerned in the electorate. The balance index is obtained by subtracting the pro-Labour percentage from the pro-Conservative percentage. The difference obviously indicates whether, and to what extent, the distribution of opinions was weighted in favour of one of the two major parties. A positive balance value reflects a Conservative advantage, a negative value a Labour advantage.

We can think of the balance of opinions over an issue as a measure of both the direction and the extent of a motivational force which pulls the electorate towards one of the parties. The direction indicates which party is being advantaged; the size of the balance indicates how much net advantage, in terms of electoral appeal, the party would have with regard to the issue concerned. As opinions on some issues affect individuals' voting decisions more than others, we can take 'the difference it makes to party choice' as a measure of the *strength* of the pull. The overall effect of the pull, it should be stressed, is not limited to contributing to vote switching. The pull will undoubtedly influence some voters to switch to another party. But for many voters the effect will be that their previous party preferences are reinforced, whilst others may continue to vote for the same party as before but with less conviction.

A balance of opinions in favour of one of the parties on one of the issues thus indicates that a comparatively large portion of the electorate could be attracted to that party (and repelled by its opponents). Whether this results in any gain of voting support will depend on several contingent factors, such as the degree of prominence of the issue in the campaign and the importance of the matter to individuals when they make their voting decisions. Individuals will, furthermore, often experience pulls in different directions on different issues. The joint impact of opinions on all of the issues on the party division of the vote will, therefore, be the result of several motivational forces of different strength, direction and extent. Some of these will reinforce each other; others will be countervailing.

These are circumstances that the parties can influence, at least to some extent, through their campaign strategies. Each of the parties will do well by steering attention towards the issues where it feels that the underlying balance of opinions is in its favour. When presenting its case to the electorate, a party will not only endeavour to win the battle of arguments: it will also seek the battlegrounds where it is most likely to succeed. But since there is more than one party, some battles will inevitably be fought on unwelcome grounds for at least one of them.

The scenario is likely to change from one election to the next. New controversies between the parties create new issues, while others fade away. Although the social and ideological dividing lines between the parties may remain unchanged, the matters that they are seen to disagree about are changeable: in 1974 as well as in 1979, the Conservatives and Labour obviously represented different views on the role of the state in the management of the economy, but the concrete issues that came to the fore in the two campaigns were quite different. And parties change their stands, too, as is exemplified by the incomes policy issue. Likewise the balance of opinions in the electorate over policies in one or more areas may change. We have seen, for example, that opinions shifted towards a less favourable assessment of Labour's ability to steer the economy between October 1974 and 1979, and that opinions on nationalisation and social services moved to the right during this period. We will look to the effects of such changes over time in the concluding section of this chapter, but first we shall examine our data on the two sides of the relationship between issue opinions and the party division of the vote in the 1979 election.

Selecting the issues that counted

As we have explained earlier, some opinion measures made little difference to the multiple correlation once the relationship between voting and other opinions had been taken into account. The version of multiple regression employed here is devised so as to select those opinion measures that jointly account for as much as possible with regard to individuals' party choice. In doing so the regression procedure deletes those opinion measures that turn out not to make any significant additional contribution. The procedure is stepwise.[11] The best single predictor of voting is selected first. Taking into account that the remaining opinion measures to some extent duplicate what has already been accounted for, the one that yields the biggest increment in the multiple correlation coefficient is selected next. The same criterion is applied in the following steps, and in each step an additional opinion measure is added. The procedure comes to a halt either when all predictors have been included or when all those left are found to be superfluous in the sense that none of them improves the joint predictive power significantly.[12]

An example may serve as an illustration of the logic of the model. Actually, our example is also of substantive interest. We have applied the multiple regression model to the four measures used to record the voters' assessments of the Conservatives' and Labour's performances in office. The multiple regression is built up in steps as is shown below:

Assessment of the Conservatives' and Labour's ability to handle:	Multiple correlation at each step
1. Strikes	0.60
2. Unemployment	0.67
3. Rising prices	0.69
4. Upholding law and order	0.70

Voters' views on the two parties' economic policy performances are good examples of correlated opinions. Those who think highly of, say, Labour's record on strikes also tend to be more favourable than others in their judgements of the party's handling of unemployment and inflation. We can think of each of these questions as a means of eliciting both an overall assessment of the Conservatives' and Labour's performance in office and a more specific evaluation of their handling of the economic problem concerned. Both of these components are reflected in the respondents' answers to the question about strikes which was first selected. Only a modest improvement in the multiple correlation is then achieved by including also opinions on unemployment, and the addition of opinions on inflation yields only a very small increment.

The law and order issue comes last. When taken separately it shows a substantial relationship to voting (though much lower than assessments relating to economic policy) but its additional contribution to the multiple correlation of assessments of the parties' performance in office is very slight. To put it another way: when we have already taken into account voters' opinions on the parties' economic records, knowing also their views on law and order adds only slightly to our ability to explain their choice of party.

This illustrative example included only four opinion measures and none of them was deleted. We will next examine a set of opinion measures which encompasses all the important issues in the 1979 election.

Constructing a balance sheet

The information contained in Table 11.8 can be likened to a still frame taken from a moving picture: the campaign is over, the votes have been cast, and the state of opinion in the electorate at that point of time is captured. The table takes in all the main issues in the campaign that are recorded in our opinion measurements: voters' assessments of the parties' performances in office, as well as opinions on policy questions. In the latter category we have included all the eight policy alternative questions discussed in Chapters 8 to 9, together with those items in the battery of questions about what a government should do (or should not do) that were concerned with specific policy alternatives rather than general goals. As before, the multiple regression analysis pertains to the three-party vote (excluding non-voters and those who voted for minor parties); the multiple correlation coefficient indicating the joint relationship between all the opinion measures and voting is again 0.77.[13]

The stepwise regression procedure described above was applied to this entire set of opinion measures. The opinion measures that were selected by the regression analysis as 'predictors' are ordered from 1 to 13 (see the left-hand side of the table) according to how much difference having a pro-Conservative rather than a pro-Labour opinion made to party choice. The difference measure used in this instance is, however, more elaborate than the one used when one reads off percentage differences in a table. The regression analysis yields a series of 'weights' (regression coefficients) which indicate 'how much difference' opinions on each of the issues make over and above the effects of individuals' opinions on all the other issues. The rank-ordering of opinion measures in the table is based on these weights.[14]

In a simplified fashion, the essence of this 'difference' criterion for ordering the opinion measures is illustrated by Figure 11.A. The horizontal axis represents a scale of opinion positions on a particular issue, ranging from pro-Labour to pro-Conservative. The ascending lines represent the Conservative share of the vote at each point along the scale. The unbroken line (Case 1) illustrates the case when opinions 'made a great deal of difference' to voting. The flatter, dotted line (Case 2) represents the case when the impact on individual party choice was noticeably weaker. It is the steepness of this line that is indicated by the 'weights'.

Table 11.8 *The issues that mattered most*

As explained in the text, the measures of opinions are *ordered* with regard to 'how much difference' individuals' opinion positions made to party choice (i.e. the values of the standardised regression coefficients). The relationship between each opinion measures, taken separately, and voting is indicated by the product moment *correlation coefficient (r)*.

 Conservative-Labour balance of opinions: For each opinion measure, we have calculated the percentages of respondents with pro-Conservative opinions, pro-Labour opinions, and ambiguous opinions ('same distance', 'don't know', etc.). *Entry* in the table is the percentage with pro-Conservative opinions *minus* the percentage with pro-Labour opinions. A + Sign indicates a pro-Conservative balance of opinions, whereas a – sign indicates a pro-Labour balance of opinions.

Opinions on:	Correlation (r) between voting and each opinion measure taken separately	Conservative–Labour balance of opinions
Conservatives' and Labour's handling of problems in the economy		
1. Strikes	0.60	+2
2. Unemployment	0.59	+1
3. Prices	0.58	–18
Policy alternatives and policy proposals on:		
4. (2) Nationalisation	0.51	+40
5. (1) Stricter laws to regulate trade unions	0.51	+35
6. (3) Comprehensive schools	0.45	+16
7. (4) Tax cuts vs. keeping up standard of government services	0.37	–16
8. (5) Social services and benefits	0.43	+17
9 (8) State control over land for building developments	0.36	+11
10. (7) Tackling unemployment and create new jobs: private enterprise or government	0.46	+32
11. (6) How wages and salaries should be settled	0.35	+15
12. Conservatives' and Labour's handling of law and order	0.42	+34
13. (9) EEC economic policies	0.27	–5
* Race relations and immigration	0.21	+13
* (10) Allowing council house tenants to buy their homes	0.24	+60
* (11) Reducing the power of the House of Lords	0.32	+6

*Opinion measures which made no significant additional contribution to the multiple correlation coefficient, when the issues listed above had been taken into account.

Data source: BES May 1979 Election Survey.

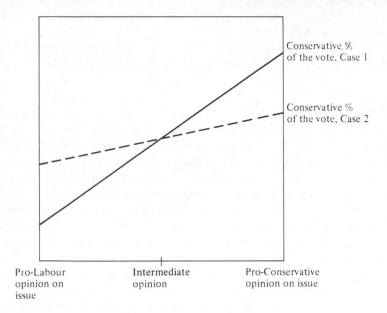

Figure 11.A

What we cannot illustrate in this simple picture, however, is the adjustment made so as to gauge only the 'net effect' of a particular issue over and above the effects of other opinions. In the actual regression analysis, furthermore, voting is represented by a three-point scale (Labour–Liberal–Conservative) rather than the Conservative vote alone.

Table 11.8 also shows the correlation coefficients for the relationship between voting and each opinion measure taken separately. In this instance, we use a measure of that relationship which is obtained as part of the regression analysis, the product moment correlation coefficient, r. It is not identical to the Tau-b coefficient used in the preceding tables but its essential meaning is the same (however, the values of the coefficients tend to be slightly higher than the Tau-b coefficients).[15]

Some of the opinion measures in our list were found to make no significant additional contribution to the multiple correlations, once the more powerful predictors had been taken into account. These appear at the bottom of the table, marked with an asterisk. These measures showed comparatively weak relationships to voting even when taken separately, as is seen from the correlation coefficients. The fact that they appear to count for even less in the regression analysis does not mean, it should be noted, that the relationships between voting and opinions on these matters were in any sense spurious or 'unreal'. It is only that they are correlated both to voting and to opinions on the thirteen issues that had already been employed as predictors of voting; therefore no significant additional information about the individuals' opinion positions could be gained by adding these measures.

The column farthest to the right in the table shows the Conservative–Labour 'balance of opinions' recorded by each of our opinion measures.[16]

The final account

We will examine the results of the analysis presented in Table 11.8, firstly, with regard to the relationship between opinions and individual voting decisions and then turn our attention to the 'balance of opinion' measures.

The ordering of the opinion measures indicates, as explained above, their importance for voting decisions in the sense of 'how much difference' opinions on each issue made to the voters' party choice. When reading down the list of opinion measures in the table, the first observation is that all the measures of the voters' views on the parties' ability to handle economic problems come forward as the most important. It must, of course, be kept in mind that these assessments involved an explicit evaluation of the parties: undoubtedly this will have contributed to make them powerful 'predictors' of which party the voter actually preferred. On the other hand, question format alone would not turn an opinion question into an efficient 'predictor' of voting. The questions asked about the parties' capability of upholding law and order were asked in the same format and yet that assessment of the Conservatives' and Labour's performances appears way down the list. It thus seems warranted to infer that it was the economic policy contents that so decisively brought the other assessment measures to the top of the list.

Then follow the two questions about policy alternatives that have consistently emerged as the most important in the 1979 election: nationalisation and stricter legal regulation of trade union activities. Why was nationalisation apparently so important in an election when the Labour party hardly made it an issue, or even advocated further nationalisation? The most plausible explanation is that the Conservatives' 'free enterprise' alternative to the economic policies of the past years made the whole question of state control of the economy a dominant theme in people's minds. That theme was easily recognisable in the nationalisation issue. In that context, the question of nationalisation became as much an ideological shibboleth as an economic policy issue in the narrow sense. Voters who knew that they wanted to support the Conservatives' alternative economic strategy would always know that it meant private enterprise rather than state ownership of industries.

It is noteworthy that trade union legislation comes so high on the list. As we have seen earlier, the voters views on the proper role of trade unions were not consistently negative towards the unions. But clearly there was strong support for stricter legal regulation of the unions. Of particular interest is the division

Table 11.9 *Voters' views on the Conservatives' and Labour's ability to handle strikes and opinions on stricter laws to regulate the trade unions – the joint effect on the Conservative share of the vote*

In this table the voters are first divided (in the columns) according to their assessments of each party's ability to handle strikes. Secondly (in the rows) they are divided according to opinions on the trade union legislation issue. *Entry* in the table is the Conservative percentage share of the three-party vote within each of the resulting nine categories. The number of respondents in each category is given within parentheses under each percentage.

Opinions on stricter laws to regulate trade unions	Opinions on the parties' ability to handle strikes			
	Pro-Labour	Ambivalent	Pro-Conservative	All respondents in the row
Closest to Conservatives	27% (162)	64% (276)	84% (450)	68% (888)
Same distance/no opinion	6% (128)	34% (129)	70% (63)	30% (320)
Closest to Labour	4% (223)	14% (74)	68% (28)	12% (325)
All respondents in the column	12% (513)	48% (479)	82% (541)	

Data source: BES May 1979 Election Survey.

of opinion among voters who were not sure whether the Conservatives or Labour were more able to handle the problem of strikes; those voters made up nearly a third of the three-party vote. A detailed analysis shows that a majority among them were closest to the Conservatives on the question of trade union legislation and, again, a strong majority (64 per cent) within that group cast their votes for the Conservatives. The combined effect of opinions on these two issues is shown in more detail in Table 11.9. The logic is by no means inexplicable: it is perfectly possible to believe both that the Labour government is about as good as a Conservative government at handling strikes *and* at the same time that a Conservative government would be more likely to cut the power of the trade unions down to size.

Returning to Table 11.8 at the bottom of the list we find the issues that have consistently emerged as those that made the least difference to individual voting decisions. The question of law and order is in that category for reasons already discussed. The question about Britain's role in the EEC – which never really seems to have been seen as a domestic economic policy issue of any great significance – is in the same category. The question of how to deal with race relations and immigration is even deleted altogether by the multiple regression, appearing 'under the line', with an asterisk, in the table. It is perhaps less surprising that the right of council house tenants to buy their homes is in the same category of issues of marginal importance, although the Conservative plan was met with broad approval; it was a matter of immediate interest only to the minority in the electorate who were both council house tenants and who wanted to buy their homes. The question of the powers of the House of Lords, a matter of at least symbolic ideological significance, appears likewise among these marginal issues, although obviously for different reasons.

An intermediate group of issues is formed by opinions on more specific aspects of economic policy, taxation and social welfare. As we have seen already, these opinions on policy choice (including nationalisation and trade union legislation) could alone muster almost as much explanatory power as the entire set. Broadly speaking, it was the questions about the country's economy and its citizens' standards of living that counted most, irrespective of how we gauge the state of opinion in the electorate.

The regression analysis brings to light, however, one exception from this pattern. The question about comprehensive schools, to which we have previously paid only passing attention, now emerges as a matter on which opinions had a strong relationship to voting decisions. Once the voters' assessments of the country's economy and the questions of nationalisation and trade union law have been taken into account, the school issue emerges as a significant matter for many voters.

The evaluations of each party's economic performance cover broadly the same ground as the more specific economic policy questions. In order to determine whether this had any appreciable impact on the rank-ordering of the policy alternative issues, we carried out a second multiple regression analysis in which the evaluation questions were not included. The rank-ordering of the issues then obtained is indicated by the numbers within parentheses immediately following the rank-order numbers to the left in Table 11.8. As can be seen from this second number series, exclusion of the evaluation questions altered the rank-ordering only in a minor way; it is interesting, though, that in this version of the analysis, the trade union issue comes to the top of the list.

In what *direction*, then, was the electorate as a whole moved by the issues that counted most when individual voters made their party choice? To answer that question we need to look at the balance of opinion measures in the column furthest to the right in the table.

As we found in Chapter 6, if the voters' evaluations of the parties' records on the handling of economic problems had alone decided the result, the Conservatives would hardly have won. Confidence in the Labour party had declined with regard to its record on both unemployment and strikes. But the Conservatives had not convinced the majority in the electorate that their record was better; and on the question of prices the Labour party had launched an effective counter-offensive. On each of these questions, around a quarter to a third of the electorate did not rate either of the parties more highly than the other. The overall result of these evaluations may almost give an impression of a stalemate.

As the example with the strikes issue showed, however, the Conservatives were able to turn the general trade union issue into an asset by proposing to do something about the power of the trade unions. In the same way, the electorate was 'pulled' towards the Conservatives on almost all the salient questions about the course that the country should steer in the future and the means that should be used in economic policies. Across the board there are pro-Conservative balances, in favour of calling a halt to nationalisation, regulating the unions, backing private enterprises rather than relying on government to open up new job opportunities, withdrawing the government's involvement in the settling of wages, and cutting back on social services. There was in fact more support for the Conservative than for Labour policies on all of the policy choice issues, except two: whether priority should be given to tax cuts, and Britain's relations with the EEC. In the latter case, the pro-Labour margin was small and the issue was not rated among the most important. With regard to taxation, it was by no means clear from the Conservatives' campaign message that a tax cut *would* necessitate any pruning of essential government services.[17] The impact of the Conservative alternative in economic policy apparently overrode many people's doubts about the Conservatives record on strikes, inflation and unemployment – whilst it combined with discontent with Labour's record to cause defections from Labour.

Opinion change and voting change: October 1974 – 1979

In one perspective, the outcome of the 1979 election can be seen as the result of the direction and strength of the motivational forces that prevailed at the time of that election. But the change since October 1974 can also be described in terms of the changes in opinion between October 1974 and 1979. We have opinion measurements from October 1974 and May 1979 for nine issues on which there was some substantial relationship between opinions and party choice.[18] On seven of the nine, opinions in the electorate shifted in favour of the Conservative party. On only one, handling of inflation, was there any change to Labour's advantage. The flow of confidence in the Labour government's handling of unemployment and strikes, which strengthened Labour's standing in the October 1974 election, had subsided and been reversed. Opinions on national-isation and social welfare policies signalled a general shift in the mood of the electorate away from welfare state politics. In the case of incomes policy, one of the issues that contributed to the election outcome, it was not so much the opinions of the electorate that had changed as the positions of the parties. In October 1974 the Labour party was still seen as the party that had ended the statutory incomes policy of the Heath era; in 1979 Labour was for an incomes policy whilst the Conservatives were against. As we saw in Chapter 10, this was not the way the issue was seen by all the voters; but Labour was nonetheless faced with a balance of opinions that favoured the Conservatives also on that score.

All the evidence we have reviewed here points to one main conclusion. The electorate in 1979 did not merely vote out of office a government that had lost much of its popularity. With one possible exception – the public's wish to main-tain the standard of public services – the prevailing mood in the electorate was broadly in line with the Conservatives' programme for economic recovery. Yet, whilst there was strong overall support for almost every plank in the Conservative platform, voters who supported some Conservative proposals did not necessarily agree with all of them, even if they cast their votes for the Conservative party. The Conservatives, as well as Labour and the Liberals, drew a significant portion of their votes from among voters whose support for the party they voted for was qualified – sometimes even to the point that they seriously thought of voting for another party during the campaign. Much of the analysis in the following chapters will be concerned with the formation of vote decisions during the campaign and the final division of the vote within this 'middle ground' in the electorate.

12

The electorate and the party system

12.1 The party system and the voters

Thinking of oneself as Conservative, Liberal, or Labour (or as a Nationalist in Scotland and Wales) is a common enough notion for most British voters. More than eight out of ten of those eligible to vote in the 1979 election said yes, they did 'generally speaking' side with one or the other of the parties in that sense. Of those who voted in the 1979 election, more than eight out of ten cast their votes for either the Conservatives or Labour. Outside Scotland, Wales and Ulster, all but a trickle of the currents of opinions in the electorate were channelled through the three main parties.

Such is the stability in voting behaviour, and such are the effects of the electoral order that the Conservatives and Labour, again, emerged as the two major parties with the Liberals continuing to play their role as the 'third party' in the system. In an earlier era, W. S. Gilbert found it comical that nature contrives to make everyone either a Conservative or a Liberal. Yet, the fact that the Liberals at one time were replaced by Labour as the Conservatives' main opponent serves as a reminder that the structure of the party system is neither given by nature nor unchangeable (although this is an historical fact, rather than a matter of personal experience for most of the 1979 electorate). Once formed, the present party system structure has been sustained. Whilst the boundaries of the social bases of the Conservative and Labour parties may be fading (as we saw in Chapter 3), the tendency for middle-class voters to side with the Conservatives and manual workers to side with Labour is still a powerful stabilising factor. So is the electoral order, which has set a high threshold against the Liberals' attempts to challenge the two major parties' dominance. Generations of voters have become accustomed to think of the Conservatives and Labour as the two real alternatives in power. Yet, the February 1974 election seemed to signal that the edifice was less safely founded than many would have believed only a few years earlier. More than one voter in five refused to act on the assumption that there were only two real alternatives.

The 1979 Conservative victory may on the face of it look like a return to

normal. The pendulum undeniably swung from the one major party to the
other. Yet, quite apart from subsequent developments, there were elements
in the 1979 election outcome that call for caution. The Conservatives failed
to recapture the share of the voters that they had normally achieved when
winning elections during the 1950s and in 1970. The Conservatives, furthermore, were helped to victory by gains among manual workers that may prove
a more fickle electoral asset than the 'deferential working-class vote' of the
past, and they no longer command quite the strong middle-class support that
they used to. On the other side of the class divide, the social trends of the
1960s seemed destined to strengthen the support for Labour among manual
workers. But the 1970s has, instead, been a period of decline for Labour's
hold over the working-class vote.[1]

If the social bases of the parties have become softer, how much did their
opinion bases differ and how sharply were the boundaries drawn? In the first
part of this chapter we make use of our measures of opinions on political issues
to answer that question. Then we go on to examine two other aspects of the
partisan division of the electorate – the extent to which voters had a sense of
allegiance to one or the other of the parties, and the voters' perceptions of
the party system: how much difference they thought there was between the
two major parties and where they thought the Liberals were placed in relation
to the Conservatives and Labour.

12.2 The opinion bases of party support

No party is supported by a homogeneous bloc of opinion in the electorate. Whilst
we have seen that voters do tend to vote for the party whose policies they agree
with, we have also found that there is a quite wide dispersion of opinions even
among voters who support the same party. Our data allow us to identify categories of voters whose policy opinions were strongly and consistently partisan,
but with regard to a great many more voters one could not do much more than
infer that their opinions made them somewhat more likely to vote for the one
party than for the other. Given that spread in the opinion bases of the parties,
their bases are bound to overlap. Among people whose opinions are neither
consistently Conservative nor consistently Labour, some will vote for one of
these parties and some for the other – even though their opinions seem to differ
little or not at all.

The opinion bases of the parties can be described for each of the issues in the
campaign, as in the preceding chapters. But we have seen that our opinion
measures jointly provided a powerful means of exploring the relationship between
voting and individuals' opinions across the whole range of issues. In this chapter,
we employ a similar technique to obtain a 'scale of partisanship in issue opinions'.
All the voters in the sample can be placed at some position on that scale and we
can furthermore describe the distribution of opinions in the electorate as a whole

as well as among the supporters of each of the three main parties. This will enable us to locate the 'centre of gravity' of each party's electoral base on the scale, delineate the areas from which the parties draw their support and the extent to which these areas overlap. Examining the electoral bases of the three main parties in this perspective will lead to a related question: who occupied the middle ground?

A one-dimensional party system?

One well-known way of describing the British party system requires the use of only three terms: left, right and centre. Draw a line, mark a position to the left for Labour, a place in the centre for the Liberals, a position to the right for the Conservatives – and there is a map of the party system. The map is pleasingly simple, and it is sufficiently true to the real world of politics to serve as a useful guide for many purposes. It illustrates, for example, what one has in mind when describing a change in party politics by stating that the Conservatives have moved towards the right. This kind of map of the party system is often implicitly referred to also in statements about the distribution of political views in the electorate. Imagine that all voters could be assigned to points on the left/right line according to the outlook of each of them. The voters would be spread along the scale, some even to the right of the Conservative party's position, and some even to the left of Labour. Some of them would be located in the mid area of the scale, not very close to either of the two major parties. If the voters themselves use the same map, they will vote for the party they are closest to on the scale. Terms like 'the middle ground in the electorate' or 'right-wing Conservative voters' have a readily understandable meaning in relation to this picture of the party system.

If this map is simple, it can also be misleadingly simplistic.[2] Firstly, not all differences between the parties can be accommodated on just one scale or dimension. When the Liberals argue the case for community politics or proportional representation, they cannot be seen to take an intermediate position between the Conservatives and Labour; rather, they stand at one pole on a completely different scale, with both of the other parties standing at the opposite pole. Questions about civil liberties, devolution, and Britain's role in Europe raise similar problems. Furthermore, even if the left/right scale is taken to represent only party differences with regard to social and economic issues (for which it appears most appropriate), it is not so certain that the distances between the parties on the scale need look the same on all the issues. The Liberals might, for example, seem closer to the Conservatives on private enterprise but closer to Labour's views on the welfare state.

We do not aim to resolve all of these problems of defining party positions in the present enquiry, although the concluding part of this chapter will throw some light on the matter by describing how the party system was perceived by the voters. At this stage we will be concerned only with voters' opinions on policies. Our data will thus reflect the opinions of Conservative, Liberal and Labour voters, rather than, say, the actual positions of their parties. The positions of the parties themselves come within the scope of this analysis only indirectly, because our opinion questions confronted the respondents with matters on which the parties advocate different policies.[3]

When we construct, as we are about to do, a summary measure of individuals' opinion positions, the result can be interpreted as just that: a summing up of the individuals' reasons for and against supporting the parties in the system. As will be seen, by this means we arrive at a description of the bases of the parties' electoral support that bears a close resemblance to the simple, left/right re-presentation of the party system. What we describe, however, are not the parties' positions but the distributions of opinions among the voters who supported each of the three parties.

The analysis technique

To obtain a summarising description of individuals' opinion positions, we use an analysis technique known as discriminant analysis. As applied here, the discriminant analysis explores the relationship between party choice and a number of opinion measurements (the same as those employed in the multiple regression analysis). As part of this analysis, it is determined whether the opinion differences between Conservative, Liberal and Labour voters can best be described by summarising all of the opinion measures in a single comprehensive scale of opinion positions. If not, each individual's position will be defined in relation to more than one 'scale' or 'dimension'. In this instance, the discriminant analysis created only one such scale ranging between two poles, one strongly Conserva-tive, the other strongly Labour.

Our account relies, ultimately, on the contents of our interview questions, most of which were concerned with economic and social welfare issues. These are the kind of issues for which the idea of a single left/right dimension appears to be most suited in the first place – that limitation has actually been imposed by the results of the previous stages in this enquiry, though. We have in fact reviewed several opinion measures that bear upon non-economic, cultural and social values (the death penalty, equality for women, abortion and so on). These opinion measures are not included in the present analysis simply because opinions on such matters bore little or no relationship to individuals' party choice.

The technical procedures in discriminant analysis cannot be presented in full here.[4] It is enough to say that the purpose of the analysis is to establish how accurately a number of 'discriminants' – for example, opinion questions – can jointly discriminate between the members of two or more groups, namely the groups consisting of Conservative, Liberal and Labour voters. The analysis actu-ally 'predicts' which party each individual is most likely to vote for, given his opinions. The proportion of voters who are classified correctly (i.e are predicted to be supporters of the party they actually voted for) can be taken as one measure of the 'goodness' of the classification. Our discriminant analysis also created a 'scale' on which all individuals are placed.[5] Individuals' positions are defined by numerical values. In this instance, the pole with a high negative value can be understood as the opinion position farthest to the left; people who consistently held opinions farthest to the right are located at the opposite pole, with a high positive value. Mean positions on that scale can be calculated for voters supporting each of the three main parties. When classifying or predicting individuals' party choice, the discriminant analysis presumes that they will vote for the party whose 'group mean' is closest to their own scale position. The group means for the three main parties' voters on this scale are illuminating; they show how the discriminant analysis yields distinctively separated model positions for Conservative and Labour voters, with Liberal voters placed neatly in between.

	Mean scale scores
Conservative voters	+69
Liberal voters	-0.15
Labour voters	-0.92

Whose votes did the parties get?

The outcome of the discriminant analysis classification of voters with regard to how they would be expected to vote, given their political opinion, is shown in Table 12.1. Each row in the table comprises the respondents who actually voted for one of the three parties, and the per cent distribution shows how they were predicted to vote by our discriminant analysis.

As can be seen from the table, very few Conservative and Labour voters held opinions that were so much at variance with the modal opinions of their fellow party supporters that they were misclassified as supporters of the opposite major party. The errors are almost entirely due to uncertainty as to who would cast a Liberal vote. In effect the discriminant analysis has defined a segment in the middle of the scale, where individuals are expected to vote Liberal. This is also the modal position of the Liberal voters. But whilst 74 per cent of the Conservative voters and the same proportion of the Labour voters indeed were predicted to vote for the party of their choice, only 39 per cent of the Liberal voters actually came from the expected middle segment on the scale. Roughly half of the remainder of Liberal voters were people whose opinions made it seem more likely that they would vote for the Conservatives, and the other half were 'predicted' Labour voters. At the same time, the Conservatives and Labour both drew about a quarter of their voting support from voters in the middle segment of the scale.

Table 12.1 *Actual vote and expected party choice according to discriminant analysis*

Actual vote 1979	'Predicted' distribution of votes per cent				Number of respondents
	Conservatives	Liberals	Labour	Total per cent	
Conservatives	74	23	3	100%	732
Liberals	31	39	30	100%	215
Labour	2	24	74	100%	586
All three-party voters	41	25	34	100%	1,533

Data source: BES May 1979 Election Survey.

The same degree of uncertainty in accounting for the bulk of the Conservatives' and Labour's voting support, in conjunction with uncertainty about the electoral base of the Liberal party, emerges if we reverse the direction of the percentage calculation. Of those expected to vote Conservative, 87 per cent actually did so, and only 3 per cent went to Labour. Among voters expected to vote Labour, 84 per cent voted for that party, whilst only 4 per cent voted Conservative. The middle area of the scale may have been the modal position for the Liberal voters, but only one in five among these voters cast their votes for the Liberals, the remainder was fairly equally divided between the Conservatives and Labour.

The Liberal party would indeed have done much better in the election if it had won the support of the whole of this middle area in the way the discriminant analysis model expected it to do, even if it had gained no votes at all from elsewhere. The Liberals would then have won 25 per cent (rather than 14 per cent) of the three-party vote in the sample. The Conservatives would have gone down from 48 per cent to 41 per cent, whereas Labour would have gone down from 38 per cent to 34 per cent (all percentages based on the sample).

For the three-quarters of the sample whose opinions placed them to the left or to the right of the middle area, our classification is impressively accurate. As a result, 69 per cent of the voters in the entire sample are correctly classified – they voted as expected.[6] So far, the result of the discriminant analysis can be seen as a reassuring complement to the high multiple correlation coefficient obtained from the regression analysis in Chapter 11.[7] But the minority that is misclassified is almost as interesting as the majority correctly classified. The classification errors indicate a spread of opinions within each party's voting support. The extent of that spread and of the overlap between the parties will come more fully to light when we look at the underlying distribution of individual opinions.

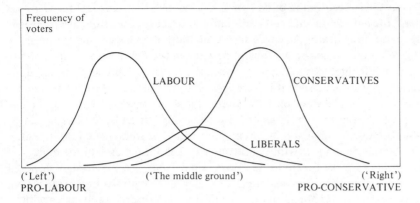

Note: The figure shows the approximate party division of the vote at each point on the scale. The total number of voters at any given point is of course equal to the sum of the numbers of Conservative, Liberal and Labour voters at that point.

Figure 12.A *The Labour and Conservative modes and the shared middle ground*

Differentiation and overlap

As explained above, the discriminant analysis classification is based on a sum-marising measure of individuals' opinions which can be represented as a scale with a numerical value assigned to each individual. In effect, the classification is arrived at by dividing the scale into three segments, each of which comprises a range of opinion positions that corresponds to predicted voting for one of the parties. The distribution of Conservative, Liberal and Labour voters along the scale is illustrated by Figure 12.A. The horizontal axis in the figure represents the range of opinion positions from left to right; the vertical axis represents the number of individuals voting for each of the three parties at each point on the scale. The curves are smoothed and the figure should therefore not be taken as an exact representation of the data (in other words, one cannot read off precise numbers from the figure). The purpose is illustrative: to show the location of the modes of the curves, the general form of the spread around the modes, and the extent of overlap between the three parties' electoral bases.

The sections comprised by the three curves indicate the span of each of the three parties' electoral bases. What becomes apparent is that the Conservatives' and Labour's electoral bases both have distinctive 'centres of gravity' from where they draw the bulk of their voting support, the one to the left and the other to the right on the scale. Labour attracts the great majority of the voters in that 'centre of gravity' part of its electoral base and also almost all of the voters whose opinions are even further to the left. The same holds true for the Conservatives on the other side of the scale.

The Liberals also have a centre of gravity, located in the middle range of the scale, but the concentration of its vote is less marked; the curve is somewhat flatter.[8] Indeed, the Liberal party is found to attract support from a very broad range, comprising nearly the entire spectrum of opinions except the extremes.

It is tempting, of course, to equate the array in the figure with the idea of an ideological left/right axis in the party system. Such an interpretation would not be wholly unjustified either, if it were applied to the voters at the two extreme ends of the scale: the views of these voters bear all the marks of ideological consistency. As regards the remainder of the scale, and in particular the middle range, it should be taken for what it is: essentially a means of summing up the extent to which individuals agree with Conservative or Labour policies. In the middle range of that scale we find individuals who, on balance, are not strongly disposed to support either of the two major parties. They agree with the Conservatives on some issues and with Labour on others, but they do not necessarily agree with each other, since there are many combinations of issue opinions that can lead to evenly balanced policy preferences. These voters may have intermediate opinion positions on comparatively many matters, but not necessarily on the same matters. In sum, the middle range of the scale does not comprise voters who all share the same 'centrist' opinions, and even less does it define a distinctively Liberal ideological outlook. What the results show instead is that the 'middle ground' in the electorate, as a source of voting support, is shared by the Conservatives, Labour and the Liberals. If that middle ground is narrowly defined as the segment of the scale in which voters were 'predicted' to vote Liberal, it includes roughly one quarter of the electorate. However, if we include also Labour voters furthest to the right within their party's scale segment as well as the Conservatives furthest to the left in their party's segment, we would be talking of a middle ground comprising perhaps as many as, say, four voters out of ten.

The 'middle ground' and the Liberals

Knowing what people think about the main issues in an election goes a long way to account for ways in which they cast their votes. As we have just seen from the discriminant analysis, a large majority of the voters could be correctly classified on this basis. To the extent that the discriminant analysis fails, it does so primarily because it operates on the assumption that the three main parties form an ideologically based party system in which one section, in the centre, is the preserve of the Liberal party, with the Conservatives drawing the support of voters to the right of the centre and Labour relying on left-of-centre voting support. (To be fair, the discriminant analysis was led to that presumption by the information provided by ourselves.)

This picture captures some significant features of the British party system but leaves out some no less important elements of the real political world. The ideological boundaries of the sections of the electorate to which each of the three parties successfully appeals are blurred rather than distinct. This is true not only of the Liberal party's voting support. The electoral opinion bases of the Conservative and Labour parties likewise overlap to a not insignificant extent. What a mapping of political opinions in the electorate cannot account for, furthermore, is the role of the social bases of the Conservatives' and Labour's voting support. Group memberships and social ties – in middle-class and working-class alike – help to hold together electoral bases that span broad ranges of political opinions.

These are all circumstances that help the Conservatives and Labour to attract voting support in the middle ground. Many of the voters in the middle ground will have felt that the things that really counted gave them good reasons to vote Conservative or Labour in the 1979 election. As we have observed earlier, there is no certainty, either, that the voters who agreed with the Conservatives on some issues, but were closest to Labour on others, must have felt attracted to the Liberal party; this would depend on how they perceived the Liberals' stands on the issues concerned. All the same, if the Liberals were to gain converts from the two major parties, they would clearly be more likely to do so from 'the middle ground' than elsewhere.

Obviously, the election system has put the Liberal party at a disadvantage. It has all but ensured that one of the two larger parties achieves a parliamentary majority and so reduced the Liberals to the role of a minor opposition party. When this is the expected outcome, at least some proportion of the voters in 'the middle ground' will be discouraged from voting Liberal for fear of wasting their votes and thus assisting the party they liked least to come to power. The election system thus has the double effect of helping the Conservatives and Labour to hold on to their voting support in the middle ground and of focusing attention at election time on the choice between government by the Conservatives or government by Labour. The machinery is not infallible, however, as was evidenced by the February 1974 election and by the erosion of Labour's tiny majority after the October 1974 election. But it did appear to work again in the 1979 election.

How would the Liberals have fared under a different electoral order? How, for that matter, would the Scottish and Welsh Nationalists have fared? One cannot even attempt to answer such questions without entering a land of might-have-beens. Had the October 1974 election been fought under a system of proportional representation, the Liberals might well have entered the 1979 election as one of the parties in a coalition. The voters who would have been attracted to a Liberal party already in office might not have been the same as those who cast their votes, in 1979, for a Liberal party tainted only a little by some degree of responsibility for government policies during the Lib-Lab pact. The ways in which the Scottish and Welsh Nationalist parties would have been affected is even harder to specify, but doubtless the situation would have been very different also for these parties.

Now, let us assume instead that a system of proportional representation had been in force, for the first time, in the 1979 election. The situation would still have been drastically different from the one in which the 1979 election was fought. With a strong possibility that neither Conservatives nor Labour could win an overall majority, the question of what coalition would be formed after the election would probably have been prominent in the campaign. Would the Conservatives have won back more or less of the support they lost in 1974 under such circumstances? Would the Liberals have gained, perhaps at the expense of both of the other parties?

If we cannot know with certainty how the voters would have responded to a very different political situation, we can at least take note of their own judgements at the time of the 1979 election. Such judgements were bound to be hypothetical, as was indeed the interview question asked of those respondents who had not actually voted Liberal: 'If you had thought that the Liberals would win a lot more seats in Britain as a whole, how likely is it that you would then have voted Liberal – very likely, not very likely, or not at all likely?' Of those who voted Conservative, 29 per cent said it would have been 'very likely' that they would have voted Liberal under such circumstances; 46 per cent said it was 'not at all likely'. Of those who voted Labour, 28 per cent said they would have been 'very likely' to cast a Liberal vote if the Liberals had looked like winning more seats, whilst 49 per cent felt it was 'not at all likely'.

These answers obviously suggest that quite substantial portions of the 1979 electorate might have switched to the Liberals, if the Liberals' electoral prospects had seemed brighter. Had all the Conservative and Labour voters who said they would have been 'very likely' to vote Liberal actually done so, the Liberals' share of the three-party vote would have risen to 34 per cent. Incidentally, with a voting support of that size, the Liberals might not have fallen much short of proportional representation in Parliament even under the present electoral system. Caution must lead us to consider this result a generous estimate of the upper limit of the potential Liberal vote in 1979. By no means all of those who said they would have been 'very likely' to cast a Liberal vote would have done so. If the prospects of a Liberal breakthough had been real rather than hypothetical, the questions about coalition formation referred to above would have arisen and, if this had happened, the Liberals might well not have been able to attract potential supporters from both the Conservative and the Labour parties at one and the same time. Granted these qualifications, there can still be little doubt that the election system discouraged a not insignificant number of voters from voting Liberal in 1979. The Liberal party's failure to surmount the threshold set by the election system even at the time of surging Liberal support in 1974 must have been one of the factors that caused voters to turn to the Conservatives in 1979, if they wanted to vote to throw out the incumbent Labour government. At the same time, the Conservative onslaught in the 1979 campaign will have led some Labour deserters to the Liberals in 1974 to return to Labour in 1979. There is some evidence – albeit not entirely conclusive – in the data that all of these factors contributed to the Liberal decline in 1979. The relevant data are presented in Table 12.2.

The table includes voters who supported either the Conservatives or Labour in both of the October 1974 and May 1979 elections, together with the 1974 Liberal voters who switched to the Conservatives or Labour in 1979. The number of cases in the two categories of party changers is small, when taken separately, but the data point to the same inference in both instances: a majority among those who switched from the Liberals to the Conservatives and Labour in 1979 felt that they would have been 'very likely' to continue supporting the Liberals if the party had stood a good chance of winning 'a lot more seats'. Yet the total potential Liberal support is much larger than the share of the vote they lost in 1979. More than one in five of the stable Conservative and Labour voters in the two elections, as can also be seen from the table, would have been 'very likely' to vote Liberal if they had thought that the party could do well.

What were the policy preferences of these potential Liberal voters, people who voted Conservative or Labour because they did not believe the Liberal party could make much impact in the election? In Table 12.3 we have calculated the mean position on the discriminant analysis scale for Conservative and Labour voters in 1979, divided according to how likely they would have been to vote for a better placed Liberal party. For comparison, the mean value for

Table 12.2 *The 'potential' Liberal support among 1979 Conservative and Labour voters*

As explained in the text, Conservative and Labour voters were asked how likely it would have been that they would have voted for the Liberals, if they had thought that the Liberals would win 'a lot more seats in Britain as a whole'. Respondents are categorised, in this table, according to their voting in the October 1974 and May 1979 elections.

How likely to vote Liberal if thought they could win a lot more seats	Voting in October 1974 and May 1979			
	Conservative 1974 Conservative 1979	Liberal 1974 Conservative 1979	Liberal 1974 Labour 1979	Labour 1974 Labour 1979
	%	%	%	%
Very likely	22	57	57	26
Not very likely	26	21	19	23
Not at all likely	52	21	24	52
Total per cent	100%	100%	100%	100%
Number of respondents	379	61	21	360

Data source: BES May 1979 Election Survey.

Table 12.3 *The relation of opinions on political issues to likelihood of voting Liberal if Liberals could 'win a lot more seats'.*

Entries are mean scores on a scale summarising opinions on political issues. The scale ranges from a strongly Conservative position (high positive values) to a strongly Labour (high negative values).

	Mean scale value for each category
Conservative voters	
'Not at all likely' to vote Liberal	+ 0.82
'Not very likely' to vote Liberal	+ 0.67
'Very likely' to vote Liberal	+ 0.55
Liberal voters	– 0.15
Labour voters	
'Very likely' to vote Liberal	– 0.72
'Not very likely' to vote Liberal	– 0.98
'Not at all likely' to vote Liberal	– 1.03

Data source: BES May 1979 Election Survey.

those who actually did vote Liberal is also included in the table. This array of mean values forms a very clear pattern. The Conservative voters who under no circumstances would think of voting Liberal are those whose opinion positions are furthest to the right in the party's voting support. Those who could have been attracted to the Liberals were on average less consistent supporters of Conservative policies. The potential appeal of the Liberal party among Labour voters depends on the same type of differentiation. The mean value for Liberal voters is based on a wide spread of opinions, as Figure 12.A indicates. By comparison with this Liberal mean, the 'potential Liberals' who in fact cast their votes for the Conservatives and Labour, were people whose policy preferences – on average – were clearly 'to the right' and 'to the left' respectively. Had the Liberals gained additional support from only one side in the party system, the 'centre of gravity' in the Liberals' electoral base would thus have moved nearer to one or other of the two major parties. Interestingly, if the Liberals had managed to attract votes from both sides, the mean would have remained the same, but the spread of opinions among Liberal voters might have become even wider.

12.3 Party allegiance and voting

What does it mean to think of oneself as Conservative, Liberal or Labour? Parties stand for different aims, different styles and values, different group interests. Elections at fairly regular intervals require that one takes sides. Whilst the issues vary from one election to the next, the differences between the parties in many ways remain the same. Parties are not merely choice alternatives on election day; they are identifiable as enduring political tendencies, each supported by different groups of people. This is the context in which many voters come to have a sense of being more or less strong supporters of one of the parties. Partisanship in this sense obviously helps to sustain a party's voting support.

Supporting one party always means rejecting its opponents. However, as we will also show, being a strong supporter of one party ('we have always been Tories in my family') does not necessarily mean feeling particularly hostile to the other parties. And, likewise, the fact that a voter has, say, a strongly negative view of one party ('I just can't stand the Tories') does not necessarily mean that he must be a strong supporter of any of the other parties. Both a positive sense of allegiance to a party and strongly negative feelings about its major opponent are related to partisanship with regard to policy opinions or ideological outlook. In this and the following chapter we will investigate how all of these aspects of partisanship bear upon voting and voting change.

The concept of party identification

In the 1979 survey, a series of questions about actual voting in the last few elections was wound up with some questions which were concerned with partisanship in a more general sense: 'Generally speaking, do you think of yourself as a Conservative, Labour, Liberal, or what?' (In Scotland and Wales, the Nationalist parties were also mentioned.) Those who did not associate themselves with a party were then asked: 'Do you generally think of yourself as a little closer to one of the parties than to the other? (If so:) Which party?' The same questions have been put in a number of electoral surveys in Britain since the early 1960s. As in the previous studies, a large majority of those eligible to vote in 1979, 86 per cent, said that they thought of themselves as party supporters. A further 6 per cent said they felt that they were at least a little closer to one of the parties (treated as party identifiers in Chapters 12-13).

Casting a vote for a candidate is an act. Being ready to adopt a party label may be taken as an expression of a more generalised attitude; it means holding a view about oneself as well as about a party. The cognitive contents of such views vary between individuals, within a range that spans from a commitment to a party's programme or ideology to a much vaguer feeling that a party is 'for people like me'. It also varies in strength, from a sense of real allegiance to mild preference. We will refer to partisanship in this sense as party identification.[9]

The strength of such party identification was captured by a single question: 'Would you call yourself very strong . . . (appropriate party), fairly strong, or not very strong?' All of these questions about party identification are deliberately phrased so as to encompass – but not distinguish between – affective attachment to a party as well as commitment to the party's policies. The intention is to allow the respondent to answer the question in terms of the meaning that is most salient in his or her own mind. Partisanship need not only mean positive support for a party, however; it also involves a stronger or weaker rejection of opposing political forces. This aspect of partisanship was tapped by an additional question about each of the parties, except the respondent's own (if he had indicated a party identification).[10] The question was phrased: 'I should also like to ask what you think about the parties that you don't support. Would you say you were *very strongly against* the . . . (party)?'

We will examine first the division of the electorate with regard to party identification, the sense of allegiance to one of the parties. Ninety-two per cent of those eligible to vote had some sense of attachment to a party. In 1979, the division of support among the parties in the entire sample of eligible voters (including non-voters) looked as follows:

	Per cent
Conservatives	40
Liberals	12
Labour	39
Minor parties	1
No party identification	8
Total	100%

For only a minority, though, could that attachment to parties have involved any strong sense of involvement. When we divide the entire sample of eligible voters (including non-voters) according to strength of party identification, the pattern is as follows:

Strength of party identification	*Per cent*
Very strong	21
Fairly strong	46
Not very strong	25
No party identification	8
Total	100%

Only one in five in the electorate described themselves as 'very strong' supporters of a party, and one in four would only go as far as to say they were 'not very strong' supporters of a party. Whether or not people had a strong sense of allegiance to a party depended somewhat, though, on which party they supported. As is shown in Table 12.4, those who thought of themselves as Liberals were particularly unlikely to be 'very strong' supporters (13 per cent only) and nearly four in ten chose to describe their support for the Liberals as 'not very strong'.

Table 12.4 *Direction and strength of party identification*

Strength of party identification	Direction of party identification		
	Conservative	Liberal	Labour
	%	%	%
Very strong	23	13	27
Fairly strong	53	48	50
Not very strong	24	39	23
Total per cent	100%	100%	100%

Data source: BES May 1979 Election Survey.

Party identification and voting.

The sense of partisanship recorded through these questions often forms a lasting element in a person's political outlook. There is indeed less change in such party loyalties than in actual voting behaviour, if we take into account both switches between parties and changes between voting and non-voting from one election to the next. Of the sample of voters eligible to vote at the elections in October 1974 and May 1979, about 76 per cent identified with the same party at both elections, whereas only 64 per cent participated in both elections and voted for the same party.[11] As we shall see, a strong sense of party identification helps to sustain loyalty and stability in voting.[12] Unavoidably, though, a person who changes his vote will often also change his more general party sympathy. The tendency between October 1974 and May 1979 was that the Conservatives gained a larger share of general, partisan sympathies in the electorate as well as more votes. The percentage of voters who thought of themselves as Conservatives (or at least felt closer to the Conservatives) increased from 35 per cent to 40 per cent, whereas Labour's share fell from 41 to 38 and the Liberals' from 15 to 12 per cent.

Table 12.5 *Strength of party identification and voting 1974–1979*

| Strength of party identification in 1979 | *Per cent of each row category* | |
	Voted in accordance with party identification in 1979*	Voted for the same party in October 1974 and May 1979**
Very strong	95%	93%
Fairly strong	89%	80%
Not very strong	76%	58%

*The percentage base is the number of respondents in each category who voted in 1979; the difference between entry and 100% is therefore the percentage who voted for another party.
**The percentage calculation for each row category includes only respondents who voted in both elections.

Data source: BES May 1979 Election Survey.

Most electors naturally vote in accordance with their general sense of partisanship. But electoral choice and party identification do not have entirely the same meaning. About 4 per cent of those who voted in 1979 cast their votes for a party without feeling that they were supporters of any party. Others had a party identification but failed to vote, for one reason or another. More interestingly, about 12 per cent of those who participated in the election voted for a party other than the one that they in general identified themselves with. Nearly one voter in six thus cast his or her vote in the 1979 election for a party to which he or she did not feel any sense of allegiance.[13]

Not surprisingly, the stronger an individual's sense of attachment to a party the less likely he was to vote for another party. Partisanship is also associated with stability in voting: the stronger an individual's partisanship in 1979, the less likely he was to have changed parties since October 1974. The data are given in Table 12.5. The party division of the vote within party identification groups is shown in Table 12.6A. In Table 12.6B the perspective is reversed and the strength of party identification is also taken into account.

Of the two big parties, the Conservatives, supported by the trend in the election, had the strongest hold over the loyalty of their 'party identifiers' in the 1979 election. Of those among them who voted, 95 per cent voted Conservative as compared to the 87 per cent of Labour supporters who turned out to vote and voted Labour (see Table 12.6A).

Table 12.6A *Voting within party identification groups in the May 1979 election*

The table includes respondents who participated in the election and stated their party choice, with exception of a small number who identified with one of the minor parties.

Party identification group	Party vote (Per cent)					
	Conservative	Liberal	Labour	Other party	Total per cent	Number of respondents
Conservative	95	3	2	0	100%	664
Liberal	19	70	9	2	100%	195
Labour	5	8	87	0	100%	620
No party identification	57	11	27	5	100%	56

Data source: BES May 1979 Election Survey.

Table 12.6B *The party identification basis of the vote in the May 1979 election*

Direction and strength of party identification (Per cent)	Conservative voters	Liberal voters	Labour voters
	%	%	%
Identified with party voted for:			
Very strongly	22	8	29
Fairly strongly	46	34	46
Not very strongly	17	20	16
No party identification	5	5	3
Identifies with other party	10	33	6
Total per cent	100%	100%	100%
Number of respondents	732	215	586

Data source: BES May 1979 Election Survey.

A strong sense of allegiance to the Liberal party was rare, as we have seen. The Liberal party in 1979 was also the party most associated with non-coincidence between party identification and voting. As many as 30 per cent of the voters who, in general, thought of themselves as Liberals actually voted for another party. But the Liberal party also attracted a more fleeting voting support than the other parties: about a third of the Liberal vote consisted of voters who would 'generally speaking' describe themselves as Conservatives or Labour (see Table 12.6B). About three-quarters of all the voters who abandoned their party loyalty to vote for another party in 1979 were either deserting Liberals, or Liberal voters who really counted themselves as Conservative or Labour supporters. In absolute numbers, it is interesting to note, the Liberals' gains and losses as the result of desertions from party identification were almost equal in size in the 1979 election.

There can be little doubt that the electoral system played a role. There were numerous constituencies where the Liberal party had little chance of winning and where its supporters would be drawn towards the major party they felt most sympathy for. There were also constituencies, albeit many fewer, where the Liberals were the incumbents or had come second in the last election; in those constituencies the Liberals were well placed to attract Conservative and Labour voters who wanted to defeat the major party they felt least sympathy for. Not all of these movements in and out of the Liberals' voting support, however, are necessarily explicable in terms of the specific circumstances in each constituency. Voters may well have responded to the national political situation when deciding either to desert the Liberals in favour of one of the major parties or to cast a Liberal vote in 1979. Indeed, it is arguable that it is precisely the Liberal party's present minority status which allows it to attract such a large portion of its vote from among Conservative and Labour identifiers. A Liberal vote may be used as a means of expressing dissatisfaction with the current performance of the party one normally supports without switching to the opposite side.[14] The data in Table 12.6A showed, however, that dissatisfied Conservative and Labour supporters by no means always stop half-way. Although it is more common for Conservative and Labour supporters to defect to the Liberals than to the opposite major party, the differences between the relevant percentages are quite slight. Perhaps this, too, has to do with the Liberals' role as a party with little prospect of influencing government policy. For a dissatisfied Conservative or Labour supporter, the Liberals may well have been the nearest alternative – but the other major party may have been seen as the only *real* alternative.

In the previous section, we gauged a potential pull towards the Liberals with a question asking Conservative and Labour voters how likely they would have been to vote Liberal if they had thought the Liberals could win 'a lot more seats'. The relationship between the Conservative and Labour voters' responses to that pull and the strength of their identification with the party they voted for is illuminated by Table 12.7. As is shown, the Liberal party held some potential attraction even among strong Conservative and Labour identifiers;

9 and 12 per cent of these categories, respectively, would have been 'very likely' to vote Liberal if they had expected it to become a strong party in Parliament. But it is among the weak supporters of the two major parties that a pull really would be felt if the voters' expectations about the Liberals' prospects were to change. Nearly half (46 per cent) of the weak Conservative identifiers and more than a third (36 per cent) of the weak Labour identifiers said they would have been 'very likely' to vote for the Liberals in 1979 under such circumstances.

If the Liberal party's place really is in the centre of a three-party system, one would expect it to be the party most often considered the 'second best' by those who regard themselves as Conservative or Labour supporters.[15] As is shown in Table 12.8 this is indeed the case. Around seven in ten of Conservative and Labour supporters who had a second preference mentioned the Liberals. Among Liberals, we find the same divide as before, inasmuch as their second preferences are about equally divided between the Conservative and Labour parties. We have already seen that a comparatively large proportion of the Liberal identifiers actually cast their votes for one of the major parties in 1979. Not surprisingly, the 'second best' party was often the electoral choice of those Liberals who did not vote for their own party, as is shown in Table 12.9. The 'defection rates' were not the same, however. Those on the right wing of the Liberal party's potential electoral base were much more likely to vote for their 'second choice' than those on the left wing. This was one factor that contributed to the Conservative surge in the 1979 election.

Table 12.7 *The relation of likelihood of voting Liberal to strength of party identification among Conservative and Labour voters*

The table includes only Conservative and Labour identifiers who voted for the party concerned in the May 1979 election.

How likely to vote Liberal if thought the Liberals would win 'a lot more seats'	Conservatives			Labour		
	Party identification			Party identification		
	Not very strong	Fairly strong	Very strong	Not very strong	Fairly strong	Very strong
	%	%	%	%	%	%
Very likely	46	26	9	36	31	12
Not very likely	21	26	27	27	22	23
Not at all likely	33	48	64	37	47	65
Total per cent	100%	100%	100%	100%	100%	100%
Number of respondents	113	291	134	84	229	142

Data source: BES May 1979 Election Survey.

Table 12.8 *Party identification and 'second preference'*

Interview question: 'Which party do you like second best?'

Second best party	Direction of party identification		
	Conservative	Liberal	Labour
	%	%	%
Conservatives	–	49	27
Liberals	76	–	68
Labour	22	47	–
Other party	2	4	5
Total per cent	100%	100%	100%
Number of cases	641	203	600

The table includes only respondents who stated a second preference.

Data source: BES May 1979 Election Survey.

Table 12.9 *The relation of voting in the 1979 election to 'second best' party preference among Liberal identifiers*

Vote in the 1979 election	Liberal identifiers' 'second best' party	
	Conservative party	Labour party
	%	%
Conservatives	34	5
Liberals	66	75
Labour	0	20
Total per cent	100%	100%

Data source: BES May 1979 Election Survey.

12.4 Aspects of partisanship

If one gathers nothing else from the battle between the parties, it can hardly escape anyone's notice that the parties disagree and that they compete for support. The great majority of the electorate, of course, knows a lot more than that about the parties. To feel that one is – at least mildly – a supporter of a party almost necessarily means feeling less than wholly friendly towards its opponents. Indeed, even someone who has no sense of allegiance to a party may still have negative views about one or more of the parties. As explained above, we used a single question to record how strongly individuals rejected each of the parties that they did not support. Although negative partisanship naturally varies greatly in degree, our actual measurement distinguishes only between two levels of negative partisanship: those who felt sufficiently strongly to state that they were 'very strongly against' a given party, and those who felt less strongly about the same party.

On this definition, a little less than half of the voters who were supporters of one of the three main parties also had a strong enough sense of negative partisanship to feel they were 'very strongly against' at least one of the two other parties. Thus, to say of someone that he is, say, a Conservative is not necessarily to say that he is hostile to the Liberals or Labour or to the policies of these parties. That will depend on how strongly the voter supports his own party and on how much difference he thinks there is between the parties.

Let us begin by examining the link between party identification and negative partisanship. When two parties are seen as each other's opponents then it is to be expected that the more strongly a person supports one party, the more likely he will be to hold a strongly negative view of the other. As is brought out in Table 12.10A, the strength of negative partisanship does depend on the strength of people's party identification in precisely this fashion – at least if someone is a Conservative or Labour supporter and is thinking of the other of the two big parties. Thus we find, for example, that 76 per cent of strong Conservatives were 'strongly against' Labour, whereas only 26 per cent of weak Conservative identifiers held that view.

This tendency is, however, much weaker among Liberal identifiers. Indeed, the Liberals are the least likely to express strong negative feelings about either the Conservatives or Labour. At the same time, the Liberal party is the party least likely to be strongly rejected by either Conservative or Labour supporters. In fact, it is quite rare for Conservative or Labour identifiers to dislike the Liberals that much, and even strong Conservative and Labour identifiers are only slightly more hostile towards the Liberals.

It is the structure of the party system that is reflected in the data in Table 12.10A just as it was in, say, the voters' 'second best' party preferences (see Table 12.8). Like most parties in the centre of a party system, the Liberals are a party of two minds. Some of its strong supporters will, in fact, be closer to the Conservatives than to Labour, whilst others will be nearer to Labour. People in neither of these categories are likely to say they are 'strongly against' more than one of the two other parties. By the same token, some who supported the Liberal party as a mediating force would not feel they disagreed strongly with either the Conservatives or Labour. Of all the Liberal identifiers in our sample, only 33 per cent were 'strongly against' either of the two other parties, as com-

Table 12.10A *Party identification and 'negative partisanship'*

Respondents are classified with regard to direction and strength of party identification. *Entries* are the percentages of each row category who were 'very strong against' each of the parties opposing their own. This percentage is zero, by definition, for the respondent's own party (indicated by − in the table).

Direction and strength of party identification	Per cent of each row category of voters who are 'very strongly against'		
	Conservative party	Liberal party	Labour party
Conservatives			
Very strong	−	10%	76%
Fairly strong	−	8%	47%
Not very strong	−	4%	26%
All	−	8%	49%
Liberals			
Very strong	39%	−	27%
Fairly strong	15%	−	26%
Not very strong	5%	−	18%
All	14%	−	23%
Labour			
Very strong	69%	13%	−
Fairly strong	38%	6%	−
Not very strong	14%	4%	−
All	41%	7%	−

Data source: BES May 1979 Election Survey.

pared to 51 per cent of Conservative and 43 per cent of Labour identifiers. Labour and Conservative supporters see the other major party as the force most opposed to their own views. The Liberals are at a shorter psychological distance from the party to their right as well as the party to their left.

A very similar relationship emerges when we relate negative partisanship to the voters' perceptions of the differences between the parties. We are able to probe this relationship with the aid of a series of questions in which we asked our respondents to make judgements on how much difference they thought there was between each pair of parties, 'considering everything they stand for': 'a great deal', 'some difference', or 'not much difference'.

The more different two choice alternatives appear, the more likely it ought to be that an individual who prefers one will also strongly reject the other. If this applies to voters' views of the parties, those who think there is a 'great deal' of difference between their own party and another party should be the most likely to have a strong sense of negative partisanship. This is obviously the relationship we would expect to find.

A great many voters, actually, did *not* think there was that much difference between the parties. When asked about the Conservatives and Labour, slightly less than half of all the voters (46 per cent) said there was 'a great deal of difference'; 29 per cent said there was 'some difference'. Conservative and Labour voters were a little more inclined to think that there was 'a great deal of difference' between their parties, but not dramatically so (54 and 49 per cent, respectively, among Conservative and Labour voters). Even less often had the voters gained the impression that there was a 'great deal of difference' between the Liberals and either of the two major parties. It depended a little on the voters' own party preferences, but within all such categories there were only some 20 to 25 per cent who thought the Liberals differed 'a great deal' from any of the other parties.[16]

When the parties are seen to differ much at all, it is again the Conservatives and Labour that most often emerge as the real alternatives in the voters' perceptions of the party system. Table 12.10B shows how negative partisanship towards the opposing major party among Conservative and Labour identifiers depends on both strength of party identification and perceived differences between the two parties. For example, 60 per cent of Conservative identifiers who felt that there was 'a great deal of difference' between Conservatives and Labour also said that they were 'very strongly against' the Labour party. Among those who thought there was only 'some difference', the percentage is 40, and it falls to 22 among those who thought there was 'not much difference' between the two parties.

Inspection of the sub-categories in the tables for Conservative and Labour identifiers reveals how judgements on the differences between the two parties and the strength of one's allegiance to one's own party affect, in combination, the likelihood of a strong sense of negative partisanship; the one factor is added on to the other. Taking the Conservative identifiers to illustrate this joint effect, one can look at the cell near the lower, right-hand corner of the table containing those Conservatives who are 'not very strong' supporters of their party and do not think there is much difference between the parties; only 11 per cent of them feel they are 'very strongly against' Labour. Among voters with a fairly strong sense of party identification who think there is 'some difference' between the parties, the proportion rises to 40 per cent. (This is the cell in the centre of the table.) Among the really committed Conservatives – those who have a very strong party identification and also think there is a 'great deal of difference' between the parties – a staggering 86 per cent express a strong sense of negative partisanship towards Labour. The pattern is the same, though slightly weaker, among Labour identifiers.

As can be gleaned from the number of respondents in the various sub-categories, the voters' views on the differences between the parties and their strength of

Table 12.10B *Relation of negative partisanship to perceived difference between the Conservatives and Labour, and strength of party identification*

Sections I and II in the table include Conservative and Labour identifiers, respectively. Each group of party identifiers are divided into nine sub-categories according to strength of party identification and perceived difference between Conservative and Labour. *Entry* in each cell is the percentage of the appropriate sub-category who were 'very strongly against' the opposite major party (i.e. Labour for Conservative identifiers and the Conservatives for Labour identifiers). The number of respondents in each sub-category is given within parentheses.

I *Conservative identifiers: Per cent of respondents with strong negative partisanship in each sub-category*

Strength of identification with Conservative party	How much difference between Conservative and Labour		
	A great deal	Some	Not much
Very strong	82% (130)	66% (34)	[29%] (7)
Fairly strong	56% (210)	40% (127)	28% (51)
Not very strong	35% (70)	24% (59)	11% (43)
All respondents in column	60%	40%	22%

II *Labour identifiers: Per cent of respondents with strong negative partisanship in each sub-category*

Strength of identification with Labour party	How much difference between Conservative and Labour		
	A great deal	Some	Not much
Very strong	76% (122)	66% (38)	40% (30)
Fairly strong	52% (153)	30% (111)	23% (87)
Not very strong	19% (48)	14% (49)	12% (56)
All respondents in column	56%	33%	22%

Data source: BES May 1979 Election Survey.

party identification are likewise interdependent: those who have a strong sense of party identification are most likely to think that there are considerable differences between the parties and vice versa.

The pattern in the data for Liberal identifiers is essentially the same but weaker and more complex. This is so because negative partisanship among Liberal identifiers depends on whether their sympathies lean towards the Conservatives or Labour. The number of respondents in the many sub-categories obtained when this is taken into account becomes so small, however, that all inferences must be based on very fragile data; for that reason these are not displayed in table form.

The message conveyed by this analysis is quite clear: the more the voter felt was at stake in the 1979 election, the more likely he was to hold a strongly negative view of either the Conservative or the Labour party. But about half the electorate did not feel that 'a great deal' was at stake.

Party identification and 'negative partisanship' can be thought of as different aspects of partisanship. They are interdependent, as we have seen, but partisanship in either sense is not a mere reflection of partisanship in the other. Party identification stands for an affective bond between the individual and a party – a sense that a party can be relied upon to espouse values and interests that one supports. Negative partisanship may only mean that one identifies one of the parties as a disliked political force. But when added to a strong sense of party identification, negative partisanship will obviously harden the individual's commitment to the party he supports. Negative partisanship without any positive party identification, on the other hand, may cause a voter to vote for the party most opposed to the one he most dislikes; but it may well mean that he votes for the party he distrusts the least.

Combining our measures of party identification and negative partisanship is one means by which we can define the 'hard core' support of the parties, especially of the Conservative and Labour parties. The negative partisanship classification, furthermore, can serve to identify two components in the Liberals' voting support: a 'Conservative leaning' and a 'Labour leaning' component. Partisanship is also bound up with opinions on issues and policies, however. The discriminant analysis provided us with a measure of partisanship in that sense. In the next section, we shall explore the relationships between all three of these aspects of partisanship: party identification, negative partisanship and opinions on issues.

12.5 Partisanship, issue opinions and voting

Broadly the same picture of the electorate has emerged in our surveying of party allegiances and partisanship in opinions on political issues. The Conservative and Labour parties have reliable electoral bases among 'very strong' or 'fairly strong' party identifiers. These are voters who are unlikely to vote for any other party and are most likely both to feel that it makes a great deal of difference which party is in power and to hold strongly negative views of the opposing major party. Both parties likewise have hard-core electoral bases of voters who hold strongly partisan views on political issues. But both parties also draw a substantial part of their voting support from among voters with a much weaker sense of attachment to the party for which they cast their votes and from the 'middle ground' of voters with more or less evenly balanced policy preferences. About one-tenth of the electorate is made up of voters who have no sense that they are supporters of either of the parties. A disproportionate portion of the voters in this category do not vote at all, but some of them do; in 1979 the Conservatives gained the largest share of these voters, whilst in October 1974 they had gone to Labour.

Our data on party allegiances have thrown light also on the role of Liberals as a party in the centre of the party system. Not many of the Liberal identifiers were strong supporters of their party, and many were pulled towards the left or towards the right when it came to voting. The Liberal party gained some compensation through its ability to attract voting support from among weak Conservative and Labour supporters. In our mapping of the voters' positions on policy issues, we found, as will be recalled, that the Liberals drew a comparatively large voting support from the 'middle ground' and yet the great majority of these voters went to the Conservatives or Labour.

Whether we rely on data pertaining to party allegiance or to opinions on political issues, the results point to the same type of differentiation between hard-core bases of party support and areas of overlap in the electorate where two or more parties can draw voting support. If the party system were to be represented by a panorama, it would be a landscape that changes gradually in character from left to right in the picture, with common land in the middle where there are no strictly enclosed areas of support for the parties on the left, in the centre and on the right.

As traits in individuals' political attitudes, partisanship in the sense of party allegiance and partisanship in policy preferences do not necessarily coincide. People can be partisan in one sense, but not in the other. This is indeed one of the reasons why the boundaries between the parties' electoral bases are uncertain and fleeting. Yet to some extent the strength – and the quality – of the support that individuals feel for a party must be dependent on how firmly they feel they support the aims and the policies of that party. It is this interdependence that we will now explore.

For this purpose we need to examine the relationships between all of the aspects of partisanship that have been discussed in the preceding sections (party identification, negative partisanship, policy opinions) and voting in the 1979 election. The data are displayed in Tables 12.11 and 12.12.

In Table 12.11 we have related opinions on political issues to strength of party identification as well as to negative partisanship. By combining these two measures

Table 12.11 *Party identification, 'negative' partisan orientation and opinions on political issues*

Entries are *mean scores* on a scale summarising opinions on political issues. The scale ranges from strongly Conservative position (high positive values) to strongly Labour position (high negative values). Number of respondents in each category are given within parentheses.

I *Conservative party identification*

Strength of party identification	Opinion on the Labour party		All
	Very strongly against	Not very strong against	
Very strong	1.13 (123)	0.72 (37)	1.04 (160)
Fairly strong	0.94 (171)	0.55 (183)	0.74 (354)
Not very strong	0.68 (36)	0.34 (102)	0.43 (138)

II *Labour party identification*

Strength of party identification	Opinion on the Conservative party		All
	Very strongly against	Not very strongly against	
Very strong	−1.37 (120)	−0.86 (57)	−1.20 (177)
Fairly strong	−1.11 (123)	−0.76 (185)	−0.90 (308)
Not very strong	−0.81 (18)	−0.40 (111)	−0.46 (129)

III *Liberal party identification*

The number of respondents 'strongly against' both Conservative and Labour is so small that the column is omitted from the table; the number of respondents in some cells is nevertheless *very small*. These respondents are included in the appropriate row of the 'All' column, however.

Strength of party identification	Strongly against Labour only	Not strongly against either Conservative or Labour	Strongly against Conservatives only	All
Very strong	0.71 (4)	0.01 (11)	−1.27 (9)	−0.35 (25)
Fairly strong	0.68 (24)	−0.03 (61)	−0.55 (10)	0.09 (95)
Not very strong	0.67 (13)	0.01 (55)	−1.05 (2)	0.10 (70)

Note that the number of respondents in some of the sub-categories is very small.

Data source: BES May 1979 Election Survey.

Table 12.12 *Party vote in the election, party identification and opinions on political issues*

Entry is mean score on scale of political opinions for each category. Number of respondents is given within parentheses.

Party vote in the election	Party identification		
	Conservative	Liberal	Labour
Conservatives	0.77 (628)	0.61 (38)	−0.04 (32)
Liberals	0.49 (21)	−0.02 (137)	−0.75 (50)
Labour	−0.04 (11)	−0.80 (17)	−0.95 (537)

Data source: BES May 1979 Election Survey.

of strength of partisanship, each of the three party identification groups (Conservative, Labour and Liberals) are divided into sub-categories. For the Conservatives and Labour we obtain six sub-categories for each party. In the case of the Liberals, the classification is a little more complex because we want to take into account negative partisanship directed against the Conservatives as well as against the Labour party. As a result the Liberal group is divided into nine sub-categories.

For each of these sub-categories, the table shows the mean value of our discriminant analysis scale of political opinions. In addition, each of the three sections in the table contains the mean values for all individuals at each level of strength of party identification (the 'All' column). A word of caution is called for with regard to the section of the table pertaining to the Liberals. The very detailed sub-classification results in some sub-categories that include very few individuals. The appropriate mean values are given for these small categories, both for the sake of completeness and because they actually fit in neatly with the overall pattern; nevertheless, they are obviously unreliable as statistical estimates.

In Table 12.12 actual voting in the election is introduced in the analysis. The three main parties' identifiers are divided according to how they voted in the election. The mean value on the discriminant analysis scale is given for each of these sub-categories.

A clear pattern emerges in each of the sections of Table 12.11 but perhaps most conspicuously so in the sections for Conservative and Labour identifiers. Among Conservative and Labour supporters, partisanship in opinions on political issues is related both to the strength of party identification and to negative partisanship. Thus, for example, the scale value for Conservatives who are very strong partisans in both respects is 1.13 as compared to a value of 0.34 in the most weakly partisan of the sub-categories. Between these two extremes, the scale values increase in a regular fashion with increasing degree of partisanship. We find the same relationship, and equally clearly, in the data for the adherents of the Labour party. The mean scale values become increasingly negative with increasing strength of positive and negative partisanship. The mean values for the weakest and the strongest groups are -0.40 and -1.37, respectively.

Most Liberal identifiers have opinions in the mid range of the scale. Interestingly, the few 'very strong' Liberals are a little to the left of other Liberals. Following the Lib-Lab pact and at an election when the Conservatives were aiming to unseat a Labour government, it is perhaps not surprising that those on the left among Liberal supporters should feel most happy about their party. Negative partisanship also makes a marked difference in the case of Liberal identifiers. Those who are strongly against the Labour party are on average considerably to the right of those whose negative partisanship is directed against the Tories.

In any election, the votes of some party identifiers will drift over to another party. The relationship between opinion positions, party identification and voting is illuminated by Table 12.12. The mean values in this table demonstrate very clearly that both the Conservatives and Labour lost potential votes in the election among voters whose opinion positions had slid towards the mid range on our opinion scale. If they voted Liberal, their opinion positions tended to be located half-way between the hard core of the party they deserted and the centre position of the hard-core Liberal vote. Those who went so far as to vote for the opposing major party, were apparently even more in disagreement with the party they were deserting without therefore being especially close to the party they voted for. In fact the average opinion positions of both Conservative identifiers who voted Labour and Labour identifiers who voted Conservative are located right in the middle of the 'middle ground'. If they were reluctant supporters of the party they deserted in 1979, they are an equally uncertain electoral asset for the party they went to.

The sharp difference between Liberal identifiers who voted Conservative in 1979 and those who voted Labour is no less noteworthy. The Liberals quite clearly lost votes on their far right wing to the Conservatives and on their left to Labour, although the policy opinions of the defectors were less consistently partisan than those of the hard core Conservative and Labour voters. The Liberals, on the other hand, attracted Conservative and Labour identifiers from much the same ranges of opinions. As is brought out in Table 12.12, these movements in opposite directions between Liberals and Conservatives on the one side of the party system, and between the Liberals and Labour on the other, resulted in exchanges of voters whose opinion positions actually did not differ very much. The rightward drift in the electorate is reflected, however, in the numerical size of the groups of voters who moved in each direction. The Labour party suffered a net loss in its exchanges with both the Liberals and the Conservatives, and the Liberals lost more of their own identifiers to the Conservatives than they gained from Conservative identifiers who voted Liberal in 1979.

Now, how hard is the 'hard core' of the Liberals' voting support, that is, those who both identify with and vote for the Liberal party? Are such voters not affected by the pulls towards the left and the right that seem inherent in the British party system? It is actually possible to take our analysis one step further by dividing this hard-core Liberal category according to which party the individuals considered 'second best'. And indeed the two groups do differ. The mean scale position for those who thought of the Conservative party as second best is +0.37, whereas the mean for those who chose Labour as their second best party is −0.39. The pulls were there; but they were not strong enough: those Liberal identifiers who actually voted Conservative were (as can be seen in the table) further to the right, just as those who cast their votes for Labour were further to the left. In much the same fashion, as we have already seen, the softer parts of the Conservatives' and Labour's voting support would have been attracted by the idea of voting Liberal if the party's electoral prospects had not seemed so bleak. Such pulls in different directions are always operating – although the strength of each of these forces varies depending on the mood currently prevailing in the electorate. The balance sheet of issue opinions that we examined in Chapter 11 explains why all of the pulls towards the right were stronger at the time of the 1979 election.

12.6 How the electorate saw the party system

Throughout our enquiry, the Liberals have emerged as a party in the middle of the party system, placed between the Conservatives and Labour. A question which naturally arises is whether this is the way in which the party system is actually seen by the voters. Do the voters perceive the parties as being positioned at different distances from each other, with the Conservatives and Labour farthest apart and the Liberals placed in between? If this is the picture of the party system that most voters behold, this would not necessarily mean that equally many were thinking of the parties in terms of their placing on a left/right ideological scale; but is would mean that the commonly held view of the party system would be compatible with such an ideological outlook. We shall conclude this review of partisanship in the electorate by examining data that bear upon the voters' views of the party system.

Most of the respondents in our sample had no difficulty in answering one of our questions on this subject.[17] We asked simply which two parties they thought were furthest apart 'considering everything they stand for' (see Table 12.13). A large majority (76 per cent) saw the Conservatives and Labour as 'furthest apart'; only 16 per cent had a different picture in their minds. There was, however, much less agreement about the positioning of the Liberal party relative to the Conserva-

Table 12.13 *The electorate's impression of 'distances' between the three main parties*

Views on distances among parties	Party voted for in 1979			All respondents
	Conservatives	Liberals	Labour	
	%	%	%	%
Conservatives and Labour are 'furthest apart'; Conservatives and Liberals are 'closest together'	54	27	21	35
Conservatives and Labour are 'furthest apart'; Labour and Liberals are 'closest together'	18	42	47	32
Conservatives and Labour are 'furthest apart'; Don't know about 'closest together'	7	8	9	9
Other placing of parties	14	19	15	16
Don't know which parties are 'furthest apart'	7	4	8	8
Total per cent	100%	100%	100%	100%
Number of respondents	732	215	586	1893

Interview questions: 'Considering everything the Conservatives, Labour and Liberal parties stand for, which two of these three parties would you say are closest together?' – 'Considering everything the Conservative, Labour and Liberal parties stand for, which two out of these three parties would you say are furthest apart?'

Data source: BES May 1979 Election Study.

tives and Labour when we asked which two parties were closest together.[18] Roughly one voter in three thought the Liberals and the Conservatives were 'closest together', but nearly as many thought the Liberals and Labour were 'closest together'. As is also seen from the table, both Conservative and Labour voters tended to pull the Liberals towards their own party in their cognitive maps of the party system. Liberal voters were nearly as evenly divided in their perceptions of the electorate as a whole, but the modal view among Liberal voters is that their party was closest to Labour.

Comparing our 1979 data with those from the October 1974 election reveals that voters' views of the Liberal party actually underwent a quite dramatic alteration during the five intervening years. We can follow how that alteration occurred with a direct question about the 'distance' between the Liberal party and each of the two major parties which was asked in 1974 as well as in 1979 ('Generally speaking, do you regard the Liberal party as closer to the Conservative party or closer to the Labour party?'). As is shown by Table 12.14, in 1974 only 17 per cent of voters thought the Liberals were closest to Labour, whereas 41 per cent had that impression in 1979. (The figure is higher than in the preceding table because we now also include people who did not think of the two major parties as furthest apart or answered 'don't know' to the relevant question.) It is hard to conceive of any factor other than the Lib-Lab pact as the main cause of this remarkable transformation.

There were thus in 1979 two dominant but competing views of the party system. In both, the Liberal party is placed in the middle. But in the one picture the Liberal party is closest to the Conservatives, whereas it is closest to Labour in the alternative picture.

Table 12.14 *Shifting views on the position of the Liberal party, 1974 and 1979*

Is the Liberal party closer to the Conservatives or to Labour?	All respondents	
	1974	1979
	%	%
Closer to the Conservatives	60	43
Closer to Labour	17	41
Don't know or no difference	23	16
Total per cent	100%	100%
Number of respondents	2335	1864

Interview question: Generally speaking, do you regard the Liberal Party as closer to the Conservative Party or closer to the Labour Party?'

Data source: BES October 1974 Election Survey and BES May 1979 Election Survey.

If there is a divide between left and right in the British party system, there is apparently no consensus about which side the Liberal party belongs to. The discord cuts right through the Liberal electoral base in 1979. It may not have mattered much which view the voters held so long as the Liberal party remained an insignificant factor in parliamentary politics. Were the Liberals – or the Social Democratic and Liberal Alliance – to achieve sufficient strength to hold the balance between Conservatives and Labour as a political force in the centre, the situation would obviously be drastically altered. The relations between a grouping in the centre and the parties to the left and right would affect almost all aspects of party strategies and might well have a pervasive impact on voting behaviour.

13

The making of voting decisions: political opinions and voting intentions during the campaign

For a large part of the British electorate, the decision how to vote in the 1979 general election was no foregone conclusion. Of the voters who participated in both October 1974 and May 1979 elections, over one-fifth voted for different parties in the two elections. At some time during the four and a half years between the elections, all of these voters must have reconsidered their party sympathies and finally decided to shift their support to another party. Changing between voting and non-voting was another cause of turnover in the voting electorate; and in addition a new age cohort had entered the electorate since the last election.

Between elections there also occurs a continuous change of a different type which could be described as a wavering of party sympathies. That type of change is reflected in the variations of the parties' fortunes which can be observed in opinion polls between the elections, whilst it is only the end result that is recorded in the election statistics. Much of this wavering does not in the end lead to any switching of votes from one election to the next. Indeed, the parties' ability to win back their reluctant supporters is one of the factors that will decide election results.

In this chapter we will first examine some data which throw light on the extent and nature of the changing and wavering of voting intentions that occurred during the election campaign, both among voters who eventually returned to vote for the same party as last time and among voters who hesitated about their party choice but eventually switched their votes. Obviously, this does not comprise all of the switching of party sympathies back and forth between the parties in the years between the October 1974 and 1979 elections. Some voters had definitely decided to switch to another party before the election campaign began and remained steadfast throughout the campaign. Therefore, the extent to which the final decisions to change to another party were delayed until during the election campaign is one of the aspects of instability in voting intentions which will be explored. Another is the relationship between the changes in voting intentions that occurred during the campaign and voters' opinions on political issues; as in

314

the preceding chapter, the summarising measure of opinions obtained from the discriminant analysis will serve as the analytic tool. Next, we shall return to the theme of Chapter 11: the opinion differences between party changers and the stable voters who stayed with the same party from the October 1974 election to the 1979 election; the same summarising measure of opinions on political issues will be used to characterise the flows of the vote between the parties. The chapter concludes with an overall appraisal of the electoral surge towards the Conservatives that was the dominant feature of the 1979 election.

13.1 Unwavering and reluctant voters

To what extent had the voters' views of the parties hardened into definite voting decisions by the time the 1979 election campaign commenced? How much of the total change in voting since the last election was the result of decisions arrived at in the course of the election campaign? How were the parties' fortunes affected by the change that occurred during the campaign?

It is an obvious drawback with a post-election survey that such questions can be answered only with data collected after the event. We thus have to rely on the respondents' memories. Memory is never an infallible source of information, and in this instance there is the added difficulty of trying to remember when an intention – perhaps an intention that was being reconsidered – became a final decision. In order to help our respondents to cast their minds back to the campaign period, we asked two different questions about their voting intentions: 'How long ago did you decide that you would definitely vote the way you did – a long time ago, some time this year, or during the campaign?' 'Was there any time during the general election campaign when you seriously thought you might vote for another party?' (If yes:) 'Which party?' Although the two questions are similar in meaning, they do not capture precisely the same recollections of how the voting decision was arrived at. The stress in the first question is on the time aspect, and it includes the decision whether or not to vote. The second question is specifically concerned with the certainty of the individual's party choice. Therefore, the responses need not always coincide. For example, some individuals who returned to an original voting intention may have felt that their party choice was in fact determined a long time ago and therefore have answered the first question accordingly. A total of 41 per cent of our respondents indicated on at least one of the two questions that they had reconsidered their voting intentions or made up their minds during the campaign, the lack of coincidence is illustrated by the fact that only 18 per cent did so on both questions, whereas the corresponding percentages were 28 and 30 for each question taken separately. Hence, when using these questions as separate measures of stability in voting intentions, one must bear in mind both that each of them probably underestimates somewhat the real extent of the change that occurred during the campaign, and also that they do not reflect exactly the same conceptions of change. On the other hand, our

inferences about the nature and direction of campaign change are obviously sub-
stantiated when they are supported by data obtained by both measures.

Nearly six voters out of ten (that is, of those who actually voted in the
election) felt that they had definitely decided how they were going to vote 'a
long time ago'. They voted as they had meant to do before both the election
campaign and the 'winter of discontent'. As is shown in Table 13.1, the time for
decision was to some extent dependent on the party choice. No fewer than 50
per cent of those who cast their votes for the Liberals waited until the election
campaign before they made up their minds. The Liberal party's potential electoral base is, as we have found, more volatile than other parties', with a very
large turnover in its support from one election to the next. It was not until the
campaign weeks that the actual size of the Liberal vote was determined.

Table 13.2 shows how the three-party vote was divided among those who
made their final choice at the different stages. The Conservative party apparently
held a majority among voters who had made up their minds before the campaign
began and never wavered. Why did the campaign bring an influx of support to
the Liberal party? One answer might be that the Liberals – and, in particular,
their leader – fought a successful campaign. Undoubtedly, that is part of the
truth. But the Liberal party was also especially well placed to attract the wavering voters during the campaign. As will be shown, wavering voters often had
reservations about the policies of both major parties. Although most of them
(see Table 13.2) ended up with a Conservative or Labour vote all the same, a
substantial share – much larger than in the more stable portion of the electorate –
resolved the question by deciding to vote Liberal.

Table 13.1 *The time of voting decision by party vote*

Interview question: 'How long ago did you decide that you would definitely
vote the way you did – a long time ago, some time this year or during the
campaign?'

| Time of definite voting decision | Party voted for | | | |
	Conservatives	Liberals	Labour	All voters*
	%	%	%	%
A long time ago	63	37	60	57
Sometime this year	16	13	13	15
During the campaign	21	50	27	28
Total per cent	100%	100%	100%	100%
Number of respondents	726	213	584	1604

*Respondents who participated in the election
Data source: BES May 1979 Election Survey.

Table 13.2 *Party division of the vote among voters making their decisions at different times*

This table includes only respondents who voted for one of the three major parties.

Time of definite voting decision	Party voted for (per cent)			Total per cent
	Conservatives	Liberals	Labour	
A long time ago	52	9	39	100%
Sometime this year	52	13	35	100%
During the campaign	37	25	38	100%

Data source: BES May 1979 Election Survey.

As we saw in Part I, the turnover in the Liberal vote is such that less than half of its voters in 1979 had voted Liberal in October 1974. Among the Liberal voters in the October 1974 election who voted also in the 1979 election, one voter in two switched to another party in the latter election. The losses were partially offset during the 1979 campaign. Of all the voters who switched from another party in 1974 to Liberal voting in 1979, 76 per cent said they had made their final decision at some time during the campaign.

The connection between party change and a delayed voting decision is not, however, confined to the Liberals. It is a general phenomenon. The contrast between stable voters (those who voted for the same party in 1974 and 1979) and the party changers is striking, as is shown by the following percentages:

Voting October 1974 and 1979	Per cent of each category who made the final vote decision during the campaign
Voted for the same party 1974 and 1979	16%
Changed party vote from 1974 to 1979	50%

It is a correlate of these findings that the voters who did not reach a definite voting decision until during the campaign form a segment of the electorate in which the vote is more volatile and partisan attachments are weaker. These differences between the early and the late deciders are brought out very clearly by the data displayed in Table 13.3.

The next table, Table 13.4, summarises the answers to our second measurement of campaign change in voting intentions. This is the question in which those interviewed were asked whether they had at any time seriously considered

Table 13.3 *Time of voting decision, strength of party allegiance and party change*

Per cent of those deciding at each stage who:	Time of voting decision		
	A long time ago	Sometime this year	During the campaign
Had only a weak or no party identification	16%	35%	47%
Thought seriously of voting for another party before final decision	14%	28%	61%
Changed party vote from 1974 to 1979	11%	30%	45%

Note: Percentages in the bottom row are based on the number in each category who participated in both of the elections 1974 and 1979; percentages in the upper rows are based on the numbers of respondents who voted in 1979. Only the three main parties' voters are included.
Data source: BES May 1979 Election Survey.

voting for another party than the one they eventually supported in the election. As the table shows, 69 per cent of all those who voted in the election said they had never thought of voting for any other party during the campaign. Well over a quarter, 27 per cent, however, had at least considered one of the three main parties as an alternative. (The remaining 4 per cent had either thought of voting for a minor party or did not specify which party they had in mind.)

The answers to this question lend further corroboration to our observation that those who switched their votes between 1974 and 1979 were much more likely than stable voters to have altered or hesitated about their voting decisions during the campaign. Of the party changers, 51 per cent said they had seriously thought of voting for another party, whereas 24 per cent of the stable voters said that they had. The latter of these two percentages is the more interesting, though. There must have been a great deal of potential volatility in the electorate in 1979, when as many as one in four of these who continued to vote for the same party as last time nevertheless felt that they had reconsidered their voting intention during the campaign.

Again, we find in Table 13.4 that the Liberal voters had been the least sure about their final party choice. Among Conservative and Labour voters, large majorities of 75 and 69 per cent, respectively, said they had not thought of voting for any other party, whereas only a bare majority of Liberal voters (53 per cent) felt they had been that certain. Similar differences are observed for the three parties' stable voters, that is, those who voted for the same party in 1974

Table 13.4 *Voters who had seriously considered voting for a party other than their final choice during the campaign*

Interview question: 'Was there any time during the general election campaign when you seriously thought you might vote for another party?' (If yes:) 'Which party?'

	Party voted for			All voters*
	Conservatives	Liberals	Labour	
	%	%	%	%
No, did not think of voting for another party	75	53	69	69
Yes: Conservatives	–	22	14	8
Yes: Liberals	15	–	14	13
Yes: Labour	7	22	–	6
Other party, or unclassifiable answer, or 'don't know'	3	3	3	4
Total per cent	100%	100%	100%	100%
Number of respondents	731	214	585	1604

*Respondents who participated in the election.
Data source: BES May 1979 Election Survey.

and 1979. As is shown below, the stable Conservative voters were the least likely to have thought of voting for another party (yet 18 per cent did so), stable Labour voters were less steadfast, and as much as a third of the stable Liberal voters had at some stage considered voting for another party.

Voting 1974–1979	Per cent of each party who did not seriously think of voting for another party during the campaign
Stable Conservative voters	82%
Stable Liberal voters	66%
Stable Labour voters	71%

It is in line with our previous findings that the 44 per cent of the 1979 Liberal voters who had considered voting for one of the two major parties during the campaign were evenly divided between seeing the Conservatives and Labour as the alternative choice. Conservative voters who felt uncertain during the campaign were – as we would also expect – definitely more likely to have thought of voting Liberal than voting Labour. It is all the more notable, therefore, that among the reluctant Labour voters just as many had been attracted to the Conservatives as to the Liberal party. This certainly had something to do with the strength of the Conservative party's appeal on some of the most important issues in the campaign, for example, strikes and trade union legislation. But it can also be taken as yet another indication of the ambiguity of the Liberals' role in the party system. On the one hand, the Liberals were seen as the party in the middle which ought to have been particularly attractive to those doubtful Labour supporters who were looking for an alternative. On the other hand, in an election where the mood had shifted towards the right, many Labour voters apparently did not think of the Liberals as a 'real alternative' to Labour. As will be shown in the next section, the Liberal party proves to have been by-passed in a similar fashion when we look at vote-switching between 1974 and 1979.

The per cent distributions for the three main parties in Table 13.4 comprise all of their voters in 1979: those who were stable voters since the last election, those who did not vote in October 1974, as well as the voters who switched parties between the two elections. In a further analysis (not shown in the table) the party changers were taken as a separate category. It turned out that the party they voted for last time was the one they had most often thought of as an alternative to their final party choice – if they had ever had any doubts about their 1979 voting. For example, a third of those who switched from the Liberals to the Conservatives said they had actually also seriously thought of voting Liberal in 1979, whereas few had considered voting Labour. A quarter of Labour switchers to the Conservatives had likewise, at some stage during the campaign, thought of going on voting Labour. Among voters who supported the same party in both 1974 and 1979, the pattern is almost exactly the same as in Table 13.4 except that the proportions who had not considered voting for any other party are, of course, much larger.

Opinions on political issues and stability of voting intentions

Why did more than a quarter of Conservative, Liberal and Labour voters give the party for which they voted such reluctant support that they seriously considered voting for another of the three main parties? Did they feel that their opinions on current politics were less in accord with those of the party they finally settled for than they would have wished? If so, one would expect the reluctant voters to differ from unwavering party supporters in their opinions on the current political issues. That hypothesis can be tested by means of the scale of political opinions obtained from the discriminant analysis. In Table 13.5, the mean values on that scale are shown for each of the sub-categories obtained when the voters for each of the three main parties are classified with regard to whether they had ever con-

Table 13.5 *Unwavering and reluctant voting decisions: opinions on political issues*

Entry for each category in the table is the mean score on the scale for opinions on political issues. The scale ranges from a strongly Conservative opinion position (high positive value) to a strongly Labour opinion position (high negative value). The number of respondents in each category is given within parentheses.

Other party seriously considered	Party voted for in 1979		
	Conservatives	Liberals	Labour
Conservatives	–	+0.31 (48)	–0.50 (80)
Liberals	+0.56 (110)	–	–0.78 (84)
Labour	+0.24 (48)	–0.66 (46)	–
None: never thought of voting for another party	+0.77 (550)	–0.09 (113)	–1.03 (405)

The table includes only respondents who voted for one of the three main parties. A small number of respondents who had thought of voting for one of the minor parties are excluded from the table.
Data source: BES May 1979 Election Survey.

sidered voting for another party and, if so, which other party they had thought of as an alternative.[1]

The data support the hypothesis convincingly. The average opinion position of Conservative voters who remained unwavering through the campaign is clearly 'to the right' of those who considered voting for the Liberals and even more so in comparison with the smaller category who considered voting for Labour. Among Labour voters the pattern is equally clear. Labour's steadfast supporters are furthest 'to the left', while the outlook of those Labour voters who thought of voting Liberal is less partisan. The average position of those who had been thinking of voting Conservative is yet one step further removed towards the right (but still definitely to the left of the midpoint).

The steady Liberal voters are almost exactly at the midpoint on the scale, whereas those who had been pulled towards the Conservatives or Labour exhibit average positions somewhat to the right and somewhat to the left on the scale, as would be expected.

The relationship between opinion positions and reluctant voting decisions emerges as a very clear pattern. The votes the parties 'nearly lost' during the campaign were those of their marginal supporters in terms of opinions on the issues. Among Conservative and Labour voters, those who seriously thought of going the whole way to the opposing major party differed (on average) more from the party's steady supporters than those who considered merely a half-way shift to the Liberals.

13.2 Political opinions and voting change: an overview

In the preceding section we described the differences in opinions on political issues among the voters whom the parties 'nearly lost' during the campaign and the average positions of each party's steady supporters throughout the campaign. Using the same analysis technique, we will now focus on the October 1974 voters whom the parties really did lose in the 1979 election. To some degree, of course, the category of voters who switched parties between the two elections overlaps with the category of voters who changed their minds, or at least finally settled their party choice during the weeks of the campaign. As we have seen, every second party changer had considered voting for some other party than the one he or she eventually supported. Looking at the proportions from another viewpoint: of those Conservative, Liberal and Labour voters who thought of voting for another party in the campaign, 35 per cent did actually switch their votes between October 1974 and May 1979.

The purpose of the present analysis is to provide an overview of the relationship between opinions on political issues and voting change 1974 to 1979. This overview serves, as well, as a summing up of the findings reported in Chapter 11, since the analytic tool we are using here is ultimately based on the divisions of opinion among stable voters and party changers reviewed in that chapter.

The relevant data are set out in Table 13.6 which comprises all the voters who voted for one of the three main parties in both of the elections in October 1974 and May 1979. These voters are grouped according to their party choice on the two occasions. The three cells on the main diagonal of the table (from the upper left to the lower right corner) comprise the stable party voters; each of the remaining six cells corresponds to one of the vote-flows between the three parties. The table gives the average opinion position (the mean scale value) of voters in each of these nine categories.

Reading the table row-wise, one can locate the average opinion position of the voters who defected from each of the three parties. As we would expect by now, the pattern accords with the positioning of the parties. The Conservatives lost support among voters on their 'left wing', whereas the Labour party lost support on its 'right wing'. Those who switched to the Liberal party were located on average somewhere half-way between the midpoint and the supporters of the party they left. Those who switched their votes to the opposite major party were even further removed from the stable supporters of their previous party. The Liberal party lost voters with opinion positions on the right to the Conservatives and on the left to Labour.

If the table is read column-wise it becomes clear that the parties were gaining marginal support just as they were losing marginal support. The voters who

Table 13.6 *Party change and opinions on political issues*

Entry for each of the nine categories in the table is the mean score on the scale for opinions on political issues. The scale ranges from a strongly Conservative opinion position (high positive score values) to a strongly Labour opinion position (high negative score values). The number of respondents in each category is given within parentheses.

Voting in October 1974 election	Voting in May 1979 election		
	Conservatives	Liberals	Labour
Conservatives	+0.82 (452)	+0.46 (26)	−0.48 (15)
Liberals	+0.57 (74)	−0.03 (98)	−0.65 (25)
Labour	+0.28 (79)	−0.63 (48)	−0.96 (451)

The table includes only respondents who participated in both elections and voted for one of the three main parties on both occasions.
Data source: BES May 1979 Election Survey (with partial use of voting data from the BES October 1974 Election Survey).

switched to Labour or the Conservatives, for example, are much less consistently partisan than those two parties' stable voters. If one compares the flows in each direction between any pair of parties, the average positions of the two groups always differ so that the one moving towards the right is showing an average opinion position to the right of the flow in the opposite direction. But there is also another feature – at least as important – in this pattern: the differences between the vote-flows in opposite directions between the Conservatives and the Liberals, as well as between the Liberals and Labour, are very slight indeed. Given individual variations around the mean values, the groups that switched their votes in opposite directions in the exchange between the Liberals and the Conservatives occupied virtually the same segment of the scale, and the same is true of the exchange between the Liberals and Labour.

One might take the average opinion positions of those who switched to the Liberals as indicating the limits of a broadly defined 'middle ground' of opinions on political issues in the electorate. The voters who switched from Labour to the Conservatives are located almost in the centre of that middle ground, while those who switched from the Conservatives to Labour are well inside the left-side limit. The size of the vote-flows is also noteworthy (see the number of respondents given for each cell in the table). The pattern is broadly the same as in the changes in voting decisions examined in the preceding section. In the switching of votes from one election to the next, however, the tendency was for disappointed Labour voters to move to the Conservatives rather than to the Liberals, despite the fact that these voters' opinion positions apparently were closer to the stable Liberal voters. The general trend in the 1979 election is further reflected in defections from the Liberal party: the loss to the Conservatives was substantially bigger than the loss to Labour. Yet, opinions on policies do count: the Labour voters who shifted to the Liberals have an average opinion position so decidedly on the left side of the spectrum that the Conservatives must have seemed even more unattractive than Labour. The fact that the average for stable Liberals was near the midpoint is the result of a quite wide spread of opinions, covering the area of competition with the major parties to the left and to the right.[2] As we have noted before, the middle ground did by no means constitute a reserved area for actual or potential Liberal voting support. It was rather an area where the Conservatives and Labour also won and lost marginal support in competition both with each other and with the Liberals.

13.3 The 'middle ground' and the surge towards the Conservatives

Our analysis in Chapters 12 to 13 has shown that both waverings in voting intentions and actual vote switching occurred largely within a broadly defined middle ground in the electorate consisting of voters whose policy preferences were neither strongly Conservative nor decidedly in favour of Labour. Much of this volatility in the middle ground involved the Liberals. Yet, we have also seen that a very significant part of the flows of support between the parties by-passed the Liberal party and took the form of direct exchange between the Conservatives and Labour. The middle ground, as we use the term here, is of course not too rigidly defined. The boundaries between, say, the less committed, middle-ground part of the Conservatives' electoral support and the party's hard-core support remain fleeting in this analysis, and the same is true of Labour's base in the electorate.

When we examined the results of the discriminant analysis, which classified voters according to their 'expected' (or 'predicted') party choice, we found that a quite broad category of voters – approximately 25 per cent of the sample – was formed in the middle range of the scale. Our model expected all of these voters to vote Liberal, but in fact only a minority of them did so. The Liberals were found to have drawn a substantial part of their voting support from the left end of the Conservatives' segment of the scale and the right end of Labour's segment. If we also include these areas in the middle ground, it obviously comes to appear as an even larger component of the electorate. We need not, for our purpose, delineate the boundaries of the middle ground much more precisely than that. As was suggested in Chapter 12, the size of a more broadly defined middle ground would comprise some 40 per cent of the voters. However, the essential facts about the middle ground are, first, that it falls outside the more reliable sources of support for both the Conservative and Labour parties; second, that the two major parties (partly because of the electoral system) both draw a significant part of their voting support from there; and, third, that this is where electoral battles are won or lost.

How stable, we need to ask, is this middle ground over time? As defined by our measurement technique, the middle ground (wherever the boundaries are set) will include voters who are attracted by some of the Conservative party's policies as well as some of Labour's, and of voters who will not go as far as either of the major parties when they steer in opposite directions. To some extent the location of a middle ground, thus defined, depends on the nature of the disagreements between the parties and on the postures they are seen to be taking. It is quite conceivable, for example, that the middle ground becomes wider when the policies advocated by the parties come to seem further apart. Even if that does not happen, it is likely that the middle ground to some extent is recreated for each election. Alas, it is beyond the scope of this enquiry to investigate such changes over time. It is enough to say that comparatively stable elements of individuals' political views - such as a strong sense of party identification - will help to sustain some degree of stability in the Conservatives' and Labour's 'hard-core' support. This will apply, also, in periods of apparent change in the party system - at least for some time. In 1979, the middle ground may not have looked the same as in 1974. But the changes of opinion that occurred between 1974 and 1979 apparently consisted mainly of a shift from the more pro-Labour side to the more pro-Conservative side of a broadly defined middle ground of policy preferences.[3]

The Conservatives' gains

In the end, what count are the votes. Although the Conservatives cannot really be said to have conquered the middle ground in the 1979 election, they certainly did make headway. Our analyses of both the trends in changing voting intentions and the switching of votes between 1974 and 1979 have shown that the net result was a movement of support in the middle ground from both Labour and the Liberals to the Conservatives. This was enough to ensure a victory for the Conservatives in the 1979 election.

Our final account of the impact of the issues in the 1979 election suggested a straightforward answer to the question of why the Conservatives won. On almost all the policy issues that were prominent in the campaign, the balance of opinion was weighted in the Conservatives' favour. When coupled with a marked decline of confidence in Labour's ability to handle the problems of strikes and unemployment, the appeal of the Conservatives' alternative strategy enabled the party to win back most, though not all, of what it had lost to the Liberals in 1974. The same factors created a direct swing to the Conservatives from among former Labour voters. As was shown in Chapter 3, this was by no means only a matter of Labour's losing marginal middle-class support; indeed, it was within its traditional working-class electoral base that Labour suffered its most damaging loss in voting support in 1979. A substantial part of Labour's voting support – not least within the working class – is drawn from what we have described as the middle ground of policy preferences. The middle-ground, in that sense, cuts across the divide between middle class and working class.

Party images and the issues in 1979

Labour did not only lose votes to the Conservatives in 1979. In contrast to the Conservatives, it also failed to recover any of the ground it had lost to the Liberals five years earlier. Yet, we found in Chapter 5 that the voters' images of the parties at the 1979 election had not really changed all that much. Labour has won elections in the past because of its commitment to social welfare policies and despite its commitment to nationalisation. Similarly, Labour has drawn strength from its working class image despite the fact that the trade unions have been unpopular from time to time. Why did the attractiveness of Labour's image seem to wear off?

Party images change slowly, if at all. They do not cause short-term electoral change. But they do set preconditions for party strategies to the extent that they can help or hinder a party to put its campaign message across to the electorate.[4] Firstly, the campaign message needs to be compatible with the party image: a party cannot, without putting its credibility at risk, propose to do things that another party is widely seen to do better, or to feel more strongly about. A Labour government may, for example, find it necessary to cut public expenditure, but it cannot expect that those in favour of such measures therefore will switch to Labour. If more people become convinced that it is time for cutbacks, the chances are that most will think of the Conservatives as the better bet, on the grounds that they would implement such a policy more wholeheartedly. Likewise, the Labour party is unlikely to win much new support by promising to cut taxes, because the Conservatives, especially in opposition, will always promise an even bigger tax cut.

Moreover, it is not sufficient for a party's pledges during an election campaign merely to be consistent with its party image; the pledges must also appear relevant and sensible to the voters whose support it is aiming to win. Campaign strategies are a matter of choosing the right issues on which to fight an election.[5] It is not all a matter of choice, however. The real choices of strategy open to a party are constrained. Party images impose constraints. So do events and the problems that ordinary voters are concerned about. And circumstances do not always evolve as expected. With hindsight, it may be argued that Mr Callaghan erred in deciding not to call an election in the summer of 1978. Whether this is true or not must remain a matter for conjecture. But it is evident that Labour's election strategy came to clash with its election timing. Labour had, indeed, a strategy, one that was congruent with its popular image: it aimed to be seen as the one party that could base its economic policy on a compact with the unions; it wanted to be seen, too, as the party that could steer a steady, trustworthy course through economic difficulties. That strategy was already looking somewhat dented by the previous summer. In May 1979 it had come to look a great deal less credible; some would say it was wrecked.

In fact, at the time of the 1979 election, the prevailing images of the parties seem to have further enhanced the Conservatives' advantage on most of the issues that were foremost in the voters' minds. Among large groups of wage-earners, feelings for the Labour party had gone sour as the result of Labour's incomes policy. Unfair though it may seem, confidence in Labour at the same time suffered because of the resentment caused by the very trade unions that had frustrated the Labour government's policy. Labour's traditional image as the party of ordinary working people must have lost some of its appeal when even many trade unionists wanted the power of the unions to be cut back to size, and the Conservatives appealed to widespread resentment of incomes policy. When loyalties to Labour's working-class image were weakened in this way, the party became more vulnerable to the Conservatives' challenges in the whole field of economic and social policies.

Labour had a potential strength in the electorate's appreciation of good public services. But the Conservatives' pledge to cut taxes was nevertheless attractive to voters concerned with take-home pay; mostly, they may have remained unconvinced that the public services they cherished were under any real threat. Labour continued to be identified with social welfare policies – at a time when public support for any further extension of welfare benefits was waning. Many more favoured the Conservative view that it was time to cut back wherever money was wasted. The Conservatives were associated with free enterprise and private industry. Labour was associated with state intervention in the economy – at a time when state subsidies to ailing industries seemed to be failing in their purpose, when public industries were doing badly, and when support for further nationalisation was crumbling. On all counts, the Conservatives' campaign message, far more than Labour's, was in tune with both the party's popular image and the state of opinion in the electorate.

A victory with a question mark

Why, then, was the Conservatives' victory not more convincing? The 1979 election left Labour much weaker than it had been in the 1950s, when commentators began to wonder if Labour could ever win. Yet, the Conservatives' electoral support was decidedly weaker than in the late 1950s, and the Conservatives failed to win as large a share of the electorate as they had held as late as the 1970 election.

The voters in the middle ground were not all persuaded by the Conservative message on all the issues. That the Liberals managed to avoid more than a moderate loss from their peak in 1974 is one indicator of the partial and qualified nature of the Conservatives' recovery. The wavering of voting intentions during the campaign, which showed up in the survey data, is another indicator.

The electorate's verdict on Labour's performance in office was far less favourable in 1979 than it had been in October 1974. But poor as Labour's rating had become, the data do not indicate decisively greater confidence in the Conservatives' performance. In that respect, the pendulum had not swung. It had just drooped. There were also other ambiguities in the 1979 election campaign. The Conservatives had strong popular support when they demanded stricter regulation of the trade unions – and undoubtedly they gained votes on that issue – but their record on handling strikes and on dealing with the trade unions was not altogether convincing. The mood in the electorate was in favour of the Conservatives' pledge to abstain from state interference in wage negotiations – but there was a fair amount of uncertainty about where the Conservatives really stood on that issue. The Conservatives could count on approval of their pledge to cut taxes – but much of that approval was given with the reservation that public services must not be harmed. None of the factors that held back the Conservatives in 1979 did much more, however, than dent the party's armour. The Conservatives won the 1979 election on their promise to take both the country and its industry on to a new start. The party could not have won, though, without the support of many voters in the middle ground who were attracted to these prospects and wanted change – rather than the 'more of the same thing' that Labour seemed to stand for – but remained less than fully convinced about all of the means.

The election result can be taken as a mandate for Conservative economic policy. But the stage was also set for the spectacular slump in popular support for the Conservative government recorded in the opinion polls in 1980 and 1981, when the prospects that the Conservatives had held out in the election campaign seemed to be receding even further into the distance.

Part III

A turning-point?

14

At the end of a decade

14.1 The elections of the 1970s in retrospect

Are we witnessing the erosion of the foundations of the Conservative and Labour two-party system which has so decisively put its mark on most of the post-war era? That question has obviously to be asked after the two general elections in February and October 1974 which showed both a remarkable increase in electoral support for the Liberal party and a new surge towards the nationalist parties in Scotland and Wales.

By the end of the decade – and after the 1979 election – the question had not lost its relevance or importance. Although support for nationalist parties appeared to have subsided in 1979, the Liberals continued to attract substantial electoral support even under circumstances which were especially unfavourable for the party. As this is being written, two years after the 1979 election, the possibility that a strong political force in the centre has re-emerged to challenge the Conservative–Labour predominance is very real. Yet, after the 1979 election the question about the party system needs to be restated. It now appears that the most crucial feature of the 1970s is the shrinkage of the Labour party's electoral base. That process may have begun already in 1970. It certainly was one of the most significant features of the two 1974 elections, and it would have been even more apparent if it had not coincided with a widespread sense of dissatisfaction with the 1970–4 Conservative government. As it happened, the Labour party was brought into office, not because of its own strength but because of the unpopularity of the Conservative alternative – and, of course, because of the workings of the electoral system. After a slight recovery in the October 1974 election, the downward slide in Labour's electoral support continued with another slight but significant fall in 1979. (However, given the Conservatives gains at the expense of small parties, Labour would still have lost the 1979 election even if it had held on to its October 1974 share of the vote.)

The 'winter of discontent' and disenchantment with the trade unions can to a large extent account for the further decline in Labour's electoral fortunes between the two 1974 elections and 1979.

331

As we have seen, it is among the working class that the Labour party has lost ground, and that is where its voting support has become the most vulner-has lost ground, and that is where its voting support has become the most vulner-able to electoral volatility. This is not to say that the working class has ceased to be Labour's single most important electoral asset. Labour still draws incomparably more support from trade union organised manual workers than from any other sector of society. But the proportion of the working class which stays loyal to Labour even when the election wind is blowing against the party is smaller than before; the proportion which votes Labour in some elections but Conservative in others has increased. It is a telling fact that Labour suffered a larger percentage loss from October 1974 to May 1979 among union organised manual workers than among middle-class voters. And not all of Labour's losses have gone to the Conservatives; in the 1979 election, the Liberals obtained nearly the same level of support in the working class as in the middle class.

The relationships between individuals' social status and their choice of party have by no means vanished. But as determinants of voting they carry less weight than before. As we have seen, furthermore, the precise meaning of such determi-nants is being gradually redefined: immediate economic interest – rather than class membership in the old sense – may increase in importance, and white-collar employees may come to differ less from manual workers in their political views.

What has occurred is not a definite shift of party loyalties within any easily definable sector of society. There has not been a political realignment within any important social group of the kind that occurred when Labour gradually became the party of the working class in the first four decades of the century. In an earlier study we have used the term 'partisan dealignment' to describe the process that had set in during the 1970s.[1] By 'partisan dealignment' we mean that none of the major occupational groups now provides the same degree of solid and consistent support for one of the two major parties as was the case in the earlier post-war era (the Conservative loyalty of entrepreneurs and the self-employed is perhaps the one exception). The process is not quite as apparent in the middle classes as among manual workers but the 1970s showed that the Conservatives have become more vulnerable than before to a Liberal challenge. In this picture of volatility, the relative stability of Labour's middle-class support stands out as an apparent deviation from the general trend. We cannot present any explanation based on hard evidence for this phenomenon, but can at least offer a plausible conjecture. Within the middle class, Labour draws most of its support from salaried employees, in particular if they are trade union members. As the bound-aries of income, working conditions and job security between manual and non-manual employees have become less and less distinctive, it is not surprising that the size of Labour's *potential* support among middle-class employees should be widening. If this is a long-term trend, then it was counteracted in the 1970s by short-term factors that worked to Labour's disadvantage. The two forces have more or less cancelled each other out.

14.2 The decline of party allegiance

Dealignment affected the electoral bases of both major parties in the 1970s. The difference between the Conservatives' and Labour's situation after the 1979 election was rather that the Conservatives proved that they – at least in competition with a Labour government in obvious difficulty – could still muster electoral support of nearly the same magnitude as in previous elections. In Part II, we have tried to show how this came about: the balance of public opinion in 1979 was weighted in favour of the free market economy alternative that formed the main theme in the Conservatives' appeal to the electorate. When disenchantment with the previous decades' style of economic politics was coupled with a lack of confidence in the Liberal party's electoral prospects, the preconditions for a Conservative electoral victory were there.

Yet, under the surface, the erosion of party loyalties continues to soften the Conservatives' as well as Labour's electoral base. We can illuminate this process with the time series of data displayed in Table 14.1. The data in the table are based on the questions, discussed in Part II, in which voters were asked whether 'generally speaking' they thought of themselves as Conservatives, Labour or Liberal, or as adherents of some other party.[2] If a person identified himself with a party in this sense, he was then asked about the strength of his attachment to that party.

In the 1970s, as in earlier years, most citizens eligible to vote in Britain did indeed think of themselves as Conservative, Liberal, or Labour. (See the grand total in the lower right-hand corner cell in each of the tables.) Yet there is a slow but unmistakable downward trend in the proportion who think in this way. In 1964, 92 per cent of the electorate thought of themselves as supporters of one of the three main parties; that percentage went down by a point or so at most of the following elections, to reach 85 in 1979.

A more significant change, however, has occurred in the proportion of the electorate who considered themselves to be 'very strongly' attached to any of the parties. In the 1960s, and as late as in 1970, such voters made up over 40 per cent of the electorate. In this time-series it becomes apparent that the February 1974 election signalled a crisis of confidence in the established party system from which it has not recovered. At the February 1974 election the percentage of 'very strong' party supporters showed a drastic fall to 29 per cent, and since then it has continued to slide – to 26 per cent in October 1974 and to 21 per cent in May 1979. Almost all of this decline reflects a diminution of strongly committed support to the two major parties. The proportion who are very strong supporters of the Liberal party has always been tiny, although it fell from 4 to 2 per cent of the electorate between 1964 and 1979. In 1964, 40 per cent of electors thought of themselves as 'very strong' Conservative or Labour supporters. By 1979, the proportion had fallen to 19 per cent. They are almost equally divided; both of the major parties must now face the fact that their hard core of supporters, with a firm sense of party allegiance, has shrunk to a tenth of the electorate.

Table 14.1 *The extent and strength of identification with the three main parties in the electorate 1964-1979*

The tables below show for each of the six elections how large a percentage of the entire electorate were 'very strongly', 'fairly strongly' and 'not very strongly' attached to each of the three main parties. The *percentage* in each cell is based on the entire sample of respondents in the election survey concerned. The grand total in the lower right-hand corner shows the percentage of respondents who indicated an allegiance to any of the three main parties. The row and column totals show the percentages of supporters for each of the parties and the total percentages in the different 'strength of identification' categories, respectively. (Small differences between the sum of entries in a row or column and the corresponding entry in the row/column total are due to decimal rounding.) Respondents who are 'a little closer' to a party are *not* treated as identifiers in tables 14.1–2.

1964 election

Generally speaking thought of them- selves as:	Strength of party identification			Total
	Very strong	Fairly strong	Not very strong	
Conservative	19	16	4	39
Liberal	4	6	2	11
Labour	21	16	5	42
Total	43	38	11	92%

Percentage base (weighted data): 1,818.
Data source: Butler and Stokes 1964 Election Survey (cross-section sample).

1966 election

Generally speaking thought of them- selves as:	Strength of party identification			Total
	Very strong	Fairly strong	Not very strong	
Conservative	17	14	4	35
Liberal	3	5	1	10
Labour	22	19	4	45
Total	43	38	9	90%

Percentage base (weighted data): 1,899.
Data source: Butler and Stokes 1966 Election Survey (cross-section sample).

Table 14.1 (*cont.*)

1970 election

Generally speaking thought of them- selves as:	Strength of party identification			Total
	Very strong	Fairly strong	Not very strong	
Conservative	20	16	4	39
Liberal	2	4	2	8
Labour	20	17	6	42
Total	41	36	11	89%

Percentage base (weighted data): 1,287.
Data source: Butler and Stokes Election Survey 1964, 1966 and 1970 (cross-section samples).

February 1974 election

Generally speaking thought of them- selves as:	Strength of party identification			Total
	Very strong	Fairly strong	Not very strong	
Conservative	11	17	6	35
Liberal	2	7	4	13
Labour	16	17	6	40
Total	29	42	17	88%

Percentage base: 2,462.
Data source: BES February 1974 Election Survey.

October 1974 election

Generally speaking thought of them- selves as:	Strength of party identification			Total
	Very strong	Fairly strong	Not very strong	
Conservative	9	18	6	34
Liberal	2	8	4	14
Labour	14	19	6	40
Total	26	45	17	88%

Percentage base: 2,365.
Data source: BES October 1974 Election Survey.

Table 14.1 (*cont.*)

1979 election

Generally speaking thought of them-selves as:	Strength of party identification			Total
	Very strong	Fairly strong	Not very strong	
Conservative	9	20	8	38
Liberal	2	6	4	11
Labour	10	18	7	36
Total	21	45	19	85%

Percentage base: 1,893.
Data source: BES 1979 Election Survey.

Table 14.2 presents the same time-series of data in a different format. The table shows, for each of the six elections, the percentage of each party's identifiers who considered themselves 'very strong' adherents of their party. The table brings out, again, the weakening of support for all the three main parties. Two observations are worth making in this context. Firstly, the growth of support for the Liberal party between 1964 and 1979 did not result in any remarkable increase in the proportion of voters who 'thought of themselves' as Liberals (see Table 14.1). There is no indication that the flowering of the Liberal party in the mid 1970s resulted in stronger attachments to the party. Instead, the proportion of 'very strong' party supporters declined dramatically just at the time when the Liberal vote reached its peak, at the February 1974 election. Secondly, it is noteworthy that the Conservative victory at the polls in 1979 was not accompanied by any strengthening of allegiance to the party among those who in general thought of themselves as Conservatives. The percentage of 'very strong' supporters continued to slide at about the same rate as among Labour supporters. Indeed, we know, from the analyses in Part II, that a good portion of the 'not very strong' Conservative voters had actually thought of voting Liberal, or said they would have been likely to do so if the Liberals had stood a credible chance of winning a large number of seats.

14.3 The 1979 election and the future

Our exploration of the electoral bases for the three main parties suggested that the Conservatives' victory in 1979 amounted to something less reassuring than a real restoration of the party's electoral support during the earlier post-war era.

In terms of the social background of the voters, a substantial part of the Conservatives' gains were made in the working class and reflected the new degree of volatility of electoral behaviour among manual workers. In terms of the flow of the vote among the parties, we found that the Conservatives recaptured a considerable share of the votes they had lost to the Liberals in 1974. If this was

Table 14.2 *Strength of party identification*

The table shows, for each election, the percentage of each party's identifiers who said they were 'very strong' supporters of their party.

Generally speaking thought of themselves as:	Percentage 'very strong' of each party's identifiers at the election in					
	1979	October 1974	February 1974	1970	1966	1964
Conservative	24%	27%	32%	51%	49%	48%
Liberal	14%	14%	12%	26%	35%	32%
Labour	29%	36%	41%	47%	50%	51%

Data source: BES May 1979, October 1974 and February 1974 Election Survey. Butler and Stokes, Election Surveys 1970, 1966, 1964.

mainly (but not exclusively) the result of a return to the Conservatives among middle-class voters, it was also the result of Conservative gains made in a sector of the electorate whose party preferences have become increasingly changeable. Moreover, our mapping of opinions on policies and on the parties' performance in office suggested that a crucial portion of the Conservative vote in 1979 was drawn from a broad middle ground in the electorate. A large part of the Conservative vote in 1979 came from voters who were less than strongly in favour of, or confident about, all aspects of the policies the Conservatives proposed to pursue. On almost all counts, however, the Conservatives met with more approval than Labour, and there is little doubt that the electorate endorsed the general thrust of the Conservative alternative. It all added up to an accumulation of short-term forces of opinion which shifted the vote towards the Conservatives.

In the 1970s the electorate became more ready to sway in response to short-term factors, especially the issues that were the cause of immediate concern. In the 1974 election this resulted in a large-scale shifting of votes to the parties of protest, the Liberals and the Nationalists. In the 1979 election, it was the Conservatives who benefited from the new volatility. On the strength of the popularity of their campaign they were able to attract exceptionally strong working-class support from among disaffected previous Labour voters and, at the same time, to win back the votes (but hardly the strong allegiance) of many of the voters who had deserted them in 1974.

The long-term, gradual changes in the political landscape we have discussed in this chapter may be seen both as a reflection of and as a cause of the softening of the Conservatives' and Labour's electoral bases. The boundaries of the traditional social bases of the two major parties are being blurred and, as they have come to be seen as less significant, they have become easier to transgress. At the same time – and perhaps partly as a consequence – an increasing portion of the voters cast their votes without any strong sense of allegiance to the party they choose to vote for in a particular election. Yet, neither the class divide nor the ideological cleavage in the party system, represented by Conservative and Labour, have vanished, and these factors do even to some degree account for the fluctuations in the Liberal vote. For many voters – especially in the middle class – a shift to the Liberals is easier to contemplate than a switch between the major parties. Switching in and out of the Liberals' voting support has therefore become the means by which an increasing number of voters express their reactions to current politics in the elections of the 1970s. Albeit to a lesser extent, voting for the Nationalist parties in Scotland and Wales was in all likelihood affected by the same factors.

What, then, are the prospects for the parties – and for the two-party predominance in British politics? Have the changes of the 1970s created the preconditions for the emergence of a new political force in the centre? Whether that will happen or not will partly depend on the performance of both the Conservatives and Labour in the remaining years of this parliament. Such factors will also decide the extent to which the Alliance of Liberals and Social Democrats can build up voting support at the expense of the Conservatives or Labour – or both in equal measure. Even if the Conservative and Labour parties survive such a challenge to their role as the two alternative parties of government, however, the setting for party competition will have changed profoundly in comparison with the earlier post-war era. Both parties will need to take into account that they are appealing to an electorate in which social group loyalties mean less than they used to, where many fewer voters than in the past have any strong sense of party allegiance, and where many more are inclined to take an instrumental view of voting. If either of the parties fails to recognise that the electorate has changed, then it will doom itself to a long period on the opposition benches in Parliament.

Postscript: realignment in the 1980s?

Many of the broader themes of this book have been brought into sharp relief by the formation in early 1981 of the Social Democratic Party (SDP) and its subsequent electoral alliance with the Liberal party. The specific occasion of the SDP's birth was the objection by a minority on the right of Labour's leadership to alterations in the party's constitution. The deeper cause was their fear that these constitutional changes foreshadowed – and reflected – the irreversible domination of the Labour party by a rigid and insular 'far left', committed to withdrawal from the EEC, unilateral nuclear disarmament, and major extensions of public ownership, trade union powers and the state's economic planning apparatus. The aim of the breakaway, therefore, was to occupy what they regarded as the recently vacated centre-left of the party battleground, ousting Labour as the major opposition to the Conservatives. Their purpose was nothing less than to 'break the mould' of Britain's post-war two-party system.

The purpose of 'breaking the mould' of the two parties, moreover, was to 'mould the break' *between* the two parties. The SDP sought not only to stop the pendulum of Conservative and Labour governments but to reshape the political choices put before the British electorate. So long as the Conservative and Labour parties remained dominant, it argued, they would continue to stamp political debate and the governing agenda with narrow, outdated, class-based appeals and doctrines. Politics would remain a battle between the presumed interests of the organised haves and organised have-nots, even though most electors' true economic interests lay away from the battlefield and in the cessation of hostilities. Under an adversary, polarised two-party system successive governments would go on dragging Britain up and down an 'ideological roller-coaster' when what was required was pragmatic, down-to-earth government pursuing stability and consensus. By winning a majority in parliament, or at least depriving the two major parties of a majority, an SDP/Liberal Alliance could breach the two-party duopoly, then destroy it through proportional representation, and thereby inaugurate a new era in British politics.

The Social Democrats are not the first party, of course, to pursue this grand design. For the last forty years its electoral partner, the Liberal party, has nurtured similar hopes – but in vain. It has failed to win sufficient seats to form part of the government or even to hold the balance of power in the Commons. This is not because its electoral support is negligible. British post-war elections have never been a purely two-party affair. There have always been a few Liberal MPs, a serious Liberal challenge in a substantial minority of seats, and surges of Liberal support under unpopular Conservative governments. But the Liberal party has always suffered at the hands of Britain's simple plurality electoral system, which severely penalises minor parties, especially those with dispersed rather than concentrated support. Some of its ideological counterparts on the European continent, where there is proportional representation (like the German Free Democrats) regularly win about the same or a smaller share of the national vote yet join coalition governments. Moreover, the penalising effects of the electoral system are self-reinforcing. Unable to convert most of its votes into seats, the Liberal party finds itself unable to convert most of its support into votes. Our study has persistently shown how the Liberals, more than any other party, underpolls its potential support. Reluctant to 'waste' their vote on a party with little chance of governing, many of its sympathisers plump for a major party when it comes to the general election.

Does the SDP/Liberal Alliance have a realistic prospect of succeeding where the Liberal party alone has failed in the past? What are its chances of clearing the electoral system's high double-hurdle of credibility and the conversion of votes into seats? Precise estimates of the vote needed for a significant parliamentary breakthrough vary, because they depend on assumptions about how the rest of the vote divides between the Conservative and Labour parties and about the pattern of change across constituencies. But it is generally agreed that the Alliance's threshold is above that for the two other parties. To become the largest party grouping in the Commons it needs from 37 to 39 per cent of the national vote; to have an odds-on chance of holding the balance of power between 30 and 34 per cent.[1] The very creation of the SDP, with its own organisation, finances, publicity and, most notably, a well-known and experienced set of leaders, obviously constitutes something of an electoral bonus for the ideological centre. Yet it is hardly enough by itself to ensure that the threshold will be crossed. Has anything more fundamental about the British electorate changed to encourage the SDP's belief that, together with the Liberals, it can remould the British party system?

The SDP's ambitious objective involves assumptions about the modern British electorate for which our researches undoubtedly offer some support. It assumes, firstly, that a sizeable portion of voters – at least a third – can be quickly persuaded to abandon old partisan habits, perhaps allegiances of a lifetime. Our study does document a gradual dealignment and slowly growing volatility in the British electorate. Earlier in this chapter we showed how identification with the Conservative and Labour parties has weakened fairly steadily since the early 1960s, so that by 1979 only one elector in five could be regarded as an unswerving partisan. Between a normally spaced pair of elections the proportion of our panel respondents who switched parties, or moved in or out of abstention, ranged from 34 to 42 per cent, and these figures exclude many others who wavered or prevaricated in their voting decision during the election campaign.

Yet the same evidence, viewed in a different light, reveals the reserve strengths of the two main parties. The *incidence* of Conservative and Labour party identification in the electorate has declined much more gently than its *intensity*: the majority are loosely attached to the two big parties, but they are not completely unattached. This is underlined by our panel analysis over three and four consecutive elections which shows the strong tendency for major party defectors at one election to return 'home' at the next. British electors nowadays might be more detachable; but they are also easily re-attachable.

The SDP's aims assume, secondly, that the Labour party is particularly vulnerable to a partisan realignment. In support is Labour's undeniably poor electoral showing throughout the 1970s and the survey evidence of a rightward drift in opinion – an ideological dealignment – among its own voters. In 1979 barely a third of Labour voters were in favour of further nationalisation, fractionally under a third opposed stricter legislation to constrain trade union powers, and only just over a quarter wanted an extension of social services. The Conservative party suffered from less faintheartedness about its policies among its own voters.

Yet too much should not be made of Labour's disadvantage. The majority of Labour voters were never committed 'socialists'; for many years people have voted Labour – and helped to elect Labour governments – despite, not because of, Labour's 'socialist' stands on issues such as nationalisation. Moreover, although the issues that came to the fore in the 1979 election may have had an ideological undertone, they were primarily tied in with more immediate material concerns. There is little doubt, for example, that the 'winter of discontent' played a major role in enhancing public concern about the powers of trade unions. In 1979 the Conservatives had an overall advantage, as we have seen, on issues involving a choice between policy alternatives. But in future elections, the constellation of salient issues need not be the same, and some of the issues may be seen in a different light. For example, Labour's stance on social welfare and on public services could become a major electoral asset again if the public come to feel that a Conservative government had neglected these areas. Issues of policy thus become intertwined with judgements on the record of the incumbent party. None of our interview questions had more bearing on party choice in 1979 than those which elicited people's comparisons of the Labour government's record on the economy with what they imagined the Conservatives would have achieved had they been the government. What shifted votes away from Labour and towards the Conservatives, however, was not the latter's hypothetical merits – on this the electorate remained fairly unconvinced – but the decline since October 1974 in Labour's *relative* standing *vis-à-vis* the Conservatives as a party capable of handling unemployment and strikes. In both these areas Labour's standing clearly suffered in the eyes of the electorate. In all probability the fate of the present Conservative government will also depend on its record – as indeed will the electoral prospects of both the Labour party and the Alliance. The relative unpopularity of some traditional Labour party tenets will make a Labour election victory more difficult, but far from impossible.

Thirdly, the SDP pins its hopes on a cross-class appeal to electors occupying the 'middle ground'. Once again, our findings could arguably be taken as evidence that such a strategy would find a ready public response. The class basis of support for the two main parties has slowly diminished over the last two decades: by 1979 only a bare majority voted strictly on class lines (and then not necessarily for class-related reasons). Judged across a large set of issues the majority of voters do adopt a set of positions that is either mixed or generally middling, rather than consistently pro-Conservative or consistently pro-Labour. In its opinions on the major issues the British electorate is not divided into united, warring camps but ranged across the territory in between. Thus, in its claim to represent intermediate stands on the old issues, and a differently mixed bundle of conventional policy positions, the Alliance should be able to draw on a sizeable pool of support.

It would be a mistake, however, to infer that all or most of this intermediate ground can be captured by the SDP/Liberal Alliance alone. Social class, whether measured by occupational status or housing tenure, remains the only enduring division in British society of partisan consequence; it still structures voting decisions, even if less decisively than in the 1950s and 1960s. The Labour party, in particular, continues to be regarded, by both its supporters and detractors, as above all else the representative of working-class interests and the political wing of organised labour. In these circumstances a rapid and substantial transfer of manual workers' allegiances to the Alliance seems unlikely.

The populous ideological middle ground, moreover, is unlikely ever to be the exclusive preserve of the Alliance, just as it has never been of the Liberal party. Our own analyses showed that the majority of electors with a moderate mixture of views have in fact voted either Conservative or Labour in the past – even if they have been more likely than others occasionally to vote, or to consider voting, for the Liberals. Moreover, even with the Conservative and Labour parties moving away from the ideological centre, and the middle ground becoming yet more crowded with electors, the Alliance could fail to capture the majority of their votes. For an elector to be placed nearer the centre than either major party is not necessarily to be placed *very* far from one or other of them. Unless convinced that the Alliance not only offers better policies but has a realistic chance of forming, or helping to form, the government many of these electors could vote for the less disagreeable of the two main parties in order to keep the more disagreeable one out. Their vote would be cast with less conviction than before and switching between the two main parties would increase; yet the number of them opting for the Alliance might still be small.

The prospect for a major transformation of the British party system is therefore finely balanced. This is vividly demonstrated by the spectacular oscillation of support for the Alliance since the SDP's emergence in January 1981. Within two months support for the putative Alliance rose to $43\frac{1}{2}$ per cent in the regular opinion polls, compared with 15 per cent for the Liberals hitherto. This figure was sustained with only minor fluctuations througout the following fifteen months and confirmed in the Alliance's by-election gains at Croydon North West, Crosby, and Glasgow Hillhead. Repeated at a general election it would have produced a majority SDP/Liberal government. For speed, strength and duration such an eruption of a third party was unprecedented since Britain's modern party system evolved in the 1920s. Yet a fall in support that was equally rapid and almost as massive occurred between the Glasgow Hillhead by-election in late March 1982 and the capture of Port Stanley by British forces three months later. As the Conservative government's popularity soared, support for the Alliance dropped to about 23 per cent – well below the threshold for a parliamentary breakthrough. The capacity of the Alliance to win over unaligned voters is matched by its incapacity to hold on to them when one of its major rivals looks more attractive.

Thus, from the limited evidence available so far,[2] electoral support for the SDP appears to be shallow as well as wide. By and large its voters are Conservative and Labour renegades, not committed partisans; it has failed to mobilise a distinctive social base; and it is not yet the beneficiary of any *major* new issue conflict or social cleavage which cuts across existing partisan divisions. Its appeal appears to be negative and diffuse, rather than positive and specific; to be based on its leadership, style and sheer novelty rather than on policies and ideology. In structure and motivation, its support closely resembles what we have reported about the Liberal vote in the past. Instead of creating a new social and ideological constituency, the SDP appears to have attracted, at least temporarily, part of the large, volatile, potential Liberal vote which this book reveals to have existed for many years.

None of this proves that the Alliance's electoral successes in 1981–2 will be as transient as previous Liberal eruptions. For one thing, past cycles of Liberal support have moved along an upward spiral. Each successive Liberal peak since the late 1950s has reached higher, lasted longer, and subsided less than its predecessor. Thus the Alliance is being launched on a higher ebb tide of support than the Liberal party enjoyed in the past. In time, moreover, as a distinctive programme develops, the Alliance might mobilise firmer support around particular interests, issues and institutions. Nor should we exclude the possibility that in future elections the consolidation of support around particular interests and issues will no longer be necessary to change the party system.

Analysis of partisan realignments in the United States points out that they are inaugurated by 'critical' elections in which supporters of the winning party are motivated by a diffuse disaffection from the incumbent government rather than by a fully fledged commitment to an alternative set of policies.[3] In Britain similar conditions for a partisan realignment would seem to exist. Dissatisfaction with the performance of successive governments of both parties is widespread. The capacity of the two major parties to pull mid-term defectors back into line has diminished. More and more voters are 'up for grabs'. This dealignment might have proceeded so far that support for the Alliance, despite its apparently ephemeral and negative quality, becomes just sufficient to breach the high threshold of Britain's electoral system and secure a beachhead in the Commons.

Whether that would be enough to transform the party system is another matter. Partisan realignments are only facilitated by significant electoral change. They are created and consolidated by the use politicians make of their newly won support. A breakthrough by the Alliance would only crack the two-party mould. Its leaders could not necessarily secure proportional representation. Even if they did, support at subsequent elections, when they were judged as a party of government not opposition, would not necessarily be enough to create a new multi-party mould in which it held a strategic position. Moreover, multi-party systems are not always conducive to the spirit of consensus-seeking and to the stable, pragmatic, innovatory and adaptable governments sought by the Alliance. Experience shows that multi-party systems which preclude enduring, cohesive majorities in a parliament can be far from desirable. Policies may come to be created in order to sustain a government in office rather than the reverse; and the centre, instead of being a fulcrum of constructive stability, can turn into a dead-lock of inertia, the scene of directionless compromise. Moreover, the feasibility of one or other major party forming a stable coalition government with the centre depends not only on the parliamentary strength of the parties, but on the readiness of their leaders and backbenchers to play the new rules, and accept the unfamiliar ethos, of the coalition 'game'. Thus the prospects for a beneficial as well as permanent change in the party system rest as much on the actions of politicians as on the votes of the electorate. That the 1980s, like the 1970s, will be a decade of dealignment seems fairly certain. Whether it will also be a decade of realignment, and if so a realignment which improves the quality of British government, remains to be seen.

Appendix

Constructing the flow-of-the-vote tables

A. The use of panel and recall data

When we came to construct the flow-of-the-vote table for October 1974 – 1979 we found ourselves in a quandary. Our preferred measure of the vote in October 1974 was the *report* of those respondents interviewed within a few weeks of that election. However, by adopting this measure we would have been restricted to the October 1974 – 1979 panel sample which, in addition to the slight biases inherent in panels, was reduced to relatively small numbers and thus subject to a degree of sampling error that was barely acceptable for a flow-of-the-vote table. We considered solving the problem by using the entire 1979 cross-sectional sample, which is over twice the size. But that would have obliged us to measure October 1974 voting by relying on respondents' recall in 1979 of a vote they had cast over four years earlier. That had its own disadvantage: quite apart from errors of memory, we suspected that some respondents would confuse the election of October 1974 with that held in February. We were faced with a trade-off between sampling error and measurement error.

In the case of earlier pairs of elections our decision was made easy. The more ample size of the panel samples (1,096 for 1970 – February 1974 and 1,830 for February 1974 – October 1974) allowed us to rely on panel respondents only and on reports rather than recalls of earlier voting – as Butler and Stokes did for the elections of the 1960s.[1] In the case of October 1974 – 1979 we resolved the dilemma by a compromise. We used the entire 1979 cross-section survey, but for panel respondents we adopted the reported measure of October 1974 voting whereas for non-panel respondents the recalled measure (the only one available to us, of course). What follows is a description of the reasoning that led to the procedure, and what it revealed about the make-up of our panel and non-panel samples.

It is well known amongst survey researchers that reliance on respondents' recall of what they thought or did in the past is risky. The longer back respondents are asked to remember, and the less central the past event was to their lives,

345

the greater the likelihood of non-response or, more often, error. For most people elections are unimportant and unexciting events. Their reports of their vote at an election of only a week or so earlier will already be subject to error (usually a 'bandwagon' effect in favour of the victorious party) but the amount is normally too small to jeopardise the validity of the survey. Such was the case with our 1979 election study in which the reported Conservative vote was only 2.1 per cent in excess of that actually cast.[2]

However, reliance on respondents' memory of their vote at elections further back in time, including the election held only a few years previously, is a different matter. According to a number of empirical, quasi-experimental investigations[3] the errors produced by such recall data are not only substantial but non-random. Respondents' disposition to project current party preferences on to claims of past party choice and to forget past instances of abnormal voting, typically results in:

(a) over-estimates of the past Conservative and Labour vote (especially the vote of whichever has enjoyed an upturn of popularity since the recalled election)
(b) under-estimates of past support for the Liberals, Nationalists and other small parties
(c) under-estimates of past non-voting
(d) under-estimates of vote-switching between the recalled election and the following election

Our own recall data are no exception, as the following two tables show. Table A.1 cross-tabulates two measures of the October 1974 vote taken from the *identical* sample of respondents, the October 1974 – 1979 panel:

(1) the respondents' *report* of their vote when they were interviewed within a few weeks of the October 1974 election
(2) the same respondents' *recall* of their October 1974 vote when they were interviewed again in May 1979.

The figures reveal substantial discrepancies between the two measures: almost a quarter of our respondents (24 per cent) recalled a vote that differed from the one they originally reported in October 1974. Moreover, these discrepancies were not randomly distributed, being far more serious among minor party supporters and abstainers. Over 90 per cent of those who in October 1974 reported a Conservative or Labour vote, re-confirmed that vote when interviewed four years later. But among those originally reporting a Liberal or other (mainly Nationalist) vote, barely half – 48 per cent and 52 per cent respectively – remembered having done so by 1979. More striking still, a majority of those who originally reported abstaining claimed in the second interview to have voted. The overall result is that compared with report data the recall data 'raise' the Conservative and Labour vote in October 1974 by 6.4 per cent and 4.5 per cent respectively, and 'lower' the Liberal and other parties' vote by 4.5 per cent and 1.4 per cent respectively. The amount of non-voting (which was anyway seriously under-estimated in the report data) is reduced by a further 5.1 per cent.

Table A.1 *Reported October 1974 vote by recalled October 1974 vote among October 1974 – 1979 panel*

October 1974 vote, as recalled in 1979	October 1974 vote, as reported in October 1974					Recalled party division of October 1974 vote
	Conservative	Liberal	Labour	Other	Did not vote	
	%	%	%	%	%	%
Conservative	90.1 (27.7)	31.0 (4.8)	3.2 (1.2)	16.0 (0.6)	25.0 (2.8)	(37.1)
Liberal	3.6 (1.1)	47.8 (7.5)	3.2 (1.2)	16.0 (0.6)	7.5 (0.8)	(11.2)
Labour	4.5 (1.4)	17.7 (2.8)	90.8 (35.4)	16.0 (0.6)	31.3 (3.5)	(43.6)
Other	0.0 (0.0)	0.0 (0.0)	0.4 (0.1)	52.0 (1.8)	1.3 (0.1)	(2.1)
Did not vote	1.8 (0.6)	3.5 (0.6)	2.5 (1.0)	0.0 (0.0)	35.0 (3.9)	(6.0)
Total per cent	100.0%	100.0%	100.0%	100.0%	100.0%	
Number of respondents	222	113	282	25	80	722
Reported party division of October 1974 vote	(30.7)	(15.7)	(39.1)	(3.5)	(11.1)	(100.0)

Notes: The table is restricted to those interviewed in both October 1974 and 1979 who disclosed their October 1974 vote on both occasions.

The figure in parentheses is the percentage of the entire sample constituted by that cell, e.g. 27.7 per cent of all respondents both reported and recalled voting Conservative in October 1974.

Data source: BES October 1974 – 1979 panel.

The discrepancies between the two measures also vary according to how the panel respondents reported voting in 1979, and the pattern of that variation confirms the findings of the earlier investigations to which we have already referred. For example, the over-recall of October 1974 Conservative voting is highest among 1979 Conservative voters (+13.9 per cent) and lowest amongst 1979 Labour voters (who *under*-recall it by 1.2 per cent); similarly the over-recall of October 1974 Labour voting is greater among the Labour than the Conservative or Liberal voters of 1979. Voting Liberal in October 1974, or not voting at all, was consistently under-recalled across the panel sample, but particularly among 1979 abstainers (perhaps because they were relatively uninterested in politics and thus particularly prone to faults of recall) and even more among 1979 Conservative voters (perhaps because many were reverting to an earlier Conservative allegiance).

The discrepancies between the two measures of October 1974 voting imply that estimates of the total amount of vote switching, and of the size of any particular vote switching category, will be affected by the measure one adopts. A glance at Table A.2 immediately suggests, for example, that reliance on recall data would produce an under-estimate of the overall amount of vote switching, because the Conservative and Labour voters of 1979 exaggerated their respective Conservative and Labour voting in October 1974. It would also lead to an under-estimate of the number switching from Liberal to Conservative because of the

Table A.2 *The discrepancy between reported and recalled October 1974 vote, by reported vote in 1979, among the October 1974 – 1979 panel sample*

Vote in October 1974	Vote in 1979				
	Conservative	Liberal	Labour	Did not vote	All
Conservative	+13.9%	+3.5%	−1.2%	+9.6%	+6.4%
Liberal	−8.9%	−2.0%	−1.9%	−6.1%	−4.5%
Labour	+1.2%	+0.5%	+7.6%	+16.2%	+4.5%
Other	−1.0%	+0.1%	−0.8%	−3.1%	−1.4%
Did not vote	−5.3%	−2.1%	−3.9%	−16.6%	−5.1%

Notes: The table displays the percentage point differences between the proportion *reporting* as opposed to *recalling* an October 1974 vote for each category of 1979 voter. A + sign denotes that more recalled than reported an October 1974 vote for the row-labelled party; a − sign denotes that fewer did. Other party supporters in 1979 were too few for separate analysis, but are included in the 'All' column. Respondents whose vote at either or both elections was not divulged are excluded.

Data source: BES October 1974 – 1979 panel.

failure of some 1979 Conservatives to recall their October 1974 Liberal vote. But the precise distortion produced by recall data will be affected by the adjustment of cell entries to total to marginal values, in the way described later in this Appendix, and can only be revealed by comparing two adjusted flow-of-the-vote tables for October 1974 – 1979, one based on recall data and the other on report data.

This is done in Table A.3 which subtracts the cell values of an October 1974 – 1979 flow-of-the-vote table based on report data from cell values based on recall data. The differences are more than negligible. As expected, recall data produce higher estimates of the level of constant voting (shown by the + signs along the top left to bottom right diagonal), and lower estimates of the proportion switching from Liberal to Conservative, Liberal to non-voting, and from non-voting to Labour. As a result there emerge two different pictures of the relative contribution made by the various components of electoral change to the Conservatives' victory (compare the second and third right-hand columns in Table A.7, at the end of this section).

So far the implicit assumption has been that a reported measure of the October 1974 vote is superior to a recall measure. But report data are necessarily derived from panel samples, which can raise special problems of their own. The first is that of diminished size. The total number of interviews in October 1974 was 2,365. In the four and a half years that followed, death, emigration, moving house and refusals to be re-interviewed took their toll, so that the number of

Table A.3 *The difference made to the cell values of an October 1974 – 1979 flow-of-the-vote table by 1979 recall as opposed to October 1974 report of October 1974 vote.*

October 1974 election	May 1979 election				
	Conservative	Liberal	Labour	Other	Did not vote
Conservative	+0.8	−0.3	−0.4	0.0	+0.1
Liberal	−0.7	+1.0	+0.2	+0.2	−0.8
Labour	+0.1	−0.8	+0.7	0.0	−0.1
Other	−0.2	+0.1	+0.3	−0.2	0.0
Did not vote	0.0	0.0	−0.9	0.0	+0.8

Note: The cell values based on reported vote have been *subtracted* from those based on recalled vote. The 'entering electors' row and 'departing electors' column have been omitted because their cell values are not estimated on the basis of panel data.

Data source: BES October 1974 – 1979 panel sample.

these respondents interviewed again in 1979 was 765. By contrast the total number of interviews in 1979 was 1,893: the 765 who were re-interviewed and a further 1,138 consisting largely of people interviewed for the first time.[4] Use of the 1979 cross-sectional sample would oblige one to adopt the recall measure of October 1974 voting, at least in the case of the non-panel element; but it would have the compensating advantage of a larger sample size and thus smaller sampling error.

Small sample size raises a second potential problem, that of representativeness. Our panel survivors constitute only 42 per cent of the entire October 1974 sample and 40 per cent of the entire 1979 sample. Do they still consist of a representative cross-section of the electorate – strictly speaking, of that portion entitled to vote at both elections? If not, it might be doubly preferable to use the entire 1979 sample, or even its non-panel element only. A rigorous test of a panel's representativeness is barely possible because we have no *independent* estimates of the partisan characteristics of the relevant portion of the electorate. But the evidence at hand strongly suggests that any bias in our October 1974 – 1979 panel is very slight.

Comparison with Office of Population Census and Surveys figures on the age, sex and region (separately and in combination) of the home population in mid 1975 reveals no serious, systematic bias in the panel sample.[5] It is no less representative than the 1979 cross-sectional sample in terms of region, and only fractionally less so in terms of age and sex (after taking into account its deliberate omission of those too young to be on the register). Less expectedly, we were gratified to discover that differences in degree of interest in politics between the panel and the 1979 sample as a whole, although in the expected direction, are also very slender (see Table A.4). More crucially still, both the October 1974 and 1979 vote in the panel are close to the actual election results (see Table A.5). Although in both instances the cross-sectional samples are even closer, their superiority in this respect is tiny. And the figures reveal no case for relying exclusively on the non-panel element of the 1979 sample because it is in fact a little less representative of the 1979 result than the panel sample (and indeed was not designed to form a representative sample by itself).

In only one respect is there some evidence to suggest more than trivial bias in the panel sample. It under-represents non-voters even more severely than the rest of the October 1974 and 1979 samples do. Non-voting in October 1974 was reported by only 11.1 per cent of respondents who were re-interviewed in 1979, but by 17.4 per cent of those who dropped out. Non-voting in 1979 was reported by 19.5 per cent of first-time respondents but by only 9 per cent of those who had been interviewed in October 1974. Housing mobility provides a possible explanation. For reasons of economy we did not seek interviews with those October 1974 respondents who had changed address by 1979 (unless the move was very local), but replaced them by a member of the new household at the same address. As a result the panel sample contains proportionately fewer movers than the

Table A.4 *Interest in politics in 1979 amongst panel and non-panel respondents*

Degree of interest in politics in 1979	Non-panel First interviewed in 1979	Panel Interviewed in Oct 1974 and 1979	1979 cross-section All interviewed in 1979
	%	%	%
A great deal	12	15	13
Some	47	50	48
Not much/none at all	41	35	40
Total per cent	100%	100%	100%
Number of respondents	1006	763	1877*

Note: Don't know responses have been omitted from the percentage base.
*Includes respondents who were interviewed in Feb 1974 and 1979, but not in October 1974.
Data source: BES October 1974 – 1979 panel sample; BES 1979 cross-section sample.

non-panel sample. It thus contains fewer respondents who, through living a distance away from the polling district for which they are registered, are liable to non-voting. But even this difference between panel and non-panel respondents is not large, and less striking than the degree to which the entire survey at both elections failed to capture the true proportion of non-voters.

Despite the encouraging evidence unearthed so far, however, we cannot entirely dismiss the possibility that panel-based estimates of the joint October 1974 and 1979 vote will be biased, in particular with regard to non-voting on either or both occasions. To gauge the difference made by reliance on panel rather than non-panel respondents, we can divide the 1979 cross-section into these two groups, and compare their 1979 recall of their October 1974 vote. Previously we compared different measures of the October 1974 vote taken from the same sample; here we are comparing the same measure taken from different samples. Once again the discrepancies turn out not to be trivial. Table A.6 sets out the differences made to the cell values of an October 1974 – 1979 flow-of-the-vote table (adjusting in the way described later in this Appendix) by reliance on panel rather than non-panel data. This exercise parallels that in Table A.3 which showed the difference made by adoption of a recalled rather than reported measure of October 1974 voting. And, despite the panel sample's representativeness, comparison with Table A.3 reveals even larger discrepancies: whether one uses panel rather than non-panel data makes more of a difference than whether one uses recalled rather than reported October 1974 voting. Again, this is so because the non-panel element is intended to *supplement* the sample – not to form a representative sample by itself.

Table A.5A *Vote in October 1974 among panel survivors and drop-outs*

Vote in October 1974	Panel drop-outs — Interviewed in October 1974 only	Panel survivors — Interviewed in October 1974 and 1979	October 1974 cross-section — All interviewed in October 1974	Actual result — Great Britain
	%	%	%	%
Conservative	36.7	34.7	36.0	36.7
Liberal	18.1	17.8	18.0	18.8
Labour	41.8	43.7	42.5	40.2
Other	3.4	3.8	3.5	4.3
Total per cent	100%	100%	100%	100%
Number of respondents	1,298	657	1,955	
(% who did not vote)	(17.4)	(11.1)	(15.4)	(27.0)

Notes: Non-voters are excluded from the percentage base, but the proportion that they constituted of each sample (after omitting those who could or would not declare their vote) is given in parentheses in the bottom row. The figure given for non-voting in the GB electorate has not been adjusted for the age of the register.

Data source: BES October 1979 – 1979 panel and BES October 1974 cross-section; *Times Guide to House of Commons October 1974*

Table A.5B *Vote in 1979 among panel survivors and drop-outs*

Vote in 1979	Non-panel sample Interviewed for first time in 1979	Panel sample Interviewed in October 1974 *and* 1979	1979 cross-section All interviewed in 1979*	Actual result Great Britain
	%	%	%	%
Conservative	47.1	45.7	46.9	44.8
Liberal	14.9	13.7	13.8	14.1
Labour	36.5	38.7	37.6	37.7
Other	1.5	1.7	1.6	3.3
Total per cent	100%	100%	100%	100%
Number of respondents	786	684	1,558*	
(% who did not vote)	(19.5)	(8.7)	(14.8)	(23.8)

Notes: See notes to Table A.5A. * Includes respondents interviewed in February 1974 and 1979, but not in October 1974.

Data source: BES October 1974 – 1979 panel, and BES 1979 cross-section; *The Times Guide to the House of Commons May 1979*.

Table A.6 *The difference made to the cell values of an October 1974 – 1979 flow-of-the-vote table by reliance on panel rather than non-panel respondents where October 1974 vote is based on recall in May 1979*

		May 1979 election				
		Conservative	Liberal	Labour	Other	Did not vote
	Conservative	+2.3	−0.2	−0.2	−0.2	−1.7
October 1974 election	Liberal	+0.8	+1.4	−0.2	−0.1	−1.9
	Labour	−1.5	−0.8	+4.0	−0.1	−1.6
	Other	−0.4	+0.1	+0.4	−0.1	0.0
	Did not vote	−1.2	−0.5	−4.0	+0.5	+5.2

Note: The cell values based on non-panel respondents (N = 828) have been *subtracted* from those based on panel respondents (N = 736). The 'entering electors' row and 'departing electors' column have been omitted because their cell values are not estimated on the basis of panel data.

Data source: BES October 1974 – 1979 cross-section sample.

Most of these discrepancies, moreover, are in the same direction. (The one important exception is switching from Liberal to Conservative.) Use of panel rather than non-panel data produces lower estimates of the amount of movement to and from abstention – as the panel's more severe under-representation of non-voters would lead one to expect. It also produces higher estimates of voting constancy – readers are again referred to the cells along the top left to bottom right diagonal in Table A.6 – which reflects, perhaps, the greater residential stability of panel members. But if one 'controls' for type of sample, adoption of a recalled rather than reported measure of October 1974 voting has a similar, although slightly weaker, effect. This suggests that errors in the construction of flow-of-the-vote tables are likely to be maximised by combining a panel sample with a recall measure, and minimised either by combining the panel sample with the report measure or the non-panel sample with the recall measure. We did both, by adopting the reported measure of vote in October 1974 from the panel element of the 1979 sample, and the recalled measure from the non-panel element. This strategy had the obvious advantage of maximising sample size and the use of report data, as well as reducing likely errors in the way we have just explained.

Estimates of the components of change in the major party lead derived from

Table A.7 *Estimates of the components of change in the major party lead between October 1974 and 1979, according to measure of October 1974 vote and to whether or not the sample is a panel*

Sample (N)	Non-panel (828)	Non-panel + Panel (1,662)**	Panel (736)	Panel (736)	Non-panel + panel (1,662)**
Measure of October 1974 vote	Recall in May 1979	Recall in May 1979	Recall in May 1979	Report in October 1974	Non-panel: recall in May 1979 Panel: report in October 1974
Components of change in the major party lead:					
Straight conversion	+5.8	+4.4	+3.2	+2.2	+3.4
Liberal circulation	+1.8	+1.9	+2.2	+3.6	+2.5
Other party circulation	+0.1	+0.0	−0.6	−0.1	−0.1
Differential turnout	+0.3	+1.6	+3.1	+2.2	+2.5
Differential abstention	+0.7	+0.9	+0.8	+1.0	+0.5
Replacement of the electorate	−1.4	−1.4	−1.4	−1.4	−1.4
*Change in Conservative lead over Labour**	+7.3	+7.4	+7.3	+7.5	+7.4
Constant voters and non-voters as a % of electors entitled to vote at both elections	56.6%	62.9%	72.4%	68.3%	62.7%

Notes: *The discrepancies in the totals arise from the rounding of cell values to one decimal place.
**Includes respondents who were interviewed in February 1974 and 1979 but not October 1974.

Data source: BES October 1974 – 1979 panel sample.

this compromise solution are set out in Table A.7, and are juxtaposed against four alternative sets of estimates based on:

(1) recalled October 1974 vote amongst non-panel respondents
(2) recalled October 1974 vote amongst panel and non-panel respondents combined (i.e. the whole of the 1979 cross-sectional sample)
(3) recalled October 1974 vote amongst panel respondents
(4) reported October 1974 vote amongst panel respondents

The compromise estimates are fairly close to an average of the four other sets of estimates. One cannot infer that they are therefore more accurate than any other single set; but the possibility of serious inaccuracies would seem to have been reduced.

The most important comparison is with the fourth set of estimates, since these are based on the customary procedures – panel data and reported measures only – adopted for previous pairs of elections in the 1970s and 1960s. One substantive difference between the compromise and customary estimates should be noted. The customary estimates suggest that the single most important contribution to the Conservatives' net gain over Labour came from Liberal circulation (+3.6 per cent), followed by straight conversion (+2.2 per cent) and differential turnout (+2.2 per cent). Our compromise estimates order the contributions of components differently: Liberal circulation (+2.5 per cent) appears to have been less important than straight conversion (+3.4 per cent) and no more important than differential turnout (also 2.5 per cent).

We need not be too distressed about these discrepancies. The customary and compromise estimates are in fact fairly similar. Both suggest that the gain in the Conservative vote between October 1974 and 1979 was the product of three forms of electoral change – straight conversion, Liberal circulation and differential turnout – and in roughly equal measures. The data bases for estimating the flow of the vote between a pair of elections are fragile in the best of circumstances. Given the vagaries of sampling bias, to insist on a more elaborate interpretation runs the risk of 'squeezing' data too hard – whatever the basis of our estimates.

B. Demographic and statistical adjustments

The previous section described the arguments for and against the adoption of a panel-based report measure of past voting, as opposed to a recall measure based on non-panel respondents, when constructing flow-of-the-vote tables. It explained the reasoning behind our choice of the former for pairs of elections between 1970 and 1974, and of an amalgamation of the two for the October 1974 – 1979 table. This section is a step-by-step description of the procedures used for estimating the magnitude and partisan impact of the physical turnover of the electorate between succeeding elections and for rectifying the small differences between the way our respondents voted and the actual election result.

Stage 1: estimating the values of the marginals

1.1 The size of the electorate

Because of Northern Ireland's very different politics and party system, all estimates, like our samples, were confined to Great Britain. To estimate the size of the electorate on polling day we subtracted from the registered electorate an estimate of the number of deaths and emigrants (among those aged eighteen and over) since the preceding 10 October, the base date from which the register is compiled. The figures for the registered electorate can be found in Craig, *Britain Votes 2* pp 238–40; they incorporate an estimate of the number who joined the register between its date of publication (16 February) and polling day on reaching their eighteenth birthday.[6] The figures on recent deaths and emigration were calculated from the returns of the registrars for England and Wales and for Scotland. The resulting figure for the electorate on polling day will remain a slight overestimate because the register includes some double-counting of those with two addresses (students, owners of two homes etc.) and is not perfectly efficient in omitting the names of those who died or emigrated before the preceding 10 October.[7]

1.2 The size of the departing and entering electorate

'Departing electors' consist of those on the register at one election who have died or emigrated by the time of the next. To estimate their number we relied largely on the Registrar-General's *Annual Abstract of Statistics* for 1980. The deaths statistics are broken down into five- and ten-year age blocs but not by nationality; our estimates of deaths will therefore include a small number who, because of their foreign nationality, will not in fact have been on the register. The emigration statistics are broken down into ten-year age blocs (including, awkwardly from our point of view, 15–24) and by nationality for England and Wales but not for Scotland. We assumed that 95 per cent of adults emigrating · from Scotland had been registered to vote.

'Entering electors' at any one election consist mainly of (1) those reaching their eighteenth birthday since the previous election day, and (2) immigrants aged eighteen and over from the Republic of Eire and the Commonwealth (which excluded Pakistan, formerly West Pakistan, after 1973). But they also include (3) those becoming naturalised citizens between the two elections and (4) those entitled but failing to register at the previous election – usually young people and immigrants. We estimated the size of group (1) by calculating the number who, according to the Office of Population Censuses and Surveys' population estimates for mid 1979, had reached the age of eighteen between the two election dates, and by then subtracting the small number who had died or emigrated in the same period.

We did not attempt to estimate the size of group (2) because Home Office and OPCS figures did not break down annual immigration by age and because estimates of the speed and level of registration among eligible immigrants are not sufficiently reliable. We could not assume that the age distribution or registration rate of immigrants was the same as that of British natives: the former is much younger; the latter somewhat lower, although the gap is slowly narrowing.[8]

Instead we combined groups (2), (3) and (4) and estimated their overall size by a simple process of elimination. For each pair of consecutive elections we subtracted the number of 'departing electors' from the previous electorate (adjusted in the way described earlier) and added the number of new electors who had come of age. The difference that remained between the resulting total and the (adjusted) electorate at the following election was attributed to immigration, naturalisation and the delayed registration of the young. We can take October 1974 to May 1979 as an illustration. During that period the registered electorate for Great Britain grew by just over one million. According to the Registrar General's figures there were during this time 2,921,000 deaths and 515,000 emigrants amongst those aged eighteen or over in October 1974 (9.0 per cent of the 1974 electorate). The number of new electors in May 1979, therefore, will have equalled the number of deaths (2,921,000) + number of emigrants (515,000) + growth in the electorate (1,032,000) since October 1974, which sums to 4,468,000, 11.4 per cent of the 1979 electorate. The Registrar General's most recent population estimates show that 3,839,000 people reached their eighteenth birthday between October 1974 and May 1979. We can therefore infer that the majority of the remaining 629,000 making up the new electorate were immigrants, and most of them, presumably, from Eire or the Indian subcontinent.

It should be emphasised that these estimates are less accurate than the precision of the numbers might at first suggest. Not all of those recorded as coming of age between two elections will have been entitled to register (e.g. most foreign students, and other aliens) or if entitled, will have done so. Similarly, not all of those who died or emigrated between the two elections will have had black or brown skins, although most of those with white skins will not have been eligible to register. It must also be remembered that a fast-growing minority of brown and black electors are not immigrants. Nonetheless, these inaccuracies are likely to have been too small to jeopardise our calculations of the proportion of the electorate made up of departing and entering electors.

Stage 2: estimating the vote of departing and entering electors

2.1 Departing electors

The next stage is the estimation of departing electors' vote at the previous election and of entering electors' vote at the following election, i.e. the cell values of the right-hand column and bottom row of the flow-of-the-vote table. These calculations cannot be made as precisely as those in Stage 1. It is dif-

ficult to discover the voting history of emigrants and impossible in the case
of the dead. We therefore adopted Butler and Stokes' strategy of calculating
the likely death rates amongst the different parties' supporters at the previous
election. These estimates are produced by combining two pieces of information:
the demographic characteristics of the party's voters at the previous election,
as revealed by our surveys, and the mortality rates for the same demographic
groups in the population at large, as supplied by the Office of Population Censuses
and Surveys. We divided our respondents into thirty-six socio-demographic
groups defined by sex, age (15–34, 35–54 and 55+) and a six-fold categorisation
of the Registrar General's socio-economic groups. Like Butler and Stokes too,
we assumed from the scanty evidence at hand that the party choice of those
who subsequently emigrated was the same as that of other electors.[9]

2.2 The vote of entering electors

The vote of those joining the electorate through coming of age was easier to
discover. From the February 1974, October 1974 and 1979 surveys we derived
the reported vote of those whose declared age defined them as ineligible to vote
at the previous election. (However, because age was recorded in units of a year
rather than months a small number of respondents will have been mis-defined
as first-time electors.)

The vote of immigrants who had come on to the register since the previous
election could not be obtained as directly. There were too few in our own
sample for reliable estimates. We therefore looked to the surveys of coloured
citizens in Britain undertaken for the Commission for Racial Equality.[10] These
are studies of various immigrant areas rather than a strictly representative
national survey, and do not distinguish between immigrants who are new to
the register from those who are not. Nonetheless, these studies are superior by
far to any others, and we took it as our guide. From a careful reading, our working assumption was that the vote of newly registered immigrants was:

	1974 (both elections)	*May 1979*
	%	%
Conservatives	7	6
Liberal	7	4
Labour	56	65
Other	—	—
Did not vote	30	25
	100%	100%

We are aware that our estimates of non-voting might appear on the low side,
but it should be remembered that the majority of newly registered immigrants
will have been from the Asian subcontinent; and the evidence from both the

Commission for Racial Equality and other researchers points to turn-out rates amongst the Asian community that are equal to or even exceed that of their white neighbours.[11]

Stage 3: adjusting the cell values to match the election result

The aim of the final stage was to rectify the difference between the vote of our respondents and the actual election result. By means of the ECTA program we adopted a technique of standardisation – colloquially known as 'Mostellerisation' after its begetter[12] – which 'corrects' an observed table of cell frequencies such that they sum to specified marginal totals while preserving the original patterns of association. In our case these target marginals are the actual election results.[13]

Notes

1. The flow of events

1   The plain term 'swing' refers here and throughout the book to 'conventional' or 'Butler' swing, i.e. the average of the increase in the Conservative percentage share of the vote and the decrease in the Labour percentage share of the vote. (Thus a plus sign means a swing to the Conservatives, a minus sign a swing to Labour.) From time to time other measures of net electoral change between the major parties are used, and these are always referred to by a different term. These electoral statistics include Northern Ireland; survey-based data presented in later chapters will not.

2   The constituency boundaries were drawn up in the late 1960s. Since then movements of population from inner city to outer suburb, new town, or country have created enormous variations in constituency sizes, largely at the Conservatives' expense. Almost a third of the constituencies deviated from the average size of 65,000 by plus or minus 15,000. Of the 95 seats with electorates above 80,000, 76 went Conservative. Of the 92 seats below 50,000, 59 went Labour. Had the Boundary Commissioners added and subtracted constituencies such that their average size was 65,000 within *every* county in 1979 the Conservatives could have expected an additional 19 seats at Labour's expense, adding 38 to their majority.

   The below average swing deprived the Conservatives of 9 gains from Labour. Although Labour lost 12 seats vulnerable to a swing of over 5.3 per cent, it saved as many as 21 seats vulnerable to a swing below. Had the Conservatives won these 9 seats, and not been 'robbed' of the 19 seats by the unequally sized constituencies, their overall majority would have been 99. For more detail on these points, see Ivor Crewe, 'The Voting Surveyed', *The Times Guide to the House of Commons May 1979* (London: Times Books, 1979), pp 249–54, on which parts of the opening of this chapter are based.

3   The standard deviation of constituency swings was the largest since the election of 1950. For an extended discussion of this point, see John Curtice and Michael Steed, 'An Analysis of the Voting', in David Butler and Dennis Kavanagh, *The British General Election of 1979* (London: Macmillan, 1980), especially pp 393–403, to which this paragraph is indebted.

361

4   See Curtice and Steed, 'An Analysis of the Voting', pp 396-400, and Crewe, 'The Voting Surveyed', p 250.

5   Details of the movement of the polls during the election campaign can be found in Butler and Kavanagh, *The British General Election of 1979*, Chapter 13; and in the chapters by Richard Rose and Ivor Crewe in Howard R. Penniman, ed, *Britain at the Polls, 1979* (Washington, DC: American Enterprise Institute for Public Policy Research, 1981).

6   A more detailed account of the course of the Labour government can be found in the chapter by Anthony King in Penniman, *Britain at the Polls, 1979* (to which our chapter is particularly indebted), and in Butler and Kavanagh, *The British General Election of 1979*, Chapters 1-5. Two left-wing critiques of the Labour government are David Coates, *Labour in Power?* (London: Longman, 1980) and Nick Bosanquet and Peter Townsend, eds, *Labour and Equality* (London: Heinemann, 1980).

7   C.B. Cox and Rhodes Boyson, *The Black Papers 1977* (London: Temple Smith, 1977). The first Black Papers were written in issues of the *Critical Quarterly* in 1969 and 1970 by C. B. Cox and A. E. Dyson.

8   As a result of complaints from parents and some teachers a public inquiry was held about the unorthodox management and teaching practices of this inner-London primary school. The headmaster and four other teachers were eventually dismissed.

9   In the January 1978 Gallup poll support for the two main parties was exactly equal; in February 1978 the Conservatives were 9 per cent ahead. In January 9 per cent mentioned immigration as one of the two most urgent problems facing the country; in February 21 per cent did.

10   Labour lost three by-elections to the Conservatives, at Woolwich West, Walsall North, and Workington. In addition, two of its backbenchers, Jim Sillars and John Robertson, had resigned the Labour whip to form the Scottish Labour Party. They normally voted with the government but could not be relied upon to support it in a vote of confidence. Labour's overall majority of three in October 1974 had therefore been turned into a deficit of seven.

11   In all but two of the by-elections held during the Labour government the Liberal share of the vote dropped below the constituency's October 1974 general election level. Excluding the two deviant by-elections, the average percentage point fall was 5.7 per cent in by-elections held before the Lib-Lab pact, but 8.1 per cent in those held after.

12   See David Blake, 'Can Mr Callaghan Fly in the Face of Electoral History?', *The Times*, 20 July 1978, p 16. The article includes a useful table of short-term economic indicators, not only for the autumn of 1978 but for the six preceding elections.

13   The most plausible account is given in Dick Leonard, 'The Labour Campaign', in Penniman, *Britain at the Polls*; see especially pp 95-101.

14   For example, a MORI poll in February 1979 found that 89 per cent agreed that 'no strikes should be called until there is a postal ballot of union members concerned'; 89 per cent agreed that there should be 'a ban on secondary picketing: that is a ban on picketing a company not directly involved in a

strike'; and 65 per cent agreed that 'social security benefits paid to strikers' families should be subject to income tax'. The proportions of trade union members who agreed were almost as overwhelming – 91 per cent, 86 per cent, and 57 per cent, respectively.

15 Labour secured the support of the two breakaway Scottish Labour party MPs, two of the Ulster Unionists and the three Welsh Nationalists, the latter in return for a promise of an early introduction of a bill that would provide compensation for those who had contracted respiratory diseases in slate quarries. One of the two pro-Catholic MPs from Northern Ireland, the Independent Frank Maguire, abstained. The other, Gerry Fitt of the Social Democratic and Labour party, voted with the Opposition. One Labour MP, Sir Alfred Broughton, was too ill to vote.

16 In the first two quarters of 1978 the proportions expecting to see an improvement over the coming year were 44 per cent and 36 per cent, respectively; by the third quarter the figure had fallen to 29 per cent and by the fourth to 20 per cent.

17 In 1978 Labour did markedly better in the three by-elections in Scotland (where the mean swing to the Conservatives was only 1.6 per cent) than elsewhere. The major reason was almost certainly the decline of SNP support, to Labour's net benefit. The pattern was repeated at the general election.

18 According to a content analysis of the two parties' leaders' campaign speeches, the proportion of their output devoted to attacking their opponents was 44 per cent in 1979, compared with 62 per cent in both 1970 and February 1974. There was a corresponding increase in the proportion of their output devoted to expounding their future plans – 41 per cent in 1979 compared with 20 per cent in 1974 and 18 per cent in 1970. See Shelley Pinto-Duschinsky, 'Manifestoes, Speeches, and the Doctrine of the Mandate' in Penniman, *Britain at the Polls*, especially pp 309–11.

2. The flow of the vote

1 If the 1945 election is included the range extends to 10 percentage points (39 to 49 per cent) but the mean swing remains 2.5 per cent.

2 In February 1974, which produced the highest constituency swings since 1950, there were five seats with swings (to Labour) in double figures; in 1979 there were thirteen (this time to the Conservatives), enough to topple such hitherto safe Labour seats as Anglesey (12.5 per cent) and Birmingham Northfield (10.2 per cent). For further details see note 3 to Chapter 1.

3 See William L. Miller, *The End of British Politics?* (Oxford: Clarendon Press, 1981).

4 See Butler and Stokes, *Political Change in Britain*, 2nd edition, pp 256, 261, 263.

5 For evidence on the 1960s see Butler and Stokes, *Political Change in Britain*, 1st edition, pp 315–19. On the two 1974 elections, see James Alt, Ivor Crewe and Bo Särlvik, 'Angels in Plastic: The Liberal Surge in 1974', *Political Studies*, 25 (1977), pp 343–68.

6 See Curtice and Steed, 'An Analysis of the Voting', pp 414–18. Previous Nationalist strength, the combination of parties taking first and second place in October 1974, by-election history, and region are among the factors cited by the authors to account for the impact on major party support of the fall in the Nationalist vote.

7 Richard Rose has produced the following formula for adjusting turnout according to the age of the register: 3.4 per cent (not registered) – 1.0 per cent (registered twice) – 0.15m per cent (effect of deaths) – 0.67m per cent (effect of removals) where m = months from the date of the register's compilation (which is effectively October of each year). See Richard Rose, ed, *Electoral Behaviour: A Comparative Handbook* (New York: The Free Press, 1974), p 494. Application of this formula to the elections of the 1970s suggests that turnout rose between 1970 (75.1 per cent) and February 1974 (79.1 per cent), but then hardly changed in October 1974 (78.7 per cent) or 1979 (78.6 per cent). However, the formula might be a little out of date by now, given the growth of residential mobility and double registration. In constructing the flow-of-the-vote tables we have used a different procedure for dealing with the age of the register which does not attempt to measure the impact of residential mobility (see Appendix).

8 Ivor Crewe, James Alt and Tony Fox, 'Non-voting in British General Elections 1966 – October 1974', in Colin Crouch, ed, *British Political Sociology Yearbook Vol III* (Political Participation) (London: Croom Helm, 1977), pp 39–109, especially pp 46–50.

9 'Conservatives are undoubtedly better at organising postal voting and middle-class people are in any case more likely to both apply and qualify for such votes. In almost every constituency there were more Conservative than Labour postal votes' (Butler and Kavanagh, *The British General Election of 1979*, p 313). The authors quote an ITN/ORC survey which found that those in marginal seats claiming to have cast a postal vote divided five-to-three in favour of the Conservatives over Labour.

10 See Butler and Stokes, *Political Change in Britain*, 2nd edition, p 257: 'Easily the largest contribution to Labour's return to power came from the physical renewal of the electorate. Indeed, either the electors who entered or those who left could be said to have supplied the last vital margin of Labour's victory . . . if the 1964 vote had been cast by the 1959 electorate, the Conservatives would have been returned a fourth successive time with a quite adequate majority.'

11 In other words, of the 46.2 million people entitled to vote in 1970 and/or 1979, or both, only two-thirds (30.0 million) were eligible to vote at both.

12 The streams of vote switching displayed in Figure 1.A can also be used to calculate other kinds of electoral change between two elections, e.g. in the Liberal share of the vote and in the overall level of voting stability.

13 These six components can be collapsed into the four components distinguished by Butler and Stokes in *Political Change in Britain*, 2nd edition, pp 247–53, when comparison requires. The combination of three of our components – differential turnout, differential abstention and circulation of minor party supporters – is the equivalent of Butler and Stokes' 'differential turnout'.

14 We use this term to distinguish it from conventional swing. The difference lies in the basis of calculation which is *voters only* for swing but *all those who were in the electorate at either election* in the case of electorate swing. The effect of widening the percentage base is to produce lower values for electorate swing than conventional swing.

15 Figures from the flow-of-the-vote tables are calculated to one decimal point in order to avoid excessive rounding errors. However, too much reliance should not be placed on the exact figures, given the size of our sample and the inaccuracies in the portion of the data based on recall.

16 Of which half a million came from the 102 additional seats contested by the Liberals in October 1974.

17 Most notably, the well publicised Wembley rally for Conservative trade unionists on the Sunday before polling.

18 On the basis of the surveys carried out by the Commission for Racial Equality, we estimated that in 1979 the vote of newly registered immigrants was Labour 65 per cent, Conservative 6 per cent, Liberal 4 per cent, Did not vote 25 per cent. See Muhammad Anwar, *Ethnic Minorities and the General Election 1979* (London: Commission for Racial Equality, 1980) and Appendix.

19 According to our 1970 – February 1974 panel sample, the proportion of Labour defectors who had voted Labour in 1966 was 91 per cent; the proportion of Conservative defectors who had voted Conservative 76 per cent (the percentage base excludes non-voters in 1966).

20 Strictly speaking, not all can count as 'homecomers' because, as the previous note reveals, a minority of those who voted Conservative in 1970 but defected in February 1974 had not been regular Conservative voters in the 1960s.

21 Unfortunately we do not possess data that extend far enough back for a sufficient number of respondents to tell us whether electors with a voting record of A-A-A-B are particularly likely or particularly unlikely to revert to party A at the fifth election; both possibilities seem equally plausible.

22 Evidence of increasing volatility is given in Ivor Crewe, 'Party Identification Theory and Political Change in Britain', in Ian Budge, Ivor Crewe and Dennis Farlie, eds, *Party Identification and Beyond. Representations of Voting and Party Competition* (London: John Wiley & Sons, 1976), p 38.

23 If 1964 is counted as year 1 and 1979 as year 15, regression analysis reveals that the amount of vote changing increased by 0.47 percentage units per annum over the fifteen-year period.

24 Readers should note that Table 2.15 is based on data adjusted to take account of sample bias (on which see Appendix), whereas Tables 2.17 and 2.18 cannot be. Precise comparisons between these tables should therefore be made with caution. Given the under-representation of non-voters in sample surveys the true proportion of persistent abstainers in the electorate will have been a little higher than presented here.

25 *Political Change in Britain*, 2nd edition, pp 268–75.

26 This is not the same as saying that vote changers were more likely to have cast a changing than constant vote at the *previous* election. This was not the

case for three of our five triads: 1959–64–66, 1964–66–70, and February
1974 – October 1974 – 1979.

27 This probably had something to do with the nature of Labour defectors between 1964 and 1966. Over these two years Labour's popularity in the
country went up. Most of the small number of Labour defectors will probably
have had a very weak Labour allegiance and many will probably not have
voted Labour before 1964. Their slender attachment will have been loosened
further by the strong fall in Labour's stock between 1966 and 1970. Readers
should also note that the percentage base is small (N = 37).

28 If the comparison is confined to those defectors who voted Liberal at both
1964 and 1966 or at both February and October 1974, the Liberals' retention rate was worse on the second occasion. In the 1960s, 12 of our 22 respondents (55 per cent) stayed Liberal; in the 1970s, 21 of our 52 respondents (40 per cent) did.

3. The lockgates on the vote

1 A separate volume devoted to a detailed analysis of the social structure, the
vote and political opinion is being prepared by our co-investigator, David
Robertson.

2 Peter Pulzer, *Political Representation and Elections in Britain* (London:
George Allen & Unwin, 3rd edition, 1975), p 102.

3 A.J.P. Taylor, *English History 1914-1945* (Oxford University Press, 1965),
p 129.

4 We have excluded from the scale those respondents whose occupational
status could not be classified because of missing information, as well as a
small number of students in full-time education. Working married women
are classified according to their husbands' occupations because it is the
latter that generally gives the household as a whole its position in the class
system. These procedures follow those adopted by Butler and Stokes, so as
to allow for comparison over time.

5 See R.R. Alford, *Party and Society: The Anglo-American Democracies*
(London: John Murray, 1964). The index is based on the total vote – and
not just the Conservative and Labour vote – cast by each of the two social
classes. This means that an equivalent class index of the Conservative vote
will not produce the identical score (although an equivalent index of the
'non-Labour' vote would). In practice the differences of score have been
very small, because the level of minor party support in the two social
classes is similar. For a further discussion of measures of class voting, see
Walter Korpi, 'Some Problems in the Measurement of Class Voting',
American Journal of Sociology, 78 (1972), pp 627–42.

6 Or nearly so. For reasons given in the previous note a perfect relationship
between class and the Labour vote does not necessarily mean a perfect
relationship with the Conservative vote: some of the middle class might
vote Liberal rather than Conservative.

7 But this is not to argue that social class has no bearing on the motives for
voting Liberal. It may well be a sense of class that makes it difficult for

some dissatisfied working-class voters to support the Conservatives and – even more often – for dissatisfied middle-class voters to support Labour. Class can have an impact not only by making one party attractive to a voter, but by making other parties unattractive.

8 When comparing the change in a party's vote share from October 1974 to 1979 between two population groups we are measuring the *difference between a difference*. When comparing the October 1974 – 1979 swing between two population groups we are measuring the *difference between the sum of two differences*. In the first case significance testing involves four groups (two population groups at two elections); in the second case eight (two voting groups within two population groups at two elections). As a rule of thumb if four groups each consist of about 1,000 respondents – as would be approached if both the October 1974 and 1979 samples were equally split – statistical significance would require the difference between the difference to be 9 percentage points; if the four groups each consisted of 500 respondents – as frequently occurs – it would need to be 12 percentage points. Almost none of the differences between differences in our tables are statistically significant by these standards, although many are of the same direction and similar size to those reported in other large-scale interview surveys of the election. Almost all conclusions based on comparisons of changes in the vote share should therefore be regarded as tentative possibilities, not firm probabilities; and this applies to comparisons of 'swing' even more.

Readers should also bear in mind that sampling and measurement error produced the following small discrepancies between our survey estimates of the change in the parties' share of the vote between October 1974 and 1979 and the actual change:

Change in percentage share of vote,
Great Britain, October 1974 – 1979

	Sample estimate	Actual result	Difference
Conservatives	+11.0	+8.2	2.8
Liberals	– 4.2	–4.7	0.5
Labour	– 4.9	–2.5	2.4
Other	– 1.9	–1.0	0.9

Our tables and text always present the survey estimates. When interpreting changes in the parties' vote shares within population groups readers can adopt a simple form of adjustment, as follows:

Increase in Conservative vote share:	deduct 3 per cent from survey estimate
Decrease in Liberal vote share:	add 0.5 per cent to survey estimate
Decrease in Labour vote share:	deduct 2.5 per cent from survey estimate
Decrease in Other vote share:	deduct 1 per cent from survey estimate
'Swing' to Conservatives:	deduct 3.5 per cent from survey estimate.

9　The Conservative share of the total GB vote was 4.2 per cent ahead of Labour's in 1959 and 7.2 per cent ahead in 1979. Its far greater parliamentary majority in 1959 (84) than 1979 (43) reflects the vagaries of the relationship between votes and seats under Britain's electoral system.

10　One may think of Somer's *d* as an extension of the Alford index to a 2 x 3 table; or of the Alford index as Somer's *d* for the special case of a 2 x 2 table.

11　The mean difference in the major party lead between men and women for all general elections between 1945 and October 1974 is 13 percentage points; the smallest difference was in February 1974 (3.5 per cent). See Henry Durant, 'Voting Behaviour in Britain', in Richard Rose, *Studies in British Politics* (London: Macmillan, 1st edition, 1966), p 125; David Butler and Anthony King, *The British General Election of 1966* (London: Macmillan, 1966), p 264; David Butler and Michael Pinto-Duschinsky, *The British General Election of 1970* (London: Macmillan, 1971), p 342; David Butler and Dennis Kavanagh, *The British General Election of February 1974* (London: Macmillan, 1974), p 263; and David Butler and Dennis Kavanagh, *The British General Election of October 1974* (London: Macmillan, 1975), p 278.

12　An ORC Survey (N = 4,328) conducted for ITN on election day reported a swing to the Conservatives of 8 per cent among men and 5 per cent among women; MORI's six election campaign polls (merged and weighted to produce an N = 6,445) reported swing figures of 7 per cent and 5.5 per cent respectively; the BBC/Gallup survey conducted on the eve and day of polling found a swing of 9.5 per cent among men and 3 per cent among women. In these three cases figures from 1979 were compared with October 1974 figures taken from the merging of three Louis Harris polls (N = 4,296); see David Watt, 'Long-term Lessons from Election Swings', *The Financial Times*, 25 October 1974, p 23.

13　About half the self-employed had no employees at all, and the self-employed members of occupational groups III to VI will normally have hired no more than two or three assistants. Because the logic of the classification of the self-employed differs from that of employees, the former are divided between grades I-II and III-IV, whereas the latter are divided between grades I-III and IV. This is for two reasons. Grades I and II include all the self-employed with more than a few employees, e.g. proprietors of large enterprises (although it also includes some with no employees, or only a handful e.g. doctors, professional consultants). In the case of employees it was important to separate out occupational grade IV - routine, non-skilled, non-manual workers - because of its marginal status between the working and middle classes. There were insufficient numbers of employees in grade III to justify separating it from grades I and II; moreover its vote was very close to that of grades I and II.

14　The proportion of the labour force employed by the public sector has risen from 24.1 per cent in 1961 to 30.0 per cent in 1978. See Central Statistical Office, *Social Trends 10* (London: HMSO, 1980), p 124 (Table 5.8); almost the entire growth occurred in central and local government rather than public corporations.

15 An analysis of P. Roth, *Business Background of MPs* (London: Parliamentary Profiles, 1975) by Patrick Dunleavy found that 44 per cent of Labour MPs but only 6 per cent of Conservative MPs (in 1974) were employed currently or prior to their election by the public sector. See Patrick Dunleavy, 'The Political Implications of Sectoral Cleavages and the Growth of State Employment, Part 2: Cleavage Structures and Political Alignment', *Political Studies*, XXVIII, 4, pp 527–49. Dunleavy offers plausible arguments for re-defining the class basis of party alignments in Britain on the basis of the trade union member/non-member and private/public sector cleavages but concludes on the basis of his analysis of data from October 1974 that 'because the influence of union membership or non-membership on alignment is only moderately strong and because the suggestions of direct sectoral effects present in the data failed to reach the levels of statistical significance suggested by a log linear analysis, the evidential basis for a sectoral interpretation must remain tentative in character' (p 549).

16 However, it should be acknowledged that we were not able to subdivide the private sector into 'monopoly capital' and 'market/competitive capital' sub-sectors, as some theoretical expositions of sectoral analysis do. (See, for example, J. O'Connor, *The Fiscal Crisis of the State* (New York: St Martin's Press, 1973) and R. Averitt, *The Dual Economy* (New York: Norton, 1968). It is always possible that such a division would have been more strongly cor-related with the vote.

17 The proportions are 38 per cent and 27 per cent respectively.

18 This is not an artifact of the higher level of Labour voting in occupational grades III and IV.

19 In technical language, tree analysis is known as the 'Automatic Interaction Detector' computer program. For a full presentation of this mode of analysis, see: J.A. Sonquist, *Multivariate Model Building: The Validation of a Search Strategy* (Ann Arbor: Institute for Social Research, 1970). For technical descriptions of the programme, see: J.A. Sonquist and James N. Morgan, *The Detection of Interaction Effects. A Report on a Computer Program for the Selection of Optimal Combinations of Explanatory Variables* (Ann Arbor: Institute for Social Research, Monograph. No. 35, 1964) and J.A. Sonquist, E.L. Baker and J.N. Morgan, *Searching for Structure* (Ann Arbor: Institute for Social Research, 1971).

20 The two-group combination of categories which shows the strongest statisti-cal association with vote will always be chosen.

21 In technical language, the split is chosen which makes the biggest contri-bution to the explained proportion of the variance. When, as in this instance, the dependent variable is a dichotomy, this amounts to choosing the split which shows the highest squared Phi coefficient.

22 In the tree analyses presented in the figures we have imposed two constraints on the further splitting of a group: firstly, the difference between two result-ing groups must meet a 'significance' criterion (a *t*-value of at least 2.0) and, secondly, none of the groups thus created is allowed to comprise less than 30 individuals.

23 For a detailed discussion of the tree analysis technique and its limitations,

see: B. Särlvik, 'Socio-economic Determinants of Voting Behaviour in the
Swedish Electorate', *Comparative Political Studies* (1969). See also:
M.N. Franklin and A. Mughan, 'The Decline of Class Voting in Britain:
Problems of Analysis and Interpretation', *The American Political Science
Review* (1978).

24 We have excluded from the analysis persons whose occupational status could
not be classified because of missing information; a small number of students
in full-time education are also excluded from this analysis.

25 The 'explained proportion of the variance' equals 0.20, when a one-way
analysis of variance is carried out for the final sub-categories in the tree for
Conservative voting. The corresponding statistic for the Labour voting tree
is 0.21.

4. Opinions on political issues and voting – the directions of the enquiry

1 The computation formula and the meaning of this correlation coefficient
(Kendall's Tau-b) is treated in most statistical textbooks, see, e.g., Hubert
M. Blalock, Jr, *Social Statistics* (New York: McGraw Hill, 2nd edition,
p 420, 1972).

   The correlation coefficient for a positive correlation has a range between
0 (no correlation) and +1.0 (perfect correlation) but the strength of the
relationship between any single opinion or attitude measure and voting does
in fact rarely approach that upper limit. As a rule of thumb applicable to
the tables in the following chapters, Tau-b coefficients with values of 0.2 or
higher are obtained when the relationship being examined is both substantive and statistically significant. That is, the relationship is substantive in the
sense that it comes forth quite clearly as one reads the percentages across
the rows or down the columns of the table. When correlation coefficients
have a lower value, the relationship may still be statistically significant, but
it will usually show up in the table only as a mild tendency. If the coefficient has an absolute value of less than 0.1, it is seldom statistically significant and the relationship will be only barely noticeable in a percentage table.

5. Why the parties were liked and disliked

1 Question texts: 'I would like to ask what you think the good and bad points
about the parties are. I'll start with the Conservatives: is there anything in
particular that you like about the Conservative party?' – 'Is there anything
in particular that you don't like about the Conservative party?' Questions
phrased in the same way were then asked about the Labour party and,
finally, about the Liberal party. The interviewer was instructed to probe to
ensure that the respondent was allowed to say what he or she wanted to say,
but not to prompt beyond that point. If the meaning of an answer was un-
clear, the interviewer would use a neutral phrase to probe for clarification.

2 The average percentage of respondents who made at least one classifiable
comment was 65 per cent for each of the four questions about the Conservative and Labour parties. 80 per cent made at least one comment on either

the good or the bad things about the Conservative party; in the case of the Labour party, 89 per cent did so. Of all respondents, 54 per cent mentioned something they liked and 46 per cent something they disliked about the Liberal party.

3 The classification shown in these tables is based on a considerably more detailed coding of contents elements in the answers.

4 See *NOP Political Social, Economic Review*, June 1979; *Gallup Political Index*, Report No. 225. See also Butler and Kavanagh, *The British General Election of 1979*, Chapter 13.

5 Question texts: 'Leaving aside your general party preference, do you think it makes any difference if an MP is a man or a woman? Which of the views on this card comes closest to your own? 1. It makes absolutely no difference. 2. A woman MP is better than a man. 3. A woman MP is not as good as a man.' — 'And again leaving aside party preference, do you, on balance, think it makes any difference if the Prime Minister is a man or a woman? Which of the views on this card comes closest to your own? 1. It makes absolutely no difference. 2. A woman Prime Minister is better than a man. 3. A woman Prime Minister is not as good as a man.'

6 This percentage includes the following subject categories in the table: prices, unemployment, general economic policy, housing and taxation.

7 It may be clarifying to think of this percentage difference as an *average* of numerical scores assigned to individuals. That is, one can assign a score of +1 to individuals who express a pro-Conservative or anti-Labour view, a score of −1 to individuals with pro-Labour or anti-Conservative views, and a score of zero to individuals who expressed no opinion at all about the policy area concerned. The percentage difference equals the *average* of these scores, multiplied by 100.

8 For a further discussion of the concept of party images, see: Butler and Stokes, *Political Change in Britain*, 2nd edition, Chapter 16.

9 In some instances, it was, of course, fairly obvious that the respondent was thinking as much about private entrepreneurs as a group as of private enterprise as an economic system. In many other instances, however, this was not the case, and the coding is based on the manifest (rather than the implied) contents of the answers.

10 Question texts: 'In general, how good a job would you say the trade unions are doing for the country as a whole — very good, fairly good, not very good, or no good at all?' With the same response alternatives, respondents were then asked: 'And how good a job do you think the trade unions are doing for their own members . . .?' — 'And now about where you work — how good a job would you say your own trade union is doing for you and your family . . .?' — 'Do you think that your own trade union at the place where you work is too ready to take industrial action or not? Please say which of the answers on this card is closest to your own view. 1. Far too ready to take industrial action. 2. A little too ready. 3. About right. 4. Not quite ready enough. 5. Not nearly ready enough.'

11 Question text: 'I would like to talk about trade unions and business in this country. First I would like to ask whether you think that the trade unions have too much power or not?'

12 Data for the period 1963-70 are given in Butler and Stokes, *Political Change in Britain*, 2nd edition, p 198.
13 Question text: 'Do you think that big business in this country has too much power, or not?'
14 The correlation between opinion on big business and three-party vote (Kendall's Tau-b coefficient) is 0.19. The correlation for opinions on the trade unions is 0.35.
15 See Butler and Stokes, *Political Change in Britain*, 2nd edition, p 198.
16 Question texts: 'Do you think that the Labour party is too willing to listen to the trade unions or not willing enough? Or that things are about right? – With the same response alternatives: '. . . how willing is the Labour party to listen to self-employed people with small businesses?' – 'And how willing is the Labour party to listen to business and industry?'. The same three questions were then asked with reference to the Conservative party.

6. Managing the economy – the Labour government's record and the Conservative alternative

1 For a longitudinal analysis of connections between economic developments, economic expectations in the electorate, and electoral behaviour, see James E. Alt, *The Politics of Economic Decline: Economic Management and Political Behaviour in Britain since 1964* (Cambridge University Press, 1979).
2 Question texts: 'All in all, would you say that the country is in very good shape, fairly good shape, poor shape, or that something is very wrong?' – 'Looking back over the last year or so, do you think that your income has fallen behind prices, kept up with prices, or has gone up more than prices?' – 'Looking ahead to next year, do you think that your income will fall behind prices, keep up with prices, or go up more than prices?'
3 Question texts: 'Looking back over the last year or so, would you say that the state of Britain's economy has stayed about the same, got better, or got worse?' – 'And what do you think will be the state of Britain's economy in the next few years – will it stay about the same, get better, or get worse?'
4 Question texts: 'Have you personally been badly affected as a result of any strike in the last year?' – 'Have you yourself or anyone else in the family been unemployed or had great difficulty in getting a job in the last year or so?'
5 Question texts: 'How well do you think the recent Labour government handled the problem of rising prices – very well, fairly well, not very well, or not at all well?' – With the same response alternatives: 'If the Conservative party had been in power at the time, how well do you think they would have handled the problem of rising prices . . .?' – 'How well do you think the recent Labour government generally handled the problem of strikes . . .?' – 'If the Conservative party had been in power, how well do you think they would have handled the problem of strikes . . .?' – 'How well do you think the recent Labour government handled the problem of unemployment . . .?' – 'If the Conservative party had been in power, how well do you think they would have handled the problem of unemployment . . .?'
6 In the case of prices, voters' assessments of the Conservative party may to

some extent have been affected by the price increases that occurred during the time after the election when our fieldwork was carried out.

7 This was found by means of a detailed analysis, not shown in the table. For a related analysis of the 1974 vote, see Alt, Crewe and Särlvik, 'Angels in Plastic: The Liberal Surge in 1974', pp 343–68.

8 The classifications were created as follows. Responses to each question were treated as a 5-point scale: 1. Very well. 2. Fairly well. 3. Don't know. 4. Not very well. 5. Not at all well. Codes 1 and 2 are considered as positive ratings, and codes 4 and 5 as negative ratings. Strong Labour = positive for Labour and at least 3 scale points lower for Conservatives. Moderate Labour = positive rating for Labour and 2 scale points lower for Conservatives. Weak Labour = positive rating for Labour and 'Don't know' or only 1 scale point lower for Conservatives. Marginal Labour = negative ratings for both parties, but one scale point higher for Labour. The pro-Conservative categories in the scale are defined analogously. The 'Trust' category consists of respondents who gave the same positive rating to both parties. The 'Distrust' category includes respondents who gave the same negative rating to both parties or a negative rating to one party and answered 'Don't know' about the other.

9 The interview question about unemployment was asked in a somewhat different format in 1974. However, the questions in 1974 and 1979 are sufficiently similar to justify the comparison we are making here.

10 For the purpose of constructing this 'scale', each of the three classifications in Table 6.5A were arranged in the form of nine categories, which were ordered from a strongly Labour to a strongly Conservative position; the mid category includes 'trust in both parties' and 'distrust in both parties' as well as 'don't know' responses. The categories were given integer scores from 0 to 8 and the scores were added for each individual. The categories in the 'scale' comprise the following score values: $1 = 0-3$, $2 = 4-7$, $3 = 8-10$, $4 = 11-13$, $5 = 14-16$, $6 = 17-20$, $7 = 21-24$. The average intercorrelation between the three component classifications (r) is 0.47; each of the three correlation coefficients is very close to that average value.

11 The similarity of the form of the relationship between opinions and voting in 1974 and 1979 can be demonstrated by means of regression analyses carried out on the data in Tables 6.6 and 6.7.

Voting was treated as a dichotomous variable with the value of 1 assigned to a Conservative vote and the value of 0 for a Liberal or Labour vote. The opinion index was treated as an interval scale variable taking values from 0 to 6. The regression coefficients in the two regression equations for the 1974 and 1979 data are nearly exactly the same: $b = 0.173$ for the 1979 data as compared to $b = 0.176$ for the 1974 data. The Y-intercept has a slightly higher value in the 1979 equation, indicating a slightly higher propensity to vote Conservative independently of the position on the opinion index.

12 The method used was to calculate a multiple regression equation in which the dependent variable was a dichotomy with a value of 1 assigned to a Conservative vote and a value of 0 to a vote for another party. All opinion measures were treated as interval scales (another necessary assumption about

the data). The 'effect' on the Conservative vote for each of the three issues was obtained by multiplying the appropriate regression coefficients by the difference between the mean values in 1974 and in 1979 for the opinion variable. The multiple regression was carried out in a stepwise fashion and stopped when no significant increase in the explained proportion of the variance could be achieved; twelve independent variables were actually included in the prediction equation. The multiple correlation coefficient for the regression is 0.71. We have not included any independent measures of party preference (or party identification) as a predictor in the regression equation. However, such a measure would undoubtedly show strong correlations with each one of the predictors that are included. When calculating the 'net contribution' of one independent variable, controlling for all the others, one is therefore effectively also controlling for general partisanship.

13 Although we describe the result in terms of 'gains' and 'losses' the calcu - lation is based entirely on actual voting in 1979. An analysis of the relationship between opinions in 1979 and individual voting change October 1974 – May 1979 is presented in Chapter 11.

14 A fully elaborated model of the kind suggested above is presented in D. Farlie and I. Budge, 'Newtonian Mechanics and Predictive Election Theory', *British Journal of Political Science*, vol. 7, no. 3 (1977), pp 413-18.

7. Responses to social and cultural change

1 See question texts in Tables 7.1 and 7.2.

2 The correlation coefficient is Kendall's Tau-b. The response alternatives are treated as an ordinal scale with the alternatives taken in the order, from left to right, in which they appear in the table. Party vote is likewise treated as an ordinal scale with the parties taken in the order: Conservatives, Liberals, Labour. Respondents who did not vote for any of the three major parties are not included in the calculation of correlation coefficients.

3 The response alternatives and party vote are treated as ordinal scales as in the preceding table. For questions marked with an asterisk, parties are taken in the order, Labour, Liberals, Conservatives; for other questions, the ordering is instead, Conservatives, Liberals, Labour. The effect is to make all correlation coefficients positive.

4 The factor analysis included all the questions in Tables 7.1-2. In order to explore the relationship between party preferences and the attitude dimensions, party vote (three-party vote treated as a trichotomous variable) was included in one version of the analysis. An oblique rotation of the factors (i.e. dimensions) was done, using the OBLIMIN criterion. As mentioned in the text, the factors are intercorrelated to some extent; the coefficients for factor correlations have values between 0.01 and 0.35. A sixth factor which could not be given any substantive interpretation was also extracted. Only the item concerning selling of council houses to tenants has a noteworthy loading on this factor. As the council house issue did not have a significant loading on any other factor, this may be taken to indicate that opinions on this issue were unrelated to all of the more general attitudes that were discerned through the factor analysis.

5 See also I. Crewe and B. Särlvik, 'Popular Attitudes and Electoral Strategy', in Zig Layton-Henry, ed, *Conservative Party Politics* (London: Macmillan, 1980).

6 Question texts: 'How well do you think the recent Labour government managed to uphold law and order – very well, fairly well, not very well, or not at all well?' – 'If the Conservative party had been in power, how well do you think they would have managed to uphold law and order – very well, fairly well, not very well, or not at all well?'

7 One can assign a score value of +1 to a Conservative vote, 0 to a Liberal vote and –1 to a Labour vote. The arithmetic means for such scores in an opinion category, multiplied by 100, is equal to the 'balance' statistics given in the table. Hence, the balance value can be taken to indicate the 'average' vote in an opinion category in this specific sense.

8. Nationalisation and social welfare policies – a rightward shift in electoral opinion 1974-1979

1 Question texts: 'There has been a lot of talk recently about nationalisation, that is, the government owning and running industries like steel and electricity. Which of these statements comes closest to what you yourself feel should be done?' (The statements in Table 8.1A–B were shown on a printed card.) – 'Still looking at the card, which statement do you think comes closest to the view of the Conservative party?' – 'And which statement do you think comes closest to the view of the Labour party?' – 'Now we would like to ask what you think about social services and benefits. Which of these statements do you feel comes closest to your own view?' (The statements in Table 8.2A–B were shown on a printed card.) – 'And still looking at the card, could you say which statement you think comes closest to the view of the Conservative party?' – 'And which statement do you think comes closest to the view of the Labour party?'

2 See the further analysis of the data in Chapter 9, especially Table 9.4.

3 Questions in a similar format were asked on several of the issues in the 1979 election. In Chapter 11, we will undertake a further analysis of the relationship between voting and opinions on each of these issues by calculating the 'distances' between the respondent's preferred position and the perceived position of each of the parties.

4 The change reported in the text is, of course, the net result of many individuals changing their opinions in different directions. Our panel sample of individuals interviewed at both elections allows us to gauge the change in individuals' opinions. Of all respondents, 43 per cent agreed with exactly the same statement on social services at both interviews (excluding those who gave a 'don't know' answer on either occasion), whereas 47 per cent gave the same answer about nationalisation in October 1974 and 1979. The correlation (Kendall's Tau-b) between opinions at the two elections was 0.38 for social services and benefits and 0.48 for nationalisation. When opinions are measured on two occasions, the data will always record some amount of random change that is due to measurement errors. This will be true also of our measurements, but the predominant feature in the data is a

pattern of directed change which could not be attributable to measurement errors. Thus 67 per cent of the voters who gave different answers about social services on the two occasions had changed to a 'more conservative view'. In the case of nationalisation, 82 per cent of the respondents who gave different answers in 1974 and 1979 had changed to a more unfavourable opinion.

5   When calculating the correlation coefficient, the parties are treated as an ordinal scale, with parties taken in the order, Labour, Liberals, Conservatives.

6   Somer's d_{yx} coefficient captures the size of the relationship between opinions and voting which is indicated by the steepness of the increase in the Conservative vote (as well as the decrease in the Labour vote) along the scale. Somer's d_{yx} coefficient is analogous in meaning to a regression coefficient. The value of this coefficient for opinions on social services is 0.28 for both the 1974 and 1979 data. For opinions on nationalisation, the coefficient is 0.48 in the 1974 data and 0.45 in the 1979 data. In all instances, 'three-party vote' is treated as the dependent variable.

7   The method employed was to calculate a regression equation with voting as the dependent variable. Voting entered the equation as a dichotomous variable which takes the value of 1 when the person voted Conservative and the value of zero if he voted for another party. The independent variables consisted of our measures of opinions on nationalisation and social welfare together with the four measures of the voters' assessments of Labour's and the Conservatives' handling of major problems (strikes, prices, unemployment, and law and order). The net gain due to changes in an opinion distribution was obtained by replacing its mean value in 1979 with its mean value in 1974 in the regression equation.

9. Policy alternatives and party choice in the 1979 election

1   For an analysis of our survey data concerning the state of opinion at the time of the February 1974 election and at the 1975 referendum on Britain's membership of the EEC, see Bo Särlvik, Ivor Crewe, James Alt and Anthony Fox, 'Britain's Membership of the EEC: A Profile of Electoral Opinions in the Spring of 1974 − with a Postscript on the Referendum', *European Journal of Political Research*, 4 (1976), pp 83−114.

2   The pair of statements on each of the issues was presented to the respondent on a printed card and preceded by an introduction. The introductions were phrased as follows: 'People have different views about whether it is more important to reduce taxes or keep up government services.' − 'Some people think that the best way to tackle unemployment is to allow private companies to keep up their profits to create more jobs. Others think it is mainly up to the government to tackle unemployment by using tax money to create jobs.' − 'There has been a lot of talk about how wages and salaries should be settled. Some people think that the government should leave it to employers and trade unions to negotiate wages and salaries alone.' − 'Some people think Britain should be more willing to go along with the economic

policies of other countries in the Common Market. Others think that we should be readier to oppose Common Market policies.' — 'People have different views about how to improve race relations in this country. Some say that the best way of improving race relations is to put a complete stop to all further immigration. Others say that the best way of improving race relations is to tackle the problem of jobs and housing in the large cities. How about you?' In all instances the introduction was followed by the phrase: 'Which of the statements A, B, or C comes closest to your view? If you don't have an opinion on this, just say so'. Always included was the 'it doesn't matter' alternative. In addition to the seven categories in the scale shown in the text, interviewers were always able to record a 'no opinion' answer.

3 The phrasing of the questions about importance was as follows: 'When you were deciding about voting, how important was this question of . . . (issue) – extremely important, fairly important, or not very important?' The following question about party preference on the issue was phrased: 'And when it comes to the question of . . . (issue), do you prefer any of the parties?' (If yes:) 'Which party?'

4 For the purpose of calculating the correlation coefficients, the opinion alternatives are ordered as in Table 9.3 and the parties are treated as forming an ordinal scale, with the parties taken in the order: Labour, Liberals, Conservatives.

5 Our measure of distances requires that the distances between adjacent points on the scale are all of the same length; this is obviously a quite strong assumption about the data. In technical terms, it is furthermore assumed that the individual's preference function is single-peaked and symmetric with the maximum at his preferred point on the scale (his 'ideal point'); see Clyde H. Coombs, *A Theory of Data* (New York: John Wiley & Sons, 1964), pp 193ff.

6 For a similar analysis of proximity between voter opinions and perceived party positions in the February 1974 election, see J. Alt, B. Särlvik, I. Crewe, 'Partisanship and Policy Choice: Issue Preferences in the British Electorate, February 1974', *British Journal of Political Science*, 6 (1976), pp 273-90.

7 For the purpose of calculating correlation coefficients, the distance to parties measure is treated as a three-point scale: 1. closest to Labour 2. same distance to both parties, or cannot place both parties, or has no opinion on the issue 3. closest to the Conservatives. The correlation is calculated with reference to three-party vote, with parties taken in the order: Labour, Liberals, Conservatives. The correlation coefficient is Kendall's Tau-b. All correlation coefficients would become slightly higher if one excluded those who had no opinion on the issue concerned. Thus, for example, the coefficient for nationalisation increases from 0.48 to 0.51.

8 For an analysis of the Liberal vote in the 1974 elections, see Alt, Crewe, and Särlvik, 'Angels in Plastic: The Liberal Surge in 1974', pp 343-68. An analysis of party preferences on issues in the February 1974 election is presented in Alt, Särlvik, and Crewe, 'Partisanship and Policy Choice: Issue Preferences in the British Electorate, February 1974', pp 273-90.

9 The distance measures are based on the assumption that all distances between

adjacent points on the scale are of the same length. This may not be the way the scale is perceived by the individual; he may prefer a party on a given issue because he actually perceives the distance to that party as shorter than our distance measure would indicate. To account for the discrepancies between distance data and preference data, one might assume that individuals have a general tendency to see distances to the party they have decided to vote for as shorter than distances to the opposite party. But this means that there is a tendency for distance perceptions to be coloured by partisanship. In effect, this is equivalent to the statement that party preferences on issues are coloured by general partisanship.

10 If the eight issues are ordered according to both importance rating and correlations with voting, the correlation between the two rank orders indicates only a modest relationship: the rank order correlation coefficient (Spearman's Rho) equals 0.35. It should be noted, however, that the *respondents* were not asked to rank order the degree of importance of the issues.

11 Including importance rating in the analysis results in the type of elaboration of the relationship between opinions and voting which Lazarsfeld has labelled 'specification', see Paul F. Lazarsfeld, 'Interpretation of Statistical Relations as a Research Operation', in Paul Lazarsfeld and Morris Rosenberg, eds, *The Language of Social Research* (New York: The Free Press, paperback edition, 1955), esp. pp 121ff.

12 Following Donald Stokes we might distinguish between 'position issues' and 'valence issues'. On valence issues it is generally agreed that a certain goal is desirable and, therefore, 'the argument turns on which party, given posession of government, is more likely to bring it about'. See Donald E. Stokes, 'Spatial Models of Party Completion', in Angus Campbell *et al*, *Elections and the Political Order* (New York: John Wiley & Sons, 1966), esp. pp 170ff. In many instances, however, what may appear as a valence issue will involve also position-issue differences between the parties. For example, when voters were asked how well the Conservatives and Labour handle the unemployment problem, the question could be answered on the basis of a general impression of how successful the two parties had been in keeping unemployment down; but it could also be answered with reference to position differences between Conservative and Labour economic policies. The fact that our pairs of assessment questions are asked in a 'valence-issue form', therefore, does not necessarily mean that all the respondents have seen them in that light.

13 If all the issues in Tables 9.8A and 9.8B are combined, some relationship emerges between the rank ordering of the issues with regard to importance rating and a rank ordering with regard to correlation between opinion and voting. The reason is that the four assessment issues rank highly on both criteria. Even so, the relationship between the two rank orderings is erratic and not very strong (Spearman's Rho rank order correlation coefficient equals 0.55).

14 The relationships discussed here can be described by a regression model comprising voting (Y) as the dependent variable and a multiplicative term which includes opinions on the issue (X) as the independent variable as well

as importance rating (Z) to account for the interaction effect. In its simplest version, the prediction equation would be of the following form: $Y = b X Z$ where b is a regression coefficient, the value of which will vary from issue to issue. See, e.g., Hubert M. Blalock, Jr, *Causal Inferences in Non-experimental Research* (Chapel Hill: University of North Carolina Press, 1961), pp 91–3 *et passim*.

10. Ambiguity and change in party positions: three special cases

1 For the calculation of correlation coefficients we have divided the original seven-point scales into three categories: 1. pro-government incomes policy 2. makes no difference; 3. against government incomes policy. For Conservative voters, the correlation between their own views and the perceived views of the Conservative party is 0.54. For Labour voters, the correlation between the respondents' views and the party's perceived view is 0.27. The weaker relationship in the case of Labour voters is due to the fact that a comparatively large proportion of these voters were against incomes policy even though they thought the party was in favour.

2 For the purpose of calculating correlation coefficients, responses to the preference question were ordered as follows: 1. prefers Labour 2. no preference or preference for Liberals or other party 3. prefers the Conservatives. The 'distance' measure was taken in the order: 1. closest to Labour; 2. same distance; 3. closest to Conservatives. The correlation for all three main party voters (top section in the table) was 0.48. The correlation for Conservative voters, taken separately, was 0.35, for Liberal voters 0.44, and for Labour voters 0.30. The coefficients are Kendall's Tau-b. If we exclude those who had no preference (or preferred a minor party), the correlation between issue preference and distances to parties for all three parties' voters (top section of the table) is 0.57.

3 In the top rows of each section of the table, the 'same distance' column includes voters who did not know the party positions, whilst such persons are by definition excluded from the 'A' and 'B' rows.

4 This must not necessarily mean that the positions of the parties are reversed in the individual's cognitive map of the situation; sometimes it means only that the opposing party is seen to take up an extreme position far away from the individual's own. For example, the Conservative voters tended to perceive the Labour party in a more extreme position on nationalisation than did the Labour voters (see Chapter 8).

5 Question texts: 'And now turning to the question of immigration, do you think that too many immigrants have been let into this country or not?' – 'How strongly do you feel about this – very strongly, fairly strongly, not very strongly?'

6 After the questions quoted in note 5, respondents were asked: 'Is it a problem around here?'

7 Question text: 'Which party is most likely to keep immigrants out – the Conservatives or Labour, or don't you feel there is much difference between them on this?'

8   Of those who believed that improving employment and housing conditions in the cities was the best way to improve race relations, 70 per cent also thought that too many immigrants had been let into the country.

9   Among those who thought that too many immigrants had been allowed into the country, 61 per cent thought that stopping immigration was the best way of dealing with race relations. In the small category who did not feel that there had been too many immigrants, only 4 per cent held that view about the race relations issue.

10 Having experienced immigrants as 'a problem' in one's own neighbourhood makes some difference to the respondents' views on the best method of dealing with race problems. The percentages who were in favour of stopping immigration and improving employment/housing conditions respectively, were: 62 and 32 per cent among those who lived in an area with an immigrant 'problem' as compared to 50 and 36 per cent, respectively, among other respondents.

11 The number of voters who had 'reversed' the positions of the parties is very small and the sub-categories become even smaller if the sample is divided into importance levels. We have therefore not distinguished between voters with different perceptions of party positions in Table 10.8, but the percentage would, in fact, be much the same if we had based the analysis only on those persons who believed the Conservatives were most in favour of stopping immigration.

12 The correlation coefficients are given in Table 9.8A.

13 See also Crewe and Särlvik, 'Popular Attitudes and Electoral Strategy', in Layton-Henry, ed, *Conservative Party Politics*.

11. The impact of the issues – an overall account

1   Tables 11.1 and 11.3–5 are based on the 1979 cross-section sample. For respondents in the panel, who were interviewed in the October 1974 survey, we have made use of the information about voting in 1974 given in the 1974 interviews. For other respondents, the data concerning voting in 1974 are based on recall responses given in the 1979 survey. In many instances, especially in Tables 11.3–5, the percentage bases for the categories are quite small, but we have included these percentage entries in the table in order to demonstrate the consistency of the pattern in the data.

2   The 'balance of opinions' is analogous to a mean value for the voter category concerned. Individuals who give a pro-Conservative answer are assigned a score of +1, those who give an ambivalent/neutral answer get a score of 0, and a score of –1 is assigned to those who give a pro-Labour answer. The average of these scores multiplied by 100 is the 'balance of opinions' for the category of voters concerned.

3   The questions concerning the Conservatives' and Labour's records on upholding law and order were asked in the same format as the questions about economic problems (see Chapter 6). The 'law and order' question is discussed in Chapter 7.

4   Multiple regression is treated in all standard textbooks on statistics, see, e.g.,

Blalock, Jr, *Social Statistics*, Chapters 17-19. The computerised program for regression analysis employed here is described in N.H. Nie, C. Hadlai Hull, Jean G. Jenkins, Karin Steinbrenner, Dale H. Brent, *SPSS Statistical Package for the Social Sciences* (New York: McGraw Hill Book Company, 2nd edition, 1975).

5 In the technical language of regression analysis, the 'predicting' opinion measures are known as the 'independent variables', whilst party choice in this instance is the 'dependent variable'. That is, the model assumes that each individual's value on the dependent variable 'depends upon' the values of the independent variables in his case.

6 For the purpose of this multiple regression analysis, the values 1, 2 and 3 were assigned to Conservative, Liberal and Labour voting, respectively. We have also carried out two different versions. One distinguished between 'Conservative' and 'non-Conservative' voting; in the other version the distinction was made between 'Labour' and 'non-Labour' voting. The results are very similar to those obtained for the 'three-party vote', but correlations are slightly weaker because the Liberal voters then are lumped together with voters supporting one of the two major parties. Each of the opinion questions is also treated as a scale in which response alternatives are assigned integer scores, i.e. 1, 2, 3, 4, etc., with the value 1 for 'the most Conservative' answer and the highest score for 'the most pro-Labour' answer. With this procedure, it is necessary to assume that these scales are equal interval scales. As always with opinion data analysis, it is questionable to what extent this assumption is justified; we have taken the view that it can be accepted as a reasonable approximation.

7 We included in this multiple regression analysis all the twenty-three opinion measures which had a correlation with voting of 0.2 or more, when taken separately. However, the multiple regression technique employed here will select an optimal set of predictors. Therefore, the multiple regression coefficient is effectively based on fourteen opinion measures.

8 Obviously, it is only with regard to the numerical scale that is used here to represent voting that it is at all meaningful to speak of a 'mean' on the dependent variable. The regression equation will yield a predicted value (in the range between 1 and 3, except for a small number of outliers); the 'error' in the prediction for each individual is the difference between that value and the score assigned to his voting. Whilst the predicted value could be, say, 1.8, the observed value can, of course, only take the values 1, 2, or 3. A portion of the 'non-explained' variance is thus due to the fact that individuals' observed scores can match exactly the predictions only when the values are equal to 1, 2 or 3. The discriminant analysis used in Chapter 12 yields a different measure of the 'goodness' of our prediction of voting which is the proportion of voters whose party choice is correctly 'predicted'. This measure has, of course, a more readily interpretable meaning.

9 This group includes all the opinion measures (in distances to parties format) discussed in Chapters 8 to 9. The race and immigration question, however, made no significant contribution to the explained proportion of the variance over and above the other seven measures.

10   The questions included in this set were: 1. Should comprehensive schools be established throughout the country? 2. Should income and wealth be re-distributed? 3. Should the state control land for building? 4. Have social welfare benefits gone too far? 5. Should the power of the House of Lords be reduced? 6. Should workers have more say at their place of work? 7. Has the reduction of Britain's military strength gone too far? 8. Should more money be put into the NHS? 9. Should more be done to get rid of poverty? Of these measures, numbers 1 to 7 made significant contributions to the explained proportion of the variance.

11   This is a version of multiple regression analysis using a 'forward (stepwise)' selection procedure; see, for example, N.R. Draper and H. Smith, *Applied Regression Analysis* (New York: John Wiley & Sons, 1966), pp 169-71. See also Nie *et al.*, *SPSS Statistical Package for the Social Sciences*, p 345 *et passim* pp 320-67.

12   This stepwise procedure was used in the regression analyses presented in Table 11.7.

13   Had we also included the remaining opinion measures in the batteries of questions about social and cultural change, the multiple correlation coef-ficient would still be affected so slightly that the difference disappears with decimal rounding. With one exception (the question about redistribution of income and wealth) these opinion measures were relatively weak 'predictors' of party choice.

14   In technical language the 'weights' are regression coefficients. Because the number of categories in the various opinion measures are not the same, we have used the standardised regression coefficients as the rank ordering criterion.

15   The r coefficient is appropriate when all variables are measured at the interval scale level. For the regression analysis it is necessary to make the assumption that this is the case; the Tau-b coefficient requires no such as-sumption.

16   The policy alternative questions were taken in 'distance to parties' format. For assessments of the parties' performance and other opinion questions, the response alternatives were grouped into the three categories described above.

17   Arguably, taxation might have surfaced both with a higher correlation with voting and with a different balance of opinions, if it had not been linked to the standard of public services in our interview question. There is no certainty that the correlation with voting would have been stronger, however; a straight interview question about the desirability of a tax cut might well have recorded a consensus of favourable opinions which would have been of very little use for the purpose of explaining the voters' party choice.

18   This includes all opinion measurements that showed a Tau-b correlation of at least 0.2 with voting in 1979.

12. The electorate and the party system

1   For an analysis of long-term trends up to the 1970 election, see Butler and Stokes, *Political Change in Britain*, esp. Chapters 8-9.

2 For a critical discussion of the assumptions underlying this type of models of party systems, see Campbell *et al.*, *Elections and the Political Order*, Chapter 9.

3 The opinion measures are the same as those employed in the multiple regression analysis. However, measures of opinions on policy alternatives (see Chapters 8-9 above) are used in their original opinion position format rather than in the 'distance to parties' format. The rationale was that we wished to classify Liberal voters with regard to their actual opinion positions rather than their 'distances' to the two major parties. In fact, as an alternative version of the analysis has proved, it makes very little difference to the result in which form these opinion measures are included in the analysis.

4 The computer program used for this analysis is described in Nie *et al.*, *SPSS Statistical Package for the Social Sciences*, Chapter 23. Good treatments of this rather sophisticated analysis technique are to be found in several advanced methodological textbooks, e.g. W.W. Cooley and P.R. Lohnes, *Multivariate Procedures for the Behavioural Sciences* (New York: John Wiley & Sons, 1962), Chapter 6, and J.P. Van de Geer, *Introduction to Multivariate Analysis of the Social Sciences* (San Francisco: H. Freeman and Comp., 1971), Chapter 18.

5 As mentioned in the text, the discriminant function analysis may locate individuals in a multi-dimensional space. In this instance, however, the first dimension (or discriminant function) derived was so predominant that additional dimensions could be considered redundant. (In technical terms, the eigenvalue for the first dimension amounted to 98% of the sum of eigenvalues.) The canonical correlation between the discriminant function and the dummy variables which represent the three parties in the analysis was 0.76.

6 The discriminant function analysis was also carried out in an alternative version in which the measures of Labour's and the Conservatives' performance in office were excluded on the grounds that these measures might boost the expected vote for the two major parties at the expense of the Liberals. In fact, the result differs only slightly from the analysis version presented in the text and it did not appreciably improve the prediction of Liberal voting.

7 This, it should be pointed out, is not surprising. The discriminant analysis and the multiple regression models become essentially similar when the discriminant analysis yields only one important dimension. Indeed, we could have arrived at very similar results by treating the predicted values on the dependent variable in the regression analysis as a 'scale' of opinion positions.

8 The standard deviation for the scores are, respectively: Conservatives, 0.6; Liberals, 0.8; Labour, 0.6.

9 These questions were introduced as a standard format of measuring party identification in the United States in the early 1950s. Since then the same questions have been used in the continuing series of Election Studies conducted by the Institute for Social Research, University of Michigan, as well as in surveys in many other countries. Butler and Stokes, in their study of *Political Change in Britain*, use the term 'partisan self-image' which they

considered more appropriate than party identification in the British context. See Butler and Stokes, *Political Change in Britain*, 2nd edition, Chapter 2. See also I. Crew, B. Särlvik, J. Alt, 'Partisan Dealignment in Britain 1964–1974', *BJPS*, 7 (1977), pp 129–90. The seminal works on the role of party identification in American electoral behaviour are A. Campbell, G. Gurin and W. Miller, *The Voter Decides* (Evanston, Ill: Row, Peterson and Co., 1954), and A. Campbell, P. Converse, W. Miller and D. Stokes, *The American Voter* (New York: John Wiley & Sons, 1960). For an overview of recent comparative research relating to the concept of party identification, see Budge, Crewe and Farlie, eds, *Party Identification and Beyond.*

10 An extended analysis – using essentially the same measure of negative partisanship as here – is presented in B. Särlvik, *Electoral Behaviour in the Swedish Multi-Party System* (Ph.D Thesis, mimeo, 1970). See also B. Särlvik, 'Voting Behaviour in Shifting Election Winds: An Overview of Swedish Elections 1964–1968', *Scandinavian Political Studies*, 5 (1970), pp 241ff, esp. p 262. See also I. Crewe, 'Negative Partisanship. Some Preliminary Ideas Using British Data', paper for Joint Sessions of the ECPR, Florence, 1980.

11 Data drawn from BES October 1974 – May 1979 panel sample.

12 For a further analysis of the interdependence between voting change and change in party identification, see Butler and Stokes, *Political Change in Britain*, 2nd edition, Chapter 2.

13 For the analyses discussed in these paragraphs and in the remainder of this chapter, the respondents who said they felt 'a little closer' to one of the parties have been included in the appropriate party group together with respondents who had stated a party attachment already in their answers to the first of the questions in the party identification series. Given that the latter group is very much larger, this has only a marginal effect on the per cent distributions in the tables in this chapter.

14 See further the study of the Liberal vote in 1974 in Alt, Crewe and Särlvik, 'Angels in Plastic: The Liberal Surge in 1974', pp 343–67.

15 Question (asked of all respondents who had indicated a party preference in answers to the party identification questions): 'Which party do you like second best?' Of all voters with a party identification, 79 per cent indicated a second preference.

16 Question texts: 'Considering everything the Conservative and Labour parties stand for, would you say there is a great deal of difference between them, some difference, or not much difference?' – 'Considering everything the Conservative and Liberal parties stand for, would you say there is a great deal of difference between them, some difference, or not much difference?' – 'Considering everything the Labour and Liberal parties stand for, would you say there is a great deal of difference between them, some difference, or not much difference?'

17 Question text: 'Considering everything the Conservative, Labour and Liberal parties stand for, which two of these three parties would you say are furthest apart?'

18 Question text: 'Considering everything the Conservative, Labour and Liberal parties stand for, which two of these three parties would you say are closest together?'

13. **The making of voting decisions: political opinions and voting intentions during the campaign**

1   The category of voters who had 'thought seriously' of voting for another party during the campaign may be subdivided further to distinguish between those who voted for the same party as in October 1974 and those who had changed parties, but several of the resultant categories become numerically small. The differences between the groups in Table 13.5 can nevertheless be traced as an equally clear pattern in the sub-categories.

2   The standard deviation of the scale scores of stable Liberal voters was 0.79 as compared to 0.58 for stable Conservative voters and 0.65 for stable Labour voters.

3   What is said above is based on a preliminary examination of opinion change data in the panel sample including the 1974 and 1979 surveys; it has been necessary – for reasons of time as well as the size of the present study – to defer the full presentation of this data material to subsequent publication.

4   For a theoretical treatment of party competition and electoral strategies adopted by parties, see David Robertson, *A Theory of Party Competition* (London: John Wiley & Sons, 1976). See also Ian Budge and Dennis Farlie, *Voting and Party Competition. A Theoretical Critique and Synthesis Applied to Surveys from Ten Democracies* (London: John Wiley & Sons, 1977), esp. Chapter 11.

5   With a different methodological approach, Farlie and Budge have arrived at a quite similar overall picture of the impact of the issues in the 1979 election; see Dennis Farlie and Ian Budge, *Explaining and Predicting Elections: Issue Effects and Party Strategies in 23 Democracies* (forthcoming).

14. **At the end of a decade**

1   Crewe, Särlvik and Alt, 'Partisan Dealignment in Britain 1964–1974', pp 129–190.

2   Respondents who said they did not think of themselves as Conservatives, Liberals or Labour, etc., were asked if they felt a little closer to one of the parties than to the others. For the purpose of the following tables, respondents who were only 'closer' to a party have not been considered as party identifiers.

Postscript: realignment in the 1980s?

1   See, for example, Matthew Oakeshott, *The Road from Limehouse to Westminster – Prospects for a Radical Re-Alignment at the General Election* (London: Radical Centre for Democratic Studies in Industry and Society, 1981), and David Butler, 'Mark Your Card for the Next Election', *The Sunday Times*, 8 November 1981.

2   For an analysis of the Alliance's electoral support and of previous Liberal surges, see Ivor Crewe, 'Is Britain's Two-Party System Really About to Crumble? The Social Democratic/Liberal Alliance and the Prospects for Realignment', *Electoral Studies*, 1 (1982), pp 275–313.

3 See Jerome Clubb, William H. Flanigan and Nancy H. Zingale, *Partisan Re-alignment: Voters, Parties and Government in American History* (Beverly Hills, California and London: Sage Publications, 1980), esp. Chapter 8.

Appendix

1 With the exception of 1959–64 when Butler and Stokes used respondents' recall in 1963 of their 1959 vote.
2 See British Election Study, *A Comparison of Respondents' Characteristics with Known Population Parameters*, Technical Paper 1980, p 16.
3 See, in particular, R.J. Benewick, A.H. Birch, J.G. Blumler and A. Ewbank, 'The Floating Voter and the Liberal View of Representation', *Political Studies*, XVII (1969), pp 177–95; Hilde T. Himmelweit, Marianne Jaeger Biberian and Janet Stockdale, 'Memory for Past Vote: Implications of a Study of Bias in Recall', *British Journal of Political Science*, 8 (1978), pp 365–75; and Richard S. Katz, Richard G. Niemi and David Newman, 'Reconstructing Past Partisanship in Britain', *British Journal of Political Science*, 10 (1980), pp 505–15.
4 Some respondents (N = 110) were interviewed in February 1974 and 1979, but not in October 1974.
5 See *A Comparison of Respondents' Characteristics with Known Population Parameters*, pp 12–16.
6 For a description of the estimating procedure see F.W.S. Craig, *British Electoral Facts 1885–1975* (London and Basingstoke: Macmillan, 1976) pp xii and 169.
7 For a recent, detailed analysis of the efficiency of the British electoral register, see David Butler and Colm O'Muircheartaigh, 'What is 40%? A Note on the Eligible Electorate', mimeo, February 1979. See also the *Home Office's Report of the Working Party on the Electoral Register* (London: HMSO, 1978) p 5 where it comments that local election registration officers are 'reluctant to remove from the electors' lists the names of those reported dead . . . or of those reported to have left the area without some first hand evidence of the fact' while being too sparing with the use of canvassers to make personal calls on households which failed to return their electoral registration form.
8 On the age distribution of Commonwealth immigrants, see Immigrant Statistics Unit, 'New Commonwealth and Pakistani Population Estimates', *Population Trends*, pp 4–7. On registration rates see Anwar, *Ethnic Minorities and the General Election 1979*, pp 34–6.
9 See Butler and Stokes, *Political Change in Britain*, 2nd edition, pp 216–17.
10 See Anwar, *Ethnic Minorities and the General Election 1979*. See also by the same author, *Participation of Ethnic Minorities in the General Election, October 1974* (London: Community Relations Commission, 1975).
11 See Anwar, *Ethnic Minorities and the General Election 1979*, pp 37–40, and for local elections M.J. Le Lohe, 'Participation in Elections by Asians in Bradford' in Ivor Crewe, ed, *British Political Sociology Yearbook* Volume 2 (London: Croom Helm, 1975) especially pp 95–101.

12 Frederick Mosteller, 'Association and Estimation in Contingency Tables', *Journal of the American Statistical Association*, 63 (1968), pp 1-28.

13 In practice this required the subtraction of the bottom row cell values (the vote of entering electors) from the column marginals and the subtraction of the right-hand column cell values (the previous vote of departing electors) from the row marginals before setting the 'targets'. The estimates of the vote of entering and departing electors were not subject to the standardisation procedure since they had largely been calculated on the basis of official statistics, not our surveys.

Index